D1527111

Liberalism in Empire

BERKELEY SERIES IN BRITISH STUDIES

Edited by Mark Bevir and James Vernon

Liberalism in Empire

An Alternative History

———

Andrew Sartori

UNIVERSITY OF CALIFORNIA PRESS

University of California Press, one of the most distinguished university presses in the United States, enriches lives around the world by advancing scholarship in the humanities, social sciences, and natural sciences. Its activities are supported by the UC Press Foundation and by philanthropic contributions from individuals and institutions. For more information, visit www.ucpress.edu.

University of California Press
Oakland, California

Library of Congress Cataloging-in-Publication Data
Sartori, Andrew, 1969–
    Liberalism in empire : an alternative history / Andrew Sartori.
        pages   cm.— (Berkeley series in British studies ; volume 8)
    Includes bibliographical references and index.
    ISBN 978-0-520-28168-4 (cloth : alkaline paper)—ISBN 978-0-520-28169-1 (paperback : alkaline paper)—ISBN 978-0-520-95757-2 (e-book)
        1. Great Britain—Colonies—History.   2. Imperialism—History.
        3. Liberalism—History.   I. Title.
        DA16.S27   2014 C. 2
        320.5109171'241—dc23
                                                                2013043066

Manufactured in the United States of America

23 22 21 20 19 18 17 16 15 14
10 9 8 7 6 5 4 3 2 1

In keeping with a commitment to support environmentally responsible and sustainable printing practices, UC Press has printed this book on Natures Natural, a fiber that contains 30% post-consumer waste and meets the minimum requirements of ANSI/NISO Z39.48-1992 (R 1997) (*Permanence of Paper*).

CONTENTS

ACKNOWLEDGMENTS

The research for this project was supported by a yearlong National Endowment for the Humanities Fellowship (FA55026). It was also supported by New York University's Faculty of Arts and Sciences, History Department, and Global Research Institute in London.

Thanks for the thoughtful engagement of colleagues and students at New York University. I have also benefited from helpful feedback over the past several years from colleagues and audiences at Columbia University, Cornell University, Dhaka University, the École des Hautes Études en Sciences Sociales, Harvard University, King's College London, New York University, Northwestern University, Oxford University, Tufts University, the University of Chicago, the University of Heidelberg, the University of Pennsylvania and Yale University. I am grateful for the constructive criticisms offered by two reviewers, and to Niels Hooper, Kim Hogeland, Wendy Dherin and Paul Tyler at the University of California Press. Thanks to the staff of the Oriental and India Office Collection at the British Library, the National Archives of Bangladesh and Interlibrary Loan at Bobst Library. I would particularly like to thank John Shovlin for encouraging me to turn an overgrown initial essay draft into a longer book project; Hylton White for insisting that this material was important; Sam Moyn for giving me invaluable criticisms, suggestions and encouragement on the entire manuscript; Mark Bevir for backing this book; and James Vernon for his insightful, constructive, patient and generous engagement throughout the process of revision.

Chapters 2 and 3 incorporate material previously published in "A Liberal Discourse of Custom in Colonial Bengal," *Past and Present* 212 (August 2011), 163–97.

Thanks, Amy and Izzie, for bearing with me through the research and writing of this book.

This is dedicated to my father, Loris Sartori; I think he would have been chuffed.

How to Write a History of Liberalism?

One of the more recent developments of the neoliberal era is a new international "land grab." In 2009, the International Food Policy Research Institute was estimating that in the period from 2006 through the middle of 2009 foreign investors had sought or secured between 37 and 49 million acres of farmland in Africa, Southeast Asia and Latin America, concentrated in areas that combined poor integration into international markets with weak land tenure security, easy accessibility, and relatively dense populations. By early 2011, estimates suggested that 115 million acres of farmland and forestland—85 million acres in Africa alone—had been bought or leased by investors. As of 2012, although the rate of acquisition was slowing, the Land Matrix database had registered reports of negotiations and/or agreements for around 500 million acres, 175 million of which had been confirmed through triangulation or cross-referencing. The biggest surge in acquisitions occurred in response to a spike in food prices in 2007–08, but the general trend has been sustained in response to rising demand for food, timber, biofuels and water, as well as concerns about food security. The rationale for capital-starved nations or regions to accept such investments is that the influx of capital will promote development. But setting aside the fundamental issues of rent-seeking and corruption, there remains the fraught question of how this rush to make huge swathes of land available to industrially organized agriculture is going to impact various groups, including smallholders, that already stake claims to a complex skein of legal and prescriptive rights (however unenforceable) over such lands.[1]

Given large concentrations of capital, expanding levels of consumption, and regional concerns about food security, it is not surprising that Indian investors have participated prominently in the land grab. But South Asian nations have long been familiar with the issues surrounding the confrontation between major capital investments and tribal and smallholder claims to control land. The Narmada Dam in western India is perhaps the best-known instance of such a confrontation. More recently, in 2007 and 2008, in the Indian state of West Bengal, the long-regnant Left Front government led by the Communist Party of India (Marxist), or CPM, used eminent domain powers to take possession of farmland for large industrial developments in new Special Economic Zones (SEZs) located in Nandigram and Singur. These efforts led to violent clashes between villagers and the police and party cadres. They also led to a most peculiar alignment (though in no sense alliance) between disaffected leftist intellectuals and the aggressively populist and anticommunist leader of the Trinamul Congress, Mamata Banerjee. Both condemned the expropriation of peasant property that the Left Front government (previously responsible for substantial land reform legislation) was effecting in the name of an aggressive policy of state-sponsored developmentalist capitalism. There is a strong case to be made that the CPM's development policy was precisely the wedge that in 2011 led to their electoral loss, after 34 years in government, to the Trinamul Congress.[2]

In all of these cases, questions about process, implementation and compensation, about environmental costs, about the conflict between the general utility of developmental policies and their disutility to particular groups and individuals (especially the poor and socially marginal), about the desirability of large-scale capitalist production, about the peculiar attachments of smallholders and tribal groups to local environmental resources and the particular challenges of displacement and transition for such groups, and about neoliberal developmental regimes and the future of leftist political visions, have understandably proliferated.

Of course, the battle over the control of land, whether waged legally, politically or violently, has as long a history in South Asia as elsewhere. It is not in its most general features a peculiarly modern struggle. Controlling land and its product has long been of enormous importance to producers as well as to dominant lineages, local gentries, states and state-agents. But that should not preclude the recognition that such struggles assume historically specific contours and historically specific stakes. Modern capital's impulse to directly control production processes, the privilege it accords to the productive capacities of labor, and the fundamental role that labor assumes as a social relation under conditions of its predominance, together generate quite particular kinds of political and economic projects and quite particular possibilities of normative judgment.

From this perspective, what is so striking about the conflicts in Bengal, as in so many other cases where smallholding agriculturists have been displaced in the name of large-scale capital investments, is that the critique of capitalism as a property regime has been undertaken *in the name of property*. Sure enough, many leftist intellectuals, deeply critical of the neoliberal developmental policies in which the CPM had been dabbling, lined up alongside the populist Trinamul Congress to denounce capital in the name of property rights. What normative assumptions undergird this defense of property across otherwise quite disparate political impulses? What conception of property made possible the convergence of right and left around a defense of petty proprietorship? I believe that there is a longer history to this possibility. It is to be found in a history of arguments about the rights of smallholders that turned on appeals to claims about the property-constituting powers of labor. These arguments emerged in colonial debates in the middle of the nineteenth century and proliferated in Bengali agrarian society itself in the course of the later nineteenth and early twentieth centuries. Seen in the light of this history, the key to these questions lies in the contradictory impulses buried at the heart of liberalism, and especially in the ambivalent place that claims about the property-constituting powers of labor have held in liberal political and political-economic thought.

In the face of what appears to be a global resource crunch, the question of how to frame claims to property has become ever more urgent. In such a context, it is worth recognizing that there is a history to the debates over how to frame claims to control environmental resources and how to specify the legitimate bases on which such property has been and should be constituted. Such debates have never been reducible to pro- and anti-property arguments; nor have they been confined to the modern West. This book is a history of the process by which property became available as the standpoint for a specifically liberal critique of capitalism and colonialism. I do not primarily mean by this a history of why some groups of people ("petty bourgeois" and "kulaks" in classical Marxist terminology) might have found it convenient or useful to assume the standpoint of property for a critique of capitalism. I mean rather a history of the kinds of arguments that were available for identifying property as a plausible standpoint for a critique of domination and exploitation; a history of the conditions of possibility for the emergence of those kinds of arguments; and a history of what kind of dynamics their embrace set in play once they had been adopted as the basis for articulating the claims of diverse social interests. We are thoroughly familiar, thanks to the rich historiography on classical republicanism, with arguments that pitch (landed) property against commerce and credit.[3] But the anticapitalist potentialities of republican ideology should not blind us to the generative ambivalences that have characterized liberalism's relationship to capitalism. We cannot afford to forget that the history of liberalism is much more than the prehistory of neoliberalism.

In some ways, other dimensions of liberal ambivalence have assumed striking prominence in recent scholarship. Thinking about the history of liberalism in empire has been one way of approaching questions about the status of universal norms in a world characterized by cultural differences. Such questions have assumed ever greater attention at a historical conjuncture when neoliberal thought and policy have intersected with a partial redistribution of global economic and political power as a result of the rise of the BRIC nations. The terms in which this conjuncture has been conceived have roots in an earlier period when developmentalist imaginations intersected with processes of decolonization. Fueled by a critical insistence on the deep roots of neoliberal politics in a longer history of European imperial preeminence, the historiography of liberalism's ideological trajectories in relation to Britain's imperial projects and territories has flourished in recent years. This literature has developed a refined sensitivity both to liberalism's alignments with the history of European imperial political and economic power, and to the subtle exclusions buried in the apparent universalism of its commitments. Such emphases have generated some exemplary analyses of the conceptualization of empire in classics of liberal political thought. They have also renewed attention to the politics of liberalism in colonial contexts and to the effects of such contexts on liberal political thought in turn. Liberalism has been plausibly implicated, with enormously varying degrees of necessity and contingency, in the conceptualization, institutionalization and legitimization of hierarchical practices of subordination on the basis of race, gender and other categories of difference; in the exploitative reordering of colonial economies, along with the political institutions that had previously organized them; in the constitution of new regimes of colonial governmentality; in the annihilationist violence against the nomadic aboriginal populations of the settler colonies; and in a vast assault on indigenous epistemological and ethical norms.[4]

This interest in the history of liberalism in empire has also generated new insights into the process by which liberal ideas came to be embraced and debated by non-Europeans in the colonies. Histories of liberalism in India, whether celebratory or condemnatory, have often turned on accounts of the development of political projects that bound the indigenous embrace of liberal norms and commitments to engagement with imperial institutions of governance and education. The most straightforward way to tell a history of liberalism in colonial South Asia is in terms of the diffusion of ideas and texts—the very story that was at the heart of Macaulay's famous *Minute on Education*. A familiarity with liberal arguments was of course most quickly and readily available to those best positioned to encounter them—that is, among those literate in English. Just as political theorists and intellectual historians have attended so carefully to the complex textual evidence represented by major liberal intellectuals in Britain, so too can the intellectual history of South Asia be construed through readings both close and wide of the most articulate sections of that region's populations. An emphasis on intellectual diffusion has much to be said for it. Liberalism did, in some sense, come from Britain to South Asia as a set of already elaborated arguments. To concede that is not necessarily to imply that South Asians could only be passive recipients of those ideas: as C. A. Bayly has recently demonstrated, South Asians showed considerable creativity in reworking such arguments in terms of their own different intellectual traditions and in relation to their own different local circumstances, thereby giving South Asian liberalism its own history, with its own trajectories and its own dynamics, even as it participated in a global conversation about "the Good Life."[5] It is not, therefore, the case that a diffusionist history has to be a Macaulayan history of derivativeness.

It has not only been intellectual historians who have embraced this kind of diffusionist approach. The history of liberalism can be thought about in terms of a top-down dissemination that tracks the intrusion of colonial institutions into indigenous cultural worlds.[6] Some important studies that we might cluster as broadly Foucauldian in inspiration have pursued the institutionalist approach in imaginative new ways, in order to reach more deeply into the domain of the social in colonial South Asia than an older literature had. These studies seek to grasp the deeper purchase of liberal concepts on the organization of everyday life and the justification of political and social norms, while maintaining an eye to the circumstances of their reception. From this perspective, colonial liberals articulated their legal and political projects of colonial governance in complex circumstances where the transparency of the universal concepts that liberalism assumed was radically compromised or complicated. This interruption of liberal thought generated unanticipatable and original responses to liberal arguments on the part of colonial administrators and intellectuals, as well as on the part of South Asians themselves. Crucial to this approach has typically been an emphasis on the role of law as a mediation between colonial discourses of rule and governance and indigenous social and political norms and practices. Insofar as it impacted everyday practices more powerfully than any other colonial institution, it was law that best accounted for the power of liberal ideas to affect the normative assumptions of a wide range of indigenous agents.[7]

These arguments serve in many ways as the point of departure of this book. I too think that the deeper impact of liberal concepts on colonial society needs to be better understood. I too think that the law has been a crucial mediating institution. And I too think that the elaboration of colonial liberalism was impacted by its interaction with the complexities of colonial contexts. Yet the story my book tells is substantially different in emphasis. It suggests that the role of colonial contexts in shaping colonial liberalisms was not only one of interrupting liberal universalisms and of demarcating spaces of exclusion and exception. It suggests that colonial contexts could, under some circumstances, resonate with projects of radicalizing and extending liberal commitments as easily as with circumscribing them. As such, colonial contexts should be understood as potentially the basis for an account of the embrace of liberal norms, not only of their strategic deployment, refraction, transformation, displacement, compromise and delimitation.[8] This in turn implies the need for an account of how practices in indigenous society constituted the conditions for a reception of liberal ideas in social spaces in which one might not readily expect to find them—without thereby succumbing to a naïve conception of the transparent universality of the appeal of liberal norms.

This book is therefore fugal in conception, if not in presentation. It juxtaposes a narrative about the elaboration of a liberal argument about property in legal debates in colonial Bengal to a narrative about the development of claims to proprietary rights in Bengali agrarian society. It argues that from the middle of the nineteenth century, under circumstances of the deepening commercialization of social relations in the countryside, one trajectory of political argument in rural Bengal came to be premised on what we might think of as specifically liberal norms articulated through a discourse of property. It was precisely at a moment when a new Toryism was in ascension in British imperial thought and policy, and when racial-cum-civilizational difference and hierarchical authority assumed renewed emphasis, that some liberals began to identify agrarian Bengal as historically organized around liberal norms.[9] This, I argue, must be understood in relation to the generativeness of a crisis in later Victorian liberal thought. This generativeness pointed not only towards the retrenchment of liberal universalisms, but also towards the radicalization of liberal aspirations. But it must also be understood in relation to demands emerging from the Bengali agrarian context itself. This book insists that an adequate conceptualization of the liberal arguments that some colonial officials espoused must therefore be matched by an adequate conceptualization of the circumstances under which liberal arguments could be endorsed by some people in the rural hinterland. This latter conceptualization should be mounted with the same degree of ambition and rigor as the former; and it should aim to grasp the *fit* between the two histories, not just their episodic moments of intersection.

How did it become possible to conceive of the smallholding society that predominated in agrarian Bengal as having developed historically in response to the binding authority of liberal norms? How did this become possible for educated liberals in colonial civil society, *and* how did it become possible among rural Bengalis? I focus this inquiry on the history of the concept of property. Property is by no means a necessarily liberal idea or institution. But arguments about what property is, what ought to count as property, and who is entitled to make claims to various kinds or degrees of ownership, were central to the process by which actors on both sides of the colonial divide began to appeal to liberal norms when they attributed specific rights and obligations to different kinds of people. Such arguments were specifically embraced in nineteenth-century Bengal to vindicate smallholding property as the cornerstone of an agrarian society based on the recognition of labor's property-constituting capacity. They were correlatively invoked to challenge the economic preferability of large estates, the power of the state to create proprietary rights, and the rationality of the market as a distributive mechanism. At the very core of such claims were "Lockean" arguments about the normative force of the property-constituting capacities of labor. To the extent that they embraced the crucial Lockean claim that legitimate property was constituted by labor, agrarian political movements in Bengal criticized existing social and political institutions without appealing to normative frameworks radically alien to the normative universe in reference to which those institutions had been constructed.[10] The invocation of the property-constituting powers of labor defined a new kind of political movement in the countryside. While deeply hostile towards the political agendas of certain self-consciously liberal voices, this new kind of politics nonetheless itself relied on certain radically liberal normative presuppositions. We need to be able to understand how this kind of agrarian politics became possible and why it was compelling.

By focusing on the particular constellation of the concepts of labor, wealth and property that I am calling "Lockean," I believe it is possible to make better sense of the broader and deeper processes that led to the increasing power of liberal norms in colonial Bengal. In the process, I seek to broaden the framework within which the history of liberalism in empire has been seen. In focusing on Bengal, I do not intend to suggest that this is an exceptional history. On the contrary, I assume that, for all its specificity, similar kinds of processes were most likely at work in many other places in the subcontinent and elsewhere.[11] Beyond the history of elite figures that intellectual history has emphasized and the history of the institutional mechanisms that Foucauldians have focused on, there is a *social* history of the movement of liberal concepts through the empire. That is what this book is about.

Ultimately, the history of liberal thought can only be adequately understood if it takes into account what we might call "vernacular" histories of liberalism. By "vernacular" here I mean less the question of language (though I shall indeed turn to Bengali sources in the final chapter of this book) than the histories of the movement of liberal concepts beyond the rarified domains of self-conscious political theory or jurisprudence into wider worlds of normative social and political discourse. Michael Freeden argued long ago that an adequate history of liberalism would have to proceed from a recognition that "political thought is to be found at any level of political action, on different levels of sophistication." The "*formulation* of politically significant ideas" therefore emerges out of wider circles of engagement and debate, not merely "the coherent speculation of isolated men."[12] But vernacular histories cannot be limited to the narrow social domains of the metropolitan and colonial literati—or even of politically articulate metropolitan plebeians.[13] Agrarian Bengal is, I suspect, the last place most historians and political theorists would think to look for the history of liberalism, unless in the form of projects of colonial and capitalist domination. Yet recognizing the vernacular history of liberalism in a place like agrarian Bengal radically challenges our understanding of the history of liberal thought by forcing us to rethink both its political trajectories and its social location.

Debate rages among political theorists and intellectual historians about the degree to which liberal thought has been structurally implicated in the history of European racial, colonial and capitalist violence, and about the possibilities of redeeming it from whatever degree of implication in such histories it might have had. Yet the debate as it has unfolded has been largely contained within a world of reference defined by intellectuals occupying a remarkably narrow range of social spaces (even when such spaces defy the division of metropole and colony). My argument is that we cannot understand the liberalism of elites without understanding the plebeian liberalisms that have haunted it, and that we have not properly understood liberalism *anywhere* if we cannot grasp how it was possible for it to ground the political aspirations of agrarian Bengalis. I argue that we cannot even recognize, let alone understand, the embrace of liberal normative commitments by agrarian Bengalis until we grasp liberalism as a form of political argument that is capable of generating a critique of domination and exploitation from the standpoint of property.

Finally, I argue that we cannot understand the appeal of liberal claims as the basis for construing and articulating determinate agrarian interests in Bengal in these terms without recognizing the ways in which liberal norms were constitutively bound to practices of commodity exchange. There can be no adequate conceptualization of the history of forms of liberalism anywhere until the reality of those forms' capacity to travel—not just horizontally across geographical space, but vertically through social space—has been taken into account. Such an account requires a form of conceptual history that recognizes the entailments that link concepts to each other and to historically specific social practices. In this sense, the history of liberalism must be thought of as part of a global intellectual history, not because liberalism's movements track the secondary elaborations or transformations of an already constituted ideological framework, but because liberalism's capacity to travel tells us something about what it always must have been, and must always have entailed, as a set of normative commitments. In this sense, to write a history of "Lockeanism" as I do in the following chapters is not to depart unproblematically from a parochially "Western" origin. It is rather to transform retroflexively our understanding of liberalism's conditions of possibility.

LOCKE AND PROPERTY

When I call the idea that property is constituted by labor "Lockean," I do not primarily mean that it is a set of theoretical arguments and problems bequeathed to theoretical posterity by John Locke's writings. There is of course a real tradition of Lockeanism in this provenantial sense, but it is not the Lockeanism that matters to the history with which this book is concerned. Rather, this book is about a Lockeanism that is "Lockean" only in the sense that it happened to be John Locke who, in the process of elaborating a theory of property as part of a radical intervention in the extended exclusion crisis of the late 1670s or early 1680s, grasped something profound about the new forms of social interdependence that were beginning to assume fundamental significance in seventeenth-century England.[14] I work from the supposition that Locke's theory involved serious reflection on his contemporary social realities. Consequently, the history of Lockeanism necessarily exceeds the comparatively minor question of intellectual provenance. We might expect to find Lockean conceptions of property even where Locke himself was unknown, insofar as reflective historical subjects confronted the opaque forms of practice to which Locke's theory had spoken; that is to say, insofar as they had confronted questions about the normative significance of newly emergent practices that were coming to organize social interdependence.

To the extent that Locke developed fundamental insights into the possible normative implications of such practices, attending to the specifics of his arguments is a way of thinking about how the idea of the property-constituting powers of labor relates to other dimensions of liberal thought. This is a set of relationships on which hangs the answer to the not insignificant question of why we should consider this theory of property a particularly "liberal" argument at all, let alone an especially significant one. If my supposition that the coherence of this argument is bound to particular practices of social interdependence is correct, then it should further follow that the sets of relationships that Locke establishes between the argument about property and other dimensions of liberal argumentation should tell us something important about the practical ecology within which liberal norms have come to assume their power, their coherence, and their persuasive force. Crucial here is the fact that Locke's identification of labor's property-constituting capacity made visible the basic conceptual space out of which both liberal political theory and political economy would be elaborated.[15]

Locke had set his sights on the theory of Sir Robert Filmer that Adam, who had been given unlimited authority over his family and over the earth itself, was the first king. Kingship was therefore a form of authority inherited from Adam. In Filmer's account, the king was endowed with a form of political authority that was indistinguishable from paternal authority, and therefore absolute in its rights over both his subjects and the lands in his kingdom. The king therefore possessed both imperium (political authority) and dominion (possession of the soil).[16] In contrast, Locke argued that Adam's succession was broken, or in effect that all men were the heirs to Adam. Government was therefore better conceived in terms of the relationship between brothers, each the master of his own (patriarchal) household, rather than one between fathers and their dependents.[17] Men were thus originally juridical equals in the state of nature, each with rights of mutual recognition. Upon what practical basis did this mutual recognition stand, and what cause would such individual householders have to unite under the superordinate authority of government? Locke's answer to both these questions in the fifth chapter of the second treatise was property.[18]

God had given the earth to mankind in common. Having withdrawn from Adam the spontaneous bounty of Eden, God had also condemned him and all his progeny to labor, as the means to sustenance and in the service of God's providential purposes. The necessity of labor, however, was evident to natural reason even in the absence of biblical authority. In laboring, Locke argued, man mixed a part of himself, in which he had an indisputable natural property, with the earth, thereby rendering that element of nature on which his labor had been expended into a compound of nature and himself. By natural right, no other man could partake of this portion of nature without unavoidably partaking also of the labor of another, so that that portion of nature was effectively removed from the common stock and became the property of the one who had first appropriated it. This right was not unlimited. The individual was entitled to withdraw from the common stock only such resources as he was able to make use of before spoilage. That limit applied not only to the fruits of the earth, but to the land itself. Legitimate withdrawal from the common stock did not represent any real infringement of the rights of others to appropriate nature for their own purposes, so long as there was more land to appropriate, as in America. And since ten acres of land brought under cultivation was at least as productive as one hundred uncultivated, "he that incloses [ten acres of] land . . . may truly be said to give ninety acres to mankind."[19]

But what was to prevent a man from infringing through theft or violence or fraud on another's property once established? Under natural law, it was only conscience and the capacity of each to defend their own. So it suited the convenience of all such property holders to come together and form a contract according to which they would be bound together in a civil society. In civil society, all men were subject to a common rule of law whose purpose was to defend the rights of property in general. Civil society was thus, as John Dunn puts it, "the state liked: the non-pathological state."[20] It was the state insofar as the state was properly performing the functions that were normatively defined for it by the conditions of its coming into existence, that is, the universal protection of the natural rights of property. Where the law failed to provide this, or where the magistrate ceased to serve as a neutral arbiter, civil society could no longer be said to exist, and men were released from their obligations to political authority. They returned in fact to the pre-contractual condition of the state of nature, in which only natural law, rather than the positive law of human legislation, remained authoritative.

I think there are good reasons to describe this Lockean argument about property as "liberal," even if Locke could not possibly have conceived of himself in such terms. What made Locke's argument about property "liberal" most fundamentally, for my purposes, was his insistence that the grounding of property in natural law rendered its normative claims *prior* to those of constituted political authority.

Property therefore provided the fundamental regulatory norms that governed the legitimate exercise of political authority. It provided grounds for positing freedom itself as a principal norm organizing political life. If we understand liberalism to be premised on a political commitment to the extension of personal liberties, there is no reason to think that the primordial sanctity of property is a necessary element of every liberal political theory. Seen from this perspective, Locke's theory of property was never necessarily the center of gravity of liberal argument, which could traverse a wide range of problems including the consent of the governed, the rule of law and constitutionalism, the role of representation in government, the right to freedom of conscience and of expression, and a whole range of projects of social reform and social intervention. Each of these concerns *can* be linked to the theory of property, but liberal arguments did not always, or even often, concern themselves with that particular vector of justification. Nonetheless, Locke's attribution of a fundamental normative priority to property, and hence his insistence that liberal norms preceded political authority, was something more than merely one more variant in a long list of liberal family resemblances. The Lockean theory of property could never be said to be the essence of so nebulous and hyperplastic a tradition of political thought as liberalism. But it is nonetheless something more than an optional add-on.

The refusal to derive rights from the structure of constituted political authority characterized liberal arguments long after many of the constitutive elements of Locke's intellectual universe had ceased to be plausible. For example, Locke's non-historicizing imagination, in which the state of nature and civil society were eternally present as normative frameworks, would be superseded in later liberal thinking by an assertively developmental historical imagination, to which even a more historicized conception of the transition from a state of nature to civil society would come to appear naïve. Yet when it came to normative judgments about the state, it was precisely the kind of normative framework that Locke had articulated that later liberals also brought to bear. Adam Smith still wrote *as if* the normative foundation of government was the preservation of property in general. In the absence of that implicit normative reference to a social contract for the preservation of property, it is hard to make sense of his critiques of monopoly, his pro-commercial suspicion of the role of merchants in government, his emphasis on the commensurability of private interests with the common good, or his defense of the state's public functions. Locke's appeal to indisputably theological conceptions of natural law and natural right would be the object of dismissive contempt from utilitarians. Yet James Mill found himself citing Locke's authority approvingly on the key dictum that "it is for the sake of property that government exists."[21] Mill clearly understood himself to be denying the possibility of grounding rights in any kind of pre-political space; but his capacity to justify the regime of legal rights he advocated relied on the pre-political logic of political economy, which itself represented an elaboration, as I shall suggest below, of the implications of Locke's theory of property. Mill effectively replaced Locke's theological notion of natural law with the science of political economy, a new kind of natural law to which the state remained normatively answerable and that reformulated the state's function of universally protecting proprietary rights. Given, as we shall see, that Locke's theory of property already was at its core a theory of political economy, this was much less of a leap than it might at first appear. John Stuart Mill would further highlight the link between Locke and his father's commitment to political economy when he specified that political economy only justified the state's role in preserving rights of property *when* property was the fruit of labor. He thereby brought the right to own land into the realm of legitimate political intervention precisely to the degree that the earth's product was partly the result of natural fertility—a disaggregating move in turn made possible by the calculation of proportionality using political economic principles.[22] The "new liberals" of the late nineteenth century might seem to be a more intransigent exception to the Lockean impulse. They argued that rights, including property rights, were constituted within the collective life of a community. They therefore treated property relations as subject to intervention whenever it was deemed that such intervention would promote broader conditions of personal liberty. Yet they were nonetheless "liberals" because they took personal liberty to be a fundamental normative principle governing the ethical life of the state. Seen in these terms, the intervention into property rights could itself be premised on Lockean first principles, including the premise that political norms ultimately derived from the property-constituting powers of labor—as I shall suggest in chapter 3.[23]

None of this is to deny, then, that liberals placed an enormous amount of importance on, and maintained a primary interest in, systems of positive law, whether legislative or customary, as the practical vehicles of liberty. Nor is it to suggest that liberals were necessarily committed to democratic political forms as the best means to preserve a liberal state. Thomas Paine famously developed Lockean premises in a radically republican direction. John Locke himself, however, would end up a defender of the post-1688 constitution.[24] Smith shared Locke's embrace of mixed regal government.[25] James Mill advocated a male franchise limited by a property qualification.[26] John Stuart Mill offset his commitment to representative government with deep anxieties about the pathological dynamics of democracy, Coleridgean appeals to a cultural clerisy, and a frank disavowal of representative government in relation to civilizations whose backwardness disqualified them from release from British quasi-paternal authority. From this perspective, a republican or democratic form of polity was a much less important liberal commitment than was the normative priority of property over the state.

Recognizing this, C. B. Macpherson argued that Locke stood alongside Hobbes, the Levelers and Harrington at the head of an English tradition of political thought that he called "possessive individualism." According to this tradition, the individual was understood to be "essentially the proprietor of his own person or capacities, owing nothing to society for them. . . . The human essence is freedom from dependence on the wills of others, and freedom is a function of possession. Society becomes a lot of free equal individuals related to each other as proprietors of their own capacities and of what they have acquired by their exercise. Society consists of relations of exchange between proprietors. Political society becomes a calculated device for the protection of this property and for the maintenance of an orderly relation of exchange."[27] Macpherson's Locke was a champion of capitalist market relations, affirming the individual right to open-ended accumulation outside any overarching moral or ethical framework provided by social norms, and naturalizing "a class differential in rights and in rationality" in such a way as to provide "a moral basis for capitalist society."[28] This critical reading was in turn mirrored on the libertarian right, albeit with a view to endorsing Locke as the font of a free-enterprise culture.[29] Crucial to these readings was the fact that Locke had argued that the limitation to the right to accumulate posed by the threat of spoilage had been effectively abolished by the invention of money, a social convention that allowed people to store the value of their labor in the form of a more durable substitute.

Locke's approach linked rights of property to a labor theory of wealth, according to which the property constituted by labor readily overbalanced claims to the primordial collective interest in land because "it is labour indeed that puts the difference of value on every thing."[30] The same activity that created property, Locke argued, also generated wealth. And so from the beginning Locke's liberal political theory was closely bound to an emergent discourse of political economy. Locke's argument that wealth derived from labor might have always been controversial, but it was in no sense new.[31] What *was* new in his theory, though, was the way in which the claim that "ninety-nine hundredths" of the "products of the earth useful to the life of man" are "the effects of labour" was set in apposition to a claim that laboring activity produced a natural right to property.[32] There is no more reason to believe that Locke himself thought that labor determined quantities of exchange than that Smith thought that property was necessarily bound to labor. But when Locke brought together a labor theory of property with a labor theory of wealth, he opened up the conceptual space within which a new formulation could emerge: when people exchanged the products of their labor, what was being exchanged was for the most part quantities of materialized labor over which the agent of appropriation could claim an absolute juridical right.

"Bread, wine and cloth, are things of daily use, and great plenty; yet notwithstanding acorns, water and leaves, or skins, must be our bread, drink and cloathing, did not labour furnish us with these more useful commodities: for whatever bread is worth more than acorns, wine than water, and cloth of silk than leaves, skins or moss, that is wholly owing to labour and industry."[33] This was precisely the conceptual space within which a further argument (that Locke himself never went on to make) would ultimately be elaborated: that wealth could be measured in terms of such commensurable quantities of labor, and that there could therefore be a science of exchange and production based on them. When Locke went on to identify money as an enduring, nonperishable proxy for wealth, he was on the brink of announcing a science of political economy that went far beyond his own more hesitant but nonetheless pioneering efforts in the field. Labor was both the basis of property and the (quantifiably) predominant source of wealth. It was also fungible and preservable in the quantifying form of money. From here it was only a very small step to the further argument that, when the products of labor are exchanged, labor is the most radical basis of the determination of the proportionality of those exchanges.

It is no surprise then that Locke has commonly been taken to be Smith's forebear as both a political theorist and a political economist, despite the many substantial intentional, theoretical and conceptual differences between them. If Locke's labor theory of wealth was not new, its connection to a labor theory of property was. It was the novelty of this connection that laid the groundwork for the classical theory of value. Locke's discussion of property, John Ramsay McCulloch would observe in the early nineteenth century, "contains a far more distinct and comprehensive statement of the fundamental doctrine, that labour is the constituent principle of value, than is to be found in any other writer previous to Dr. Smith, or than is found even in the *Wealth of Nations*. But Mr. Locke does not seem to have been sufficiently aware of the real value of the principle he had elucidated."[34]

There is little historical reason to doubt Locke's credentials as a champion of the vibrant commercial society that had developed in seventeenth-century England. Even his criticisms of the unproductive activities of "brokers" were undertaken from the standpoint of a firm commitment to productive activity as a basis for commerce.[35] Locke was a founder of the Bank of England; he was deeply entrenched in the Atlantic colonial world, employed first by the new American colony of Carolina and the English Council for Trade and Foreign Plantations, and two decades later again by the English Board of Trade; he was an articulate advocate of agricultural improvement; and in the chapter on property itself, he had argued that the invention of money represented an implicit collective acceptance of inequality of property since it made possible the open-ended accumulation of fortunes.[36]

Nonetheless, there are good reasons to think that that commitment should not be taken to imply that he was therefore an unambiguous champion of unfettered capitalist development on the model of the Macpherson thesis. A host of revisionist scholarship has argued that Locke's entire argument about property was deeply rooted in premises that, far from representing a radical shift into the amoral world of unlimited accumulation, remained fundamentally oriented by Protestant theology and natural law jurisprudence. Consequently, far from exploding the moral coordinates governing the creation of wealth, Locke elaborated a theory whose fundamental starting point was God's gift of the earth to mankind in common as the basis for subsistence through the calling to labor. Such a theory was intrinsically ill equipped to justify a society based on an open-ended process of capital accumulation fundamentally indifferent to such human (or divine) purposes.[37] The revisionist point is well taken. Indeed, the significance of such skepticism about the characterization of Locke as a champion of capitalism only increases when we recognize that his impulse to analyze the rights of property within a larger framework of natural justice could ultimately subsist independently of the narrower theological and jurisprudential worlds within whose terms his theory was elaborated.

I am not myself staking any very strong claims about the status of these themes in Locke's own writings. I do, however, want to argue that the history in which this dimension of Lockean thought was preserved and rearticulated through the subsequent several centuries is one that is most intelligible in relation to the practices organizing interdependence in capitalist society. Revisionists have used a displacement of the problematic of capitalism very effectively as the means for redirecting our attention to aspects of Locke's thought that were obscured by Macpherson's account. A more complex understanding of the contradictions of capitalist society might make it possible to grasp the specifically *anticapitalist* trajectories of Locke's thought in terms of ethical norms whose force was nonetheless bound to practices constitutive of capitalist society. To inhabit a capitalist society and to participate in its practices might, in other words, generate the possibility of subscribing to norms that were critical of capitalist accumulation while remaining fundamentally premised on capitalist social forms for their normative power. I have little investment in the question of whether Locke's normative presuppositions were proximately grounded in Protestant theology and natural law jurisprudence. Much more important for my purposes is the argument that the history of Lockean thought, which quickly left the radical contingencies of late seventeenth-century English political and economic debates behind without losing any of its vibrancy, was deeply engaged with these larger normative dimensions, and normative contradictions, that capitalist society itself generated.

From the standpoint of classical political economy, Locke's theory of property could be restated more or less in these terms: first, that the relationship between man and man is normatively constituted prior to political relationships; and second, that those normative relationships are determined by the action of man upon nature. Locke's theory of property effectively identified human labor not merely as the activity of nature appropriation, but also as a medium of social relationships.

Locke assumed that land was plentiful and that it was bountiful once subjected to labor. From that perspective there was little obvious reason for human beings to exchange other than their own natural cupidity.[38] Nonetheless, Locke's central concern in his discussion of property was with the question of the normative relationships existing between property holders. The fact that people were engaged in relationships of exchange was a fundamental premise of his analysis.

That the basic relationship that should pertain among property holders was in fact exchange was implicit in the category of property. The parting of individual and property could only happen legitimately on the basis of free volition, so (except for a benevolence to which Locke only considered men bound in extremity[39]) the relationships between such individuals were necessarily ones of exchange. Exchange then becomes the basis of a prosperity-generating interdependence.

> [F]or it is not barely the plough-man's pains, the reaper's and the thresher's toil, and the baker's sweat, is to be counted in the bread we eat; the labour of those who broke the oxen, who digged and wrought the iron and stones, who felled and framed the timber employed about the plough, mill, oven, or any other utensils, which are a vast number, requisite to this corn, from its being seed to its being made bread, must all be charged on account of labour, and received as an effect of that: nature and the earth furnished only the almost worthless materials, as in themselves. It would be a strange catalogue of things, that industry provided and made use of, about every loaf of bread, before it came to our use, if we would trace them; iron, wood, leather bark, timber, stone, bricks, coals, lime, cloth, dying drugs, pitch, tar, masts, ropes, and all the materials made use of in the ship, that brought any of the commodities made use of by any of the workmen, to any part of the work; all which it would be almost impossible, at least too long to reckon up.[40]

The human capacity for labor constituted a society based on relationships of free exchange. It was the remarkable social potency that Locke ascribed to labor that in turn brought into existence civil society, or government. And government was then normatively dependent for its legitimacy on the kinds of social relationships that labor had set in motion. Locke thus ascribed a remarkable role to labor. Labor was an activity that normatively regulated social relationships at a much more fundamental level than social relationships normatively regulated labor. Whatever role Protestantism may have had as the proximate cause of Locke's own preoccupation with labor, the resonance of his claims in subsequent centuries turned on the plausibility of his attribution of such remarkable social agency to it. Lockeanism mattered because its normative framework was construed in reference to practices organizing social interdependence.

It was precisely the peculiarity of the way in which laboring activity functioned as a social mediation that the concept of "value" in classical political economy was used to grasp. Central to Karl Marx's mature critique of the tradition of classical political economy, however, was the attempt to show that labor did not possess this socially mediating role intrinsically, as a function of an unalterable human nature. For Marx, what Locke and the tradition of classical political economy that followed him understood to be natural law was in fact a socially specific form of collective life. In all societies, something we would call labor had been necessary. But such labor processes and the distribution of their product were organized by social and cultural norms. There was therefore little reason to think that specific labor processes in those societies were, in any real practical sense, particular instances of "labor in general."[41] Labor, in other words, was socially mediated more fundamentally than it was socially mediating. Of course, in capitalism too labor would always remain in various ways socially mediated. But the radical transformation of laboring activity into a fundamental social mediation was an epochal characteristic of modern capitalism. This was the cornerstone of Marx's analysis of the constellation of social practices that organized capitalist society and of its dynamic tendencies.[42]

Marx had argued that when labor was generally undertaken as a means to acquire the goods of others, qualitatively different kinds of laboring activity were in practice treated as a qualitatively uniform expenditure of socially necessary labor time—what Marx called "abstract labor." As a result, the commodity effectively became a bearer of value. As a bearer of value, a commodity was exactly the combination of property and wealth that Locke was intuiting. That is, it mediated social relationships precisely insofar as it was the product of human action on nature. Outside of this transformation of the role of labor in collective life, there was little basis for a science of political economy to develop.[43] But Marx *also* argued that the tendency of capitalist development was to abolish the property-constituting capacity of labor, insofar as capitalist development turned on the separation of labor from its product through the subordination of labor to capital in the production process. For Marx, famously, the relationships of exchange in capitalist society generated the normative conception of "a very Eden of the innate rights of man. There alone rule Freedom, Equality, Property and Bentham."[44] But the practices through which such norms were lived necessarily entailed other practices, as for example in the sphere of production, that were incompatible with those norms, and that appeared to render them anachronistic. Thus liberalism could be a celebration of capitalist development as the practical foundation of freedom. But it could also become a critique of capitalist development as the abolition of the conditions of freedom. This dialectical contradiction at the heart of the relationship between liberal thought and capitalist society was fully self-evident at the beginning of liberal political thought in the ambiguities of Locke's theory of property.

The historical resonance of Locke's theory of property thus turned on the way in which his characterization of labor as simultaneously property-constituting and wealth-creating served as a way to grasp a specific form of social organization in which the practice of labor was coming to possess peculiar properties as a social mediation. Locke's political purposes are less important here than the theoretical categories out of which he built such arguments. It is very hard to understand the long afterlife of Lockean theory, absent its capacity to function as a mode of self-conscious reflection on the part of historically specific social agents trying to make sense of a historically specific form of life and its normative implications. From this perspective, Locke's argument begins to assume two different aspects—one directed towards the affirmation of *development* premised on capital formation, the other directed towards the affirmation of *right* premised on lateral relations among self-owning property holders. There is as little reason to think that these two aspects can be coherently resolved with each other as there is to think that they can be thought of separately. This condition of antinomic theoretical vectors was not an idiosyncrasy of Locke's thought. It was a reflection of the seriousness of his attempts to grapple with the form of life of which he was trying to make sense.

On the one hand, Locke's theory was a strong defense of the claims of individual proprietorship against any redistributive ambitions grounded in the common ownership of nature before its appropriation. It radically undid landed property's claims to special political status by grounding its existence in the same property-constituting powers of labor as determined property in movables. It allowed for the hiring of labor by the property holder, and treated such labor not as itself property-constituting but as an instrument of the property holder's agency. It recognized money as a legitimate means for the abolition of natural limitations on accumulation, and invoked money's invention as the basis for affirming an implicit common consent to inequality of property among men. It thus suggested that the unequal distribution of property, although built on social convention, was nonetheless fully consonant with natural justice. Furthermore, it aligned itself in implicit practical terms with an agenda of agricultural improvement that pointed towards the desirability of unequal property and the separation of labor and land as the foundation of increasing levels of productivity. In other words, even outside of the patriarchal family, Locke still condoned relationships of vertical subordination; and he condoned these on principles internal to commercial society, rather than by reversion to the kinds of paternalistic political authority against which his argument was primarily directed.[45]

On the other hand, Locke's defense of individual property against the claims of community seemed to rest at least in part on the continued availability of unappropriated wasteland (i.e. America) capable of sustaining subsistence. It was only if nature was bountiful that individuals could emerge as property owners *before* political relations had come into being. Otherwise, under conditions of scarcity, the apportioning of nature would have had to have happened as part and parcel of the constitution of property. People would have been brought into political relationships with each other by the necessary struggle to acquire the means to subsistence. This in turn would have compromised the core liberal commitment to the normative privileging of free social relations among individuals over political ones.[46] Furthermore, since the state of nature was not merely a temporal origin but a perpetual default possibility whenever the state failed to meet its normative requirements for legitimacy, the capacity of property to maintain its status as a normative standard for political life depended on the continued possibility of creating property.

Labor did not always have to constitute property, for labor could be done by servants on behalf of a master. It did, however, have to continue to be *capable* of constituting property. If it no longer could, the inauguration of civil society would effectively have abolished the law of nature, and political life would have come to determine its own normative standards of legitimacy, including the determination of property itself. The liberal impulse of Locke's argument depended on the fundamentally lateral nature of social relationships. These were relationships of exchange among property owners. That fundamental impulse was ill fitted to a society of open-ended capital accumulation, in which labor had precisely to be separated from its property-constituting capacities in order to become productive. (Adam Smith would imply much the same point when he argued that the development of capital and landed property rendered real price anachronistic as a measure of wealth.[47]) That same impulse was also one, however, most immediately intelligible *within* capitalist society. It was in capitalist society, after all, that people labored primarily as a means to acquire the goods of others. It was in capitalist society that horizontal relations of exchange among primordially free and equal individuals could be most readily imagined as normatively binding. Liberal norms could thus become the standpoint for a critique of capitalism as being inimical to free commerce among productive, property-constituting individuals.

I am not concerned here with the question of Locke's "influence" on subsequent liberal thought. The relevance of Locke as a political theorist lies in the way that he rendered visible certain normative dilemmas attendant to liberal thought. These dilemmas are inescapable insofar as liberalism's conceptual framework is bound to a set of practices that turns on the role of labor as a form of social mediation. However right C. B. Macpherson and Neal Wood might have been to characterize Locke as a thinker of early-modern capitalism, John Dunn and James Tully were equally right to emphasize that his thought was resistant to the unqualified endorsement of capitalist accumulation. This ambiguity haunted the history of liberal thought. Richard Ashcraft was surely right to conclude that "liberalism as a theoretical expression of social life supplied the values, assumptions, and arguments for both a defense and a radical critique of the existing social order."[48] This book will attempt to elaborate that characterization by reference to the social practices in which liberal norms assume their significance.

Twentieth-century libertarians sought to read Locke as a champion of free enterprise. Yet the specter of Lockeanism that has haunted the liberal tradition has more forcefully manifested itself historically in the form of invocations of the property-constituting capacity of labor; and such invocations were symptomatic of liberalism's enduring discomfort with the dynamic implications of large-scale and open-ended capital accumulation. These were discomforts that, as I argue in chapter 3, assumed a pervasive force in later nineteenth-century Britain, when dynamic capitalist development intersected with processes of political democratization. Such a reading does not turn on the intentional status of Locke's writings as advocacy or repudiation of "capitalism." He could neither advocate nor repudiate something that had not yet been conceived as an object of thought.[49] Rather this reading turns on an account of the continued power of Locke's understanding of property (even among people who could not possibly have read him or even heard of him) as an articulation of specific normative possibilities that were internal to liberal thought. Here liberal thought is understood to be premised on a set of norms whose coherence and force have been bound to practices of capitalist social interdependence, yet that have been in complex tension with the trajectories of capitalist development.

LIBERALISM AND EMPIRE

Empire has provided a key thematic for some of the most sophisticated analyses of the practical entailments of liberal thought in recent political theory. The most rigorous representative of this approach remains Uday Singh Mehta's *Liberalism and Empire*.[50] Mehta's work targeted the peculiarly abstract conception of individuality that has been fundamental to liberal argument since Locke. He took a close reading of Locke's writings as his point of departure for much larger claims about liberalism's deep implication in the violence of empire more generally.

In Locke's account of the social contract, the individuals who come together to form a civil society are devoid of any specifying characteristics beyond self-ownership. As such, their rights are apparently constituted outside of any determinate political status or qualifications beyond answerability to natural law. That is as much as to say, individuals had simply to possess a capacity for natural reason. Mehta argued, though, that Locke's conception of "reason" was necessarily bound to "a thicker set of social credentials that constitute the real basis of political inclusion." Those social credentials rested on "social structures and social conventions" that "delimit, stabilize, and legitimize, without explicitly restricting, the universal referent of his foundational commitments."[51] This covert reliance on a thicker ecology of particular cultural norms becomes clearest in a domain of life that Locke went to some lengths to juxtapose to the contractual domain of civil authority; namely, the patriarchal family, where authority is directly constituted by natural law. Complementing Carole Pateman's argument that equality in civil society was premised in Locke's writings on an affirmation of patriarchal authority in the family, Mehta noted that the individual only assumes his natural rights in civil society upon the achievement of his majority. Only then can he be said to have acquired the capacities for reason necessary to render him capable of holding himself answerable to the requirements of natural law. Switching his attention then to Locke's writings on education, Mehta noted that the acquisition of adult reason was actually bound to remarkably parochial practical and affective qualifications. These qualifications were nonetheless rendered invisible in Locke's political theory, so that liberal abstraction seemed to possess its own independent normative force despite its real concrete entailments in the form of child-rearing practices.

It follows that when liberal thinkers, blithely blind to these entailments, encountered forms of life that did not share familiar norms of personhood and sociability, they were intrinsically predisposed to regard such unfamiliarity as a sign of political disqualification. As a result, cultural difference was dismissed as the immature unreason of an incomplete humanity.[52] "Liberalism . . . was self-consciously universal as a political, ethical, and epistemological creed. Yet, it had fashioned this creed from an intellectual tradition and experiences that were substantially European, if not almost exclusively national."[53] Mehta thus construed the abstractness of liberal individuality as obscuring the actual social or affective densities that constituted its real conditions of possibility. He argued that the "psychological aspects of experience," including reason itself, "always derive their meaning, their passionate and pained intensity, from within the bounded, even if porous, spheres of familial, national, or other narratives."[54] Nineteenth-century British liberals (his analysis focused on the Mills) found themselves confronted forcefully by the hidden parochialism and exclusionary underpinnings of their political abstractions in colonies like India, where social relations were characterized by dense relations of sentiment, hierarchy and dependence that differed radically from those of contemporary Britain. Cushioned by the asymmetry of power at the heart of the colonial encounter, however, they were able to foreclose this implicit challenge through an intellectual sleight of hand that transposed the conception of immaturity that organized Locke's discussion of readying children for full social responsibility onto the concepts of "history" and "civilization." These concepts reorganized the difference between European and non-European societies into a hierarchy of readiness for adult self-government. Thus emerged the liberal conception of Britain's imperial civilizing mission.

Mehta's analysis of the institutional entailments of liberal norms is brilliant and lucid. Nonetheless, it must be observed that his notion of practical entailment remains narrow. It is possible to see how the liberal idea of the free subject presumed an indoctrination into conventions that limited that subject's freedom. It is much less clear how the abstract idea of the free subject or of the self-interested individual per se partook of the same mode of contextual contingency. That is to say, it is easy to see how the viability of a liberal conception of personhood depended on a penumbra of cultural practices, but it is less easy to understand in these same terms the conditions for the emergence of a liberal conception of personhood in the first place. Mehta's interest, like Pateman's, is in how liberal abstractions entail the kinds of overt, normative relationships that one finds in social institutions where people are bound to each other by concrete social statuses: father, husband, wife, mother, son, daughter, teacher, student, lord, servant. These are statuses that can be readily recognized as practices of social power insofar as they represent forms of unequal authority. They can also be recognized as practices that involve very particular skeins of affective attachment that do not lend themselves easily to the kind of abstract social and political concepts that liberalism turns on.

My purpose here is not to question the existence of those entailments, or their importance. Rather, I question whether the tracing of these specific *kinds* of entailments is capable of explaining the impulse to abstraction that liberal political thought manifests. "The efficacy of these structures and conventions in moderating the potentially exorbitant and unlimited claims of an individual who is naturally free," Mehta notes, "is proportional to the degree to which these structures and conventions are taken for granted." Their effectiveness derives "from a tacit allegiance to a particular ordering of society" operating "below the threshold of consciousness and theoretical discourse."[55] This, however, only explains why a political theory committed to abstract concepts needs to repress its practical reliance on concrete social statuses and institutions. It does not explain the impulse to abstraction in the first place, nor the practical conditions of its plausibility, nor the specific forms of abstraction from which liberal theory proceeds.

To approach this larger problem of liberal abstraction differently, we might instead consider the long and complex relationship that liberal political thought has maintained with political economy. This is an intimacy that Locke's theory of property classically articulates. Like much political theory, Mehta's account radically marginalizes political economy as an element of liberal thought. To the extent that political economy could feature in an analysis such as his, it would presumably have to share the same status in relation to concrete institutional entailments as political-theoretical abstractions. Indeed, political economy most certainly does entail such concrete institutions. It is far from clear, however, that political economy can be adequately understood as a displaced expression of such institutions.

Smith famously argued that in "civilized society [man] stands at all times in need of the cooperation and assistance of great multitudes, while his whole life is scarce sufficient to gain the friendship of a few persons." It is therefore "vain for him to expect [that cooperation and assistance] from their benevolence only." Rather he must appeal to mutual self-interest to make an advantageous exchange. "Give me that which I want, and you shall have this which you want, is the meaning of every such offer; and it is in this manner that we obtain from one another the far greater part of those good offices which we stand in need of."[56] In what amounted to a direct reference back to Locke's discussion of the loaf of bread, Smith identified as the ultimate symbol of civilized prosperity neither gold nor silver, but rather the common day-laborer's woolen coat. This was a commodity that embodied the "joint labour of a great multitude of workmen" whom the laborer rarely considers and never could feasibly meet.[57] This kind of "civilized" or "commercial" society is a network of objective interdependencies. Those interdependencies fundamentally condition the individual's capacity to acquire the goods individuals need to live, without in any sense being dependent on their conscious intentions or their instinctive sociability. It is a society of essentially abstract relationships, in which the points of direct exchange between individuals are based only on the contingent confluence of individual self-interest. They form only moments in much longer chains of interdependence constituted out of such contingent confluences, and are determined in their quantities, proportions and possibilities by the larger context of all other such exchanges. Each of these other exchanges in turn is undertaken in reliance on, but not necessarily with conscious regard to, those longer chains of interdependence.

We can begin to see why it might make sense to locate Locke's theory of property within the context of the emergence of the first "truly self-conscious commercial society" in 1650s England. This was a context where protoliberals developed specifically political-economic arguments that were radically incompatible with the core postulates and ultimate social aims of neo-Roman republicanism. Most defenders of the Commonwealth in the 1650s, Steve Pincus has argued, began to distance themselves from the hostility of Harrington and Milton towards commercial society. That hostility was grounded in the republican assumption that "the only proper basis of political power lay in landed wealth." Instead, these protoliberals saw in the "massive expansion of English trade, domestic and foreign, in the early modern period" the basis for a new theory that "valued human choice [and] the human capacity to produce wealth" as the most powerful forces that could be harnessed and deployed to promote both the public good and the strength of a newly emerging state.[58] By the 1680s, this radical Whig espousal of human labor as a potentially infinite source of wealth underpinned the embrace of both the anti-absolutism of the Glorious Revolution and the radical embrace of credit and commerce represented by the creation of the Bank of England immediately thereafter.[59] Here liberal abstraction most fundamentally entails the practical abstraction of a commercial society based on commodity production and exchange.

In fact, we can go one step further than Smith did in specifying the conditions of possibility under which abstract personhood could have emerged as a fundamental presupposition of liberal political theory. "When the division of labour has been once thoroughly established, it is but a very small part of a man's wants which the produce of his own labour can supply," observed Smith in the first book of the *Wealth of Nations*. "He supplies the far greater part of them by exchanging that surplus part of the produce of his own labour, which is over and above his own consumption, for such parts of the produce of other men's labour as he has occasion for. Every man thus lives by exchanging, or becomes in some measure a merchant, and the society itself grows to be what is properly a commercial society."[60] Yet in a developed commercial society as Smith described it, where land, capital and labor have assumed distinct functions in organizing production, the laborer works only in order to acquire the means to the means to life, the wage. Labor has no property in the products of labor. It follows that it is no longer merely the "surplus part of the produce of his own labour, which is over and above his own consumption," that the laborer must use to supply himself with the majority of his wants. It is now rather his *entire* laboring activity (as a means to the acquisition of a wage) that becomes a means to exchange (i.e. to commanding the labor of others). This in turn radicalizes the condition of commercial society that originated, according to Smith's own conjectural history, in the exchange of bows and arrows for meat in the forest.

It is only at this moment of the separation of labor and capital that social abstraction becomes a pervasive condition of social dependence in general. The abstractions of political economy apply in some conditional sense to any form of commercial society. But they really only assume coherence as a way of describing social dependency more generally when this radical process of commercializing social relations began taking place. That was precisely why Marx insisted that the commercial society Smith described represented a qualitative discontinuity from the forms of exchange that his conjectural history projected as origin (where exchange occurred among independent producers each engaged in a trade); but at the same time that the origin Smith projected (the exchange of bows and arrows for meat as a self-interested exchange of labor) was really itself a one-sided projective fantasy from the standpoint of the *actuality* of a capitalist form of social dependence based on commodity exchange.[61] From this perspective, liberal political economy and liberal political theory both entailed the constellation of social practices that I follow Marx in calling *capitalist* society.[62]

What difference does recognizing this make to the kind of argument that Mehta and Pateman elaborated? It certainly does not vitiate the significance of the kinds of institutional entailments on which they focused. It does, however, transform the range of questions we can ask about their significance. For Mehta, the practical projects implied by liberal commitments were ones primarily shaped by liberalism's necessary denial of its constitutive institutional or relational entailments. Liberal abstraction is essentially a denial of institutional or relational concreteness. But liberal abstractions entail forms of sociality that are themselves abstract, and the determinateness of liberal abstraction is itself in some sense bound to the determinateness of those practical forms of social abstraction. It necessarily follows that the relationship between abstraction and concreteness becomes bidirectional. That is, it can no longer be a question of only treating liberal abstractions in terms of their dependence on concrete institutional or relational forms (of domination, of affect, etc.). Concrete institutional or relational practices might *themselves* depend, for both their practical significance and their conditions of possibility, on abstract forms of social dependence. If conceptual and normative abstractions are grounded in practices of social abstraction, then their relationship to concrete institutions cannot be reduced to complicity or hostility as necessary correlatives of familiarity and unfamiliarity. James Mill's infamous hostility to Indian society and culture was only different in degree, rather than in kind, from his hostility to the forms of aristocracy, priestcraft, custom, poverty and ignorance that he considered prevalent in Britain itself. Indeed, as Javed Majeed has argued, the attack on Indian culture in his *History of British India* had primarily metropolitan political aims.[63] Mill's was not, in other words, primarily a hostility towards what Mehta termed the "unfamiliar." Mill's hostility to the unfamiliar in India would appear to have turned on prior negative judgments about deeply familiar institutional forms, and we need to grasp the conditions of possibility for those negative judgments in order to make any sense of his judgments about India.

Mehta's critique of liberal abstraction was undertaken from the standpoint of what he called the "liberalism of sentiment," which he identified above all with Edmund Burke. Mehta's Burke sustained a deep reluctance towards the empire that Britain had been building for itself in Ireland, India and the Americas. Importantly for Mehta, this reluctance was not just based on political prudence, but on a sense that empire was providing the occasion for the corruption of British liberties into vehicles of unchecked power. In Mehta's account, Burke recognized that for liberty to be sustained as a practical reality, it had to be rooted in the thick lifeworld of experience, affect and everyday practice—the domain of custom, habit and prejudice. From this standpoint, Burke critiqued abstract commitments to liberty, which he associated with philosophes, moneyed men, and Jacobins, as tending to the production of license, irresponsible adventurism, demagoguery and despotism. Burke thought that liberty had to be rooted in prescriptive practices and positive laws that could never be derived from or reduced to abstract principles (even if they had nonetheless to remain always consonant with natural law). He was therefore resistant to the tendency in the liberalism of reason to treat the unfamiliar forms of life that the British encountered in the colonies as forms of disqualifying unreason. On the contrary, hermeneutically alert both to the inevitably local and finite nature of experience and to the impossibility of justifying Britain's own constitutional forms by reference to abstract reason, Burke demanded that Britain recognize that its relationship with India was not of the kind that pertained between a rational adult and an irrational child, but rather of the kind that pertained in the meeting of two strangers—with all the obligations of cautious patience and mutual respect that such a meeting required. If Britain's own institutions could not and should not be reduced to abstract rational principles, then the prescriptive force of India's institutional and affective forms correlatively demanded a default respect. Burke's liberalism of sentiment was, according to Mehta, one that respected diversity.[64]

I freely admit that I do not find the sympathetic interpretation of Burke that Mehta offers persuasive. Burke portrayed the commercial aggression of the East India Company's exploits in South Asia as a grubby free-for-all that unleashed the animal passions of greedy parvenus against legitimate authority. His respect for Indian difference and Indian sovereignty turned most fundamentally on deference to a gentry whose landed, aristocratic status (as in a famous comparison of India to the Holy Roman Empire) he invoked as a check on the corrupting agency of money.[65] His juxtaposition of the youth of the British adventurers and the age of Indian civilization was not an inversion of the ideology of imperial pedagogical responsibility, as Mehta suggested. It was a juxtaposition of the dangers of money against the orderliness secured by the ancient inherited estates of great families. As with James Mill, so too with Burke: where he spoke of India, he as often spoke of Britain itself. Any reluctance Burke did have towards empire certainly did not extend to the "gangs of savages," whose (alleged) failure to constitute stable structures of authority left them outside the framework of Burke's sympathies entirely. Indeed, it seemed to render them in his view much closer to the radicals against whom he inveighed.[66] Burke is surely as important for upholding a vision of the British Empire as a vehicle of providential moral governance as he was for his critique of the abuses of the East India Company.[67] Finally, despite his reputation, Burke was no advocate of a Smithian political economy. Smith critiqued the East India Company as a monitory example of what happens when political power intrudes inappropriately into the domain of free commerce, and his critique was articulated from the standpoint of commerce; Burke critiqued the East India Company as the manifestation of commerce ungoverned, and his critique was from the quite different standpoint of political-constitutional order.[68]

Regardless of such differences of historical interpretation, however, the fundamental issue runs deeper. Mehta affirmed the concreteness of experience as the standpoint for a critique of liberal abstractions, and thereby treated such abstractions as means of mischaracterization. Insofar as the advocates of liberal abstraction purported to use abstractions as a means to make sense of social relations, they failed to understand that social relations could never be properly grasped through abstractions. The question inevitably arises, however, as to how we are to assign normative value (positively or negatively) to such forms of concrete immediacy. The issue is not whether there is an outside to liberal abstractions, but rather why we should normatively or ontologically privilege that outside over liberal abstractions. As soon as we further accept that liberal abstractions are not derived, either mistakenly or distortively, from concrete institutional forms, but are also premised on social practices that are themselves radically abstract, then the prioritizing of the concrete ceases to be adequate as a standpoint of social or political critique. To the extent that concrete social forms are truly outside of forms of social abstraction (as in the conception of "subalternity," for example), it is not clear how they would carry normative significance in relation to liberal abstractions. To the extent that they are themselves implicated in forms of social abstraction (as, for example, the modern household is in its relationship to the wage and to commodity consumption), it is not clear that they can serve as an *adequate* standpoint for the critique of such abstractions. Minimally: if we were to adopt the immediacy of concrete affective and institutional complexes as the standpoint for a critique of liberal abstraction, it would have to be on the basis of a careful analysis of their relationship with such abstractions rather than on the basis of a straightforward opposition to them. The force of Mehta and Pateman's critique of liberalism in terms of concrete institutional entailments needs to be complemented by a critique of liberalism in terms of its abstract entailments. This is what this book attempts.

The problem with Mehta's argument is not that it identifies a certain kind of Eurocentrism in liberal political and political-economic thought. It is rather that it conceptualizes the relationship between abstraction and cultural concretion in an overly schematic manner. It implicitly maintains that that relationship, once constituted by the violence of empire, must necessarily remain static. It suggests that the relationship between the West and the non-West is permanently that between (pretended and violent) abstraction and (actual and normative) concretion— between liberal and nonliberal, capitalist and noncapitalist. In Marxian terms, we might call this a relationship of perpetually arrested "primitive accumulation." The history of liberalism in the context of the British Empire cannot be adequately treated in terms of a constant called "cultural difference." Cultural forms are not *always* discrete institutions free of abstract entailments implicit in the determination of lifeworlds. The history of liberalism must therefore rather be treated as a dynamic process bound in no small degree to transformations in the role of commodity exchange in social relations on both sides of the colonial relationship. Such transformations, on the side of the colonized in India, must be taken to involve long-term processes of the commercialization and de-commercialization of social relations both before and under the impact of modern capitalism. The transformations in the epistemological and political status of liberalism in colonial society can only be grasped in terms of a history in which the relationship of liberal concepts to the social practices of the colonized varies in relation to the modes in which, and degree to which, such social practices were themselves implicated in practices of social abstraction.

It is only by maintaining an eye to these kinds of relational complexities that a history of liberalism that looks beyond the narrower realm of elites in South Asia can be written. For if, as I shall argue, liberal norms came to play a crucial role in the development of political claims in the commercialized agrarian society of later nineteenth- and early twentieth-century Bengal, it is surely because the forms of life that agrarian Bengalis maintained were ones that admitted the plausibility and purchase of liberal concepts, starting most radically with the plausibility and purchase of the abstractions of political economy. There is no reason to assume that these concepts will find such plausibility and purchase in every historical context to which they travel. That means we must inquire carefully into the circumstances of their reception when they do. The role of colonial institutions in making available liberal concepts and of rendering them unavoidable in the negotiation of legality in colonial society has now been definitively established, and I have no intention of questioning that account. But the process by which these norms came to achieve a dynamic of their own in agrarian Bengal, such that agrarian Bengalis themselves recognized liberal concepts as possessing normative force, is one that requires further analytical consideration.

THE NARRATIVE

My account of Lockeanism in Bengal takes for its point of departure, in the following chapter, mid-nineteenth-century debates over the principles on which hung the determination of a "fair and equitable" rent. The "Great Rent Case" of 1865 (as it was known at the time) is conventionally seen as a watershed moment in the reversal of Bengal tenancy policy, which had tended to uphold and gradually extend the privileges of landlords in levying, wherever possible, market-level rents from their tenants. The new impulse was to confirm tenants' interests in the soil, and to ground those interests in the authority of custom. The customary system of rent collection in India turned on the idea of a division of the gross product of the soil between the state and the agriculturist. From this perspective, the zamindar's proprietary interest in the soil was derived out of the state's portion. That division had left the agriculturist with a default interest in the rental value of the land. It therefore implied that the agriculturist was customarily endowed with a separate and independent interest in the soil. Such rights could not be derived from the landlord. But alongside arguments from prescription, another more specific argument about the origins of the agriculturist's independent interest in the soil haunted the decisions in, and debates around, the Great Rent Case. That argument held that custom upheld the agriculturist's claims to an interest in the soil because the agriculturist, or his ancestors, had reclaimed the property from waste. From this perspective, native custom around land instituted a system of social relations premised on the role of labor in mediating forms of political rights and political-economic interdependencies. On this basis, it elaborated a critique of the colonial state for its failure to maintain its legitimate function in protecting property.

In chapter 3, I then elaborate the broader trajectories of this Lockean impulse in colonial policy in Bengal in the context of wider imperial circuits and metropolitan-centered concerns about capitalist development. Discussions of land reform in Ireland concatenated with such discussions in India, and together they formed a crucial field in which metropolitan intellectuals could work out their own anxieties about the status of property as a normative foundation of liberal polity in an age when mature and dynamic capitalist development intersected with political democratization. The liberal discourse of custom was thus part of a wider liberal attempt to renew the social foundations of liberal polity in an age when political personality was ceasing to be bound to property qualifications. It was in the context of these larger liberal anxieties that we can understand the impulse on the part of colonial administrators and public intellectuals to endorse the claims of the smallholder to a proprietary or quasi-proprietary interest in his holding; and to do so specifically in the name of custom. This discourse of custom represented a radical departure in its identification of normative models of social obligation in native agrarian society as liberal in fundamental impulse.

In chapter 4, I then reverse gears to examine the object of liberal projection, and ask instead how it was that the smallholder was identified as an appropriate vehicle for liberal attempts to renew property as a political form. I argue that the "fit" lay in demands that had emerged from Bengali agrarian society itself in a period of the deepening commercialization of agrarian social relations. Agrarian society was not a passive object onto which these liberal anxieties were projected. It was rather an increasingly politicized subject that bore the burden of this liberal projection—a subject who staked a claim to the status of independent commodity producer in no small part on the grounds of an adverse interest in their tenancy holdings. Commercialization was not in itself new to the region in this period. But the nineteenth century saw a deepening of the role of commercial interdependence in mediating social relationships in agrarian society. At the same time it brought long-term processes of agrarian commercialization into deeper interaction with the dynamics of the mature capitalism that had come into fruition in the imperial metropole. Under these circumstances, concepts that had been generated in the context of capitalist social forms assumed ever greater plausibility in relation to forms of commercial interdependence in general. The aim of this chapter is not to show that the liberal discourse of custom was being adopted in agrarian Bengal as a political language. It is rather to argue that Lockean norms resonated with demands for the consolidation of peasant property that had emerged in the mofussil (the rural hinterland) specifically under circumstances where those demands expressed an aspiration to deeper participation in commodity production.

The concatenation of imperial discourses of property with agrarian political energies generated the condition of possibility for a strong embrace of Lockean discourses of property in agrarian Bengal in the early twentieth century. But this Lockeanism did not remain wedded to the vehicle of "custom." Rather, it tended to point either towards a radically secularized discourse of natural rights, or towards a discourse of Bengali Muslimness. The latter is the focus of the rest of the book. In chapter 5, I turn my attention to Muslim political discourse in eastern Bengal in the early twentieth century. I argue that appeals to Muslim piety as the foundation for individual and collective improvement are best understood in the context of the wider affirmation of Lockean conceptions of property. That is, Muslim piety represented a set of practices that were held up as means of securing and intensifying the connection between the smallholder and his land in a period of widespread peasant immiseration in eastern Bengal. The discourse of Muslim piety was less a gospel of Muslim prosperity than it was a vision of freedom grounded in property. The stereotypical Muslimness of the Bengal peasant was thus reinforced by an argument that identified the Muslim as the quintessential smallholder by virtue of the especially intense connection he maintained with his property through labor.

I then pursue the implications of this insight into the domain of late-colonial Bengali Muslim politics. Lockean claims about the nature of peasant property intersected with identitarian claims about Muslim self-determination that had emerged among Muslim gentry. I argue that the success of Muslim politicians in giving voice to the political aspirations expressed in the agrarian discourse of Muslim self-determination was crucial in shaping the larger political trajectories of the subcontinent, including Partition itself. I also argue, though, that the wider saturation of agrarian political discourse by claims about the property-constituting capacity of labor meant that, while the Lockean discourse of property provided a framework for formally commensurating agrarian interests, the substantial incommensurability of the interests of different strata of agrarian society narrowed the purchase of the politics of the Muslim cultivator to those strata of agrarian society who had been able to retain possession of their holdings through the difficult decades of the 1920s, 1930s and 1940s. The emphasis on Muslimness in this final chapter is not intended to distract from the larger claim that Lockean conceptions of property were ubiquitous across the diverse terrain of agrarian political discourse. On the contrary, it is intended to show how even a discourse that seems very distant from the concerns of either liberal norms or political economy is in fact intelligible only within an ideological field defined by both. Late-colonial agrarian discourses of Muslim piety may not have been "liberal." Some kind of embrace of liberal norms under circumstances of the capitalist transformation of already highly commercialized social relations, however, was constitutive of their meaning in that context.

The sources for the second part of this book are by their nature limiting. Until the early twentieth century, very little vernacular literature that was substantially addressed to agrarian issues from the standpoint of the tenantry was published in the mofussil. Of course, members of the educated Hindu gentry, the famous Bengali bhadralok, wrote extensively on agrarian issues. But whether advocating reform or the status quo, and whether dependent on rentier income or on clerical labor for their livelihood, they did so in the context of a colonial public sphere that stood at a considerable distance from the kinds of agrarian political demands that are the focus of the discussion in the second part of this book. The colonial record therefore forms the inescapable archival foundation of the argument made in chapter 4. Only in the early twentieth century did a vernacular pamphlet literature emerge out of the peasant and Muslim political mobilizations of the period. It is therefore only in the final chapter of this book that I draw on vernacular sources to any significant degree. The recognition that the colonial archive is something less than transparent as a source of information about the colonized has been immensely productive.[69] Yet an insistence on the opacity of colonial discourse risks becoming a dogmatism no less problematic than naivete about its transparency. Without granting the colonial archive the capacity to function as a source base, it is hard to see how we could recognize its refractive agency as a function of colonial power. I believe that the need to provide a plausible interpretation of the emergence of the kind of articulate peasant political organizations that we do find in twentieth-century Bengal—the kind of peasant politics that chapter 5 of this book discusses—outweighs the epistemological uncertainty to which these archival problems give rise. It is clear from the Bengali-language pamphlet literature that discourses about the property-constituting powers of labor were indeed available in the twentieth-century agrarian context. Giving an account of that availability is surely necessary.

Obviously, this is an intellectual history that departs sharply from the familiar terrain of intellectual-historical inquiry. It is a history of liberal and political-economic concepts in the vernacular. The result is, I hope, a kind of history of liberal thought that has not been written before. It proceeds from the social-theoretical attempt to understand liberalism in relation to the abstract social mediations that are constitutive of modern capitalist society. At the same time, however, it attempts to track liberalism's trajectories more deeply into social spaces that intellectual historians have generally avoided as the domain not of political thought, but of either "culture," or of its opposite, a denuded and naturalized conception of "interests." But interests need to be *construed,* and the act of construing belongs to the field of subjectivity as much as to the field of objectivity. What I argue in this book is that the construal of agrarian interests in Bengal came to be built to some degree on specifically Lockean claims about the nature of property. To that extent, agrarian political demands can be understood as internal to the history of liberalism. I do not mean to suggest, at any point, that the history of Lockeanism exhausts the history of defending small property in Bengal (let alone anywhere else). My aim is simply to show that it was possible, in the context of later colonial Bengal, to articulate agrarian interests in these terms; that that possibility was indeed widely taken up; and that, once that had happened, liberal norms could no longer be treated (whether in the name of the imperialism of a Henry Maine or the revolutionary subalternism of a Ranajit Guha) as straightforwardly alien to Bengali agrarian society.

It is probably clear that my aim in constructing this account is not redemptive. I am not trying to "recover" a liberal tradition in India in the way that Bayly is, though certainly I have no qualms about embracing liberal norms when the alternative proffered is a romantic projection of precolonial or decolonial otherness. But liberal thought has always been shot through with profound ambivalences that render liberal thought both unstable and contradictory in relation to its practical entailments. To recover the anticapitalist Lockean impulse in liberal thought is inevitably to drag along its broader capitalist entailments with it. Yet in this sense we can say that liberalism has always pointed beyond itself. The approach that I undertake in this book suggests that we must recognize, in the kinds of struggles between property and capital that have become endemic in the age of the global land grab, the persistent dilemmas of what it means to inhabit capitalist society as a conscious subject of political thought; and what is at stake in the effort to move beyond those dilemmas while nonetheless remaining committed to liberalism's universalistic aspirations for human freedom.

The Great Rent Case

The early-modern British discourse of custom turned on "prescriptive" or "presumptive" claims. As a form of law that emerged in response to the particularities of a place and a people, custom did not depend on abstract reason as the basis for its authority. It instead rested on antiquity, the sheer fact of its preservation over time.[1] Custom was a foundation of English liberties to which Parliament could appeal in its battle against absolutism in the seventeenth century; and appeals to its authority survived the upheavals of that century and would even undergo something of a revival in the eighteenth century.[2] But despite its long-standing intimacy with conceptions of liberty, the concept of custom is not an obvious place from which to begin any history of liberalism. By the nineteenth century, liberals most often identified custom as a system of constraint rather than as a vehicle of liberties. It is only after clearly grasping this historical antagonism that the novelty of the new discourse of custom elaborated by liberals in 1860s Bengal can be recognized. For in this new discourse, custom would be construed as the vehicle of liberal abstraction.

From the standpoint of the nineteenth century, the foremost exponent of the legal force of prescription was Sir William Blackstone. The great body of unwritten law subsumed both *general customs, the common law properly so called*," and "*particular laws,* that are by custom observed only in certain courts and jurisdictions." It was a collection of customs whose authority "depends upon its having been used time out of mind," and whose "principal and most authoritative evidence" was a history of judicial decisions serving as precedents.[3] Customs must not directly conflict with natural or divine law, Blackstone acknowledged; but neither need they be logically deducible from or reducible to principles of natural or divine law. The doctrine of the law was that "precedents and rules must be followed, unless flatly absurd or unjust: for though their reason be not obvious at first view, yet we owe such a deference to former times, as not to suppose that they acted wholly without consideration."[4]

Eighteenth-century radicals could also still sometimes look to custom as a domain where popular liberties might be confirmed. Yet by the end of that century the invocation of custom tended to index an impulse to limit plebeian demands for the further extension of liberties or of political voice. Emblematic here was Edmund Burke's critique of the French revolutionaries and their British radical supporters, whose greatest offense was to have slighted the proper understanding of liberty as "*an inheritance from our forefathers*" properly rooted in a "reverence to antiquity."[5] Burke insisted on the significant gap that necessarily separated the general injunctions of natural law from the particular injunctions of positive law. The Revolution, Burke argued, had appealed to abstract rights sundered from the ancient constitutional arrangements that had developed over time as modes of liberal governance—arrangements opaque to abstract reason, but nonetheless compelling obedience on the basis of their grounding in an accumulation of practical experience. In their impatient "spirit of innovation," revolutionaries expressed "a selfish temper and confined views" that ignored the weighty claims to respect that the authority, dignity and majesty of ancient landed families, the established church and the Crown all properly commanded. They favored the "monied interest," whose nature was to be "more ready for any adventure," and a "literary cabal" bent on forcible innovation on the basis of irresponsible theoretical speculation devoid of reference to practical experience.[6] "Society is indeed a contract," Burke argued; but it was a contract "not only between those who are living, but between those who are living, those who are dead, and those who are to be born."[7] The living thus had only a limited right to self-legislate. Custom was one of the crucial names of this *limitation*. In this capacity, it became closely associated in the minds of nineteenth-century Britons, whether conservative or liberal, with a domain of usage whose prescriptive authority was opposed both to abstract freedom and to the kinds of abstract social relationship that were the special object of the science of political economy.

It had been in direct response to Burke's denunciation of the French Revolution that Mary Wollstonecraft would declare that "there are rights which men inherit at their birth, as rational creatures," and that, "in receiving these, not from their forefathers but from God, prescription can never undermine natural rights."[8] Also responding to Burke, Thomas Paine would state the irreducible opposition between liberty and the authority of the past as clearly as anyone could: "Man has no property in man—neither has any generation a property in the generations that are to follow . . . I contend for the right of the living, against their being willed away, and controlled, and contracted for, by the *manuscript* authority of the dead."[9]

For Paine as for Wollstonecraft, to dig in the intermediate past for "precedents" was to stop short of a deeper archeology that would uncover the original moment "when man came from the hand of his Maker." This was the moment of the "origin of his rights" to liberty, property and security.[10] The continuous time of custom was sharply juxtaposed to the originary time of natural law. It was out of the latter that radicals derived man's eternal right to self-legislate.

Utilitarian radicals certainly had little patience for Paine's enthusiasm for natural rights: "nonsense on stilts," Jeremy Bentham famously declared them.[11] Yet they shared Paine's aspiration to liberate living reason from the strictures of prescriptive authority. "Of all tyrannies," wrote Bentham, "the most relentless is that of the dead"—and there can be little doubt that he had in mind Blackstone's "spirit of obsequious quietism."[12] Bentham, James Mill and John Austin ruthlessly criticized those "past authorities" who had grounded the legitimacy of English common law in the force of antiquity. The advocacy of mere precedent could not obscure the fact, Austin argued, that "many of the legal and moral rules which obtain in the most civilized countries rest upon brute custom, and not upon manly reason. They have been taken from preceding generations without examination, and are deeply tinctured with barbarity. They arose in early ages, and in the infancy of the human mind, partly from the caprices of fancy (which are nearly omnipotent with barbarians) and partly from the imperfect apprehension of general utility which is the consequence of narrow experience."[13]

For Victorian liberals, both improvement and emancipation entailed, in the well-known words of Walter Bagehot, "breaking the cake of custom."[14] John Stuart Mill denounced the authority of custom in an age when "human beings are no longer . . . chained down by an inexorable bond to their place in life."[15] In *On Liberty,* he had made the point even more categorically: "The despotism of custom is everywhere the standing hindrance to human advancement, being in unceasing antagonism to that disposition to aim at something better than customary, which is called, according to circumstances, the spirit of liberty, or that of progress or improvement."[16] Liberals could under some circumstances make a legitimate pact with despotism; but it appeared that they could never enjoy an equivalent peace with custom.[17] In *Principles of Political Economy,* Mill further noted that political economy had been unable to emerge as a science so long as "all transactions and engagements" took place "under the influence of fixed customs."[18] Political economy presumed that individuals rationally determined their own interests when it predicted the aggregate effects of individual actions. It followed that "only through the principle of competition has political economy any pretension to the character of a science."[19] Where there was custom, there could be no political economy—and fundamentally that was because there was no liberty.

Yet Mill also argued that political economists needed to attend more carefully, not only to "what will happen supposing the maximum of competition," but also to "how far the result will be affected if competition falls short of the maximum," as was typically the case in "the actual affairs of life."[20] The resilience of custom was not always to be regretted, for its remarkable tenacity could sometimes be made to serve liberal ends. Custom's great historical role had been to act as "the most powerful protector of the weak against the strong," a power that even "tyranny is forced to some degree to respect."[21] Malthus and Ricardo had presumed that rent was determined by a competition among capitals. In an imperfect market such as Ireland or India, however, competition for access to the land was instead between subsistence farmers. Under such circumstances, rental rates were not constrained by the expectation of a standard rate of return on capital invested. Nor were agriculturists able to transfer their labor to another productive sector in the absence of a developed alternative to agriculture. Rent would then be purely the outcome of the pressure of numbers upon a limited supply of land, rising ultimately to the maximum possible while still leaving the cultivator a bare subsistence. Free competition would then produce only an immiserating tendency to rack rent.[22]

Precisely because it defied the logic of political economy, custom could under these circumstances serve humanitarian purposes by mitigating the dynamics of competition. In any society predominantly agrarian, the only safeguard against the simultaneous deterioration in the prosperity of the general population and the stagnation of agricultural production was "the growth of a custom, insuring a permanence of tenure in the same occupant, without liability to any other increase of rent than might happen to be sanctioned by the general sentiments of the community."[23] Mill had no qualms about recommending that custom's authority be enforced as a legal means to promote the conditions for renewed agricultural improvement. Under these circumstances, custom and political economy might indeed be brought into complex and fruitful articulation. It was nevertheless custom's defiance of political economy that rendered it useful to liberal political and developmental agendas.

By the mid-Victorian period, custom had developed into a key concept used, whether approvingly or disapprovingly, to name the geographical and historical limits of the epistemological and normative purchase of liberal political theory and political economy. In its most familiar British deployments under "indirect rule" in twentieth-century colonial Africa, custom connoted a proto-ethnographic thickness and concreteness in its codification of specific kinds of gendered and generational norms and modes of personhood.[24] In nineteenth-century colonial India itself, John Lawrence and Richard Temple spearheaded an administrative system in the Punjab premised on a sturdy yeomanry bound together by ties of custom defining property rights, marriage patterns, inheritance, and collective rights on village commons. These were customs that, within a few years of the region's conquest in 1848, had begun to be systematically codified on the basis of ethnographic inquiries into the extant usages organizing coparcenary village brotherhoods.[25] These policies themselves drew on precedents in early nineteenth-century colonial India. Sir Thomas Munro, Sir John Malcolm and Sir Charles Metcalfe had made common cause against the principles underlying Bengal's Permanent Settlement, which they denounced as abstract and deductive. They sought instead "to conserve the original institutions of Indian society" under the state's universal proprietorship over the land.[26] Custom, the very linchpin of the "decentralized despotism" that the British innovated in nineteenth-century India and perfected in late nineteenth- and twentieth-century Africa, was a concept that, as Mahmood Mamdani has argued, sat at the intersection of modern governmentality and ethnographic specificity.[27]

It is well known that the British Empire would experience a broadly Tory turn in the second half of the nineteenth century. In the face of the contradictions and failures in which their imperial projects became mired, liberals increasingly retreated from the more ambitious and aggressive universalisms to which they had been committed earlier in the century. Disillusionment was transformed into what Karuna Mantena has called "alibis of empire," whereby the political failures that were generated by the institutionalization and operationalization of liberal political commitments in the colonial context were attributed to the racial or cultural inadequacies of the colonized.[28] The Sepoy Mutiny of 1857 was a particularly acute moment of disillusionment that accelerated a turn to visions of India as a land of timeless traditions whose tenacious hold over native society could be challenged only at the grave risk of undermining the stability of British rule.[29]

Yet far from representing the closure of an era of substantial debates over the appropriate policies and principles of British governance in India, there clearly remained significant divergences in impulse even *within* the overarching contours of this new Toryism. Fortifying structures of vertical authority, for example, sometimes implied a new emphasis on the authoritarian and utilitarian rationality of a colonial state founded simply on the right of conquest. But it could also sometimes imply a valorization of "traditional" forms of indigenous authority. Such traditional authority in turn might look like princely rule. But in post-Mutiny Awadh, it meant a newly secured absolute proprietorship for a previously displaced revenue-collecting gentry under a restored colonial regime that upheld a combination of traditional authority and contractual, market-determined tenancies.[30] Meanwhile, alongside both of these possibilities, the desire to cushion traditional society from the destabilizing effects of abrupt transformation under the impact of social reform or agrarian upheaval could also lead to the reinvigoration of custom as a medium of social stability. "I am firmly convinced," Sir Charles Wood, the Whig Secretary of State for India, would observe monitorially in 1866, "that our permanent hold of India would be fearfully loosened if the cultivating population felt that their customary rights were in danger."[31] On the same basis though, those of a more frankly conservative inclination could also pitch custom's status as the foundation of Indian agrarian life against the kinds of radical utilitarian programs of social and economic reform championed by reformers.[32]

Even if we recognize how internally fractured and contradictory the different strands of post-Mutiny colonial ideology were, there still seems little reason to question the assumption that the renewed endorsement of custom in this period of neo-Tory imperialism was simply part and parcel of a broader postliberal retreat from an earlier aggressive universalism.[33] From this perspective, even the frequent invocation of the authority of John Stuart Mill on custom's capacity to correct the pathologies of imperfect competition would seem to fit the parameters of this broader retreat.[34]

The discourse of custom that proliferated in the Bengal Presidency in the 1860s, however, demands that we qualify this account. I do not mean to dispute that there was a shift in imperial ideologies starting around the mid-nineteenth century; nor that that shift was to a large extent in a conservative direction. The question, however, is whether the loss of confidence in aggressively universalistic liberal projects of reformist intervention *only* pointed in the direction of an intensified politics of hierarchical-cum-traditional authority and civilizational-cum-racial difference. The concept of custom that emerged to prominence in public debate in 1860s Bengal in the course of the Great Rent Case dispute was strikingly devoid of any sense of ethnographic richness. The major personalities involved in customary relationships were identified in terms of general legal categories derived from the vocabulary of Mughal revenue practices. Legal categories like "zamindar" and "raiyat" were used to conceptualize social relations that were in turn characterized as political-economic in nature. In the process, some liberals came to identify custom as a vehicle of liberal values. Indeed, as we shall see in the next chapter, the most radical exponents of this discourse would go on in the 1870s to identify customary law with a long-standing agrarian civil society. Custom could thus serve as the basis for a critique of the existing juridico-political regime in Bengal from the standpoint of property rights. In this discourse, custom's prescriptive authority was ultimately rooted in a form of natural law whose scientific elaboration took the form of political economy. This conception of "custom" was both liberal and political-economic in nature. It stood at a crucial distance from the conceptions of custom that organized colonial governance in the era of indirect rule.

The discourse of custom that emerged in 1860s Bengal thus fits rather uncomfortably into both the more general narrative of custom's formation as a core concept of modern conservatism, and the more proximate narrative of post-Mutiny reaction. In many ways it represented not a retreat in the face of ideological crisis, but a *radicalization* of certain liberal commitments. It stood at a crucial distance from John Stuart Mill's position on the utility of custom. It treated custom as an already intrinsically liberal mechanism of social organization rather than as an alien instrument of effective liberal governance operating under constrained circumstances. It is the emergence of this new conception of custom out of the thick tangle of debates over tenancy law in the early 1860s that this chapter reconstructs.

TOWARDS REFORM

A ferocious debate over the respective entitlements of Bengal's landlords and peasant smallholders raged more or less continuously from the late 1850s through to the mid-1880s. At the core of this debate were questions about the socio-economic condition of the peasantry and the desirability of rival projects of reform. More fundamentally though, this debate was about general principles. As such, the debate returned to basic questions about the proper interpretation of the Permanent Settlement, a quasi-constitutional document that had established what Ranajit Guha called the "rule of property" for Bengal in the late eighteenth century. Coupled with this issue was the question of determining the parameters of custom's enduring capacity to establish prescriptive rights. Such rights were presumed to have remained legally binding alongside the legislative history of the colonial state, absent specific legislation to the contrary. Threaded through these quasi-empirical questions was a deeper issue still: what were the principles that determined the legitimacy of any particular property claim. This in turn was bound up with even broader questions, first about what kind of social relations did in fact prevail in the Bengal countryside, and second about what kind of social relations ought to prevail there. As such, the seemingly narrow concern with "rent" and "land revenue" was in fact a placeholder for arguments about fundamental political and normative claims and commitments.

Zamindars (literally, landholders) had been a stratum in the Mughal revenue hierarchy composed of heterogeneous social groups: some princes governing principalities, some large landowning lineages holding massive estates, some minor gentry with tiny estates. Zamindars were initially drawn from rural power-brokers after the Mughal conquest of the region in the sixteenth century. Their authority was formally derived from their imperial office, but in practical terms it was grounded in the local networks of power that rendered them effective instruments of revenue collection. In the seventeenth and eighteenth centuries, however, many zamindars had also arisen through official favor out of the clerical and functionary classes, and had been established either as tax farmers or as a new hereditary gentry. Others were created through the ex post facto legal recognition of the claims of individuals who had undertaken land clearances or purchased lands on their own initiative. Many zamindars were, by the eighteenth century, already effectively treating their claims to a portion of the revenues from the lands of their estates as both heritable and alienable property.[35]

The Permanent Settlement of 1793 had declared these zamindars "proprietors" of their zamindaris. It fixed the revenue obligations of each estate in perpetuity, and granted zamindars rights over all revenue from land subsequently brought under cultivation within the bounds of their estates. Their proprietorship was, however, subject to the so-called Sunset Rule, whereby any delay in the payment of quarterly revenue obligations subjected the estate to immediate foreclosure. The Permanent Settlement was primarily instituted with a view to reforming the relationship between the colonial state and the zamindars. It had relatively little to say about the relationship between zamindars and their tenants beyond general commitments to the protection of customary rights. Indeed, in large swathes of its territory in 1793, relationships between zamindars and tenants constituted a domain largely beyond the practical competencies of the colonial state. It was only in the wake of widespread defaults on revenue obligations (resulting from the initially high demands set under the terms of the Permanent Settlement, compounded by a slump in agricultural prices) that the colonial state was forced to reconsider the chain of authority and obligation below the level of the zamindar in a more systematic way. When it did so, it was primarily with a view to strengthening the hand of zamindars through new coercive powers (embodied in the 1799 Haftam and 1812 Punjam regulations) intended to consolidate the flow of much-needed revenue to a fiscally hungry state.[36]

In this context, the orthodox position on entitlements to land and its product in nineteenth-century Bengal was a shifting synthesis. On the one hand, colonial officials defended the Permanent Settlement on the basis of a political-economic argument about the role that security in substantial landed property might play in promoting agricultural "improvement" through the reclamation of wasteland and investment in infrastructure. On the other hand, they defended it on the basis of a jurisprudential argument about the residual legal authority of local "custom" in governing the relations between zamindars and raiyats (also spelled "ryots"), the people at the bottom of the state's revenue-paying hierarchy (though, as we shall see, not therefore necessarily at the bottom of the rent-paying hierarchy).[37] In this context, "custom" could be interpreted as justifying the preservation of the ancient patriarchal authority of zamindars over their tenant-subjects, and/or the protection of the ancient privileges of those tenant-subjects. Within this ambiguous terrain, there was ample room for controversy over how the state should construe and hence enforce different entitlements to land and its product.

John Kaye's *The Administration of the East India Company* (1853) articulated a commitment to the virtues of the Permanent Settlement that was widely shared in the Bengal services. It was, Kaye acknowledged, "an uncomfortable necessity . . . to raise revenue for purposes of government" out of "the scanty means of subsistence enjoyed by the mass of people" in India.[38] But given its unavoidability in the face of the "embarrassed condition" of Indian finances, the East India Company deferred to the Indian's instinctive "horror of change" by hewing closely to Mughal precedent.[39] Applying themselves to the problem of instituting a system that would respect the established social order while correcting the abuses of the ruinous tax-farming model prevalent before the Permanent Settlement, the leading servants of the East India Company of the 1770s and 1780s gradually came to the conclusion that the best way to "respect the rights both of the Zemindar and the Ryot, and to develop the industrial energies of the country," was to recognize "the claims of the Zemindars, as proprietors of the soil," and grant them "permanency of tenure."[40] Kaye rejected the argument (voiced most famously by James Mill) that "the Zemindarree settlement was an idea hastily conceived by Lord Cornwallis—the aristocratic plan of an aristocratic statesman—an ignorant *Englishism,* in short, utterly unsuited to the country in which it was designed to make it strike root." The Permanent Settlement was not "of aristocratic conception, English importation, or precipitate execution. It was emphatically the work of the Company's civil servants—members of the middle classes, who had come out to India in their boyhood—and they had been incubating it for a quarter of a century."[41] Despite "errors of detail," the settlement's basic aim of giving "the landlord such a beneficial interest in the improvement of the land as would induce him to venture upon this reclamation of the jungle" had been broadly successful.[42] "There is hardly a rood of land not under cultivation. The jungle has entirely disappeared . . . . The provinces under the Perpetual Settlement are the most thriving provinces in India."[43] Taken on balance, Kaye concluded, the zamindari settlement had been more successful in producing general prosperity than raiyatwari rivals that purported to uphold "the interests of the cultivators of the soil."[44]

The defense of concentrated landed property could lead to an overt hostility towards the prescriptive rights of raiyats. Typifying the strong pro-landlord position of the Bengal civilians was the Bengal Board of Revenue's defense of "the place of natural contracts between the *owner* of the soil, and the *tiller* of it, with which in a healthy state of society, it would be injudicious, if not unjust, on the part of Government, to interfere in any shape or degree."[45] As the Whig Secretary of State for India, Lord Argyll, would explain in the 1870s, curtailing landlords' power to enhance rent would effectively mean withdrawing a portion of the gross product paid in rent "from the reproductive fund out of which improvements can be effected." It was possible to "transfer from the owner to the occupier, for a time, the whole margin of profit" resulting from the ever increasing margin separating a permanently fixed rental rate and the "natural rise" in the value of the product. Yet the occupancy raiyat would not hesitate to charge the full value of the land as determined by competition to any incoming subtenant or raiyat subsequently purchasing that right of occupancy from him—thus becoming in turn a petty landlord.[46]

Advocates of political-economic orthodoxy generally assumed that the relationship that bound zamindar and raiyat had already generally come to be defined in terms of a free contract between the owner of land and someone desiring to use the land for productive purposes. In reality, under circumstances where labor was scarcer than land, the entire system of zamindari property relied on a remarkable degree of extra-economic coercion down through at least the first half of the nineteenth century.[47] But advocates of political-economic orthodoxy saw the state's interference in tenancy relations as anachronistic and harmful.[48]

"Capital and Land," an anonymous essay published in 1863 in direct response to the judicial controversies with which this chapter is primarily concerned, gave voice to a particularly trenchant example of this reasoning. If Bentham had been right in positing his famous maxim of "greatest good of the greatest number," then the promotion of greater production was a logical corollary. Furthermore, if "we should contrive to make this increased production coeval with the employment of a lesser quantity of manual labor upon the land," then food would need to become cheaper while labor would need to be directed "into new and profitable channels." Pointing to the development of railways, tea and coffee plantations, the cultivation of silk, cotton and indigo, the mobility of populations, and modern education, the author insisted that "no one can look at India now without seeing that we are on the eve of a great industrial development." This nascent development could best be advanced by bringing about "a marriage between capital and land." That in turn required that capital should "find no difficulty thrown in the way of its free alliance with land, whenever it found its interest to point that way."[49] "Capital and Land" identified three forms of such obstruction in India. First, coparcenary rights, a form of joint proprietorship that prevailed outside of Bengal proper and Assam, prevented the formation of "considerable estates [held] by single individuals" and hence should be abolished as "relics of a former stage of society."[50] Second, the binding power of custom led to an unacceptable degree of interference in the private contractual relations between individuals, and defeated any "hope of progress" by creating an "almost impassable barrier to any healthy change."[51] Finally, the extension of occupancy rights and rental protections to raiyats distorted the normal functioning of the market.[52]

Rent, the Malthusian author of "Capital and Land" explained, was the portion of the value of the gross product that remained with the owner of the land after the normal costs of labor and capital had been paid. This surplus increment was generated not by human productive powers, but by the natural fertility of the soil. The comparatively scarce tracts of fertile land had the peculiar capacity to generate a rising demand for its own product by sustaining a growth in population. Land became property through the application of labor to it. Having naturally chosen the most fertile land available, however, the original claimant eventually became a proprietor and landlord who allowed others to work his property in return for the payment of rent. The rate of such rent was determined by the degree to which the productivity of the soil exceeded that of the less fertile land brought under cultivation in the wake of the rise in food prices that inevitably followed increases in population.[53] "It follows from this that the natural state of an advancing society is

to create property in land in the hands of its original cultivators, who then naturally cease to be cultivators and become landlords."[54] Since rents rose in response
to capital accumulation, population increases, agricultural improvements, and
rises in the prices of agricultural products, it followed that "increasing rent must
be allowed to be a good thing," indicative generally "of a nation's prosperity." Rent
is the "stimulus" that forces the soil's cultivators to "yield its full fruits."[55] If a "progressive steady increase" in rental rates was to be achieved, the government must
"refuse to fix any man's rent" and grant the landlord "the power of ejecting a cultivator at pleasure."[56] This was in accordance with the basic principle of leaving the
private individual free to make contracts and do "what he likes with his own,"
without "communistic" interference from the government. If we "do not regulate
the prices of commodities, why should we regulate that of land?"[57]

In comparison, John Kaye was a much more moderate advocate of zamindari
rights. If there was one "great blot" on the record of the Permanent Settlement in
Bengal, he noted, it was surely that it had failed to define the claim that the landlord could make on his tenant in the process of permanently specifying and fixing
the amount the state could levy from the landlord. As a result, the zamindars generally set out to "exact from the Ryots as much as they can be made to pay; and
there is no doubt that what is left to the actual cultivator, after all these exactions,
is little more than suffices to keep the souls and bodies of the peasantry together."
Warren Hastings, Kaye argued, had "maintained that it was the duty of Government 'to fix the deeds by which they hold their lands and pay their rents, to certain
bounds and defenses against the authority of the Zemindar.'" The Permanent Settlement had enshrined the same noble intentions, but later administrations had
abandoned them entirely in the face of fiscal challenges. "It was decreed, indeed,
that the Ryot had no rights, and he was left to fight it out with the Zemindar." In
this, the fate of the raiyat was identical with the fate of the laborer everywhere; but
at least in Bengal, thanks to the delta's renowned fecundity, "the peasant is as well
supplied in that flourishing province as in any part of the world."[58]

These arguments were all variations of laissez-faire liberalism of a familiar
nineteenth-century kind. They focused on the role of security of property in
unlocking the potential for economic growth in a society stunted by a history of
despotism, superstition and custom. But there were most certainly rival positions
in play as well that would achieve increasing momentum in the course of the nineteenth century. The raiyatwari critics of the Permanent Settlement deplored the
unnecessary and wasteful subjection of raiyats to exploitative zamindar middlemen. They also denounced the inability to reassess revenues on estates periodically as fiscally irresponsible.[59] Thomas Munro, a key figure in the Scottish School
of colonial administration, had identified raiyats as holders of long, renewable and
transferable quasi-proprietary leases under the superordinate universal sovereign
proprietorship of the state. He appealed to customary modes of apportioning the

gross product of the soil between sovereign and subject as the proper mechanism for regulating the extraction of revenue. Raiyatwari settlement would also find support at the opposite end of the political spectrum, in the hands of James Mill. Mill shared Munro's hostility towards intermediary landholding classes; but rejected Mughal precedents of product apportionment in favor of the Ricardian doctrine of differential rents as the appropriate mechanism for the regulation of revenue demands. This was a doctrine that, in the absence of a functioning market-mechanism of the kind classical political economy presumed, would have to be operationalized through the technocratic expertise of trained Company officers.[60] Such arguments impacted attitudes even in landlord-friendly Bengal, even if most Bengal civilians (that is to say, members of the Indian Civil Service) continued to perceive it as a wrong-headed heterodoxy. The force of their arguments was intensified by the failure of the Permanent Settlement to generate sufficient revenues to keep the Company out of debt. Such pressures led the Bengal government to insist on direct control over most of the lands that fell outside the estates recognized in 1793. Large portions of the shifting alluvial lands and jungles of (especially eastern and southern) Bengal thus became *khas mahal,* land that was leased directly by the government to cultivators or farmers in what amounted to a raiyatwari system.[61]

But alongside debates about revenue settlements, a robust juridical discourse that bound the legal rights of raiyats to the continued prescriptive force of native custom also thrived in nineteenth-century Bengal. This was an argument that remained self-consciously faithful to the quasi-constitutional framework established by the Permanent Settlement. It nevertheless identified custom as the vehicle of a petty proprietorship that had survived 1793 intact. In the Bengal administration itself, John Herbert Harington was perhaps the weightiest voice advocating this position. Harington had been active in the Company's revenue institutions since before the Permanent Settlement. His commentaries on the Bengal revenue regulations were, in the words of W. S. Seton-Karr many years later, "for Indian legislation what Coke on Littleton is for English law."[62] Harington argued that, if

> by the terms *proprietor of land, and actual proprietor of the soil,* be meant a landholder possessing the full rights of an English landlord or free-holder in fee-simple, with equal liberty to dispose of all the lands forming part of his estate as he may think most for his own advantage, to oust his tenants, whether for life or for a term of years, on the termination of their respective lease-holds, and to advance their rents on the expiration of leases at his discretion; such a designation, it may be admitted, is not strictly and correctly applicable to a Bengal *zemindar,* who does not possess so unlimited a power over the *khoodkasht ryots* and other descriptions of under-tenants, possessing, as well as himself, certain rights and interests in the lands which constitute his zemindary.[63]

In other words, whatever proprietorship the Permanent Settlement had invested in the zamindar had not superseded or abolished claims over the soil that were based on different sources of authority.

In 1827, Harington sought to reverse the tendency of decades of legislation strengthening the hand of the zamindar over tenants. He drafted a declaratory Regulation that would secure the customary rights of raiyats, which he considered to have been legitimately established under the Mughal constitution. These included rights to occupancy and to the limitation of rent to either a hereditary fixed rate or the rate of the pergunnah (subdistrict), depending on the specific status of the raiyat. The Permanent Settlement, the draft stated, was never intended to "abrogate or abridge in any degree the prescriptive rights and privileges of . . . under-tenants or cultivators of the soil of whatever denomination." The zamindars therefore "must be considered to possess only a restricted property and interest with respect to the lands occupied by permanent under-tenants." Such permanent under-tenants were entitled to an "equitable rent" calculated "to leave to the tenant a fair and reasonable profit, after providing for the wages of labour and every other expense of computation, with due attention to the contingencies of season and other casualties, and to any charges beyond the rent payable to the landlord."[64]

Harington's proposal was roundly defeated. His critics questioned the authenticity of such customary rights among a class of cultivators who were really "only agricultural labourers"; the compatibility of the proposed Regulation with the proprietorship guaranteed to zamindars by the terms of the Permanent Settlement; the justice of a Regulation that threatened to reallocate an increasing portion of the rent fund to the raiyat; and the wisdom of entrenching customary rights that hindered the access of capital to the land.[65] By the mid-nineteenth century, supported by these kinds of arguments, the legal position of the zamindar had achieved its zenith.[66] The advocates of absolute zamindari proprietorship and of the customary rights of raiyats were both polemically and substantively polarized.

Yet the tide of policy would in the 1850s begin to manifest a distinct shift in favor of the advocates of custom. This impulse found its most significant expression in Act X of 1859, "a real and earnest endeavor to improve the position of the ryots of Bengal, and to open to them a prospect of freedom and independence which they have not hitherto enjoyed, by clearly defining their rights and by placing restrictions on the power of the zemindars, such as ought long since to have been provided."[67] The act distinguished three tenant statuses: (1) For tenants who could show that they had paid an unaltered rate for twenty continuous years, Act X established a legal presumption in favor of a hereditary rent fixed in perpetuity. Such tenants would no longer have to provide proof of their continuous status since before the Permanent Settlement; they merely had to answer evidence to the contrary. (2) For tenants who had for twelve years uninterruptedly occupied raiyati land (that is, land outside the landlord's personal demesne holdings), the act recognized a right of occupancy at "fair and equitable" rates. It guaranteed that the landlord had no right to evict the tenant from possession of the lands they cultivated or to raise rents arbitrarily. (3) Tenants who could meet neither of these criteria were consigned unambiguously to the category of tenants at will. That is, such tenants were fully subject to rates determined by market competition, and their tenancy could be terminated at any time or as stipulated by lease terms. Furthermore, the entitlement to "fair and equitable" rents that accompanied the right of occupancy granted by to the second category above was also the basis for a limitation of the legitimate grounds of rent enhancement to only three circumstances: (a) when the rent paid by the tenant was below the prevailing rate for comparable lands in the subdistrict; (b) when the value of the produce had increased due to causes other than the cultivator's own activities; and (c) when the area of the holding was found to be greater than previously understood.

The bill was not primarily intended to reform the law on questions of the prescriptive entitlements of tenants. On these issues, the framers understood the legislation to be declarative of existing law. Its primary purpose was rather "the revision and consolidation of the distraint and summary suit laws" that had existed since the Haftam and Panjam regulations. It sought to clarify the entire disparate body of laws surrounding the procedures for settling disputes over and recovering rent. It especially set out to remove the zamindars' extensive coercive powers, which it blamed for "a large amount of oppression inflicted by the more wealthy and powerful, upon the poorer classes."[68] It was thus primarily a bill about jurisdiction and procedure. It created, in the words of Justice Phear of the High Court in Calcutta in 1865, a "right to oblige the other side to submit to the arbitration of the Collector with regard to the terms upon which the holding shall be continued." This was a right that could be "invoked at any time, when either party is dissatisfied with the existing relations between himself and the other, or on as many occasions in succession as the dissatisfaction may arise."[69] From 1857 to 1859, the bill was debated primarily as a measure that would dramatically enlarge the role of the state in contractual relations concerning the land.[70]

Yet in the course of the debates leading up to the passage of the bill, other issues were already beginning to emerge. The British Indian Association, the voice of Bengal's zamindars, complained about "encroachments on the rights secured to landholders by immemorial usage and the laws."[71] H. T. Raikes of the Sudder Dewany Adawlut (Chief Civil Court) agreed. He criticized the draft legislation as tending to "make the ryot's tenure permanent and his rent *fixed*," so "aggrandis[ing] the ryot at the expense of the zamindar," who was "the party entitled to derive benefit from any rise in the value of land consequent on the increase in the price of landed products."[72] Charles Currie, a senior civilian, acknowledged that hereditary rights existed. He nonetheless insisted that "the system of arbitrarily determining the amount of rent to be paid by tenants is contrary to the true principles of political economy." This was especially the case in Bengal, a country that had already "obtained a natural state" based on market relations of free and mutually advantageous commercial exchange.[73]

In contrast, A. Sconce, at that time a judge of the Sudder Dewany Adawlut (and soon to be appointed Bengal Member of the Legislative Council), saw the legislation as grounded in the promise of the 1793 Regulations to "enact laws necessary for the protection and welfare of ryots and other cultivators of the soil."[74] The Permanent Settlement, he argued, was supposed to have settled the rates paid by raiyats to zamindars as permanently as those paid by zamindars to the state. Sconce invoked the prescriptive authority of "common law" and "customary law." "Resident, permanently-occupying ryots" derived their rights over the soil not from zamindars but from "labour and occupancy." The resulting entitlements were enshrined in "the sacred force of common law in this country."[75]

In March of 1859, the Report of the Select Committee appointed to consider the proposed legislation reported that the "principles on which the Bill is founded have met with very general acceptance from the local officers of both the Revenue and Judicial Departments in the Lower Provinces, as well as from the two Boards of Revenue and the Lieutenant-Governor." They recommended no alterations at the level of principle. But the alterations of detail they recommended represented a substantial departure from the established legal discourse of customary entitlements in Bengal. The bill clarified that the status of "hereditary ryot" was no longer to be established by reference to proof of "title antecedent to the Permanent Settlement," but rather on the basis of a presumption arising after twenty years' continuous possession at an unchanged rate of rent. It replaced the old term "at pergunnah rates" (rates whose existence had been plausibly called into question) with the language of "customary and fair" rates. This would in turn end up being enshrined as "fair and equitable" rates. It replaced the term "khudkasht ryot" ("self-cultivating" or "own-cultivating," generally understood in these debates to refer to a cultivator who resided in the village of the lands he cultivated) with the term "resident ryot." Then, having determined that residency was not a criterion for occupancy rights in the North-West Provinces (to which the act would also apply), it erased the criterion of residency in favor of twelve years' continuous possession.[76] Thus the ultimate relationship between the rights enshrined by Act X and the domain of custom from which they purported to derive their legitimacy was attenuated in ways that opened up the space for the enormous controversy that would follow.

FAIR AND EQUITABLE

In the long trail of judicial fallout following the passing of Act X, it was the crucial intermediate category of the occupancy raiyat that would prove the most troublesome to the courts. In the case of *James Hills v. Ishwar Ghose,* Sir Barnes Peacock, the first Chief Justice of Calcutta's new High Court (which superseded the Sudder Dewany Adawlut, or Chief Civil Court, in 1862), had issued a series of judgments on appeal in the period 1862 through 1864. His decisions doggedly applied Malthusian principles to the interpretation of Act X's "fair and equitable" stipulation.[77]

An English indigo planter, self-described elsewhere as "the most extensive planter in India," brought suit as a middleman in the tenure hierarchy to recover arrears of rent at an enhanced rate from a cultivating tenant holding under him.[78] At stake in this suit was primarily a new strategy on the part of indigo planters. Hills argued that tenants had been the beneficiaries of unnaturally low rents in return for their cooperation as growers of indigo. After indigo-growing raiyats had begun a collective boycott of the plant in 1859–60, planters had sought to use the provisions in Act X allowing enhancement of rent as leverage over tenants unwilling to plant. They did this either to get them to return to indigo cultivation or to recoup some of their losses. Hills based his claim for enhancement on the basis that the value of the produce had increased independently of the agency of the raiyat. In the original decision, the Additional Judge of Nadia had allowed an increase, but he had limited it proportionally to the increase of the value of the product. That is, the rent could be increased only to the same degree that the value of the product had increased.

When the case came before the Calcutta High Court on appeal, Chief Justice Peacock delivered a judgment that unequivocally rejected the principle of proportion on which the lower court had based its decision: "The Act does not say that the increased rent shall bear the same proportion to the original rent, as the increased value does to the original value, but merely that the rate shall be fair and equitable." The real question, he noted, was how to determine a "fair and equitable" rate. The judge of the lower court had been correct to say that "enhancement can take place only so far as the ground on which it is claimed has been proved." Peacock interpreted this to mean the rent could not be enhanced "beyond the full amount of the increased value."[79] Working from the presumption that the former rent had been fair and equitable, that rent had by definition left to the raiyat sufficient income to compensate him for the expenses of cultivation, the full wages of labor, an appropriate return on capital (whether his own or borrowed from a moneylender), and a fair allowance for the risk of seasonal losses. The question then left to be decided was, if all other expenses remained constant, how was the new income that the increased value of the raiyat's product represented to be distributed?

The answer, Peacock insisted, lay in the very concept of "rent" as defined in Malthus's *Principles of Political Economy:* "he there defines rent to be—'that portion of the value of the whole produce which remains to the owner of the land after all the outgoings belonging to its cultivation of whatever kind have been paid, including the profits of the capital employed estimated according to the usual and ordinary rate of agricultural capital at the time being.'" Under circumstances where the value of the product was ever increasing and the state's claim on that product was permanently fixed, the landlord might claim the entire amount of every increase in the value of the product and still leave the raiyat in exactly the same condition as before the increase—that is to say, receiving the same fair and equitable return for inputs of labor and capital. The increase in value would then be properly considered part of the "unearned increment," or "rent" as it was understood in classical political economy. In consequence, Peacock concluded, there was no reason to think that the right of occupancy should mean that the occupancy raiyat was entitled to pay a rate of rent lower than a tenant at will. A fair and equitable rent would be figured on exactly the same principles for both classes of tenants.[80]

Peacock insisted that Act X's provision for a right of occupancy was a legal innovation. The expansive interpretation that a right of occupancy further entitled the raiyat to a lower rental rate would constitute "an unjust interference with the vested rights of the landowners in the permanently settled districts."[81] Indeed, allowing the occupancy raiyat to retain a portion of the unearned increment would amount to granting the raiyat a proprietary interest in the soil. "I cannot think that it was the intention of the Legislature by Section 6 of Act X of 1859 to give to a ryot who obtained possession only 12 years ago, when he had no right to the land, and when the zemindar was not even bound to accept him as a ryot or to admit him into possession, any proprietary right which would entitle him to participate, beyond the period of his tenancy, in any increase in the value of the land not caused by his own agency, or at his expense."[82] As such, the "fair and equitable" rent to which the occupancy raiyat was entitled must surely be the rate that the market determined of its own accord, leaving the landlord his full share in the rent after fully compensating labor and capital: "To be fair and equitable, it must be fair and equitable so far as both parties are concerned, not fair and equitable as regards the ryot, and unfair and inequitable as regards the proprietors of the land."[83]

Peacock was not denying the binding force of established custom. As a member of the Legislative Council when the bill was being framed, he had been especially concerned "not to interfere with any well-known usage or recognized rights of the ryots."[84] But he took it as given that such customary entitlements were local in nature, and insisted that the burden of proof lay with the raiyat. "It is not because some old rights may exist without the means of proof that rights are to be created which never existed before, and in favor of ryots who never had any rights in the land at all."[85] This narrow construction was particularly justified given the undesirability of such rights in the first place, insofar as they tended "to perpetuate small holdings which must ultimately become injurious to the best interests of the country," and to burden the courts with the necessity of intervening in disputes that might have been better left to the contracting parties to settle on their own.[86]

Despite Peacock's verdict, unclarity still haunted the law. The concurring but separate review of judgment delivered by the junior justice presiding over the *Ghose v. Hills* appeal, Shumboonath Pandit, had already, without altering the actual mechanics or broad impulse of Peacock's decision, sounded a subtle but prescient note of inconsistency with the principles outlined by the Chief Justice.[87] Justice Pandit had confirmed the principle that any increase in the value of the product not resulting from the agency of the cultivator (and not offset by increased costs of production) could be claimed by the landlord.[88] He explicitly acknowledged, however, that raiyats who cultivated lands outside of the zamindar's demesne "have been, according to custom, allowed a share out of the profits of the lands cultivated by them beyond the bare wages of a hired laborer." Zamindars could not therefore claim "by law or custom that complete right over the lands and tenants which parties called proprietors enjoy in other countries."[89]

Meanwhile, a series of cases had had to struggle with the problem of defining just what constituted a raiyat at all in the terms of Act X. In the 1820s, Harington had wanted to institute appropriate protections to "under-tenants" in general, from "dependent talookdars" all the way down the tenure hierarchy. In 1853, Welby Jackson, a judge of the Sudder Court, had identified patnidars, or perpetual lease-holders, as the agents of "improvements in the state of agriculture and manufactures," and hence as the tenants most deserving of rights to occupancy. (He clearly had in mind British indigo planters.) If raiyats had a just complaint, it was against the arbitrary and improper procedural powers of the landlord, not his rental demands.[90] It had not been until a Minute of February 19, 1850, by A. Sconce (at that time the Collector of Chittagong) that the cultivator, rather than the intermediate tenure-holder, had been specifically identified as the exclusive beneficiary of legislative protections of this kind.[91]

Throughout the 1850s and 1860s, the legal category of "raiyat" was, in keeping with long precedent, identified with the sociological category of "cultivator." Yet neither fact nor law suggested any perfect congruence between the two. After all, not everyone who claimed to be a raiyat seemed to be engaged directly in cultivation. Conversely, the terms of Act X made clear (as Peacock had pointedly observed) that not all cultivators could be considered raiyats. After all, the legislation specifically precluded the under-tenants of raiyats from acquiring occupancy rights.[92] In a series of cases, judges were forced to determine whether specific parties in suits should be considered to be raiyats as contemplated in the relevant sections of Act X, or whether they were really holders of intermediate tenures and hence not entitled to its protections. In *Harish Chandra Kundu v. Alexander,* the court noted that Act X "draws a distinction between ryots and farmers of lease-holders, but contains no definition of the sense in which the terms are to be understood." In this case the defendants were indigo planters seeking protection under Act X. They were "realizing rents from ryots on the land in question," and their lease "purports to be a farming lease" that not only gave to the owners of the indigo factory "a mere right to hold and cultivate," but also to "under-let the whole or any part of the land to ryots for the purposes of indigo cultivation or otherwise." The lessee, the court concluded, was clearly "something more than a ryot, which according to Wilson's Glossary and Shakespear's Dictionary, appears to mean 'a subject, cultivator, or peasant.'"[93] In *Bindrabund Chunder Chowdhree v. Issur Chunder Biswas,* the court held that the village lessees being sued could not be deemed raiyats in the absence of compelling evidence that they had "ever cultivated these lands or sublet them to the other actual cultivators of the soil (thus keeping alive their rights of occupancy)."[94] And in *Baboo Dhunpat Singh v. Baboo Gooman Singh,* the court held the lower court's decision to have been in error in designating "the holders of a tenure comprising 11,000 beegahs [about 3,700 acres] of land" as khudkhasht raiyats, or indeed "as ryots at all. It is very difficult to lay down any general interpretation of the word 'ryots,'" the court acknowledged. "As a rule they are cultivating tenants, but they may not be cultivators at all themselves; they may cultivate their land by hired labor or by under-tenants. In this case the amount of land included in the tenure is, we think, sufficient evidence that the tenants are not ryots."[95]

Peacock's decision did nothing to resolve these kinds of difficulties. Moreover, it was simply too controversial to stand as settled precedent, provoking criticism from both pro-raiyat and pro-indigo lobbies. "No Act of the Legislature in this country was ever passed," observed Justice Jackson in 1864, "which has been the subject of more contention than this."[96] In 1859, the Protestant missionaries of Bengal had enthusiastically applauded the progress of the rent bill as the "most important boon ever offered by the British Government to the mass of the people of Bengal." Unsurprisingly, they were horrified by Peacock's decision.[97] G. N. Taylor of the Revenue Department condemned Peacock's decision as "a doctrine which is full of danger and injustice to the whole body of occupancy ryots."[98] Henry Maine, Law Member of the Viceroy's Council, considered Peacock's judgment to be "determined by what is his chief intellectual characteristic, extreme subtlety confining itself within very narrow limits." In this case, those were limits that willfully excluded "the ancient historical relations of landlord and tenant."[99] If Peacock had properly understood the distinction between rent by competition and rent by custom, he would have realized that "all quotations from politico-economical writers were entirely irrelevant" to the issue at hand.[100] Ashley Eden, then Secretary to the Revenue Department, noted that Peacock's "exposition of the law apparently leaves no room for distinction between a fair and equitable rent and a rack-rent." He argued that in the wake of such a precedent "the law as it stands does not seem to be in accordance with the received theory of rent in India, with the whole course of legislation down to 1859, or with the intention of those who passed Act X of that year." All such precedent properly amounted to a "theory of rent" as "the proportion of the produce to which the ruling power is entitled," a rate determined "according to local custom and usage."[101]

Meanwhile, indigo interests, self-described as "the very roots which spread into the ground and enabled the tree of European civilization in the East to derive nourishment from the soil," fought a vicious political battle in the wake of the act. When the new Lieutenant-Governor, Sir John Peter Grant, failed to back them unequivocally in their battle against insurgent raiyats refusing to grow indigo, they denounced him as the head of a "Despotic Government" that combined the old Company proclivity for monopoly with a new radical proclivity for socialism. In the face of a "universal combination to refuse the payment of rents" among the raiyats of Nadia and Jessore, complained the indigo planter R. T. Larmour, "the landlord in Bengal has . . . in reality no means of recovering his rents."[102] The ostensible victors in the case Peacock decided could find little comfort in the decision. A determination of rental rates based on "minute inquiries into the value of the produce, and the expense incurred by the ryot in its production and conversion into money . . . guided by the definition of Malthus" only offered the planters the prospect of endless "litigation equally ruinous to their peace and their pockets."[103]

Henry Maine considered "a judicial reversal of the decision as the best settlement of the question." It would avoid the uncertainty attendant on frequent legislative changes, as well as provide an occasion to elaborate a new principle to supersede Peacock's precedent. Maine knew from his friend George Campbell, a judge of the High Court, that "the great majority of the Court are in favour of the view taken *at first* by the District Judge" (the principle of proportion). He was pushing Campbell to bring the issue before the full bench of fifteen justices.[104] The government meanwhile requested the judges of the High Court to provide separate (and as it turned out deeply conflicting) opinions on possible amendments to the act. It grudgingly moved to draft new legislation that would put an end to the "state of uncertainty" exacerbated by subsequent decisions in the High Court in which the "presiding judges appear to have proceeded upon a different principle" from that laid down in Peacock's judgment.[105] For while the court consistently upheld Peacock's Malthusian principles in relation to tenants at will, the judicial waters surrounding the occupancy raiyat in 1864 grew ever murkier. Led by George Campbell, members of the court bucked Peacock's precedent outright with respect to the determination of fair and equitable rents for occupancy raiyats. They held that the raiyat's rent should be adjusted "according to the method of proportion; that is, the increased rent must bear to the old rent the same proportion as the present value of the produce of the soil bears to its former value."[106]

The judicial process came to a head in 1865 in the appeal of *Thakurani Dasi v. Bisheshwar Mukharjya*, referred by Justices Campbell and Jackson on appeal to the full bench of all fifteen justices of the High Court.[107] The plaintiffs had sued for enhancement on the grounds of an increase in the value of the product. In response the defendant, having failed to establish a claim to a fixed rent, was declared to have rights of occupancy. The question then arose as to "the principle on which the calculation [of the new rent] should be made." The case was referred to the full bench to determine, firstly, whether the "fair and equitable rate to be awarded" was "that which might be obtained by commercial competition in the market" or "a rate to be determined by the custom of the neighbourhood in regard to the same class of ryots." Secondly, if the neighborhood rate had not adjusted itself to the increased value of the produce, "then on what principle is the customary rate to be adjusted."[108] The lead opinion was written by Justice Trevor and concurred in without further comment by Justices Loch, Bayley, Jackson and Glover. Justices Macpherson, Phear, Campbell, Pandit, Seton-Karr, Kemp, Morgan, Norman and Steer provided separate judgments broadly concurring in Trevor's opinion. Chief Justice Peacock stood alone in a dissenting opinion that restated his original position.

Under the Mughals, Justice Trevor explained, the gross product of the land was divided in fixed proportions between the state and the raiyats. The zamindars were entitled to a fixed cut of the revenue they collected on the state's behalf. The final decades of the Mughal empire and the early years of the British accession to the diwani saw the collapse of this system into a chaotic grab for revenue. The zamindars seized the opportunity to enhance their share through the levying of cesses, additional taxes. That zamindars resorted to this "circuitous mode of increasing the payments" demonstrated the endurance of custom's authority throughout this period. It "assuredly would not ... have been resorted to, *if there had been an acknowledged right in the landlord to increase the rent. Its adoption is a proof that there was once an effective limitation, or real customary rent.*"[109] When the Permanent Settlement limited the demands of government revenue from the zamindars, it left "*the zemindar to appropriate to his own use the difference between the value of the proportion of the annual produce of every beegah of land which formed the unalterable due of Government according to the ancient and established usage of the country, and the sum payable to the public.*"[110] Thus while the zamindars were named the "actual proprietors of the soil," this status fell far short of a concession of an "*absolute* estate" to the exclusion either of the government's interests in the soil or the raiyat's.[111] The privileged rights associated with khudkasht status could therefore still be acquired even after the Permanent Settlement had been instituted. All khudkasht raiyats "have a right of occupancy so long as they pay the customary rents" merely by virtue of being cultivators of the lands of their own villages. They further possess "an interest in the produce over and above the mere wages of labor and the profits of stock." The customary rates were the "pergunnah rates."[112] These local rates were fixed by custom. Where the condition of the country was improving, however, and the rent was "calculated in money," that same pergunnah rate would necessarily be represented "by an increased quantity of the precious metals."[113] The fixity of custom therefore admitted of the inevitability of enhancement.

It was under these circumstances, Trevor explained, that the legislature had passed Act X of 1859.[114] The act had introduced a radical innovation that granted occupancy rights at "fair and equitable" rates to all those who fulfilled the twelve-year qualification without regard to village residency. It implied, however, that such "fair and equitable" rates were "the equivalent of the pergunnah rates . . . or rates fixed by the law and usage of the country."[115] If "the rate of rent which a ryot with a right of occupancy has paid shall be considered fair and equitable until the contrary be shown," then that former rent represented the "customary rent." Where, as in this case, "the increase of the produce has arisen from circumstances independent both of the zemindar and the ryot, the zemindar is entitled to a rise in his rent proportionate to the increased value of his share of the produce . . . .This method of calculation, on the supposition that the costs of production have risen in the same ratio, leave the parties as to each other in exactly the same relative position as they were."[116] All else being equal, the "terms 'fair and equitable,' when applied to tenants with a right of occupancy, are to be construed as equivalent to the varying expressions, pergunnah rates,—rates paid for similar lands in the adjacent places,—and rates fixed by the law and usage of the country,—all which expressions indicate that portion of the gross produce, calculated in money, to which the zemindar is entitled under the custom of the country."[117]

The majority opinion thus established an unprecedented degree of clarity in the principles governing the determination of rents. Customary rates prevailed over competition rates; and the law of proportion was enthroned as the procedure for determining fair and equitable enhancements. The "Great Rent Case," as it was known at the time, established that Act X, read in the light of established custom, guaranteed to raiyats an interest not only in that portion of the gross product that repaid the costs of labor, materials and capital, but also in the "unearned increment" that resulted from the relative fertility of the soil.

The earlier opinions submitted as Minutes at the government's request in 1864 were at once more candid and more expansive in their treatments of the complex issues at hand. There many of the justices of the High Court had already invoked the authority of custom and common law in relation to the provisions of the Rent Act and the relations of landlord and tenant in Bengal. George Campbell, the chief instigator of the rebellion against Peacock, had insisted that the relationship of zamindar and raiyat in India differed in principle from that between landlord and tenant in England. The raiyat's rental payments therefore did not constitute "'rent' in the strict sense of Political Economists."[118] Justices Bayley, Campbell, Jackson and Seton-Karr, along with W. J. Allen of the Revenue Board, had all insisted on the continuity of the force of custom across the constitutional rupture of the Permanent Settlement.[119] Since custom retained the capacity to constitute new rights,

Act X's legal recognition of a right of occupancy among tenants who could not claim direct hereditary continuity from before the Permanent Settlement was entirely justified.[120] "I am not aware that at any time of our rule," noted Justice Kemp, "the payments of the ryots have been regulated by competition. There has always been a pergunnah rate, or some rule common to a neighbourhood founded upon custom and usage."[121] W. J. Allen suggested that the wording of the act might be amended from "at fair and equitable rates" to "*at fair and equitable rates, according to the established usage and custom of the pergunnah, place, or village.*"[122] Justices Bayley, Jackson and Seton-Karr were especially explicit in juxtaposing the actuality of the determination of rents by force of custom to the "abstract theories of European political economy."[123] Common to most of these approaches was an insistence on moving beyond a narrow reading of the legislative history of the colonial government since the late eighteenth century (typified by Justice Loch) to consider established usage as having the prescriptive authority of "the unwritten common law of the country." Chief Justice Peacock was held to have ignored that authority in implicitly contending that tenancy relations in agrarian Bengal were fundamentally commercial in nature.[124]

Justices Campbell and Seton-Karr were both concerned in their 1864 Minutes to insist that the raiyat's customary interest in the soil was independent of the claims of both the zamindar and the government.[125] In his concurring judgment, Justice Morgan insisted that the "ryots having rights of occupancy did not derive their rights from [the zamindar], but from a title anterior to his; and the Government, in its bounty to the zemindar, gave only what it justly could give, that is to say, what belonged to itself, not what belonged to others."[126] Justice Campbell's Minute was quite explicit in calling for the customary impulse underlying the occupancy provisions of Act X to be elaborated more explicitly into a fully proprietary interest in the soil. "I would limit the rights of sub-proprietary occupancy to a class whose claims are more indubitable than those of some of those now classed as occupant ryots; but I would render those rights more tangible and more secure; would acknowledge them as strictly, in every sense of the word, property; and would declare them to be freely transferable, and capable of being in every way dealt with, as property."[127] The independent raiyat represented a yeomanry whose wealthier members rose, in Seton-Karr's words, "into that substantial middle class without which communities have neither strength nor vitality . . . I hold theories which would tend to make the Bengal ryot a mere recipient of wages, and which would expose him to the chances of ejectment, and competition, and change, on the plea of 'giving free play to capital,' to be mischievous and very ill-suited to the state of the country."[128] The aim should rather be to "give security and confidence to a large, valuable, and old-standing class of the agricultural population, who it is, on every account, political, commercial, social, and moral, most desirable to preserve in their homesteads and villages, to save from the exposure to ruinous rack-rent and competition."[129]

Custom might have been juxtaposed to "abstract theories of European political economy," but customary rights were intimately bound up with questions of political economy. Justice Macpherson argued that if the landlord was entitled to the full value of any increase in the unearned increment, the substance of the occupancy right was rendered devoid of value: "The right, if it exists, must needs be worth something."[130] Supporting the force of custom through legislation would, Justice Campbell contended, serve to render economic transactions smoother and more predictable by clarifying the different rights at stake in real property.[131] Justices Campbell and Glover both drew attention to the new urgency of clarifying customary claims under circumstances of a rising population pressure on the land.[132] For Campbell, Peacock's judgment was certainly mistaken in general when he applied Malthusian principles to the determination of rents in India. But under these demographic conditions, a "fair and equitable" rent could mean only a "rack rent" on the Irish model.[133] The custom of India was opposed to European political economy insofar as the latter was fundamentally premised on free competition. It was yet further opposed to it, Justices Trevor and Bayley, as well as Mr. Trevor of the Revenue Board all agreed, insofar as custom conceded to the raiyat the right to retain a certain proportion of the unearned increment.[134] Justices Seton-Karr and Jackson even called for an amendment to Act X specifying the entitlement of the raiyat to a portion of the gross profit beyond the due rewards of labor and capital.[135] So while Justice Trevor's lead opinion in the Great Rent Case might have presented customary rents as simply a proportion of the gross product determined by the interaction between governmental fiat and customary expectation, it was also clear that this was readily translatable, for those who espoused the principle of proportion, into the correlative political-economic claim that raiyats enjoyed a stake in the gross product that included a portion of the unearned increment.

"One could easily hazard the view," wrote S. Ambirajan, "that customary rates, which were very different from competitive rents, became the accepted policy" after the Great Rent Case's decisive overthrow of British models of agrarian development.[136] We might then assume that the shift being marked by the Great Rent Case was an unambiguous moment in the larger post-Mutiny, mid-Victorian retreat from the more aggressive universalism of early nineteenth-century reformism into a politics of racial, historical and civilizational differences.[137] Yet the argument offered in favor of customary rent did not represent any simple repudiation of the applicability of "abstract theories of European political economy" to India. To conflate their critique of particular political-economic arguments with a straightforward recourse to the authority of prescription would be misleading. This is true even when, as in the case of Trevor's lead opinion, the logic of the decision defended apportionment of the product on the basis of common-law precedent. The judges disagreed about how best to apportion the various components of the gross product among the different interests connected to the land. They all concurred, however, in applying the same abstract categories of wages (labor), profit (capital) and rent (land) in justifying their decisions. They also all assumed that the existing ratio of apportionment bore some predictable relationship to these categories. They thus implicitly understood custom to be regulative of particular kinds of social relationships that could only be grasped through categories of political economy.

Classical political economists had held that, under conditions of perfect competition, the sum paid to the landlord would gravitate naturally around the value of the unearned increment. Defenders of custom argued, however, that the sum payable to the landlord in India fell short of the full unearned increment. They nonetheless grounded their reasoning in the concept of rent as a determinate portion of the gross product of the land. The abstractions of political economy were not being contested. It was rather the determinate forms of their expression in the particular social context of agrarian Bengal that was in question. "Whether Political Economy, meaning by the term the science as it exists and is taught in Europe, can fairly or advantageously be applied to Indian administration, we have some doubts," explained a defender of the pro-raiyat impulses of Act X in 1864; "but that a science of Political Economy, which takes its date and forms its inferences from the state of society we find here, ought to be so studied and applied, we are very certain."[138]

In authorizing their opinions, the majority in the Great Rent Case invoked the force of prescription as the social mechanism regulating the distribution of the distinct elements of the gross product. That could represent a conservative affirmation of custom; though as the example of John Stuart Mill makes clear, it could be readily adapted to liberal political ends as well. Nonetheless, it was precisely here, at the interface of prescriptive rights and the abstractions of political economy, that a new conception of agrarian social relations would be framed. This conception rooted the customary rights of the raiyat more profoundly in the premises of political economy. George Campbell's detailed judgment in the Great Rent Case followed Trevor's judgment in grounding the principle of proportion strictly within the idea of the state's historical claim to a portion of the gross product. Reading this narrower opinion in the context of Campbell's earlier Minute and of his judgments in contemporary cases, however, a different grounding for the principle of proportion becomes evident—one radically distinct from the logic of prescription.

If the landlord had been the sole agent of improvements, Campbell conceded, no right of occupancy could reasonably accrue to his raiyats, even after twelve years' continuous possession.[139] But unlike English landlords, zamindars were not generally the agents of capital improvements to the productivity of land. Rather, the zamindar "makes arrangements with ryots who are in no sense 'coolies,'" (a "word expressing, as I understand it, laborers receiving wages,") "but who are, in their own small way, capitalists."[140] In this way, "considerable tracts of jungle have been cleared wholly at the expense, or by the labor of the ryots."[141] The general principle of customary rents prevailing on raiyati lands was based, according to Campbell, on the presumption that raiyats had played a substantial role in enhancing the productivity of the soil. They had therefore correlatively assumed a hereditary stake in the rent fund. On this basis, Campbell concluded that the custom of occupancy implied a fair and equitable rent at a rate that effectively left the raiyat with a continued interest in the unearned increment. This entitlement was founded in turn on a presumptive recognition of the historical role of the raiyats in improving the condition of the land and rendering it cultivable: "the land was originally brought into its present state of culturability (if I may coin a word) and productiveness, by the labor and capital of the ryot," and "to so much of the surplus produce as results from the labor and capital so sunk, the occupant ryot alone is entitled."[142] Similarly in his decision in *Choudhury Khan v. Gour Jana*, just a few months before the Great Rent Case, Campbell had held that if a raiyat "has had to do more than bring into cultivation uncultivated land, if the land was not only uncultivated jungle, was in its then state impractical for cultivation, if it was salt land which could only be made sweet by special works of the ryot . . . then I think the ryot who made those works or expended that special labor, would be entitled to hold at exceptionally low rates," indeed "only the ordinary rates paid for land of the same quality irrespective of the special characters impressed on it by himself."[143] This was also the deeper implication of Seton-Karr's observation that the "law that fixtures become the property of the zemindar, is, in Bengal, absolutely unknown, *even in theory*."[144] By combining commercial interest with proprietary rights, Campbell argued, the legislative endorsement of custom could be instrumental in consolidating a class of small "capitalists" who in time might accumulate larger holdings, and ultimately make real contributions to India's general prosperity.[145]

In this kind of argument, custom was far from functioning as a limit to political economy. Custom rather represented a different instantiation of political economy: one that sought to distinguish natural fertility from capital improvement, and on that basis apportion the rent fund between zamindar and raiyat. Custom itself had developed, Campbell effectively argued, as an informal system for organizing the fair distribution of these elements of the gross product. That is why, as Justices Kemp, Loch, Campbell and Jackson all agreed, even "pergunnah rates" were presumed to gradually adapt themselves to the increased value of the gross agricultural product—and where they had not, to be legitimately susceptible to enhancement.[146]

Seen in this light, the decision in the Great Rent Case introduced into juridical discourse a new conception of custom that has escaped historiographical recognition. For all its frequent invocations of Henry Maine's authority, this new discourse of custom had very little to do with Maine's historicist understanding of customary law. For Maine, where custom governed rents, the theoretical concepts of political economy were by definition rendered irrelevant as determinations of the distribution of the product. Maine's analysis of the Aryan "village-community" contained within itself a strong relativizing impulse that asserted the status of "the great body of custom and inherited idea" as "equally natural, equally respectable, equally interesting, equally worthy of scientific observation."[147] Yet Maine saw his role as Legal Member of the Viceroy's Council primarily as an opportunity to cultivate a system of civil law capable of governing the emergent contractual relations that he saw as the germs of modern civilization in India.[148] Maine saw the role of custom as residual. He argued in the wake of the successful overthrow of Peacock's precedent that it would be best "to abolish occupancy rights altogether as a future institution, i.e. I would protect all existing occupiers of 12 years standing in the privilege affirmed by the H[igh] C[our]t decision, but say that nobody shall *acquire* a right of occupancy for the future."[149] Whether Maine and Campbell understood the depth of their differences is doubtful. It is clear though that the conception of Indian custom that Maine so qualifiedly defended from the unhistorical assault of political-economic and utilitarian universalism was by definition inaccessible to the categories of political economy.[150]

In his 1874 novel, *Govinda Samanta* (later retitled *Bengal Peasant Life*), the Reverend Lal Behari Day would still recall the passage of Act X of 1859 as having established the "Magna Charta of the peasantry of Bengal." The act had effected the raiyat's "legal emancipation" by finally recognizing the great common law principle that "the tenure of land in Bengal is based on the right of labour. He who clears the land of jungle becomes its owner. It is true he pays a certain share of his profits to Government, or to the zamindar, who is usually a collector of tax appointed by Government; nevertheless, the right of ownership lies with the clearer of the jungle and the occupant of the soil. This theory underlies all legislation of land in this country."[151] Such a claim represented a serious break from the Scottish School. For Sir Charles Metcalfe, the justification of the mahalwari settlement model in 1830 demanded a leap of the ethnological imagination, rather than a return to first principles, to grasp the possibility of raiyat proprietorship. "What mind purely English could connect the idea of the proprietor of land with that person following the plough, who paid one half of his gross product to Government? Yet, in India these two characters are the same."[152]

Custom had been used since the late eighteenth century in Bengal to ground a conception of a pre-political space outside the institutional structures of the colonial state.[153] That conception of custom clearly stood at the core of the broad judicial consensus that allowed the principle of proportion to be established by a majority of 14 to 1 in the Great Rent Case. George Campbell accepted this framework when he joined the majority, but he also transformed it dramatically. He construed custom as a distributive mechanism the internal principles of which expressed forms of normative social relationships whose fundamental determinations could only be grasped through the categories of political economy. The force of custom thus had two layers: first, the legitimacy possessed by long-standing usage; and second, underlying that usage, the rationality of natural law as construed through the categories of political economy. Already implicit here was the suggestion, not merely that custom could serve as an instrument of liberal policy, but that custom represented a practical reality in which liberal norms already exercised a binding social power in agrarian Bengal. The proper legal role of the colonial state would seem to have been to acknowledge and uphold the normative force of entitlements constituted and recognized pre-politically in the domain of custom as the vehicle of natural law. In conceptualizing custom in these terms, Campbell carved out a radically new conceptual space in which, as we shall see in the following chapter, the pre-political status of custom was rearticulated in specifically liberal terms.

3

Custom and the Crisis
of Victorian Liberalism

Custom had long been defensible on identifiably liberal grounds. As attested by the ubiquitous invocations of his name among advocates of raiyat interests in India (including the lawyers arguing the raiyat case in *Hills v. Ghose*), John Stuart Mill had elaborated a widely recognized way of connecting customary rights to desirable political and political-economic outcomes. Mill defended custom as a moderator of despotic power, and as a limit to competition under circumstances where the market tended to produce systematically inequitable outcomes.

Nevertheless, as we have seen in the preceding chapter, some of the very liberals who were invoking Mill's authority in the Great Rent Case would suggest much deeper connections between agrarian custom and liberal norms. They invoked the authority of a system of prescriptive entitlements constituted outside of and prior to colonial legality, in the domain of everyday established usage. They grounded the legitimacy of such customary rights, however, in a new kind of historical argument. This was an argument that rested proximately on the authority of precedent and the promise of general utility, but ultimately on the normative entailments of political economy. Since it had been the raiyats rather than the zamindars who had reclaimed wasteland and rendered it cultivable, they argued, raiyats were entitled to that portion of the rent fund that was the result of improvements resulting from their own labor and capital, or the labor and capital of their forebears. The customary entitlement was thus conceptualized *constitutively* through the categories of political economy. Custom's claims to normative authority could be elaborated strictly out of liberal political and political-economic principles. It followed that any authority custom carried in Bengal's existing agrarian society was an index of the degree to which that society was already organized normatively and institutionally by the binding force of liberal commitments.

This chapter analyzes the radicalization of the relationship between customary right and political economy in Bengal as a moment in the wider elaboration of liberal arguments in the Victorian imperial world. What emerged, I show, was a specifically liberal discourse of custom. I do not mean this in the sense that it was the only way that liberals could conceptualize custom or render it compatible with their own political projects. Rather, I mean that it was a specifically "liberal" construal of the principles governing custom's own inner constitution. This new discourse placed custom at the intersection of liberal political theory and political economy. It placed it, in other words, precisely where the Lockean proposition that property arises from the mixing of labor with nature stood. The liberal discourse of custom developed within a wider context of debates and dilemmas in liberal thought and liberal politics in the Victorian period. Indeed, the ideological impulse that impelled colonial administrators like George Campbell to articulate this new conception of custom was partly generated by challenges to the coherence and persuasiveness of liberal ideas in the imperial metropole. What was at stake when some liberals began to prioritize the property-constituting power of labor over more conventional liberal commitments to the rationality of the market and the security of established property rights? This broader imperial context makes visible the specifically liberal concerns that underpinned the new turn to custom. In the process, it makes visible an important dynamic at the very core of Victorian liberalism.

CUSTOM AND RIGHT

The liberal credentials of George Campbell, the chief instigator of the judicial rebellion against Peacock in the Great Rent Case, are hard to dispute. "My father was a great reformer, and very actively engaged in the Reform movement [i.e. the Reform Bill agitation of 1831–32] at a time when his neighbours looked upon such a man as a kind of mad dog. As a child, I came to sympathise in an active agitation of a more thorough character I think than anything we have seen in these days, and as it were drank in Radical ideas with my mother's milk."[1] In 1868, Campbell was back in Scotland serving as Chairman of the Fife Liberal Committee and starting an ultimately aborted run for parliament on the platform of a self-declared "good Radical."[2] In 1874, while Lieutenant-Governor of Bengal, he sketched a vision of political self-governance emerging out of the associational vitality of Bengali civil society, and developing into a "real Parliament with real powers . . . a Bengalee House of Commons."[3] He ended his career back in Britain representing Kirkcaldy in the (actual) House of Commons as an Advanced Liberal from 1875 until his death in 1892.[4] So although he forged a close friendship with Henry Maine in 1860s Calcutta, there can be little doubt that his political commitments diverged significantly from those of the conservative Maine. So too did his understanding of custom.

Of course, Campbell had not always held the views on custom he would give voice to in the 1860s. In *Modern India* (1852), he had postulated a racial difference between the ancient Hindus and the later invaders from whom the Jats and the Rajputs were descended. These later invaders never really penetrated to the south and east, leaving these latter regions as a refuge for ancient Hindu society. "The Bramins and Soodras colonized Bengal, and probably found and incorporated some aboriginal tribe, forming the Bengalee people and language, which seem to be among the most purely Hindoo in India."[5] The later invaders were democratic tribes that had established in their village-republics a collective proprietary right over land. In contrast, the caste-based Hindu village lacked both democratic spirit and a strong sense of proprietary right. Property in land in the ancient Hindu polity, Campbell acknowledged, was claimed on the first tillage of it. But the right established by this mixing of labor with the soil extended no further than the area directly cultivated, as the basis of subsistence. The entirety of the rent fund was owed to the governing agency. "[T]he rent being excluded from the property, the mere right of cultivating . . . could have little market money value," whether for sale or rent. "This then is the lowest description of property in the soil, and amounts to little more than a sort of very strong tenant-right."[6]

Brought up among "moderate landholders," Campbell did not share the anti-landlord zeal of mid-century Manchester radicalism. Despite his early years in the North-West Provinces and Punjab, whose civilian cadre were generally hostile towards the Permanent Settlement, he never considered himself to be "a rabid Ryotwar or anti-aristocratic man."[7] As a Scot, Campbell's evolving sympathy for the customary rights of tenants must in part have been nurtured by the pro-crofter sentiments that became commonplace in response to the Highland clearances in the 1850s following the potato famine.[8] Campbell happened to be in Britain on furlough in the early 1850s, at a moment when these clearances were at their peak. By the 1860s, this sympathy was sufficiently developed to lead him into a headlong struggle against the policies of Sir Charles Wingfield in post-Mutiny Awadh. Wingfield was attempting to consolidate the social position of the independent talukdars of the region (comparable to zamindars in Bengal proper) by reducing agrarian social relations to the simple "relation between landlord and tenant on English principles of contract."[9]

Campbell was chased out of Awadh and onto the bench of the High Court, a position he held, like many of his fellow justices, despite having no formal training in law.[10] There Campbell pressed the claim that a "man who holds certain fields at fixed and regulated rates may do what he likes with his land, and build wells, plant trees, etc., without additional taxation. It is by such small tenures, I believe, that most improvement of the land may be effected."[11] This was a utilitarian argument not radically different from the kind of position we could readily find in other contemporary defenders of smallholding, including John Stuart Mill. But Campbell would soon move beyond this narrower argument to arrive at a further claim founded on liberal principle:

> [I]n regard to the position of small tenants in India, Ireland, or anywhere else, I have always held that, in the absence of positive law, the claim of tenant-right is founded not only on a moral basis, and the necessity of protecting the weak, but also on the strict and economic ground that, where the landlord does not provide the buildings and improvements, cultivation cannot properly be carried on without such a security of tenure as may enable the tenants to do these things; and that, when the tenant does make the improvements, his capital being intermixed with that of the landlord, it is generally recognized that he ought not to be ejected. Curiously enough some of the ignorant Oude ryots seem unconsciously to have put their case upon this economic basis. Thus one man says he claims to hold the land "because he has made his field so nice, and spent so much in manure he would not stand being turned out by any but the Government." Another says, "he has cultivating rights; has done so much tilling and manuring that it would be a shame to turn him out; he could not live if he were ousted."[12]

The argument from utility is still there; but it is now coupled with a much broader claim that the utility of affirming tenant right depends not only on the insight of the colonial official formulating policy, but on a deeper sense common to both the official and the cultivators themselves that the cultivator could claim such a right on principle. The ignorant peasant's intuitive sense of his rights over the soil turned on an understanding of the intrinsic nature of property rights as fundamentally grounded in an investment of labor that served to increase the productivity of the land. If custom could instantiate natural law, it was surely because of the universality of this intuitive sense of right.

Campbell's concern with the primordiality of the property-constituting powers of labor did not end with his posting in India. He continued to discuss it extensively in the years after his return to Britain, elaborating in ever more detail the analysis he had first given voice to in the Great Rent Case. "As soon as we pass beyond the monkey stage we cannot satisfy our wants in respect either of dwellings or of food and clothing, without some kind of improvement of the land, and if we recognize private property of any kind, these improvements must be private property," Campbell argued in 1890. "The private improvements of the land necessarily become so mixed up with the land given by God, that some distribution and recognition of a possessory right of some kind is inevitable." On the basis of this original foundation, one man might through his "superior industry" be able to enlarge his holdings or increase their value, without contravening the basic principle constituting the right of property. Just as, in the beginning, all the world was

America, so this basic principle "is so far, and may continue to be, the history of land in the United States." But in the "Old World," the foundation of property had been radically divorced from this "original basis." A long history of conquests had, despite leaving "the tillers of the soil in possession of most of the land," bequeathed to the conquerors "the unearned rent, and probably a good deal more—a good deal of the ancient improvements of the aboriginal inhabitants." The "feudal title" of the conquerors thus superseded the "allodial title" of the original improvers. Property in land ceased to be independent. It became instead conditional on sub-servience to a lord who could claim a rent. While these conquerors had subse-quently "established a right in the land" through a long history of improvements, this could not vitiate the natural rights of the original improvers of the soil.[13]

The landlords of Great Britain had succeeded in becoming absolute proprietors of the soil only through a protracted process of ousting the "holders of subordinate rights." In Ireland, in contrast, subordinate rights still retained their moral force even after their legal status had been undermined. Furthermore, with the reconfir-mation of these rights under Gladstone's Land Acts, "[w]e have in full force the dual ownership—the landlord, owner of the unearned rent—the farmer, owner of the 'dominium utile,' holding the possessory right and the improvements. We must realize that this is not an extraordinary and exceptional state of things, but is really the normal, and it may be said the natural tenure in almost all the countries of the Old World, whether in Asia or in Europe."[14] What the landlord claimed in the English system was that portion of the gross product that was the result of the natural fertility of the soil. The right to this unearned increment, the natural basis of the public fund, was something "to which no individual has any economic claim, and which an individual only holds by service grant from the State, or quit of the service, because he has long so held it." In contrast, the "possessory right is the right of the individual founded on economic law." Depending on neither polit-ical authority nor prescription, this was a natural right of which the holder could not be rightfully divested.[15]

As his repeated arguments for the abolition of the House of Lords indicate, Campbell was fully aware of the radical implications of this argument. In practice, he was more moderate. "I should very much like to see the land re-nationalized and re-distributed if it were possible, but we all feel that so many interests have grown up around it, and it is so intertwined with the whole institution of private property and private credit that this cannot now be done violently."[16] Rather than press for a radical reconfiguration of property relations in Britain, Campbell invoked the public ownership "of the God-given portion of the value of the soil" as a principled basis for the state to shift the burden of taxation onto the landed classes. He also advocated the forcible purchase of land near concentrations of population to give proletarian workers access to a form of proprietorship in the form of "garden-plots."[17]

For Campbell, it was "revolting to strict logical reasoning, and invidious in democratic days," that a small class of landowners should continue to appropriate the natural gifts of the soil.[18] "At present I believe the country is daily becoming more and more a rich man's country," he would observe sometime in the mid-1870s, "while at the same time we are drifting towards democratic institutions inconsistent with plutocracy." If the inevitable social "convulsion" was to be avoided, democracy would have to be actively embraced against plutocracy.[19] That could only be done by renewing the connection between labor and property that plutocracy had rent asunder. Campbell's democracy was implicitly a democracy of *small property*. "Hence arises a sort of radical reaction—a disposition on the part of some of the most advanced reformers [among whom he very much counted himself] in some things to revert to earlier phases of society, when wealth in the hands of individuals was less exclusively king; when castes and classes were less widely separated; and when institutions prevailed which admitted greater numbers to the privileges and enjoyment of property and of common rights."[20]

This "Radical" espousal of a "return to the good old times of a simpler society when the people had their own, and money did not always make right" was a kind of liberal primitivism. The invocation of the originary status of Lockean right was at the core of Campbell's defense of the rights of the Bengal raiyat. The raiyat's shortage of land and abundance of industriousness made him the ideal colonizer not only of the Bengal jungles but also of Britain's many other underexploited tropical possessions. Raiyats would not undertake such colonization as "coolies" replacing the slave labor lost to planter-masters. They required a system of "free colonization and settlement on the soil under a liberal system similar to that adopted in the United States."[21] The raiyats of Bengal should now have the opportunity, as free settlers, to repeat elsewhere in the empire what they had already accomplished in their own jungles.

The British worker had been peculiarly disadvantaged by a "monopoly of land" that "causes the working classes of our towns to be cooped up in insufficient space and unwholesome dwellings and prevents their expanding into crofts and gardens in the outskirts."[22] The result was that

> Englishmen and most Scotchmen have been too long divorced from the responsibilities of property and of complete self-dependence. I take it that the more people cease to work for themselves and become labourers for others, the less the necessities and forethought that beget prudence influence them. When a man cultivates a bit of land on his own account, or carries on any trade on his own account, he must look to the vicissitudes of the season and market. He cannot live from hand to mouth from day to day or from week to week. He must have either money by him or credit to enable him to tide over a rainy day, a bad harvest, or a bad market.

British society was confronting a great problem. How could "a great manufacturing system" based on proletarian labor be reconciled with the preservation of the kinds of virtues that made liberal citizens capable of political life.[23] A land reform that would distribute ownership more broadly through British society, Campbell insisted, was the only path through this dilemma. Land was "the form of property or privilege on which the comfort, well-being, and contentment of the nation most depend, the most visible national inheritance in respect of which the inequalities of condition are most glaring, and in a desire for the possession of which the prudence and economy of prudent nations is chiefly founded."[24] Campbell was bringing the lessons of the Great Rent Case right to Britain's front door.

Campbell was driven to elaborate a sharp critique of Bengal officials' conventional commitment to the "*laissez-faire* system, or want of system," as the highest principle of political-economic science.[25] Campbell had little patience for the "pharisaical spirit" with which Bengal's Board of Revenue "held by the most rigid rules of the driest political economy, and the most unwavering faith in the 'demand and supply' theory," even in the face of catastrophic famine.[26] He was intensely aware of the apparent irony of the peculiar alliances to which his defense of custom and his critique of laissez-faire led him. In India, Tories could champion the raiyats, while radicals led the charge for their subjugation to landlords and aristocrats.[27] Campbell was aware of a persistent geographical inversion of conservative and radical allegiances between the British and Indian contexts. For Clive Dewey, this geographical inversion of political alignments was the relatively straightforward reflex of the victory of laissez-faire capitalism in Western Europe. Before its victory, radicals who advocated laissez-faire as an instrument of change in Europe could also advocate the overthrow of established custom in India on the same basis; and conservatives who defended the established order in Europe could do the same in India. "But once laissez faire became the established economic system, metropolitan conservatives and radicals were forced to exchange labels: proponents of laissez faire became conservative apologists of the status quo; critics of laissez faire became radical malcontents . . . . The result was a real, not merely a terminological confusion." Outside of the developed West, however, the old alignments still remained valid, so that a now-conservative defender of laissez-faire became a radical proponent of change in India, and a now-radical opponent of laissez-faire might become a conservative defender of Indian custom.[28]

Dewey's argument no doubt makes sense in many cases, but it nonetheless stumbles in the face of the specific kind of argument we have seen Campbell making. Campbell was not defending custom on conservative grounds. Nor was he in the least inclined to uphold a "socialist" vision of primitive communal property as an antidote to laissez-faire.[29] He was defending custom on strictly liberal principles. Furthermore, he considered the principles that underwrote his critique of zamindari eminently transferable back to a plutocratic metropole. If the "good Radical" Campbell became an advocate of Indian and Irish custom, the real question to be considered is this: How did liberal principles themselves lead some-one like Campbell to defend custom as a vehicle of liberal values?[30]

THE SPECTER OF LOCKE

When Campbell identified custom as a vehicle of Lockean right he was not operat-ing in an ideological void. The basic temporal structure that rendered the identifi-cation of Lockean natural law with custom possible was already present before the elaboration of a liberal discourse of custom per se. Indeed even those whose sym-pathies lay unambiguously with the rights of substantial landed property and cap-ital could feel obliged to answer the claims of Lockean natural right. Indeed, they even did so in ways that acknowledged the originary status of such rights in the formation of societies and polities. We can see this quite clearly in the writings of George Poulett Scrope, a Whig parliamentarian, a notoriously prolific pamphlet-eer, a geologist and a political economist, who also happened to be an enthusiastic advocate of Irish land reform.[31]

Scrope wrote extensively on many of the issues that would concern Campbell. But as an ardent and unequivocal champion of established rights of property, Scrope was certainly safe from any accusations of radicalism. In his *Principles of Political Economy* (1833), he insisted that the "maintenance of the right of property is the *sine qua non* of production, wealth and civilization."[32] He was also implaca-bly hostile towards Ricardo's conception of labor as a substantive measure of value. Value, he argued, could mean nothing but "*value in exchange*," meaning that the "value of a thing" simply meant "the quantity of other goods or of money, that is, the price, it will command at a particular time and in a particular place," subject to supply/demand ratios.[33] Yet neither his skepticism about the labor theory of value nor his broadly conservative Whiggism prevented Scrope from beginning with "natural rights" as the first principles of political economy. Man, he argued, has a natural right to personal freedom and a natural right to the bounties of creation. From these two natural rights, the right to property can then be derived. Since there must be a limit to the rights of individuals to appropriate nature to their own use, this limit is established on the basis of a "simple rule" that "appears to have been universally adopted by every fraction of the human race," namely, "that what a man obtains from nature *by his own exertions* becomes *his property* . . . The ideas of *meum* and *tuum*, founded on the natural law of appropriation by labour, are as old as the union of any two or three human beings in society." Scrope then quoted Locke at some length to establish his claim that "the right to property acquired by labour is derived from the right to personal freedom," grounded in the property one has in one's own person.[34]

Scrope was hardly shy about elaborating the political implications of such explicitly Lockean premises. All these natural rights, he argued, culminated in the right to good government, since only government could secure the enjoyment of any of the preceding rights.[35] Scrope insisted that the political rights of man could be defined as "the claim of every individual to have his interest promoted and protected to the same extent as that of every other member of society by the combined power of the whole body."[36] In other words, man's natural right to freedom, the enjoyment of nature, and private property were all dependent on his duty to submit to the law, but only insofar as the law upheld such rights universally. This was precisely the condition that Locke called "civil society." Scrope went on to argue that the "natural and equitable title to property in land which arises from its appropriation 'per industriam,' by the labor necessary to render it productive, must always have required the sanction and support of the law."[37] But this in turn gave rise to the possibility of political inequity in the administration of such rights. For with the establishment of government through social contract, power was consensually centralized in a manner that also potentially gave rise to despotism. So Scrope then matched his espousal of a Lockean theory of rights and of consensual government with a critique of Filmerian patriarchalism: "Wherever despotic power exists, whether the result of domestic treachery or foreign invasion, there property, as well in land, as of all other kinds . . . is of course held only at the will of the ruler. And, accordingly, we find in countries which appear to have been subjected to this form of government, that the exclusive proprietorship of the land, as the primary source of all wealth, has been claimed by the sovereign."[38]

At this point, Scrope unsurprisingly turned his attention to the history of property in India. Scrope sought to distinguish between, on the one hand, "the simple principles on which land is originally appropriated from a state of waste, by the industry of the labourer," and on the other hand, its subsequent seizure as a valuable possession by a sufficiently powerful ruler. According to Oriental law, the sovereign must be either the proprietor or the source of all proprietary claims, since the law itself is merely "the *will* of the sovereign." Yet that sovereign both theoretically and customarily recognizes the claim of the raiyat to a heritable right of continued occupation of his land, even if he always leaves the fruits of his improvements susceptible to confiscation as revenue. This amounted to a "compromise between the usurped and unlimited power of the despot, and the ancient and natural privilege of private property as the result of appropriation by private labor." Seen in this light, the Asiatic *theory* of peasant proprietorship approximates "the most natural, equitable, and beneficial arrangement," so that "the misery suffered by the land-cultivators of Asia and the wretched state of their agriculture are a consequence not of the original rule of the country, but of its continual infraction" by its despotic sovereigns.[39] Scrope contrasted this situation not only to the historical growth of liberty out of the limitation of the Western sovereign's power by the existence of a landed aristocracy in the feudal system; but, more radically still, to the colonies of the New World, in which could be seen emerging "a system approaching perhaps as nearly as is desirable to the natural and equitable law of land proprietorship." Free of ancient monopolizing landlords and despotic rulers, the colonists of the New World could each claim as much land as they found it convenient to cultivate, while rejoicing at the contiguity of adjoining properties that made possible a division of labor. Scrope thus unabashedly defended Locke's theory of the property-constituting powers of labor from Edward Gibbon Wakefield, who had insisted that the prosperity of the settler colonies demanded the limitation of the availability of land to the wealthier colonists so as to assure a supply of free labor for its cultivation. Ironically, Scrope found himself defending these Lockean commitments despite being an ardent and articulate exponent of Wakefield's colonization schemes as the solution to Britain's social and economic woes.[40]

Scrope never directly identified "custom" as the vehicle of Lockean right. Nonetheless, we can see in this argument the temporal structure that would underpin such a conceptual linkage. Property emerged from the appropriation of nature through labor, and government arose as a necessity out of that first appropriation. Not only despotism but also substantial landed property (in excess of the needs of the cultivator) necessarily therefore represented secondary developments that unleashed new developmental dynamics (just as money had in Locke's argument, and the emergence of capitalists and landlords had in Smith). Scrope would mount a strident defense of the contribution of substantial landed property to the progressive dynamism of British commercial society. That defense turned, however, on the characterization of natural right as historically anachronistic.

> The only consequence of a complete abolition of monopoly rents [on the basis of an appeal to natural rights] would be to put them in the pockets of the farmers, under the name of extra profits—in short to turn the farmers into landlords. But society would gain no advantage [thereby]. . . . And, on the contrary, there is a very evident advantage accruing to society from the existence of an independent and wealthy class of persons, disengaged from the necessity of constant personal attention to their affairs, and therefore enabled to give their time gratuitously to literary and scientific studies, or the performance of public, but unpaid duties. . . . And it is, moreover, from the elevation of mind and manners, the refinement and intellectual polish which leisure and easy circumstances enable this class to attain, that much benefit descends to all the other classes, in the example afforded them of a higher taste for the comforts and decencies of life, and a higher standard of enjoyment than the gratification of mere animal wants.[41]

So the natural rights on which civil society and government were founded came to be superseded by a Malthusian logic according to which substantial property in land had become an inevitable and beneficial feature of civilized societies. This structural relation between originary natural right based on the property-constituting powers of labor and progressive civilizational development based on the dynamic powers of accumulation was precisely the temporalization of Lockean principles that would open the conceptual space for the identification of custom as the vehicle of liberal norms.

It is important to recognize that Scrope was not dredging Lockeanism from obscurity when he wrote these pages. Even the writings of a liberal utilitarian like James Mill preserved to some degree a Lockean substratum. Despite his complete lack of interest in the question of the origins of government (and its correlates, the state of nature and the social contract), and despite his utilitarian skepticism about natural rights, Mill saw the primary purpose of the state as being to protect property—and specifically to protect it insofar as it was the product of labor. "It may be remarked, that the conclusion to which we have thus arrived coincides exactly with the doctrine of Locke."[42] Mill did not believe in the social contract, but he certainly argued *as if* he did. "That one human being will desire to render the person and property of another subservient to his pleasures, notwithstanding the pain or loss of pleasure which it may occasion to that other individual, is the foundation of Government."[43] Mill thought that private property should be justified on grounds of utility rather than by appealing to chimerical natural rights. It followed that private property was sacrosanct only insofar as its protection promoted the greatest good for the greatest number. But the capacity of private property to produce the greatest good turned on a conception of political-economic regularities that rendered private interest commensurable with the general interest. In other words, natural law was not abolished in Mill's utilitarianism. It was the special distinction of the science of political economy to make intelligible "the laws of nature, on which the condition of man depends" (and foremost among these laws, "the necessity of labor").[44] Natural law was thus merely reformulated as the practical framework within which the prospective utility of any law was to be understood. (Indeed, when Thomas Babbington Macaulay criticized Mill's deductive analyses of government and political economy as residues of pre-Baconian scholasticism, surely he was simply questioning whether Mill had brought natural law down to earth enough.)[45]

Scrope's need to subsume Lockean arguments into his schema must be understood in the context of the vibrant currency forms of Lockeanism possessed, not just among middle-class radicals like Mill, but also among the plebeian radicals of the late eighteenth and early nineteenth centuries.[46] As early as the mid-1750s, Thomas Rutherforth, Regius Professor of Divinity at Cambridge, had recognized the potential for Locke's theory of property to transform into a radical assault on established structures of landholding in Britain. He envisioned the terrifying prospect of hired labor swallowing the landlord's inheritance by appealing to the claims of natural right, founded on the false premise that labor was responsible for most of the value of the product.[47] (This was the very accusation that orthodox defenders of the Permanent Settlement brought against the advocates of Act X in the

1860s.) In the eighteenth century, Locke's name would be closely associated with assertions of popular right against the closed circles of the parliamentary classes. From the 1760s, a resurgent conservatism would take special pains to excoriate Locke's political philosophy as a ubiquitous reference point for the vocal popular radicalism of the period.[48] Scrope seems to have been reprising Blackstone's earlier audacious attempt to neutralize the potential radicalism of Lockean property theory.[49] But such efforts to contain the implications of Locke's political philosophy nonetheless represented a symptomatic recognition of the continuing historical force of its categories.

The connection between labor and property was already present in the radical responses to Burke's defense of landed aristocracy. It was a position that would lead Thomas Paine to denounce Babeuf's communism in the name of property grounded in labor, but also to advocate universal franchise for all those who labored (because all laborers met the basic property qualification of having a property in their own labor).[50] Indeed, Paine's essay on *Agrarian Justice* represented a classic example of the radicalization of Lockean conceptions of property:

> It is a position not to be controverted, that the earth, in its natural uncultivated state, was, and ever would have continued to be, the COMMON PROPERTY OF THE HUMAN RACE. In that state, every man would have been born to property. . . . But the earth in its natural state . . . is capable of supporting but a small number of inhabitants compared with what it is capable of doing in a cultivated state. And as it is impossible to separate the improvement made by cultivation, from the earth itself, upon which that improvement is made, the idea of landed property arose from that inseparable connection; but it is nevertheless true, that it is the value of the improvement only, and not the earth itself, that is individual property. Every proprietor therefore of cultivated land, owes to the community a *ground-rent* . . . equal in value to the natural inheritance [a property constituted by labor] has absorbed.[51]

Paine identified the natural fertility of the soil, the cornerstone of Malthusian conceptions of property in land, as an irreducibly common property—just as James Mill would when recommending that the rent fund form the basis of the colonial state's finances in India, and just as the majority in the Great Rent Case would when they derived zamindari out of the state's interest in its share of the product. By this logic, the only really legitimate form of private property, at least on grounds of fundamental principle, was a property constituted by labor. Thomas Spence's influential egalitarian and communitarian assault on existing structures of landholding drew on an essentially identical Lockean understanding of natural property as an extension of the person.[52] This was a trajectory of British political thought that would find perhaps its most full-throated articulation in the thought of socialists like Thomas Hodgskin. Hodgskin's Ricardian commitment to a labor theory of value was a direct extension of his Lockean commitment to a labor theory of property, both of which served as the standpoint for his critique of capitalism.[53]

It was perhaps with regard to the question of Irish agrarian politics that these Lockean themes would achieve their most urgent public airing in nineteenth-century Britain.[54] In 1835, William Conner, an Irish agrarian radical, published *The True Political Economy of Ireland*, a tract that brought the Lockean specter of natural right to bear on the nineteenth-century Irish political present.[55] "I submit to the candour of the enlightened reader, whether experience does not teach us, that the Creator has established a connection between labor and the fruit of labor—between the laborer and the produce of labor . . . In the first stage of human society, this law is so predominant as to form almost the only law of property; in other stages it is less clearly discernible; while in others, it becomes greatly obscured and almost entirely effaced; but in all stages of the progress of human society, I submit that it is discernible to be a great, original law of the Creator."[56] On the basis of this Lockean premise, Conner concluded that the "great law which established the connection between the laborer and the produce of labor, must have given the laborer the right to the full value of his labor." This was not to contest the obligation to pay rent, but rather to insist that the cultivator was entitled to the entirety of the difference between "the fair value of the land, and the full value of the crop."[57] Whereas the supply of other commodities could be increased to meet increased demand, land was a finite resource. The rise in demand for land could therefore inflate the price of land (i.e. rent) beyond its "fair value," thus "taking from the industrious farmer and laborer the fruit of their labor" in a proportionate degree—i.e. rack rent.[58]

Since the ever increasing demand for land must always be met by its inevitable scarcity, Conner argued that "the property of the industrious class—that which arises to them from their industry on the soil—cannot be protected from the encroachment of the landlord in any other way, than by the state's abridging the landlord's power over the land—by giving the tenant, in all cases, a fair valuation of his land."[59] This necessarily involved overriding the market through political intervention. Furthermore, the tenant would have to be provided with security of tenure against the "avarice and capricious whim of the landlord." The state would have to prevent evictions for reasons other than nonpayment of rent, and establish full legal recognition for "what in England is called *the tenant's right*, a valuing that right at so many years' rent; which sum to be paid the tenant by the landlord, should he be put out at the expiration of his lease."[60] If parliament were to "reanimate the law of industry . . . and call that great law once more from its grave," the result would be the promotion of the accumulation of capital in the hands of tenants. They could then use it to pursue further agricultural improvement, thereby raising the real value of land, reinstituting the authority of the law, and restoring harmony between the "two great classes—the industrious class, and the property class."[61]

In 1846, Peary Chand Mittra, a member of the Young Bengal group educated by Henry Derozio at Hindu College, was sketching a similar, albeit much less strident, argument for Bengal.[62] As a fertile land "bountifully intersected by noble rivers" that, "constituting links of communication, stimulate and promote the alacrity and bustle of traffic," Lower Bengal at once seemed naturally inclined to commercial prosperity, yet at the same time depended mainly on "agricultural resources" for its wealth.[63] At the inevitable base of Bengal's prosperity was therefore the raiyat, the agent of labor: "It is he who clears and fertilizes the land. . . . It is he who supplies the necessaries of life—infuses activity and vigor into commerce, and keeps up the vitality of the whole country. . . . His welfare, and the welfare of his country, are so much linked with each other, that it behoves every one to interest himself in his cause."[64]

So what had been the condition of the raiyat under ancient Hindu law? Mittra adapted the claim that the gross product of the soil was customarily apportioned between the cultivator and the state as the foundation for an explicit assertion of raiyat proprietorship based on labor. "The right in the cultivated land did not exist *in the sovereign, but in him 'who cut away the wood, or who cleared and tilled it'*. . . . The rights of the agricultural classes were in no way feudal; and what they paid was not *rent*, but a *tax* 'as the price of protection.' This tax was a portion of the produce."[65] Here Mittra drew from Sir William Jones's translation of the Laws of Manu, which held that "Sages, who know former times, consider this earth (*Prithivi*) as the wife of king PRITHU; and thus they pronounce cultivated land to be the property of him who cut away the wood, *or who cleared and tilled it*; and the antelope, of the first hunter, who mortally wounded it."[66] Prithu was the mythical Vedic sovereign who convinced the earth-cow to yield her milk in return for his stewardship, thereby becoming her husband (or father), and hence the model of a patriarchal right to subsistence from the earth.[67] Mittra concluded on the basis of this passage that the raiyat had since ancient times held land as private property appropriated through labor, adopting the notion of lordship over the earth into an essentially juridical social relation between householding men. Although the Muslim invaders were "bigoted, intolerant, and looked upon those who did not embrace their creed as *Kafirs*," they nonetheless "respected (at least in theory) private property."[68] Under their despotism, however, the former administrators of the land tax acquired the confusing title of zamindar, or landholder, and gradually came to engross larger and larger domains under their fiscal responsibility. This in turn gave rise to a class of tax farmers who "were neither the actual collectors, nor did they in any way bring themselves in contact with the people." Under these "Zemindar Talukdars" exactions grew to such an extent that "there was *practically* an annihilation of property rights," insofar as these exactions engrossed the entirety of the rent fund.[69] It was with this class that a well-intentioned Lord Cornwallis, his "mind saturated with the ideas arising from the institutions of his father-land," mistakenly and disastrously undertook to permanently settle the revenues, recognizing them as the "actual proprietors of the soil" rather than the "tax-gatherers" they really were.[70]

It was thus the British who, in assuming the right to grant such recognition, had introduced an entirely new doctrine of land ownership that fundamentally contradicted the Lockean social contract that had been the foundation of India's ancient constitution. When Sir John Shore, a key driver of the initiatives that would lead to the Permanent Settlement, argued that 'the Ryots paid in the proportion of one-half of the gross product of their lands,'" he had "virtually established a doctrine inculcated neither by the Hindus nor by the Mahommedans—We mean the proprietary right of the sovereign in the land. Such a tenet, subversive as it was of the existence of private rights, was an exotic in this country; and in itself an unnatural and unjust one," since it inverted the natural relationship between government and private property.

> Whatever diversity of opinion there may be on the origin of Government—whether it was traceable to contract, heavenly ordination, or the natural course of events, there can be no question as to political institutions having been subsequent to the existence of private property. The idea of property, as being the product of labor, is *natural* with man. Land unreclaimed from sterility is common property. It is the first tillage and cultivation which constitute private property. In proportion as agricultural pursuits are thus carried on, the curtailment of the natural liberty and the want of mutual protection are felt; and it is private property which gives rise to Government, and not Government to private property.[71]

Despite the claim to be agnostic as to the origins of government, Mittra was here narrating a classically Lockean narrative about the origins and normative foundations of political life. Condemning the Permanent Settlement for subjecting raiyats to the "arbitrary will" of their zamindars, and thus opening the door to exactions that "prevent the ryots from creating a capital," Mittra called for protections that would allow the raiyats to "create a capital for their agricultural pursuits" and "feel encouraged to lay out capital in the cultivation of waste lands and to the carrying out of improved modes of culture."[72] In effect, he denounced the zamindari settlement as an illegitimate political infringement on the naturally constituted and historically recognized property of cultivators. This class of cultivators might otherwise have grown through the rewards of their own productive labor into farmers whose prosperity might in turn have generated the kind of thriving commercial society that Bengal so desperately needed.

FROM NATURAL RIGHT TO CUSTOM

In their discussions of tenant-right, "custom" seemed no more central to Conner's or Mittra's appeals to natural reason than it was to Scrope's discussion of the theory underlying Indian tenancies. Nor for that matter did it play an overt role in the attempts by Sharman Crawfurd, the Irish parliamentarian, to introduce a bill in the 1830s requiring the compensation of evicted Irish tenants for improvements they had made to their holdings.[73]

It was in fact William Neilson Hancock, Professor of Political Economy at Dublin University, who appears to have been the first to establish custom as the bearer of rights whose intrinsic constitution followed the logic of political economy. *The Tenant-Right of Ulster, Considered Economically* (1845) was written in response to the detailed and surprisingly critical findings of the Devon Commission report on Irish landlord-tenant relations. Hancock set out to "explain the nature of the custom [of tenant-right] as it actually exists" in Ulster, and to identify "the real foundation on which it is based." This real foundation was, it transpired, "the principles of political economy."[74] Hancock was certainly no agrarian radical. He denounced the prospect of peasant proprietorship in Ireland as an "open confiscation of property." He was a fierce advocate of laissez-faire and the commercialization of land. And he advocated the contractual models of landlord-tenant relations that would form the basic impulse of the 1860 Landlord and Tenant Act, which largely followed his own recommendations.[75] The larger trajectory of his intellectual career, however, moved him towards a deepening commitment to a recognition of the specificities of the evolution of Irish society. On this basis, he increasingly emphasized the need to give customary tenant-right in Ireland the full force of law.[76] Yet because of the very specific way in which he construed custom, his championing of its authority in no sense compromised his commitment to political-economic orthodoxy.

The Ulster tenant-right, as Hancock characterized it in 1845, was composed of three primary elements: (1) the right to continue possession in the absence of a legitimate reason for eviction (i.e. nonpayment of rent); (2) the right of an outgoing tenant to receive a sum of money from the incoming tenant "for the peaceable enjoyment of his holding"; and (3) the right of the tenant (subject to his landlord's approval) to sell or bequeath this interest in the farm.[77] The substance of tenant-right turned on the difference between the sum paid as rent to the landlord, based on the "fair value of the ground" *excluding* "the buildings and other permanent improvements made by the tenant," and the full value of the land when such improvements were taken into account. What the incoming tenant was buying, at a price "determined by competition," was in essence "his estimate of the value of the land . . . over and above the rent payable to the landlord."[78] Hancock was following Ricardo's analysis closely in separating out that element of the rental value of the land resulting from natural fertility (which Hancock called "land-rent") from that due to the labor and capital of the tenant (which Hancock called "inherited profit").[79] On the basis of this distinction, Hancock argued that the custom of tenant-right guaranteed the tenant's interest in improving the productivity of the soil. This it did by securing his just entitlement in the inherited profit of past investments of labor and stock otherwise amortized into the rent. This was especially necessary in a society where it was the tenant, rather than the landlord, who was generally responsible for undertaking improvements.[80] "*The tenant-right of*

Ulster, when considered economically, is only a recognition, by long-established custom, of the right of the tenant to the fair profit of the capital vested by him, by purchase or expenditure, in the permanent improvements of the land, or to the inherited profit arising from such improvements, when made by some of his ancestors.[81] It was precisely because this custom was grounded in natural reason (political economy) that the Ulster landlord did not generally feel morally entitled to raise rents, even though the law allowed such enhancements. The landlord understood that, in raising the rent, "he would be taking, by means of the power which the law gives him, what is not his own."[82]

Thus the landlord's demand properly stopped at the limits set by the property constituted by labor; and it was custom that effectively defended that limit. This was a principle put into practice by Sharman Crawfurd. In his own dealings as an Irish landlord, Crawfurd recognized the Ulster tenant-right so long as the tenant could "show that he has expended labour or capital in some form so as to increase the value of the premises."[83] Unlike the radical tradition stemming from Paine and Spence, Hancock preserved the presumptive claims of a private property in the rent fund against counterclaims in favor of mankind's common inheritance of the land. Nonetheless, the value of such private property was limited in accordance with the rival customary claims of a property in labor. Hancock no longer required an overt appeal to an originary "state of nature" of the kind Locke had invoked. Custom's peculiar combination of extralegal normative authority, historical depth and timeless iteration allowed it to fulfill the same conceptual function, while still remaining plausible to the deeply historical consciousness of nineteenth-century intellectuals.

Mainstream exponents of political economy did not confine their construal of the rationality of custom to discussions of the problem of land in Ireland. Philip Pusey, a Peelite Tory virulently critical of the stinginess of Radical policies towards the poor, had spearheaded a campaign in the 1840s to consolidate the legal standing of custom in the regulation of English agricultural relations. This campaign was predictably routed by the combined hostility of landlords and free traders.[84] In the report on agricultural customs he authored for the House of Commons, Pusey argued that the tenant's right at the termination of a tenancy to compensation for improvements was a long-standing conventional practice prevailing in many areas "as the custom of the country." Even where it was not long established, it seems to have sprung up as a more "modern usage." This was because it was "highly beneficial to agriculture, to the landlord, and to the farmer" insofar as it promoted "the full powers of the soil," especially under circumstances of "improved and spirited systems of farming, involving a large outlay of capital."[85] For Pusey, custom was closely linked to the productive functions of capital, and the tenant he had in mind was a capitalist farmer. The custom of tenant-right simply effected an extension of the distinction between capital and land from the domain of trade, where it was universally recognized, to that of agriculture, where the tendency of English law to subsume improvements into the rental value of the land was contrary to "sound reason."[86] Pusey thought that parliament should "render the principle of tenant-right for improvement general throughout England, by giving it prospectively the validity of a custom."[87]

It was broadly this same conception of custom as a vehicle of political-economic rationality that was lurking in much of the liberal discontent with Peacock's decision in *Hills v. Ghose*. In 1864, in the midst of the controversy provoked by Peacock, Sunjeeb Chunder Chatterjee's *Bengal Ryots: Their Rights and Liabilities* argued with lawyerly moderation that a right of occupancy could accrue to the raiyat regardless of any proprietary claim on the part of the zamindar. Chatterjee was not making any revolutionary claims. The zamindar might indeed be a landowner rather than a mere tax officer—whether originally so or not being less immediately important, though called deeply into doubt by the authorities Chatterjee chose to invoke. Nonetheless, even understood as a tenant, the right of the raiyat to his land extended beyond the limited term of his lease.

> The rent once paid, [the raiyat] has a right to enjoy the remainder of the fruits of his labour. To the full enjoyment of this right it becomes necessary, under certain circumstances, that he should be allowed to retain the land he cultivates, longer than the caprice or the love of gain of his landlord might allow. Thus his labour might have increased the productive powers of his land, and it is but fair that it should not be in the power of the capricious or unjust landlord, to deprive him of the land, which he has laboured to improve. Thus a secondary right, the right of occupancy, may spring up from the first.[88]

Having thus established the right of occupancy strictly on grounds of political economy, Chatterjee immediately went on to map this onto the customary rights of raiyats. The rent paid by the raiyat to the zamindar, he argued, was not in fact best understood as "rent" at all in the classical Malthusian sense, where the rate was regulated by the competition of capitals in the market for access to the land as a means to profit. On the contrary, following John Stuart Mill, Chatterjee considered the rent paid by the raiyat to be the payment of "a peasant proprietor to a co-proprietor," at a rate entitling many classes of raiyats not just to recompense for labor and capital expended, but also to a share in the unearned increment. Such rental rates were regulated not by competition, but by custom.[89] The resulting apposition of these two arguments may not have been terribly coherent, but together they amounted to the claim that the raiyat's customary entitlements expressed the commonsensical conception of a form of property constituted by labor.

Writing a decade later, Sunjeeb Chunder Chatterjee's more famous younger brother, Bankim, would reiterate these same principles, albeit in much less refined terms. In "The Cultivators of Bengal," a series of contributions published in *Banga-darshan* in 1873, Bankim bemoaned the poverty of the cultivators despite the threefold or fourfold increase in the region's gross income: "This wealth is the product of cultivation—it is due to the cultivator—readers will immediately think that the cultivators receive it. In fact they do not. . . . The rightful owner of that wealth does not possess it. He who produces the harvest out of the sweat of his brow is not to be found among those with a share of the profits."[90] Why? Because even though the raiyats had always been the real "landlords" (*bhusvami*), the Permanent Settlement had completely extinguished their "immemorial proprietary rights."[91] After the Pancham regulation of 1812 strengthened the hand of the zamindar, the cultivator could retain "no relationship with the land" and "became a laborer."[92] "We have no objection to the English renouncing their own proprietary right to the land, making the people of the country the owners, and renouncing the right to enhance revenue demands . . . We only say that this Permanent Settlement should have been made with the raiyats rather than with the zamindars."[93] If Cornwallis had recognized the customary proprietary rights of the raiyats, then a commercial society based on free exchange might have been possible. "If the people were free and no one was too great, then everyone would become fully human."[94]

The liberal discourse of custom achieved its most elaborate and remarkable formulation, however, in a voluminously overgrown pamphlet entitled *The Zemindary Settlement of Bengal*. Published anonymously in 1879, it is generally attributed to R. H. Hollingbery, who in that same year retired from uncovenanted service as Assistant Secretary in the Financial Department of the Government of Bengal.[95] The extensive documentation and analysis of the history of the Bengal regulations, acts and case law in the appendices to this work would serve as something of a general sourcebook for pro-raiyat critiques of high landlordism and colonial law for decades to come. Hollingbery argued that the framers of the Permanent Settlement had not only intended to settle permanently the revenues payable by zamindars, but also "to fix the ryots' rents for ever at the old-established pergunnah rates of 1793."[96] In contrast to the "so-called principle, that the unearned increment belongs to the zemindars," any aggregate increase in the rent fund therefore ought correlatively to have remained wholly in the hands of the raiyats.[97]

Just a few years earlier, Sir Richard Temple, Lieutenant-Governor of Bengal and himself a key figure in the Punjab School with considerable pro-raiyat sympathies, had noted that, "[a]lthough the permanent settlement in Bengal did clearly imply protection for the tenantry, it did not promise that their rents should never be enhanced. Such a promise would have involved a special and perpetual subsettlement with the ryots, which was in fact never attempted."[98] Only on the most abstrusely "abstract grounds" did Temple consider even remotely plausible the proposition (apparently already circulating sufficiently in the mid-1870s to require refutation) that "the landlord is not entitled to *any* share in the increased value of the land and its produce."[99] Hollingbery set out to refute these kinds of arguments through a detailed analysis of the history of colonial legislation, rendering political practicability answerable to abstract principle.

Hollingbery began by arguing that the results of the failure to follow through legislatively on the Permanent Settlement's original impulse to protect raiyats had been baneful to general utility. From the perspective of a revenue-collecting state, "[t]he simplicity of 1793 has been superseded by a complication in 1879 so embarrassing, that, as testified by the Bengal Government not long since, a man must know all about political economy, agricultural economy, trade routes and prices in Bengal, and other things besides, before he is able, to determine what rent ryots should pay to zamindars."[100] All levels of rural society had been negatively impacted. The frequent enhancement of rents "destroys in the ryot all motive to improvement, or to greater exertion than suffices for a bare subsistence," leaving raiyats vulnerable to famine.[101] Meanwhile, "were it not for the proverbial unthriftiness and indebtedness, as a rule, of classes that live on fixed incomes from the land, it would be surprising to learn . . . that the majority of the zemindars are in debt, and that the money-lenders are the only class who have benefited by the permanent zemindary settlement."[102] As such, the best way to "simplify the substantive rent law" and "root out the middlemen or farmers of rent, who are the curse of Bengal," would be to simply prohibit any further enhancement of rent.[103]

From these utilitarian concerns, however, Hollingbery then shifted to arguments derived from basic principles. He directly disputed the claim that the Permanent Settlement had acknowledged the zamindars to be the owners of the land. He equally repudiated the premise, fundamental to the raiyatwari model, that the state was the universal proprietor of the land. Furthermore, he established this double refusal on the basis of a radically Lockean claim about the proper relationship between property and government. "The reason of the State's existence is the security of individual rights and of private property; and it would have been strange if the State (among the millions of its subjects) had been the sole proprietor of the land, though originally it was reclaimed from waste by individuals, each family for itself, and though it was more generally distributed than other kinds of property."[104] In fact, "the proprietary rights in land of the members of the village communes constituted a perfect title (free from accidental or accessory elements), which was derived from the acquisition (or by descent from the reclaimers) of land that had been *res nullius.* The union, for mutual help, defense, and protection, in a village commune, of the holders of these perfect titles, did not derogate from those titles as against the rest of the world, including any germs, or possible embryos or germs, of zemindars."[105]

In Bengal, village communities had long been in a state of advanced disintegration as a result of "the usurpation by the zemindars of the functions and lands of village headmen." Yet this very "disintegration only perfected the khoodkasht ryot's title, by freeing him from obligations towards the other members of the village commune which, in other parts of India, trammeled the possessor of a holding in his transfer of it by mortgage, sale, &c."[106] In the face of the "joint and several property of the members of a village commune," the only way that zamindars could have established proprietary rights was either through violent dispossession (for which there was no evidence); through purchase (for which the capital could not have existed); or through subsequent legislation or binding legal decisions (of which, at least until recent years, there was no record).[107] Hollingbery concluded that "the zemindar's was an office, and that he was not proprietor of the lands which constituted his zemindary."[108] There was therefore no sound reason to doubt that the "ryot's right . . . was a substantive definite right, such as no legislator in the present day would attempt to destroy by a mere fiat that the right (which, as a fact, inhered in the ryot) belonged to someone else."[109] The prescriptive authority that upheld raiyat proprietary claims was thus derived out of rights based on reclamation.

The Mughal state had instituted a land tax at "a pergunnah rate that had been established by ancient custom." This did not, however, "alter the proprietary right of the khoodkasht ryots as against individuals."[110] On the contrary, this land tax was itself evidence of the reality of raiyat proprietorship over the soil. The tax had generally been a tax in money in Bengal since the time of Akbar. As a cash amount fixed at the customary pergunnah rate, it did not, and could not, vary from year to year with the value of the produce of the soil (as a proportional rent in kind would). The raiyat, rather than the sovereign or the zamindar, was therefore implicitly recognized as the owner of any increase in the rental value of the land. Furthermore, "the way in which proprietary rights commonly grew up was through custom, the ever-surviving law of the East." The tax rate was itself therefore the product of the collective will of the raiyats, rather than of specific agreements with zamindars.[111] Tenure under "pottahs" or written agreements was characteristic only of "pykhasht" or nonresident raiyats, and in any case was typically at a rate *lower* than the customary pergunnah rate. As such, there was no grounds to think that the rate had been liable to enhancement. "It is the practice of the majority which determines custom; and the great majority of the cultivators were the khoodkashts [resident raiyats], who paid the maximum pergunnah rate. . . . In 1793 . . . there was a competition of zemindars for ryots; the *custom* of the pergunnah rate was necessarily imposed, therefore, by the ryots, who were in myriads; not by the zemindars, who were few. The latter could not create the custom; the former, perforce, would not destroy it."[112] In Bengal, custom enshrined rights whose authority had been constituted prior to any specific legislative or executive command: "The proprietary right of the cultivator in the holding was derived from a custom more ancient than law, and long anterior to the permanent settlement."[113] These were rights whose rational foundation lay in the historical reclamation of wastelands through human labor: "the ryots have done everything, the zemindars nothing, for the extension and improvement of cultivation. . . . The outlay of capital by zemindars . . . was not worth mentioning."[114]

Hollingbery did not deny that the Permanent Settlement had assigned zamindars some form of proprietary right in the soil. But what was legally transferred could only be what it was in the legitimate power of the state to transfer. The only claim that the zamindar could make to an interest in the raiyat's lands was necessarily "carved out of the Government's rent or share of the produce of the soil. The ryot's was the dominant right, which represented *dominium* or property in his holding; the gross amount payable by him as rent was *servitus* or easement—a fraction or particle of dominion broken off from the ryot's property, and limited, so that the power of user remained with the ryot, subject to this restricted *servitus* to the State, rendered through its representative the zemindar."[115] What the state transferred to zamindars in 1793 was considerable: "a gross amount of permanently limited demand upon ryots, less the permanently limited amount which the zemindar had to pay to the Government." This was a right not "confined to the State demands on the ryots then cultivating the land," but "extend[ing] also to the demands leviable thereafter from the ryots who might bring waste lands into cultivation."[116] Nevertheless, "the so-called proprietary right of the zemindar was a very limited one; it was so greatly restricted that it was not *dominium*, but *servitus*—a rent (or, strictly speaking, a revenue) charge upon property which belonged to another, and which the zemindar had no power of turning to any use he liked without buying it from that other, who was the proprietor."[117]

That being the case, the rent that the raiyat owed the zamindar was not actually "rent" at all. Rather, like the payment owed by the zamindar to the state, it was a form of tax. If "rent is the surplus profit of land after deducting the wages of labour and the interest of capital expended on the land," then "what the ryot paid was revenue, not rent."[118] The Permanent Settlement thus granted to zamindars something more like a property in office. Their proprietorship was more in the nature of a "personal privilege . . . transmuted into a heritable alienable right" that "did not include a right to the unearned increment." It was rather only a right to a permanent share in the state's revenue. For this very reason, Hollingbery would reserve some of his most vehement criticism for Act X of 1859 and the majority decision in the Great Rent Case. Hollingbery construed their pro-raiyat argument for a more equitable apportionment of the rent fund between zamindar and raiyat as a novel capitulation to the idea that zamindars had a proprietary interest in the soil. Zamindari proprietorship was an idea that had emerged only in the "long interval of lawlessness" during which zamindars had enhanced rents through "highhanded oppression." The result of Act X could only be a general enhancement of rents through the conflation of "established pergunnah rates" (revenue) with "fair and equitable rates" (rent).[119] The "tendency of the legislation of 1859 is to reduce, in time, all ryots to the position of tenants-at-will." In destroying "the restraining force of custom," it would ultimately lead to a competition between raiyats "who can do nothing else if they do not cultivate," and must thus be reduced to a rack rent–paying "cottier tenantry." This situation had nothing in common with a competition between capitals, in which "the rent is limited by the rate of interest obtainable in other pursuits or investments."[120]

Hollingbery's practical solution was to call for a complete freeze on the enhancement of rents, and to commute the land tax into a freehold property.[121] Without such a broadening of the property base in Bengali society, "the people will continue a population of servants, instead of holding, as peasant-proprietors, a position of social independence," in keeping with their original and rightful state.[122] Elsewhere, Hollingbery had characterized this generalization of property as fundamental to a "vision of true conservatism," whose purpose was to restore "to land its former supremacy in moulding the spirit and strengthening the will of the nation, among whom commerce has had free course to work its will, during the past thirty years, and has failed in those more essential objects of national welfare which are dearest to the patriot."[123] Hollingbery was here reaching deeply into the rhetoric of early-modern republicanism. But despite the centrality of land to this "conservatism," Hollingbery's political vision was premised on the twin Lockean postulates of labor's status as the source of social wealth, and of the role of property constituted by labor as the foundation of liberal personhood.[124] The upholding of landed property as the basis of political participation, and commerce as the source of debilitating luxury, is no doubt rhetorically beholden to republican thought, as well as to the Tory agrarian romanticism that drew upon it. Nonetheless, Hollingbery's concern to consolidate raiyat proprietary claims proceeded from radically different, and radically Lockean, theoretical premises about the relationship between land and liberty.[125] The problem of virtue was here indistinguishably wedded to the problem of the viability of a liberal polity in the age of capital. In this sense, it belonged to a larger imperial moment of crisis in Victorian liberalism.

Hollingbery understood zamindari to be a form of politically constituted property whose legitimacy ended at the limits of the properly political (that is, as an interest in the state's revenues rather than in the rental value of the land). In contrast, he affirmed the authority of custom because it expressed the rationality of liberal political economy. Custom preceded the state. It also served as the inherited memory of the state's normative raison d'être, to provide "the security of individual rights and of private property." Hollingbery's polemic makes the genuinely extraordinary claim that, in the colonial context, it was agrarian society that embodied the universal rationality of liberal civil society. In contrast, the colonial state had drifted from its legitimate station as defender of property and liberty to become a vehicle of an arbitrary political will divorced from the rationality of natural law.

What I assume we all assume to be the conventional ordering of colonial differ-ence—colonizer is to colonized as universal is to particular—would appear to have been utterly inverted here.

There is no reason to see this Lockean inversion of the "rule of colonial differ-ence" as necessarily proto-anticolonial, let alone proto-nationalist.[126] Hollingbery clearly identified the presumed liberal potentialities of the British imperial state as the practical condition of possibility for his defense of raiyat proprietorship . If it was the peculiar duty of the colonial state to ignore the voice of public opinion from the perspective of this kind of liberalism, it was only because native "public opinion" in Bengal included only the voices of zamindars and leaseholders. The liberal discourse of custom was thus not necessarily opposed, in practical terms, to the political vision of utilitarian reformers, who appealed primarily to legislative fiat as the appropriate vehicle of a rationality inaccessible to the allegedly servile, improvident and imbecile raiyats of Bengal.[127] In both cases, the imperial state would have to act as a "trustee for a people without representatives, and destitute of any organisation for making itself heard."[128] Or as George Campbell himself put it, "the very utmost social freedom" enjoyed by Bengalis could not yet correlate with "political freedom"—though "social freedom" vigorously pursued might one day form the foundation for India's future self-governance.[129] This kind of liberal politics did not therefore set in motion a necessary struggle between the colonial state and indigenous society. When a politics that turned on the opposition of Western and Asian values did finally emerge to prominence in later nineteenth-century Bengal, the kind of Lockeanism to which the liberal discourse of custom gave voice would have little appeal to a new generation of thinkers bent on a more radical critique of liberal norms.[130]

Yet nor was the liberal discourse of custom ultimately confined to an inelucta-ble loyalist commitment. It was perfectly possible and, indeed, quite plausible to denounce the British regime in India as radically illiberal and hence intrinsically illegitimate. In the 1870s, for example, we find Anandachandra Mitra's *Byabahar darshan* laying the groundwork of a theory of popular sovereignty (*prajasakti, pra-jatantra*) and popular rights (*prajasvatva*) as the basis for a critique of colonial rule. In drawing our attention to this text, Partha Chatterjee notes that "although Anandachandra is expounding a theory of popular sovereignty based on the gen-eral will, and although his republicanism is far more explicit than would be usual in any contemporary British text of political theory, he does not coin a term for *citizen* but uses the word *subject* to mean 'the people.' *Praja* in Bengali stands une-quivocally for 'subject'; a *praja* is one who is under the authority of a ruler, and in colonial Bengal the most familiar meaning of *praja* would have been the tenant in a landlord's estate." Chatterjee concludes from this that "the leaders among the colonized have still not mastered the means to think of themselves as 'citizens.'"[131] In British political discourse, the "citizen" was never as significant as a bearer of liberties as the "British subject." More importantly though, in the more specific context of the liberal discourse of custom in Bengal, it was precisely these agrarian associations of the word *praja*, the common Bengali translation of "raiyat," that most powerfully invoked the figure of the Lockean liberal subject.

A NEW TENANCY ACT

The Bengal Tenancy Act of 1885 shifted the basis of occupancy rights from twelve years' continuous possession of specific plots to a more general *khudkasht* "status" achieved through twelve years' continuous possession of any village lands. It gave the raiyat a new legal presumption of occupancy, curtailed the capacity of the raiyat to contract away such rights, streamlined the procedures for settling disputes over rent, instituted procedures for compensating tenants for any improvements they may have made in the event of eviction, and limited enhancement of rent to a periodic reassessment every fifteen years. The act was the culmination of a long-expressed desire to reform the confusing and ultimately unsuccessful legislation of 1859, and thereby to "restore to the ryots their original position and rights" as established by custom.[132] New legislation was deemed necessary in the face of widespread unrest provoked by conflicts between zamindars and raiyats, especially in the eastern districts of Bengal where raiyats were relatively prosperous, well acquainted with their legal rights, and often the beneficiaries of favorable leases as jungle reclaimers. The aim was to get behind the legislative force of Act X of 1859 to recover the continuing prescriptive force of a customary right to occupancy at regulated rental rates.[133] "[W]e think . . . that it is expedient," wrote Lord Ripon in 1882, "for the cultivation of the soil to be kept in the hands of a substantial peasantry, able to bear up against the vicissitudes of season and the pressure of bad times; and with the Famine Commission, that a system of holdings guaranteed by conditions of permanency and protected from arbitrary enhancement of rent will tend materially to promote the accumulation of property, the sound growth of credit, and the progress of agricultural improvement."[134] In effect, the 1885 act marked the end of high landlordism, and with it, the increasing displacement of rent-based mechanisms of surplus extraction by credit-based ones that penetrated much more deeply into processes of agrarian production.[135]

At the same time though, the Tenancy Act also aspired, as Peter Robb has argued, to be an exercise in "social engineering." It aimed to broaden and deepen the state's presence in agrarian society, and to promote social progress through the creation of a new class of raiyat-capitalists with proprietary rights over occupancy holdings.[136] There is little doubt that George Campbell for one was indeed the "enlightened paternalist" that Eric Stokes considered him to be. He was a consistently fierce advocate of a more vigorous form of colonial governance in Bengal.[137] But the peculiarities of the liberal discourse of custom should make us pause at the adequacy of accounts that emphasize only the political dimensions of colonial rule. It would seem that any new project of colonial governance necessarily rested on presuppositions about the nature of the society to be governed. Only after the liberal discourse of custom has been grasped at the level of ideology, in other words, can the impulse underlying it be analyzed at the level of colonial governmentality. The emphasis among the advocates of the liberal discourse of custom was sometimes on identifying the occupancy raiyat specifically as an affluent class of rich peasants capable of substantial investment in an improved capitalist agriculture. This emphasis featured less consistently, however, than the more general assertion of the raiyat's yeoman-like independence, grounded in a proprietary right stemming from a historical investment of stock and labor to render the land cultivable. That the act was intended to produce prosperity (or at least security against dearth) is unquestionable, but the immediate issue here is *why* this specific strategy was thought to be a plausible means to that end.

I am not suggesting that the Tenancy Act that ultimately passed in 1885 was the direct outgrowth of the liberal discourse of custom. The Rent Law Commission of 1879 was formed at the initiative of Lieutenant-Governor Ashley Eden and represented the first round of struggle to bring about legislative reform. Its deliberations were structured around three distinct factions within the committee, resulting ultimately in a final report that was "a compromise between widely divergent opinions."[138] The final report was drafted by the commission's president, H. L. Dampier, a member of the Board of Revenue. Dampier gave most immediate voice to a faction composed of himself, H. L. Harrison (Secretary to the Board of Revenue) and C. D. Field, a judge who had been given the important duties of compiling a digest of the history of relevant legislation and then of drafting the bill.[139] This faction's position was rooted in what might be called a "raiyatwari" interpretation of the Permanent Settlement. This was an interpretation that proceeded from radically different presuppositions from those underpinning the liberal discourse of custom. They held that:

> according to ancient and established usage the dues of Government from the land in India have from time immemorial consisted of a certain proportion of the annual produce of every *bigha.* . . . It is not so very material whether the proportion of the produce so taken by the State be called rent, or revenue, or a tax; nor is it necessary to our present purpose to determine whether the property in the soil belonged to the State, or to the cultivators, or in coparcenary to both. Once land was cleared and brought completely under cultivation, this proportion of the produce was taken in every case. The ryots cultivated for subsistence, not with any immediate view to profit. . . . The proportion taken by the Government was determined by the Government itself; and . . . the well-being or comfort of the people depended on arbitrary discretion exercised with despotic power.[140]

In the absence of either a capitalist farmer of the European type or any rule of custom sufficiently clear to directly regulate the rates of rent, it was left to the ruling power "to determine the rent payable . . . by the ryots to the zemindars. In this view, the appropriate theory of Rent is . . . that it is such a proportion of the produce of the soil, deliverable in kind, or payable in money, as the Government shall from time to time determine shall be delivered or paid by the cultivators to the zemindars or those to whom the zemindars have transferred their rights."[141] Just as the government had in 1793 determined the permanent revenue obligation of the zamindar to the state by fiat of its own inherited despotic authority, so the colonial government should now fulfill the intentions of the framers of the Permanent Settlement by fixing the rental obligations of all tenure holders, undertenure holders and raiyats, with each "hypothecated for its own rent" just like a zamindari, and subject to periodic enhancement.[142] The difference between rent and revenue was, this group concluded, a moot one of abstract theory. Under the ancient systems of Hindu and Mughal rule, the state had taken "the full market rent of the land for its own use," making it the proprietor of the land in every real sense.[143]

Dampier, Harrison and Field were arguing a position directly rooted in the arguments of Thomas Munro. Munro had insisted that, if the colonial state was to commit itself to leaving a portion of the unearned increment to the raiyat, it did so on principles of its own (benevolently despotic) devising rather than on the basis of any right of property inherent in the raiyat. Munro had identified a historical tendency for raiyat property to assume individualized form as an expression of the pursuit of individual economic interests, and recognized the prescriptive status of such rights. Yet he had also insisted on the state's historical right to demand revenue at a very high rate, at its own discretion, and to treat raiyat property as security for this obligation. He did advocate the maintenance of modest revenue rates that would leave the raiyat with a stake in the rent fund to promote the development of saleable property. He nonetheless held that it was the state that effectively created or destroyed property through the ongoing practice of its revenue assessments. In that sense, he considered property entitlements to be always the product of political power. The natural law of property could not serve as the measure of the state's legitimate authority where it was the state itself that brought property into existence in the first place.[144]

The despotic power that Dampier, Harrison and Field claimed for the colonial state was now being mobilized to check the power of zamindars to enhance rents. The bill's avowed authoritarian-utilitarian principle was that "the land of a country belongs to the people of the country, and while vested rights should be treated with all possible tenderness, no mode of appropriation and cultivation should be permanently allowed by the Ruler, which involves the wretchedness of the majority of the community."[145] From the perspective of Peary Mohun Mookerjee, who along with Mohini Mohun Roy represented the zamindar interests, such a theory "assails the very foundation of private property. Whether they are the outcome of prescriptive enjoyment, or the result of the acquisition by labour or money, rights of property should be scrupulously respected."[146] Fighting a rearguard action against the gradual strengthening of raiyat entitlements, this faction of the commission defended Campbell's principle of proportion and the force of custom side-by-side with the assertion of the absolute proprietorship of the zamindar.

But as we have seen, liberal commitments to the protection of property could also point in a quite different direction. It was left to Alexander Mackenzie (a future Lieutenant-Governor of Bengal) and James O'Kinealy to elaborate a position on tenancy reform that was firmly located within the liberal discourse of custom. They insisted, against the utilitarian impulse of the majority faction, that customary claims must remain the starting point for any future legislation. The commission was too riven by dissent to form the basis of immediate legislative action. In the end though, it was only because of concessions to this last faction that it was able to be issued as a majority opinion at all. These concessions proved sufficient for Mackenzie and O'Kinealy to consider the final report to have "practically endorsed" the view that there remained in force "both in law and fact, a living tenant-right in Bengal."[147] Unlike Dampier, Harrison and Field, Mackenzie and O'Kinealy did not hesitate to assert the radical difference between "rent" and "revenue" that was also central to Hollingbery's pamphlet (produced in the same year). "For my part I have no doubt whatever," Mackenzie insisted, "that it was from the earliest times an axiom in Indian Land Law that every settled cultivator was entitled to be maintained in the quiet occupation of the land he tilled, so long as he paid the established quota of land-tax to the State, or (in Bengal) to the zemindars, as under contract representing the State; and that this was a right inherent in the cultivator, and did not in any way emanate from the zemindar."[148] Since this conception essentially left the substantial proprietary right with the raiyat, it followed that, even after 1793,

> ordinary landlords had originally under our legislation no legal power of raising the customary prevailing rates at all. . . . [The raiyat] is entitled in virtue of his ancient rights, and of the reiterated orders of the Home Government to secure him those rights, to be protected against arbitrary ejectment; he is entitled to demand that his rent rates shall be those prevailing in, or legally established [in substitution for the pergunnah rates where these had been destroyed] for, his neighbourhood; and he is entitled so far to benefit by the intentions of the Government in 1793, as to derive from his holding not merely maintenance, but a reasonable profit. . . . If it once be admitted that the ryot has a beneficial interest in his tenure, the corner-stone of agricultural prosperity may be considered laid.[149]

O'Kinealy went even further: "in Bengal the State never claimed as such any proprietary rights in the soil. In all the regulations the State claimed only a definite share in the produce, and nothing more."[150] The implications of this formulation were radical, for it amounted to the position that the zamindars could claim a property only in the state's revenue demand, not in the land, which belonged to the raiyats. "What Lord Cornwallis asserted, what the regulations affirmed, and what the Court of Directors held, was that the ruling power claimed nothing as proprietor; but as sovereign it claimed a certain share of the produce which had from the earliest period been commuted into fixed money rates in Bengal. The payment of the revenue, calculated on these fixed money rates, is leased in perpetuity to the zemindars, and any unauthorized attempt on their part to increase the State's share would be simply an assumption of the powers of the ruling power which would not be tolerated."[151] Beyond the specific entitlements granted in the regulations, the zamindar was left "in relation to persons other than the ruling sovereign almost as he was before, *i.e.* governed by the customary or common law of the land."[152] O'Kinealy was assuming a position fundamentally identical to that of Hollingbery. Furthermore, he was doing so from within the confines of the Rent Law Commission itself. No wonder C. T. Buckland (among others) would fulminate that the proposed bill was "full of Irish poison," the victim of "a certain clique of Irishmen," all thinly veiled "Fenians," who had declared war on landlordism wherever they found it.[153]

BACK TO BRITAIN

The 1885 act may well have ultimately represented, as Robb argued, an aggressive but largely failed attempt at state-led social engineering underpinned by an authoritarian utilitarianism. But the act also represented, for some of the fiercest advocates of legislative reform, the culmination of a specifically *liberal* project to recuperate custom as a category of colonial rule. This defense of custom was in part underwritten by a broader ideological disposition to recognize and uphold such rights in the context of metropolitan anxieties about liberalism's ideological viability in an age of simultaneous democratization and mature capitalist social relations.

The concern for smallholders' rights over the product of their labor would persist not only among Irish and Indian agrarian reformers, but also among those most deeply committed to liberal political economy back in metropolitan Britain itself.[154] John Bright would condemn the landlords of Ireland as the beneficiaries of a conquest and confiscation that had robbed the Irish people of their own soil. That conquest had instituted what for a Manchester radical was an all too familiar form of "feudalism" that contrasted unattractively against the "free institutions" and "free people" of America, the land of smallholders.[155] Bright took up the arguments of Hancock and Crawfurd to advocate "security to the tenant for the improvement which he may make upon his farm. . . . If at this moment every Irish cultivator and farmer could be told that every farthing he hereafter expended upon his land should not become the property of his landlord, but should remain his property, you would find a new spirit infused into the whole of this population."[156] That other great spokesman of mid-century liberal Radicalism, Richard Cobden, would elaborate a similar pro-smallholder impulse in an 1864 letter to the *Morning Star* published not long before his death. There he denounced the claim that granting laborers a proprietary right in the soil they cultivated would be "a retrograde movement in agriculture."[157] Cobden's hostility to substantial landed property cannot of course be disaggregated from the more general hostility of middle-class liberalism (whether of the Cobden-Bright or the utilitarian variety) to feudal aristocracy and to monopolistic impediments to capital's free circulation.[158] Yet the core of Cobden's argument for a free trade in land to match the free trade in corn was an endorsement of small property on grounds of both political economy and political ethics. Cobden coupled criticism of the monopolistic nature of great landed estates with considerable sympathy for claims about the productivity of Continental models of *petite culture*. But Cobden was also confident that "no man will deny the advantages which the possession of landed property must confer upon a man or a body of men—that it imparts a higher sense of independence and security, greater self-respect, and supplies stronger motives for industry, frugality, and forethought than any other kind of property." Actually, the relative virtues of different kinds of property were really irrelevant, for the "question really is between owning land or possessing nothing." The great mass of laborers could reasonably aspire to no other form of capital when production had generally become so capital intensive. Without property in land, workers would be consigned to a perpetual condition of wage labor without hope of improvement, and without motive to industry and frugality.[159]

In making these arguments, Cobden was voicing a wider anxiety that capitalist social relations were failing to generate a broad-based extension of liberal values within a society composed of free producers. Commercial society promised to generalize individual freedom. Yet at the very same time it seemed to generate an erosion of independence, self-respect, industriousness and forethought among the propertyless. With proletarian labor divorced from a property in its product, it was correlatively deprived of precisely the property-constituting capacity that was both the premise of the liberal subject's entry into political life and the basis of that subject's commitment to liberal political norms. What is more, it offered no prospect of improvement. That perceived collapse of the practical foundations of liberal character, however, was occurring at exactly the moment when the metropolitan British polity was being democratized. Gladstone's championing of the extension of male suffrage was premised on the moral character he attributed to "the people." Workers who had elicited recognition in principle of their right to sell their labor at its full value were surely bourgeois subjects with the attendant rights and capacities. Yet the culmination of this trajectory in the 1860s was the incorporation of the propertyless into the political life of the state. The very claim that workers possessed a property in their labor went hand in hand with forms of collective organization that seemed distinctly threatening to most middle-class liberals, whose conception of political life was centered on individual property. Cobden's advocacy of small property in land thus stemmed from a commitment to individual ownership of property in general, not to the ownership of land per se. His repudiation of the necessity of large estates for social and economic progress was not just a symptom of his hostility to the removal of part of the surplus into the hands of nonproductive aristocratic magnates. It was also an expression of his utopian retention of an assertively liberal commitment to individual property rights as the universal foundation of freedom and general prosperity.

Especially when faced with the Irish agrarian question, liberals who were committed to the property-bearing individual as the normative standpoint of both liberal political theory and political economy embraced the kind of argument Cobden was invoking here. On this basis, however, they were able to articulate, from a specifically liberal standpoint, a broad critique of the adequacy of the very laissez-faire commitments that remained the cornerstone of Cobden's own political vision. Writing in the *Fortnightly Review* in January 1870, John Elliott Cairnes, the benchmark of orthodoxy in classical political economy at that time, would return directly to themes that Hancock (a predecessor in the same Chair of Political Economy at Dublin University) had introduced years earlier. "Various as have been the schemes recently offered to public notice for the settlement of the Irish land question, one feature is noticeable as more or less prominently characterizing all of them—a profound distrust of Political Economy."[160] This was, Cairnes explained, a result of political economy's history of "collision with numerous regulative codes," leading it to be identified among the general public "mainly as a scientific development of the doctrine of *laissez-faire*."[161] But in the face of problems like those endemic in the Irish case, Cairnes objected to the stark choice between a disastrous inaction in the name of laissez-faire and a repudiation of political economy. In fact, Cairnes argued, the principles of political economy fully authorized the government to interpose its authority in the determination of a fair rental rate in all cases where the market did not itself effect this outcome. This was generally the case whenever agriculture was not undertaken by capitalist farmers in a developed commercial society.[162]

Following John Stuart Mill, Cairnes held that land differs fundamentally from forms of mobile wealth. As the product of human labor, mobile wealth "can be produced in indefinite quantity." The recognition of "a right of property in the thing he has produced" serves as a stimulus to an individual's industriousness without infringing on the rights or entitlements of others. But since land is fundamentally limited in quantity, its "appropriation, when there is not enough left for all, is, at the first aspect, an usurpation on the rights of others."[163] The claim to property in land must therefore be differently grounded than that of property in mobile wealth, for the value of land is intrinsic, and the reward of labor applied to it takes the form of the product of the soil rather than the land itself. Only labor that permanently improves the quality of the soil would seem to constitute any form of property right parallel to that which applies to mobile wealth.

But recognizing this only underscored the radical disjuncture separating the efficacious basis for recognizing property in land from the legal basis of actually existing property rights. The system of landed property prevalent in Britain was "wanting in that foundation—in the judgment of most people, I apprehend, the strongest of all those on which property rests—the expediency of securing the labourer the fruits of his toil."[164] Following Ricardo, Cairnes assumed that a farm on the least fertile land brought under cultivation was productive of no rent. Providing its productivity owed nothing to the landlord's outlay, the product of the soil would rightfully belong entirely to the cultivator. Furthermore, where that cultivator had increased the land's productivity through his own efforts, the cultivator could claim a permanent property in the surplus product so generated, and therefore a permanent interest in the soil. By extension, even on more fertile land, the same principle held: the totality of the rent fund would have to be discriminated, as Ricardo had argued, into that portion generated by the natural fertility of the soil, which was the (Malthusian) unearned increment due to the landlord, from that portion resulting from improvement, which was the (Lockean) inherited profit that by right should stay with the cultivator whenever it was the cultivator who was responsible for the improvement.[165]

For Bright, Cobden and Cairnes, custom was hardly central to their affirmation of smallholding or tenant-right. Yet it should come as no surprise, in the light of what we have already heard of the arguments of Hancock and Campbell, that when Cairnes came to the immediate practical crux of his discussion, the question of Irish land reform, the appeal to custom would find its way into his discussion as the preeminent historical vehicle of the natural rights of labor. Indeed, Cairnes's essay would endorse a recently published scheme for the resolution of the Irish land problem. This was a scheme published in 1869 by George Campbell. Campbell's proposal turned on the recognition of a tenant's customary right to the full value of improvements made at their own expense, and to a right of occupancy at a fair rate. Campbell had justified such entitlements by reference to the fact that "in Ireland a landlord is not a landlord, and a tenant is not a tenant," because "there are two sets of laws [there]—the English laws and the laws or customs of the country." Under these circumstances, the "extreme theory of property is everywhere overborne and modified by the custom."[166] For not just in India and Ireland, but wherever it is the tenant who "supplies the fixed machinery of cultivation, [and] the capital permanently attached to the soil . . . his capital and his property being permanently conjoined to the property of the landlord, the feeling of the people is that they have a claim to remain on the land so long as they pay a fair rent."[167] This linking of capital, labor and property constituted the very principle that Campbell had advocated in the Great Rent Case. In conjunction with recommendations pre-pared for the Irish administration by William Neilson Hancock, Campbell's essay on *The Irish Land* would provide the immediate catalyst for Gladstone's grudging concession to the need to intervene in Irish property relations. The outcome of Gladstone's leap was the Irish Land Act of 1870, passed just a few months after Cairnes's own essay was published. Its legislative assault on high landlordism rested on the intrinsic connection between Irish custom and the property-consti-tuting powers of labor.[168]

THE NEW LIBERALISM

The liberal discourse of custom must be located within this much wider unsettling of classical liberal commitments. The catastrophe of the Irish and Scottish potato famines of the 1840s had been used as an argument against laissez-faire, insofar as it prevented coordinated intervention to alleviate hunger and threatened to lower the price of whatever produce the Irish peasantry did bring to market. But it had also been widely invoked as an argument in favor of laissez-faire, insofar as the repeal of the Corn Law would render the importation of food grains easier and cheaper.[169] By the 1870s, however, the dramatic industrialization and economic growth of a newly unified Germany and of the United States, along with the ter-ritorial ambitions of the Russian empire, rendered the unilateral laissez-faire com-mitments of the high Victorian era vulnerable to the skepticism of national econo-mists and imperial tariff-reformers. At the same time, the sustained impact of what Alfred Marshall identified as "a depression of prices, a depression of interest, and a depression of profits," lasting from 1873 through 1896, would profoundly undercut the optimistic belief that economic activity could, left to itself, continue to generate endless growth and generalized prosperity.[170] In the early 1870s, J. A. Froude would lead the intellectual charge to reconstruct an empire that would more aggressively protect and pursue its interests in what amounted to a radical repudiation of classical liberalism and liberal imperialism.[171] Froude's mentor, Tho-mas Carlyle, had already been committed to the idea that "work is alone noble," and therefore that "[l]abour must become a seeing rational giant, with a soul in the body of him, and take his place on the throne of things."[172] This was something it could only do, Froude agreed, under heroically paternalistic, authoritarian and charismatic leadership.

Joseph Chamberlain had emerged from the heart of Midlands radicalism in the 1880s to become the preeminent champion of a postliberal politics opposed to Irish Home Rule and unilateral free trade. He shared nineteenth-century British liberal imperialists' concern for the maintenance of Britain's industrial and com-mercial preeminence. He had become skeptical, however, that unilateral free trade was the best policy for achieving this. He instead advocated a stronger and more interventionist state, most famously in the form of a protectionist tariff and a reformed empire. The necessity of such measures turned to a great extent on the fact that "capital has acquired so predominant a power that it is not safe to leave labour to look after itself."[173] He radicalized Cobden and Bright's land reform projects, calling for a wider dispersal of landownership and denouncing the historical despoliation of the agricultural laborer, upon whose prosperity ultimately rested the well-being of the nation as a whole.[174]

The emergence of a more assertive and increasingly illiberal British right in this period, whether in British India or in Britain itself, cannot be identified as the straightforward continuation of some ongoing tradition of Toryism. It must also be located within the history of what Karuna Mantena has called liberalism's "political entailments"—just as I have argued elsewhere that the emergence of a specifically postliberal form of culturalism among Bengali Hindu intellectuals from the 1880s should be so understood.[175] As his Radical roots suggest, Chamberlain's ideological commitments were shot through with ambiguities. While his career was marked by a party-political drift from liberalism to conservatism, his drift away from mainstream liberal politics initially took the form of an embrace of "Socialism" as "the path of legislative progress in England."[176] It had arguably been liberal concerns that led Chamberlain to embrace a more assertive and activist role for the state. First his radicalization and later his drift to the right both seemed to have stemmed from flagging confidence in the capacity of commercial society to generate the conditions of liberal subjectivity without the active intervention of state-agency. This trajectory in conservative British politics would be further expressed in the idea of "property-owning democracy" espoused by Hilaire Belloc, G. K. Chesterton, Noel Skelton and Anthony Eden.[177]

Those who remained firmly committed to liberalism also contemporaneously began to evince a deepening skepticism about the adequacy of laissez-faire individualism as a means to realize, perpetuate and extend liberal values. As Michael Freeden has argued, communitarian concerns were part of an unfolding liberal tradition, and the new liberalism was the key moment of the elaboration of this trajectory of liberal thought.[178] In Bengal itself, the 1870s had seen the emergence of a new protectionist political economy driven by a concern to restore the vibrancy of Indian commercial society and thereby to salvage the viability of a colonial liberalism that was seen to be sinking into a crisis of relevance.[179] Change was also contemporaneously evident in metropolitan Britain. Charles Trevelyan had been the most infamous symbol of unyielding laissez-faire dogmatism in the face of the social catastrophe in Ireland and the Scottish Highlands in the 1840s. Yet Trevelyan would not only denounce Peacock's decision in *Hills v. Ghose*. He would be the one to pass George Campbell's pamphlet on the *Irish Land* so fatefully to Gladstone in 1869.[180] In the 1860s, old anti–Corn Law radicals like Cobden and Bright turned towards an interest in social reforms like land redistribution. The later

Gladstone grudgingly came to accept (in the words of his son, Herbert) "the demonstrated necessity of State action on a large scale" to supplement the efficacy of individual action in preserving liberal society.[181] Liberals of the generation of L. T. Hobhouse and J. A. Hobson began to embrace more systematically both social ethics and social spending in their elaboration of what they themselves described as a "new liberalism" that endorsed forms of communitarianism. They argued, as John Morrow has put it, that "private property is a necessary condition for liberal subjects," but that only state action could "secure substantive rights to private property for all members of the community and . . . thus give reality to the idea of a liberal subject."[182] Then from the 1890s, H. H. Asquith and David Lloyd George would begin to advocate "new liberal" policies within the framework of parliament politics. In the wake of the fallout of universal male enfranchisement, the Liberal Party looked to the new liberalism for an ideology through which to speak to the aspirations of working-class people.[183] This ideological tendency would see only further elaboration with the emergence of the British Labour Party, at its core "a radical extension of the Liberal Party."[184] Herbert Spencer was already grumbling in 1884 that "[m]ost of those who now pass as liberals are tories of a new type."[185] By this he clearly meant that liberals were increasingly embracing the agency of the state as a means to actively reconstitute the conditions of liberal subjectivity on a broader social basis. The turn to the state, or to some form of communitarianism, was a compelling recourse under circumstances where the propertyless were now recognized as political subjects in a liberal polity.

The liberal discourse of custom should thus be seen as a crucial moment in the elaboration of a new impulse to rethink the relationship between labor and civil society at the intersection of democratization and developed capitalism. "[I]t was the Liberals with Indian experience, like the younger Mill and Sir George Campbell," noted Eric Stokes, "who first taught their party that the State might justly lay hands on the sacred institution of private landed property."[186] Indeed, given that the 1870 Irish Land Act marked Gladstone's first significant endorsement of state intervention in civil society, it might well be suggested that the liberal discourse of custom marked one of the first substantial political articulations of the trajectories of the "new" British liberalism. This was a development that expressed not just anxieties about the permanency of Britain's economic hegemony, but more fundamentally anxieties about the plausibility of liberalism itself.

4

An Agrarian Civil Society?

The liberal discourse of custom carried with it no guarantees as to the accuracy of its claims about the political-economic and normative principles prevailing in agrarian society. Obviously, there are no grounds to assume that the account of the "common law" of the country that the liberal discourse of custom offered bore any discernable relationship to an actually existent set of customs practiced on the ground in agrarian Bengal. As Peter Robb has observed, the actual "tendency of custom" in relation to land in Bengal, even in the second half of the nineteenth century, remained geared "towards specific rather than general rates of rent—rents which changed in accordance with status, soil, crop, and supply and demand too. Average rent rates certainly differed from place to place and, less dramatically, between the different categories applied by the British; but the greatest variations were from village to village and holding to holding."[1] Such unevenness in rental rates would normally be taken to suggest a radical opposition between custom and political economy, insofar as the tendency of market relations would be to equilibrate prices around uniform variables. In any case, there is little basis for assuming that the flourishing markets in capital and commodities in nineteenth-century Bengal would automatically lead to a correlative extension of vibrant markets in land and labor.

So far we remain on the safe and familiar ground of a general skepticism about colonial and elite discourse. I have no hesitation in conceding that the conception of custom worked out by people like Campbell and Hollingbery was something substantially less than a transparent description of the (many and varied) forms of usage organizing Bengali agrarian social relations. Indeed, theirs was not so much a misrepresentation of the "common law of the country," as a misapprehension that there was any such "common law." Even so, it is far from clear that this easy skepticism is not itself a form of historiographical blinker. In this chapter, I want to suggest that when Campbell construed Bengali agrarian society as regulated by forms of relationship that political economy was competent to conceptualize, he did not do so arbitrarily. Nor were his motives merely instrumental to the purposes of colonial governance. Campbell's conception of custom could find a referent in agrarian society. Yet that referent was not in any straightforward sense present as a stable structural reality in agrarian life, a fact simply discoverable through colonial sociological or anthropological inquiry. Rather, Campbell's embrace of a new conception of custom was a response to normative claims that emerged from agrarian society in the form of major episodes of raiyat mobilization through the 1860s and 1870s.

To be clear, at no point did this raiyat politics rest its demands substantially upon the platform of "custom" in the generalized sense in which it was invoked in the Great Rent Case. Nonetheless, there was an important dimension of commensurability that connected the political-economic conception of custom to the demands for raiyat independence articulated in the same period. The liberal discourse of custom, on the one hand, posited an agrarian civil society governed by the normative obligations that the property-constituting capacities of labor entailed. It thereby implicitly posited a society of independent individuals bound to each other by their productive interaction with nature. Raiyats, on the other hand, framed normative claims over environmental resources. They did this not primarily as a basis for securing the viability of the subsistence food production that remained crucial to the reproduction of most agrarian households. They more immediately sought to secure and extend their participation in independent commodity production. They thus posited the labor they put into the land as the practical foundation of a form of social relationship that political economy was specifically competent to grasp. Liberal custom's insistence that agrarian society was deeply structured by political economy mirrored the demands on the part of raiyats that exchange between independent producers be recognized as the normative foundation of social relations in what implicitly amounted to an agrarian civil society.

I am not suggesting that raiyats in this period had generally anticipated the Lockean discourse that would feature with such explicitness in Campbell's arguments—though there are definitely suggestive moments. I am rather arguing that, in advancing a conception of independence that rested on commodity production, raiyats were in effect occupying a space of political argument that was deeply commensurable with Campbell's conception of an agrarian civil society based on the role of labor in shaping normative obligations. By hitching their interest in the soil to commodity production, raiyats opened the crucial conceptual space into which the liberal discourse of custom—and with it, the discourse of political economy—

would step. I mean this in two senses: first, in the sense that the plausibility of the liberal discourse of custom was tied to its emergence partly as a response to these very kinds of agrarian political demands; and secondly, in the sense that raiyat politics would find in the liberal discourse of custom a powerful set of conceptual tools through which to articulate its demands. These conceptual tools would allow it to incorporate an ever more explicit repertoire of political-economic concepts into the articulation of peasant interests.

THE INDIGO PROBLEM

Connecting the liberal discourse of custom to raiyat politics does not rest on speculative homologies. The conception of custom that emerged into the domain of legal debate in the Great Rent Case was elaborated under the immediate practical pressures of incidents of agrarian unrest that erupted in the interval between the passing of Act X of 1859 and Peacock's judgments in *Hills v. Ghose*. When George Campbell argued in his 1864 Minute that customary rights were the practical foundation for the raiyat's status as a kind of "capitalist," he was not introducing an entirely novel claim. In fact, the argument that the raiyat was a capitalist whose labor constituted part of his investment, rather than a laborer employed by capital, had already been voiced at the very highest levels of the Bengal Presidency's government, in the course of a series of debates that provided the immediate background to the suit for rent enhancement that James Hills had brought before the court.

In 1850, A. Sconce had played a key role in championing the cultivator as the chief beneficiary of future tenancy reforms. In 1854, Sconce set a second controversy in motion when, assigned as a judge to Nadia district, he wrote to the Secretary of the Government of Bengal, Cecil Beadon, to propose a commission of inquiry (never formed) into relations between the mostly European indigo planters and the raiyats who cultivated the plant. Cultivation of indigo was concentrated mostly in central and western Bengal, where it usually took place on raiyati lands rather than on whatever demesne (*nijabad* or *khas khamar*) planters might control as part of a zamindari or intermediary leasehold. The advantages of this system were several. The expenses of direct farm cultivation, especially credit, could be avoided. The risk of crop failure could be transferred onto the cultivator. And the cost of production could be further reduced through exploitation of the unpaid labor of the cultivator's household. Throughout the 1850s, planters had relied on a combination of advances, forged contracts, the inheritance of raiyat debt, control over grain stores, and direct physical coercion to keep raiyats cultivating the crop even in the face of net losses. Compared to rice, indigo represented only a small proportion of Bengal's commercial agriculture, even at its height. But it enjoyed a disproportionate profile in the concerns (and archives) of the colonial

government for at least four reasons. Firstly, indigo was an export crop, so it necessarily passed into customs records and was factored into balance of payments calculations. Secondly, indigo's financing was drawn largely from local capital, and its
cultivation was initially accelerated by the need to find means for the remittance of
personal savings back to Britain. As a result, the indigo industry was vulnerable to
periodic withdrawals of capital and an impulse to overproduction, which in combination with its susceptibility to international price fluctuations, rendered it subject to intense periodic crises (most dramatically in 1829–33, and again in 1847–
48). Thirdly, indigo cultivation enjoyed strong support from orthodox advocates
of political economy because it brought European capital into Indian agriculture,
and so was considered a key means of agricultural improvement. Finally, with the
rising price of other agricultural products relative to indigo, planting was a source
of growing unrest in the countryside. This was especially true after the collapse of
the financing structure of indigo production in 1847–48, when coercion necessarily emerged more prominently as an instrument of profitable cultivation.[2]

Sconce had pursued some initial inquiries into whether the "indigo system"
was founded on "contentment and profitable industry" or on "constraint, bank-
ruptcy, undeliverable bonds." He concluded with the "general impression" that it
was "sustained throughout by compulsion, and by the advantages gained by arbitrary and unrighteous dealing." Raiyats, it was said, were coerced into growing
indigo on their best land and giving the plant their first attentions. Their contracts
to grow the plant were measured in unusually large beegahs, and the resulting
plant was then systematically undermeasured. The plant was generally unremunerative to the cultivators, especially after necessary payments had been made to
corrupt factory servants. "Ryots, it has been said to me, have nothing, and can have
nothing; they are working cattle merely, not men reconciled to labour by their
gains."[3] Sconce was marking out the initial impulse of a pro-raiyat stance on the
indigo system. This was an impulse that turned, however, on the affirmation of the
raiyat's rights *as a free laborer* whose agreement to produce indigo ought to have
been grounded in the prospect of just remuneration for labor, rather than fear of
violence.

This conception of the indigo-cultivating raiyat as a laborer was also the basis
of the pro-planter position. In 1854, the joint magistrate and deputy collector of
Pabna district, F. Beaufort, submitted a report calling for the criminalization of
breach of contract to cultivate indigo. His basic motivation was to provide planters
with greater means of redress when raiyats took advances and then failed to cultivate. In the face of legal delays and the raiyat's lack of means to make redress, a
remedy in civil court, he complained, was tantamount to no remedy at all. Furthermore, as the law stood, the planter was deprived of any capacity to command
the labor he had hired. "[I]f the planter brings a suit before [the magistrate] . . . as
having a *quasi* possession of the land, as obtained through advances in money and

seed for its cultivation, he cannot interfere, since the Sudder Court have expressly ruled that the ryot who has cultivated, and not the person who has made advances, is to be held to be in possession of the land; and that the lien or interest which the planter holds ... should not be considered in such cases." Because indigo raiyats labored on land that was not generally under the direct control of their employers, labor could not be properly disciplined to perform its task. It was therefore the duty of the law to provide the proper means to achieve this discipline. Only this could avert the need for the extralegal means, "acts of violence," to which the planters had in desperation been driven.[4] As A.C. Bidwell, Commissioner of Nadia Division, would argue in support of Beaufort's proposal, the fact that planters "resort to physical force, in order to obtain their rights from the ryots," was itself prima facie evidence against the claim that the "interests of planters are sufficiently protected by the law in force."[5] Planter violence was thus symptomatic of the difficulty of enforcing the contract for indigo cultivation rather than the precondition for the existence of the contract.

Beaufort's critics had little patience for this kind of argument. They contested its factual basis. They also appealed to the general jurisprudential principle that the law of contracts belonged to the civil jurisdiction, making criminalization unsound. Sconce responded forcefully, insisting that the reason that planters preferred cultivation by raiyats on raiyati land was because "planters cannot cultivate indigo by their own hired labourers. They cannot make it pay. The returns do not remunerate them with sufficient profit over and above the expenses of labour." Given the unremunerativeness of the crop, it was impossible to deny the coerced nature of the cultivation: "knowing that the ryot is an unwilling party to the covenant, knowing that in his judgment the cultivation of rice or of oil-seeds would be more profitable to him, shall we aggravate the anomaly by constituting the rejection of the contract a crime, and imprison the criminal?"

The crux of the issue for Sconce was that the "connexion of the planter and the ryot is not simply one of a cultivator working upon the advances of a capitalist. The planter is and yet is not the cultivator. He selects the land; he directs and compels the ploughing, and the sowing, and the weeding. The land is 'his cultivation'; and the ripened crop is cut for his vats." The result was, he conceded, an improved agriculture. Yet the "interference which he exercises and the rights he asserts" implied a degree of responsibility appropriate to a "cultivating farmer," including the "adequate remuneration of the ryot's enforced, but possibly, judiciously directed labour." Planters advanced two rupees per beegah to be cultivated with indigo. They claimed extensive rights over the direction of the cultivation. They then, however, "practically disavowed" the labor "to whatever extent the crop fails," with the "money paid in anticipation ... written back as debt against the ryot." This was the very "reverse" of a proper capital-labor relationship. "An advance of two rupees a beegah cannot justify the assertion of every sort of right;

nor is it, in any fair sense, a measure of the ryot's duty to labour, or of the remuneration of his labour and of his expenses additional to his own labour."[6]

This conclusion pointed in two antithetical directions. H. B. Lawford, Officiating Magistrate of Nadia, would take up one: "in my opinion the planter ought to
have no claim whatever against the ryot, after the ryot has sown and delivered the
crop of the specified quantity of land which he (the ryot) agreed to sow. It is not the
ryot's fault if the crop turn out a bad one, and if so, why should he be obliged to
bear the burthen of the loss of it; if the planter had sown and cultivated the indigo
himself, and an adequate crop had not been produced, the planter would have had
to bear the loss himself, and because the ryot has sown the crop, why should he
have to bear the loss for the planter?" Lawford supported Beaufort's draconian
proposal, but insisted that the law should include an additional feature, namely
that "if, owing to a bad season, or any other cause out of the control of the ryot, the
produce of the land which he had sown did not cover the advances which he had
received, the planter should have no claim against the ryot on that account, it
being manifestly more equitable that the loss consequent on a bad crop should be
borne by the planter than by the ryot who was obliged to sow it for him."[7] If the
raiyat was to be treated as a laborer, then the planter was obliged to assume the
responsibilities of a capitalist, including the risk.

But it was again Sconce who would adumbrate the alternative approach that
would ultimately prove ascendant in subsequent policy. If planters could not find
raiyats to cultivate freely with a view to earning a fair wage, nor were willing to
assume their responsibilities as capitalists by themselves shouldering the risks of
their investment, then the government's support for a coercive indigo-system
could not be justified on the grounds of political economy: "Under such circumstances, it is a striking scientific error to commend or justify the employment of
advances" as a means to bring capital into agricultural production. "Capital super-
fluously spent is mis-spent; and labour misdirected is lost and wasted." The contradiction between the raiyat's status as laborer and his status as bearer of risk might
instead be resolved in favor of the latter, by asserting the status of the raiyat as an
independent commodity producer. "Let then the ryot cultivate his land in his own
way, with indigo if it be profitable, and with advances if advances be desirable to
him, paid at the risk of those who are willing to accommodate him . . . . Hear what
the Pubna ryot says: He says he is prepared to cultivate his own land; it will not
therefore lie waste by the withdrawal of the planter; and what is more, he is persuaded that the products he will himself cultivate, will pay him better than indigo."[8]

In responding to Beaufort's proposition, a number of civilians drew attention to
the fact that all the "great crops of Bengal rice, sugar, silk, fibres, oil seeds, etc."
were being grown on advances, and on a much vaster scale than indigo. Yet they
did not seem to require any special legislation or physical coercion. The difference
was of course not only the nonremunerative nature of indigo cultivation that

underpinned the system of raiyati (rather than demesne) cultivation. It was also the rising prices of other agricultural products. "I cannot show in figures that indigo is less profitable than other crops," noted G. U. Yule, Officiating Judge of Rangpur. "The ryots believe that it is so, and they ought to know best."[9] But this was an issue that extended beyond concerns about opportunity cost and utility maximization. It spoke instead to the more fundamental question of the political-economic status of the raiyat. For one of the great differences "between contracts for indigo plant and those for other produce" was, according to Yule, that "by the terms of an indigo contract . . . the ryot must give the whole of his indigo plant to the factory at the same fixed rate; in contracts for other produce the ryot only agrees to repay the advance with interest, &c., in cash or in produce, at a fixed market rate, while all the surplus is his own to dispose of as he pleases."[10] In the first instance, the raiyat was in effect a laborer working for capital, for the product always already belonged, by hypothecation, to the capitalist whose advance it represented. Having once accepted advances, and thereby having entered into a "condition of hereditary debt and servitude to indigo," the raiyat "came subject to the supervision of the factory omlah."[11] In the latter instance, the raiyat was an independent producer engaging in market exchange. The raiyats of Barasat, for example, insisted that "they will not sow indigo for this very sound reason, that they find tobacco and other crops far more profitable." Even when the rate paid for indigo did not represent an absolute loss, they said, it was nonetheless "never viewed as advantageous to them, because far below the rate of profit attainable from other crops."[12] They were thereby asserting their rights as independent producers, cultivating crops on land that was theirs. Against this claim, the indigo planters insisted that that freedom could only be available to the raiyats once they had paid back all their debts from past and present advances, thus fulfilling their contractual obligations. (Of course, as any number of civilians noted over the years, the whole premise of the indigo system was that, once a raiyat accepted an advance, whether freely or "by intimidation and by fraud," they would never be allowed to successfully pay it off.)[13]

The unrest of indigo cultivators would accelerate in intensity in 1859 and peak in 1860 in central and western Bengal. Raiyats launched a concerted effort to refuse to plant indigo by forming combinations to collectively resist planters. The Bengal government was faced with a dizzyingly complex and contrary set of concerns in the face of these conflicts between European planters and Bengali raiyats. In the wake of the recent suppression of the 1855 Santhal Rebellion against coercive debt-bondage on the western margins of Bengal, not to mention the seismic upheaval of the Mutiny of 1857, the government's overwhelming immediate preoccupation was the maintenance of law and order. This implied the suppression of raiyats whenever they threatened any kind of unfair combination to elude contractual obligations, coercion to promote acquiescence to such combinations, or physical action against planters. But it could also give rise to impatience with planter law-lessness, to the assertion of a rule of law binding upon Europeans and Indians in the mofussil, and to a desire to unveil the root causes of the unrest.

Alongside this primary issue, however, were several other concerns that worked variously with and against that overriding preoccupation. Some civilians, led by Lieutenant-Governor Grant, tied the rule of law to a conception of free commerce. This in itself pointed in two quite contrary directions. On the one hand, Grant and Ashley Eden (recently returned from the campaign against the Santhals) criticized the extralegal coerciveness of the indigo system in Bengal as indicative of its unre-munerativeness for the raiyat. They pointed to its inconsistency with the funda-mental principle of commercial society, that exchanges be freely entered into, with a view to the interest of both seller and purchaser. As such, it was frequently argued that raiyats were simply acting on the basis of a rational estimation of their self-interest when they repudiated indigo, and were perfectly within their rights to do so. On the other hand, indigo planters frequently argued that many raiyats were seeking to repudiate contractual obligations for which they had accepted advances from the planters. This was a point conceded to a greater or lesser degree by most civilians. As Henry Maine stressed from the moment of his arrival in India as Law Member in 1861, commercial society was unimaginable without a reliable institu-tional arrangement for enforcing private contracts.[14] Indigo planters argued on this basis that legislation was required to compel raiyats to fulfill contractual obli-gations to planters for the season. Grant obliged, on a temporary basis, in 1860.

Yet this impulse to compulsion was expressed, under the practical exigencies of the moment, in the form of a criminal penalty under summary jurisdiction. This was a repudiation of the principles of civil contract, and an outcome strenuously criticized by Maine as part of his advocacy of a reformed system of civil courts.[15] Why this recourse to compulsion on the part of a government that repeatedly declared itself to be above the competition of private economic interests? Surely because, as zamindars, patnidars or other intermediate tenure holders, indigo planters' capacity to recoup returns on their investments directly impacted the capacity of the state to collect its revenue from the land. Furthermore, indigo had long been understood by colonial administrators to be a means to introduce Euro-pean capital and management into agrarian production, and hence to promote agri-cultural improvement. Such improvement was urgently needed to increase govern-ment revenues in the medium term. These were always the arguments to which indigo planters ultimately appealed in their addresses to the government.[16] The colonial state could not anticipate the prospective dissolution of the indigo industry in Bengal without trepidation. Yet even here there was a contrary concern: that the lawlessness of planters in the mofussil might serve to undermine the (racial) pres-tige of British rule, ultimately rebounding negatively back onto the government's most immediate preoccupation with the maintenance of law and order.[17]

As debates over the indigo system heated up in response to the increasingly widespread disturbances, positions polarized. Planters emphasized their rights as capital over labor. Critics of indigo emphasized the illegitimacy of coercion exercised over free producers. Backing indigo, the Commissioner of Nadia Division, A. Grote, proposed in 1859 a law to allow planters "to sow against the ryot's will" when the raiyat refused to fulfill his contractual obligations. The law would allow planters to seize the land they had in effect leased when making an advance to the raiyat, and to substitute other labor for the raiyat's as necessary.[18] Indigo planters, consistently characterizing the intensifying conflict over indigo as "a dispute between capital and labour," freely admitted that the raiyats' desire to throw off indigo cultivation was driven by the rising prices of other crops. Planters dismissed this desire, however, as in conflict with raiyats' contractual obligations, which, once made, could not be simply forgotten.[19] Planters were incensed by officials who told raiyats that they were not obliged to cultivate indigo. They especially targeted Ashley Eden, who was said to have instructed the police in Barasat that "the ryots are to keep possession of their own lands, sowing thereon such crops as they may desire," and that "indigo planters shall not be able, under pretense of the ryots having agreed to sow indigo, to cause indigo to be sown by the use of violence on the lands of those ryots." Planters increasingly shifted blame from the meddling of zamindars to the government itself. They accused it of providing implicit support to raiyats who refused to fulfill their contracts. "[S]uch interference . . . between the capitalist and the labourer, is unwarranted by the practice of any civilized country."[20]

Ashley Eden would emerge as the indigo system's most eloquent civilian critic in the course of the disturbances of the late 1850s and early 1860s. Lieutenant-Governor Grant tried to maintain the government's role as neutral arbiter. On the one hand, he affirmed the "legal and moral right" of raiyats to choose whether or not to engage in indigo contracts. On the other hand, he simultaneously and contradictorily upheld the planters' claims that their advances represented a binding contract that required fulfillment before the raiyat could justly reclaim that freedom.[21] Eden, in contrast, elaborated a persuasive explanation of the increased unwillingness of raiyats to continue to submit to planter coercion. First, he linked their unrest to rising land, food and wage prices that rendered ever more disadvantageous the cultivation of a crop whose price was monopsonistically and coercively fixed. Second, he emphasized the increasingly painful opportunity cost of wasting land, labor and prime sowing time on a disruptive and unremunerative crop when the value of other market crops like rice, tobacco, oil seeds and jute was rising so dramatically.

> The whole of the crops in Bengal are grown under advances, yet we never hear of the mahajuns complaining that the ryot wont sow his rice, or jute, or tobacco crop; the reason is, that they sow their crop on what land they like, and sell it at the market

price. Ryots have been known to get over 100 rupees per beegah from their tobacco crop this year. The average of an indigo crop is two per beegah, that is 10 bundles, at 5 bundles for the rupee; at the very highest rate known the crop never exceeds 25 bundles, which would give 5 rupees, from which the advance, the price of seed and cultivation are to be deducted, for the price never varies; there is no market price. . . . The planter's sole object is not to recover his advances, but to prevent their recovery. I believe that there is scarcely a ryot in Bengal who would not pay up his advances to-morrow if it would exempt him from future cultivation of indigo.[22]

The reliance on coercion deepened the "more it became for the interest of the ryot to sow crops other than indigo." Yet this intensification of coercion was occurring at the same time as an extension of assistant magistracies deeper into the mofussil, making raiyats more aware of their legal right to resist that coercion. If the raiyats concluded from the government's unwillingness to support planter violence that the government was opposed to indigo cultivation—a rumor rife in the indigo-producing districts that did much to fuel unrest—this was also unsurprising, since indigo was only cultivated under coercion.[23]

Eden was thus forthright in his belief that "contracts, *i.e.,* engagements voluntarily entered into by both parties for the purpose of mutual benefit, are almost entirely unknown" in the indigo system. As such, the advances planters claimed to have made to cultivators, and the debts accumulated by raiyats who had been unable to pay off past advances, represented no true claim on the raiyats' labor at all. It was on the basis of this analysis that he affirmed, in his role as Magistrate of Barasat, that the role of the police in indigo pursuits was "to protect the ryot in the possession of his lands, on which he is at liberty to sow any crop he likes, without any interference on the part of the planter or any one else."[24] Or as he would put it even more forcefully in his evidence before the Indigo Commission of 1860: "the land is the land of the ryots, they are the best judges of their own interests, and so long as they object to the cultivation of indigo, for whatever reason, I can conceive no principle upon which it can be argued that it is justifiable for a third party to come in and insist upon a ryot sowing that to which he objects, although it may be in his opinion beneficial to the ryot."[25]

Faced with ever-sharper criticism from planter lobbies, Lieutenant-Governor Grant would gradually drift into a more and more explicit defense of the rights of raiyats as free cultivators. Already, when championing legislation to make breach of contract for indigo a summary offense in March of 1860, he recognized that the "same men who fight for the privilege of cultivating a field with rice, for sale in the open market, are now almost in rebellion in order to escape the calamity of cultivating a field with indigo for sale (if sale it can be called) to the planter."[26] Planters had recourse to addressing a petition over Grant's head to the Viceroy. They demanded that the Viceroy order Grant to "refrain from pursuing a course of conduct which cannot but be ruinous to the indigo planters in Bengal" and to desist from meddling in the "due course of the administration of the law by the regularly appointed judicial officers." Such meddling, they argued, was "especially indiscreet in the case of a dispute between capital and labour."[27] In response, the Lieutenant-Governor formulated his approach to this question in newly rigorous terms.

> The commercial disagreement in question is designated a dispute between capital and labour. . . . I am aware of no such dispute. . . . The disagreement actually existing is between the manufacturers of the dye, and the producers of the plant, which is the raw material of the dye. *Both classes are capitalists,* and so far from it being true that the capital of the producers is so small, comparatively, that they may be truly described, for practical purposes, as labourers, their capital, in the aggregate, infinitely exceeds the capital of all the manufacturers of indigo dye. The capital of the ryot is in his land, his crops, and his cattle, and in very many cases in his means of hiring labourers, over and above the value of his own bodily labour. The whole cultivation of Bengal is in his hands; and the ruin of this mighty interest would be the ruin of the country. The capital of the manufacturer of indigo dye is partly in his manufacturing premises and utensils, and in his means of hiring labourers, but mainly in the debts due to him by the former class of capitalists, namely, the ryots.[28]

There is no reason to think that by "capitalist" here Grant understood that raiyats were agents of ongoing open-ended accumulation. He did, however, understand them to be surplus generators who carried on cultivation on the basis of their own stock and on that basis independently produced commodities for the market. As a relationship between "capitalists," the proper course to be followed by the government was to ensure that commerce follow its natural course so that contracts were made for the mutual benefit of both parties. This required the government to defend the raiyat's rightful possession of his land and his right to grow whatever crops he desired on it.[29]

Indigo planters responded to "Mr. Grant's facetious assertion that [the raiyat] is the real capitalist of Bengal" with skeptical irony.[30] They declined "to enter into an argument as to the correctness of the Lieutenant Governor's view of the position of the ryot as a capitalist, as they believe that such a theory is one wholly new, and one particularly opposed to the general idea of what constitutes a ryot in Bengal."[31] James Hills, the indigo planter who would soon set in motion the entire litigational process that led to the Great Rent Case, had already in September of 1860 recognized the connections with the Rent Act of 1859. He identified as two of the "chief causes which originated the disturbances" Section 6 of the act, "giving the right of possession, after 12 years' occupancy, to a class of men who, a few years ago, were the coolies who were employed to clear the jungle off the land on which they have since squatted," and Section 11, which withdrew from zamindars their power to compel their tenants' attendance for the adjustment of rents, thereby "breaking the link between ryot and his liege lord."[32]

Led by W. S. Seton-Karr, soon to be one of the High Court justices that decided the Great Rent Case, a Commission of Inquiry produced a majority report deeply critical of the indigo system. Grant was now positioned to press his argument further. He observed that the few planters in eastern Bengal generally opted for demesne cultivation using unambiguously waged labor. Indigo cultivation there had not provoked the same kind of unrest. This implied that it was where planters sought through illegitimate violence to reduce independent producers to the status of inadequately remunerated waged labor, in central and western Bengal, that the system had become untenable. "Now, if one remembers that these ryots are not Carolina slaves, but the free yeomanry of this country, and, indeed, strictly speaking, the virtual owners of the greater part of the land in the old cultivated parts of Bengal, so heavy a loss as this will fully account for the strength of the opposition to indigo cultivation which we have just experienced."[33] Grant was effectively recognizing that the constitution of a legitimate commercial society based on free exchange had to be grounded in the raiyat's proprietary rights over the soil.

The 1860s and 1870s saw a precipitous decline in indigo cultivation throughout Bengal proper.[34] When it became clear by 1861 that the raiyats would be successful in their campaign against indigo, planters resorted to rent enhancement under the terms of Act X as a means either to coerce obedience from *ilaka* raiyats (who held land directly under them in the tenure hierarchy), or to recoup some of their losses.[35] But Hills's enhancement suit had much more at stake than merely the capacity to extort higher rents from a few tenants. He fully understood that the very status of the raiyat as an economic and legal subject was at stake in the interpretation of Act X. Chief Justice Peacock held that if the raiyat was a "mere laborer, who is obliged to borrow his daily food at the rate of 50 per cent. interest, and the necessary capital at the rate of 37 per cent.," he could stake no claim to the profits of capital, which "must go to the person who supplied the capital."[36] Such a raiyat was really a laborer, not even a capitalist. As such, there could be no reason to imagine that he should be further entitled to an interest in the rent fund. "The ryot contends that a share of the net profits ought to have been reserved for him; that he, being a ryot, possessing a right of occupancy, had an interest in the land. . . . It is a mistake to suppose that such a ryot has any interest in the land which gives him a right to a share in the rent."[37] If the raiyat lacked capital of his own and had to borrow it from the mahajan, "he must make such a bargain with the Mahajun as will throw upon him who receives the profits of the capital the risk which is run by so employing it."[38] The overthrow of this precedent in the Great Rent Case effectively asserted the raiyat's right to a portion of the rent fund on the basis of his historical role as investor of labor and stock in the land, regardless of any present dependence on subsistence or capital loans. The securing of the right of occupancy and the limitation of enhancement consolidated the Bengal raiyat's position as a free commodity producer by affirming his claim to be a "capitalist." This was a term that referred not primarily to the narrower stratum of affluent raiyats who held large holdings farmed by under-raiyats, sharecroppers and hired laborers, but to occupancy or hereditary raiyats *in general*.

RAIYAT POLITICS

The role of money in Bengal's rural economy had been broadly accelerating since the thirteenth century; again in the wake of Mughal integration in the sixteenth century; and again with the inflow of precious metals from the West from the mid-seventeenth century. With its extensive participation in the Islamic and Indian Ocean trading worlds, a developed system of cash rent as the basis of state revenue, and a differentiated population substantially engaged in nonagricultural activities, it is clear that parts of precolonial South Asia must have seen a substantial portion of the agricultural product directed into commercial transactions over a very long span of centuries.[39] Yet in Bengal at least, the second half of the eighteenth century seems to have set in motion a new dynamic in the nature and extent of this commercialism. Its effects penetrated to a much deeper level of everyday production and consumption. "[I]t was the late eighteenth century which provided the distinctive point of departure [for a significantly new commercial phase in the nineteenth and twentieth centuries] by bringing about the commercialization of the province's *rice producing economy and of the social relations which were embedded in it.*"[40] This impulse, initially centered on the old Bhagirathi delta of western Bengal, would extend more deeply in the course of the early nineteenth century into the younger, more active delta of eastern Bengal.[41] The period 1859–85 appears to have been another key period of transformation in the role of commercial agriculture. Regional commercial agriculture became more deeply integrated into international commodity chains underpinned by imperial rule. Commercial crops (including staple crops) became more important in the reproduction of peasant households. A new cash crop emerged in the form of jute, the extension of whose acreage was necessarily at the expense of rice. Even though most of the rice trade was intraregional, rice exports expanded dramatically until the mid-1920s.[42] In combination with the expansion of jute acreage, this would set the conditions for the region's subsequent dependence on cheaper Burmese rice imports. Finally, capital penetrated more deeply into the agrarian sector in the form of networks of credit distribution.

Bengal had been a major rice exporter since at least the sixteenth century—though how significant the scale of this trade was to the internal economy of the region has been disputed.[43] It is likely that the expansion of this commerce had been driven in large part from the late seventeenth century by "land developers" who purchased permanent rights in uncultivated land from provincial authorities (whether prospectively or retrospectively). These taluqdars assigned parcels of uncultivated land to subtenants who in turn organized bands of colonizers to reclaim their tenures from waste. There is thus little question of the role that monetization and cash advances already played in the reclamation of new lands as the delta shifted eastward in the seventeenth and eighteenth centuries. And there is also little question that this process involved a highly active and dynamic sector of what Richard Eaton has called "capitalist speculators, or classical revenue farmers."[44]

Even in the heyday of speculative land development through revenue farms, however, there is little evidence that reclamation was driven by an interest in commercialized production. The colonization of new lands meant first and foremost the expansion of land revenues in the form of rents. The more active deltaic regions combined high levels of climatic risk, the mutability of a delta environment, limited transportation and communications (especially in the wet season), and rampant piracy throughout the early-modern period. As such, these remained areas of shallow political integration and limited agricultural commercialization.[45] Only in the late 1780s do we begin to find reliable evidence anywhere in Bengal of grain merchants regularly using advances to raiyats to gain sustained control over their product and their production process. Meanwhile, the waste-reclaiming jotedars and gantidars of the eighteenth century would for the most part only become village landlords capable of serving as agents of the furtherance of agrarian commercialization and capitalist social relations in the course of the nineteenth century.[46] So while it makes a great deal of sense to locate the commercialization of the nineteenth century within the longer trajectories of commercialization in the early-modern period, we should nonetheless be leery of collapsing the society with which colonial officials were grappling in the mid-nineteenth century into the uninterrupted continuities of the preceding three centuries.

Furthermore, we should recognize that the long process of expansion in Bengal's rice trade represents evidence primarily of the relatively consistent production of a substantial agricultural surplus across an expanding frontier, coupled with a highly developed mercantile-commercial network.[47] It tells us almost nothing about the degree to which commercialization affected agricultural relations of production and reproduction per se. It might be objected that the scale of cotton and silk production in the same period seems to weigh against such excessive caution. In fact, however, even in the core areas of silk and cotton production, rice remained the predominant crop throughout this period.[48] Tirthankar Roy estimates that the net employment generated by the Dutch and British textile trades in the early eighteenth century represented less than 1% of the total workforce. This was a segment that could be fed, along with their families, all year round on the product of less than half of a percent of the estimated cultivated land.[49] Of course, before the late eighteenth century the archive is especially opaque. Furthermore, there is no reason to doubt that the kinds of mercantile capitalism that preexisted the constitution of this archive most likely did sometimes generate their own impulses to reach for closer control of the production process.[50] Nonetheless, there seems little reason to be surprised that sixteenth-century discussions of wealth and production were organized around a "zero-sum logic." In such texts, realistic portrayals of "expansion of settled agriculture on the agrarian frontier, and a degree of commercialization of the instruments of kingship," were in no way connected to any conception of "a general and secular growth of the economy," let alone to an "attempt to find a human explanation" for such growth.[51]

Colonial officials' identification of the Bengali raiyat as a "capitalist," a free commodity producer, has to be understood as a response, in part, to the substantial intensification of commercialized social relations that had made substantial headway by the middle of the nineteenth century. More immediately, however, it echoed political demands being voiced by raiyats themselves. Raiyats seem to have drawn on the potentialities of their highly varied, but overall deepening, participation in the sphere of circulation as a basis for repudiating their identification and subordination as "mere laborers." Their claim to the status of independent producer substantially rested on the raiyat's claim to an interest in the soil. It was this interest in the soil that represented the most generalizable form of raiyat capitalization. It was typically on this basis that reliance on planter or moneylender credit could be distinguished from the reduction of the raiyat to the status of a laborer working for capital.

The argument I am making here should not be confused with a more conventional sociological interpretation of peasant political formations as organized around homogeneous class interests. The claims of the raiyat to be an independent producer indexed neither the general interests of a traditional subsistence peasantry with customary rights to possessory dominion, nor the exclusive interests of the more affluent peasantry (who did indeed figure prominently in peasant mobilizations). The category "raiyat" named a legal status in the revenue hierarchy, but it was of indeterminate sociological significance even within any given subregion of Bengal, let alone across them. As Sugata Bose and Partha Chatterjee have argued, only in eastern Bengal did the conception of raiyats as a relatively homogeneous class of smallholding cultivators hold to any degree true. And as Iftekhar Iqbal has argued, in the wake of the 1885 Tenancy Act even in those areas raiyati would become an increasingly opaque category.[52] Yet the forms of peasant politics at stake in this chapter were articulated across the variations of subregional agrarian social relations in the second half of the nineteenth century.

I suggest we read the politics of raiyat rights as an ideological framework through which specific normative potentialities of participation in commodity production could be articulated in the form of demands for the legal constitution of (occupancy) raiyats as a definite economic class of independent producers. This is not to deny the fact that raiyats in fact participated in many other forms of social obligation and relationship whose norms were not constitutively bound to practices of commodity exchange. But the plausibility of raiyat politics rested on minimizing such heterogeneous participation in order to emphasize the force of the normative assumptions implicit to their claims to the status of independent producers. Of course, it was in fact the more affluent raiyats who, unsurprisingly, would emerge as the leaders of the new peasant politics in many instances. But from the cultivating smallholder of eastern Bengal to the more affluent entrepreneurial farmer, diverse agrarian interests could be voiced through the single ideological framework provided by raiyat independence. That was what made this raiyat politics so potent.

The general thrust of this political discourse had already arguably been foreshadowed by the Faraizi movement. Faraizism was an Islamic reformism that emerged amongst the weavers and cultivators of eastern Bengal in the 1820s. It was subsequently dynamized politically in the 1830s, however, under the leadership of Dudu Mian. In the newly formed alluvial islands (churs) of the active deltaic regions of eastern Bengal, raiyats sought to bring new land under cultivation, while zamindars and indigo planters sought to claim such lands as demesne, to restrict raiyat access to them, or to subordinate raiyat claims to their own. The Faraizi movement had arisen in the course of the resulting conflicts. In a period of rising agricultural prices driving extensive land reclamation, the Faraizi movement appealed to the predominantly Muslim peasantry through the famous slogan, "*langol jar, jami tar*"—that is, the land belongs to the owner of the plough that tills it.[53] "They not only resist successfully the levy of all extra or illegal cesses by the Zemindars and Talookdars," noted the Commissioner of Dhaka Division in 1843, "but with equal ability to pay their land rent, they give much more trouble than others in collecting it—they would withhold it altogether if they dared, for it is a favorite maxim with them, that Earth is God's, who gives it to his people—the land tax is accordingly held in abomination, and they are taught to look forward to the happy time, when it will be abolished."[54] The Faraizi movement would continue to play a key role in the organization of agrarian leagues right through the 1870s in the active deltaic parts of Dhaka, Faridpur and Backerganj districts, even when the political and economic programs being espoused were strictly secular.[55] Indeed, the centrality of agrarian issues to the popularity of the movement was not least testified to by the extensive cooperation of Hindus with the hierarchical administrative structure maintained by Dudu Mian and his son, Noa Mian.[56]

Classical jurisprudence of the Hanafi school (the school to which most South Asian Sunnis adhered, including the Faraizis) had endorsed the primordial claims of the cultivating peasantry to a property in the soil. But by the sixteenth century Hanafi scholars had come to insist on the role of the state as the primary source of rights over the land. The jurisprudential defense of property rights in this period, whether in the Ottoman or the Mughal domains, therefore took the form of asserting the legitimacy of the historical process by which those rights had been derived *from the state*. In these terms, property was primarily understood to refer to revenue grants and awkaf (religious trusts) rather than smallholdings.[57] Nonetheless, some Hanafi scholars from the Ottoman domains began in the late seventeenth and early eighteenth centuries to link proprietary rights more directly to productive activity, albeit primarily with an eye to the commercial interests of revenue estate holders and religious trusts.[58] In Bengal as in the Ottoman Empire, it is clear that land use, rather than state rights over revenue, was becoming the key reference point for the development of new conceptions of property in the same period. The Muslim pioneers of the eastern delta played a crucial role in organizing land reclamation and establishing shrines and mosques as the institutional centers of agrarian life in eastern Bengal. In the process of transforming jungle into agricultural land, they affirmed the primacy of the state's claims over the soil. Yet they nonetheless generated parallel claims to a property in the soil on the basis of reclamation itself, which did not in any obvious sense rely on the state's authority. It was in this context, Richard Eaton has shown, that Islam would come to be "locally understood as a civilization-building ideology, a religion of the plow."[59] It was precisely in these eastern and southern deltaic regions that Faraizi political mobilization would assert a similar identification of Islam with cultivation in the first half of the mid-nineteenth century.

Nonetheless, the Faraizi movement was not passive in its inheritance of these older associations between Islam and agricultural civilization. Its reformist assault on local and syncretic practices also transformed that association. It effectively severed Islam from the very mediating institutions (pirs and shrines) on which the spread of Islam as a religion of the axe and plough in Bengal had been built. As a result, Adam-the-original-cultivator (a thoroughly Bengali motif) ceased to be the primordial source of patriarchal authority (implying a top-down distribution of entitlements through the patrimonial inheritance of founder-lineages). He instead became something more like the prototypical householder (implying lateral relations among brothers each with property independently constituted through the tilling of the soil). This was a move with striking parallels to the conceptual patricide that underpinned Locke's own theory of civil society.[60] Faraizism seems to have forged a precocious set of connections between independence, productive activity and religious authority that were strikingly novel for agrarian Bengal. This set of connections put labor at the core of the determination of social obligations.

Among Faraizis, the relationship of man to nature had become a normative foundation for the relationship of man to man precisely under circumstances of accelerating commodity production and commercialization. The reclaimed lands in the active deltaic regions, especially in the thick jungles of the Sundarbans, were not only centers of Faraizi mobilization. They also featured some of the most intensely commercialized processes of agricultural expansion, undertaken by both small cultivators and wealthier farmers who had some capital to finance the expensive and slow process of land clearance and preparation. In 1871 James Westland described the process by which tenurial claims were created in the Sundarban jungle-lands of southern Jessore district (a region that would become Khulna district in the following decade). The distinctive tenure hierarchy characteristic of the region began at the top with a "taluqdar." In this district, a taluqdar was the counterpart of a gantidar or jotedar, a farmer of means who paid rent for substantial holdings, often a village or half a village. The taluqdars who led this reclamation process were sometimes zamindars from farther neighboring regions, "but a great number of them appear to belong to the comfortably circumstanced class of people residing immediately north of the Sundarbans." These men generally "have just enough money to enable them to carry on Sundarban reclamation with success, and they are not rich enough to leave everything in the hands of agents, and by forgetting their direct interest, relax their enterprise; many of them also have ryots of their own in their old settled lands [immediately to the north of the Sundarbans], and can use them for their newer lands. It is to the class to which these men belong that the greater part of the agricultural improvement and extension since the permanent settlement is owing."[61] To bring the land into cultivation, the taluqdar created "hawaladars" beneath him, who then created "nim-hawaladars," who "are almost always of the pure ryot class, and engage personally in agriculture."

As Ramshunker Sen explained a couple of years later, a raiyat would cultivate his homestead further north in April and May. Then in June he would cultivate his "jungle-cleared lands" to the south, "where he with the assistance of his *krishans* or cultivators ploughs them up, having at the outset spread his dhan [rice] on a well-chosen seed bed." Then he returned to his homestead again to plant the upland rice. Then he would return south again "with his party of *dawals* (grain-cutters) in order to reap the harvest." The crop was then divided up between wages for the grain-cutters and threshers (a fifth of the harvest), rent for the superior tenure holder, a stock of seed-grain, a store for personal consumption, and finally, "the bulk of the surplus . . . to the rice-dealer." Sundarbans agriculture, in other words, was an entrepreneurial farming venture, in which "[r]yots who are well-to-do in life (and there are very few here who are not) do not cultivate land with their own hands," for they were "sufficiently comfortably circumstanced to hire out labor."[62] This was a vast farming enterprise in which capital was invested in the production of commercial crops through the direct deployment of agricultural labor.

All tenure ranks down to and including nim-hawaladars enjoyed rights of occupancy. Even the cultivating raiyats "call themselves 'abad-kari' or reclaiming ryots, and esteem themselves to have a sort of right of occupancy in their lands." Only tenants below nim-hawaladars were tenants at will. This lead Westland to conclude that "these [higher] tenures have their origin . . . in rights founded upon original reclamation. A ryot who gets a small piece of land to clear always regards himself as having a sort of property in it,—an 'abadkari swatwa' or 'reclamation right.' As reclamations extend, he begins to sub-let to other ryots, and we have a 'hawaladar' with his subordinate hawaladars in a few years."[63] Those with the capital to reclaim created through that process a form of proprietary claim over the soil, which was thereafter not compromised by the deployment of hired agricultural labor for year-to-year cultivation.[64]

On these deltaic frontiers, raiyats were not always looking for long-term rights in the land. While land remained plentiful (in some areas, this continued into the early twentieth century), raiyats were often loath to take on such long-term responsibility when short-term commitments carried less risk. Even in the later nineteenth century, it was not always easy to find tenants to take long-term leases in the *khas mahals* (government estates) of the active delta. Officials described a "system of shifting cultivation, expanding and contracting with the rise and fall of the price of rice" in these regions. The raiyats were "for the most part nomads, who are on the land one year and away the next, and whose settled holdings are under the zemindars of the neighbouring main land."[65] It is possible that the "abadkari swatwa," the quasi-proprietary right derived from reclamation, was the necessary cost of inducing the raiyat to undertake reclamation of wasteland and maintain a permanent revenue commitment. The occupancy right seems, according to Westland, to have been built into the contract between the original lessee of the land (the taluqdar) and the raiyat to whom he in turn leased some portion of it. This is confirmed by Robert Morrell, the largest landholder in the Jessore Sundarbans, who observed that when contracting with hawaladars to clear forests for cultivation and settlement, the "abadkars would take up pottahs (written rights of possession)" for the most part only if they were given "a permanent right of possession."[66] What is particularly worth noting here is that what colonial administrators like Campbell and Westland would construe as "custom" was itself in part something generated out of a reclamation process driven by a certain kind of commercial agriculture. At one level, this process reconstituted associations between reclamation and property that had been present in Hanafi jurisprudence for centuries, and that had been restated unambiguously in the *Fatawa-i Alamgiri*. At another level, it seemed to echo the Faraizis in emphasizing less the primacy of rural and religious gentry as founder-reclaimers than the binding authority of labor's property-constituting capacities throughout the social space of agrarian society.

The result of this commercial colonization of the Sundarbans was "a great rice-producing tract" over "one vast plain" the wealth of whose rice fields it was "difficult to give an idea of." This agricultural tract was cultivated either "with the ryot's own capital" or through "advances from merchants" and, indeed, from talukdars, who were all rice lenders.[67] Its rice mostly entered "a general westward movement" so that "most of the rice grown in the Jessore Sundarbans" ended up feeding Calcutta, leaving the rice-deficit zones of northern Jessore "to be supplied from

Backerganj," the district neighboring to the east.[68] This trade in Sundarban rice, coupled with an equally valuable trade in firewood, constituted a highly developed commercial agriculture. At just one hat (weekly market), Chandkhali, "3,000 or 4,000 rupees worth of rice on an average change hands every hat day, and during the busiest season the amount probably reaches twice that quantity; and about 1,500 boats are brought up by people attending the hat." But Chandkhali was "only one out of many hats," and all these in turn represented only a portion of the overall trade, which was also shadowed by an "immense traffic carried on, less conspicuously, by traders all over the Sundarbans," some of whom traveled the delta in "large ships," and others of whom were "stationed at some village."[69] "It may be noted as a measure of the progress of commerce and the advance in administration since the time to which the statements made in this chapter refer," Westland noted, "that while for the police tax of 1795 the trading *capital* of the district was assessed at Rs. 8,90,000, for the certificate tax of 1868 the trading *profit* of the district was estimated at Rs. 32,00,000."[70]

Outside of the Sundarbans, in other parts of nineteenth-century Bengal, commercialization took place on a different footing. In western Bengal, commercialization had (possibly since the late eighteenth century, but certainly by the second half of the nineteenth century) been partly driven by credit dependence that deepened mercantile and zamindar control over agricultural production. The direct involvement of zamindars and other higher leaseholders in agricultural production, using hired labor on substantial demesne lands, further spurred commercialization in these areas.[71] In eastern Bengal, in contrast, the relative paucity of zamindar demesne lands, the relative homogeneity of a smallholding tenantry working fertile soils at relatively low rents, and a still-expanding agricultural frontier combined to restrain the expansion of capital's hold over labor until later in the nineteenth century. In eastern Bengal, wealthy farmers did not enjoy the same prominence in agrarian society that they did further west and north. Commercialization seems to have occurred as an intensification of older trajectories. Commercial crops probably began as an opportunistic response to the rise in prices for specific cash crops that were suited to cultivation in the delta environment. Jute was the best-known commercial crop in later nineteenth-century eastern Bengal, the fabled source of a new prosperity among at least those agriculturalists with sufficient resources to benefit substantially from its cultivation and weather the fluctuations in its price.

But commercialization was not an unambiguous process. On the one hand, although the impulse to commercialization was ubiquitous, it was not for that reason experienced uniformly. Starting in the early twentieth century there was a widely recognized tendency across Bengal to replace cash rents with product rents; that is to say, to settle sharecroppers on holdings. B. C. Prance was already reporting in 1916 that 28.5% of the land under cultivation in the riparian tracts of Pabna district was sublet on produce rents, whose rental rates could effectively be four times those of comparable cash rents in the area. This process of what might well be thought of as de-commercialization was driven by developments in the law governing rents and tenures. But it was also premised on sensitivity to rising crop prices, and as such was itself an effect of processes of agrarian commercialization.[72]

On the other hand, the role of capital in sustaining agrarian production and reproduction, most often in the form of credit but sometimes also in the form of organized commercial agriculture on demesne lands, could generate tendencies for capital to attempt to intervene more directly in the production process and take command of peasant labor as labor. This was precisely the development that raiyats were resisting in their repudiation of indigo. This tendency did not necessarily involve the general formation of a rural proletariat through large-scale expropriation. According to Rajat Datta, credit was already beginning to function as a lever for the subordination of labor to mercantile capital in the later eighteenth century—at least in northern and western Bengal. In the early 1870s in northern Jessore, the raiyat typically depended on food loans to survive the agricultural cycle, seed loans to plant the new crop, and money loans to pay rent installments or purchase clothes and other necessities. There "the money-lender to whom the ryot binds himself is termed *jater* . . . and *pater* . . . *mahajun, i.e.* the guardian of his honor and supplier of his food."[73] Credit was thus already functioning as a condition for the reproduction of a commercially oriented agrarian smallholding society; and the mahajan was "the motive power by which [the social structure] is kept working."[74] In northern Jessore, the creditor was entitled to appoint a guard over the crop that had grown from his seeds, making clear its hypothecated status. He was said to gradually become in effect "the ryot's accountant," making equally clear the substance of the relationship that connected them.[75]

As Sugata Bose has argued, the tide of indebtedness would undergo a secular rise in the late nineteenth and early twentieth century even in the more prosperous parts of the eastern delta. By 1888 Peter Nolan was reporting, on the basis of extensive government inquiries, that the "ryots, even where most prosperous in the Backergunge district, where it is said that each holding averages 9 acres, producing 13 maunds of cleaned rice an acre—are said to be very generally in debt, at least from the sowing time till harvest."[76] Late in the nineteenth century, the rising pressure of population on the land, coupled with the ecological degradation of the delta system, increasingly rendered a dependence on cash crops the only viable way to maintain subsistence on smaller holdings. This was especially true of capital-intensive jute. But the expansion of jute production also encouraged the growth of a more affluent stratum among those in agrarian society able to weather its vagaries and benefit from periodic high prices. It was these wealthier peasants who were best positioned later to extend their economic and social power as the sequential ravages of the collapse of jute prices during the First World War, the prolonged Depression of the 1930s, and the 1943 Famine cumulatively eroded the foundations of smallholding reproduction.[77]

It was in a context where commercialization could point towards very different possible trajectories, then, that the cultivation of commercial crops emerged as a crucial plank of a model of raiyat independence across otherwise diverse agrarian regions. In Central Bengal, the heartland of indigo planting, raiyats were generally less affluent than in either the eastern delta or the southern jungles. But even here other cash crops besides jute could serve the purpose of grounding the sense of raiyat independence. In northern Jessore, for example, the "majority of ryots live from hand to mouth" and generally labored with their own hands. Yet despite that, Ramshunker Sen noted a "growing unwillingness of the Bengal ryot to undertake the degrading work of a cooly."[78] "The profession of agriculture is now considered so incompatible with the degrading work of a cooly, that the ryots have fairly given up that employment, so that no offer of a pecuniary award or persuasion will induce them to betake to a task which they think it beneath their dignity to perform."[79] Such work, notably on the declining indigo plantations that lingered on in the 1870s, was increasingly left to migrant tribal laborers, who were attracted by the higher wages generated by the limited availability of local labor. In fact, there is little question that many raiyats did continue to supplement their income from their own holdings with other kinds of waged labor. They had limited options if their holdings were insufficient to provide them with a reliable income.[80] No doubt the unwillingness that Sen noted was also especially acute in relation to indigo planting.

Yet the sheer ubiquity of observations about the resistance of raiyats to waged labor suggests a broader impulse on the part of raiyats to defend a conception of independence deeply bound to independent commodity production. "So many people . . . derive from [date] sugar all that they have above the mere necessities of life," Westland had already earlier suggested, "that it may be considered that the sugar cultivation and trade is the root of all their prosperity."[81] Sen went further, recognizing this branch of native industry as "one of the most important, as it is carried on by the ryot quite voluntarily, without the aid of compulsory advances, as is the case with indigo cultivation. In the production of food grains, the ryot is impelled by that most powerful of incentives, hunger, to which the inexorable demands of the *mahajun* tend to give additional momentum. But the date-tree is his own. He has received no equivalent in kind, nor hypothecated the produce at 50 per cent. interest."[82]

Sen was outlining a conception of raiyat independence that was not only opposed to the subordination of raiyats as labor to various forms of capital. It was also at sharp variance from a model of subsistence autarky based on the direct production-for-consumption of food crops. It was as a producer of commodities for exchange that the raiyat claimed to be independent. It was only as someone who could plausibly stake some claim over those date palms that such a conception of independence made sense. The raiyat's sense of independence was thus founded on the connection between a property in the products of the soil and commercial production.[83]

So it was not just Faraizis on the deltaic frontiers who invoked raiyats' rights over the soil they plowed as a basis for a claim to independence. The claim was common in the testimony of rebellious raiyats protesting indigo in 1859 and 1860. "Because of indigo," sang Kubir Gosain, the renowned poet of the Sahebdhani cult popular among the rural Hindu lower castes of the indigo districts of Nadia, "those wily, wicked men [who deal in indigo] have taken away all our homesteads."[84] In an 1859 petition from Barasat, raiyats who had sowed their lands "with sugar-cane and tobacco," cash crops with "fair prospects," complained that the local indigo planter had first tried to raise their rents to cover the costs of his lease, and upon their refusal had violently forced them to replow some of those lands with indigo. The petitioners complained that they had been "forcibly seized . . . like judgment debtors" and even yoked to their own plows: "we, poor ryots, find no means for the protection of our honour, lives, and property."[85] The value of such seized property, noted another group of petitioners from Nadia, could amount to "six or seven thousand rupees" once one figured in the cost of "brick-built houses," the value of "paternal jammy lands and trades," and "upwards of twenty or twenty-five thousand rupees" advanced to debtors.[86] The assumption that raiyat property was so easily converted into monetary terms is a striking indication of how far we are from an understanding of independence in terms of subsistence autarky here. In another petition from Nadia, not only was the monetizability of the holding also assumed, but rights over the holding were specifically grounded in the property-constituting powers of labor: the planter, the petitioners complained, had "dispossessed them of the greater part of the estates what their forefathers did by their labour, and has driven them off from the abodes of their ancestors."[87]

Testifying before the 1860 Indigo Commission, many raiyats and gantidars (affluent farmers with more substantial holdings, more generally known in historiography as jotedars[88]) declaimed indigo as irreducibly linked to oppression in the form of direct interference in and regulation of productive activity. They declared themselves unwilling to plant indigo again under any circumstances: "The ryots who appeared before us . . . are loud in denouncing the . . . [planters'] supervision, as harassing and vexatious," noted the Indigo Commission report; "they say that they are required, again and again, to plough, to crush the clods, to remove stalks, to smooth the ground, to sow at the precise moment which the planter may dictate, *until neither their time nor their labour can be called their own*."[89] Indeed, Kubir Gosain identified the entire collection of revenue- and rent-collecting officials as "all of them together . . . my opponents."[90] Raiyats identified the indigo system both as offensive to their honor and dignity, and as ritually polluting, especially in its demands on family labor—an attack on the very core of the patriarchal peasant household.[91] It is true that raiyats complained most immediately about violence and unremunerated labor. Several also clearly considered themselves lawfully subject to the planter's authority as their superior leaseholder (though it should also be remembered that these raiyats were giving evidence before an official commission, so such professions might well be taken with a grain of salt).[92] But many expressed a willingness to pay off the balances that planters so determinedly maintained against them. Freed from their debts to planters, they imagined (just as Sconce and Eden had suggested) being able to cultivate more remunerative crops, whether of their own choosing or by arrangement with their creditors— especially rice, a source of immediate subsistence but also of rising market value, and the timing of whose cultivation conflicted directly with indigo.[93] They overwhelmingly attributed their degree of indebtedness to the burden of unremunerative indigo cultivation. They imagined a future without coercive debt-bondage to indigo as one where, producing freely for the market, they would also readily be able to pay off their debts to mahajans and achieve independence and affluence, often through the leasing of their holdings to subtenants and sharecroppers.[94]

Unsurprisingly, raiyats responded with great enthusiasm to magistrates' declarations of the limits of planters' entitlements, and rumors of government hostility to the indigo system significantly fueled mobilization. Indeed, administrative proclamations of the kind that caused such controversy around Ashley Eden were clearly important sites for the interaction between colonial discourses concerning raiyat's rights and the dynamic impulse of the political demands of raiyats themselves. Several raiyats observed the close connection between *ilaka* status (tenants holding directly under the planter) and declining rates of remuneration for indigo cultivation.[95] Others insisted on their right to collect fair rent from their own superiors in the tenure hierarchy for use of lands within their holdings.[96] Such claims in turn set up the obvious correlate that it was only by clarifying the raiyat's adverse rights against the zamindar or other superior tenure holder's claims as landlord that the independence of the raiyat as a free producer of commodities could be consolidated. A petition from Nadia stated the conflict between raiyat property and planter power clearly in its complaint that the leaseholding planter "destroys date plantations and pepper which they grow on their lands, saying there would gradually be a scarcity of indigo lands if the ryots be suffered thus to appropriate their lands to their own use."[97] Date plantations, recall, were a cornerstone of raiyat independence in this part of Bengal (immediately adjacent to the northern Jessore of Ramshunker Sen's description); and pepper plants were a standard commercial garden-crop. Their loss was more than a merely financial issue. The demand to limit the power of proprietorship represented by the planter's interest in a superior tenure was driven, then, not merely by some timeless peasant subsistence ethic. It was the raiyat's increasing participation in the sphere of circulation as a producer of commercial crops that elicited opposition to the indigo system. The Reverend James Long for one was quite clear that "the lower orders of Bengal have lately adopted more independent habits of thought" as a result of the "rise of prices and the increased value of labour." He considered this to be one of the roots of the indigo disturbances. The Reverend Cuthbert thought that "the connexion of the ryots with indigo planting tends to repress that spirit" of independence.[98]

Santosh Mundal, an affluent raiyat from Nadia who also had interests as a village grocer, sold clothes and wood, and lent money and rice, would put it most clearly. When asked as to the conditions under which he would consider planting indigo again, he declared that if "the land belonged to the Queen, and the Sahib had nothing to do with it, but only dealt with us as a mere merchant and paid for the plant in cash right down, we should be satisfied." And should there be any unclarity around the significance of this invocation of the Queen as sovereign-proprietor, Mundal laid it to rest a few answers later when he unequivocally denied that the zamindar had any right to enhance his rents or was entitled to any share in the profits of his cultivation: "The profit and loss are both mine."[99] In other words, the invocation of the superordinate authority of the Queen was precisely the means of securing the raiyat's claim to adverse possession against his superior tenure holders, not a means of relinquishing it to the Crown. The connection between commerce, the consolidation of the raiyat's occupancy rights, and a conception of raiyat independence could not be clearer.

A decade later, the trajectory of peasant politics would find powerful articulation in eastern Bengal. The Commissioner of Chittagong reported in 1875:

> The inhabitants of this division are mostly agriculturists, and as such share in the general prosperity attaching to that class. . . . The rate of labour has within the last few years doubled, and it is yearly becoming more difficult to obtain workmen, as the people are becoming more and more independent and averse to seeking employment. A great change has of late years swept over the peasantry of this division as well as over those in most parts of Lower Bengal: increased prosperity among members of the agricultural classes has brought with it a sense of their importance, and a wish to throw off all old feelings of feudal attachment and set up their own interests in opposition to those of their landlords, a course in which they believe they have the support and sympathy of the Government.[100]

In fact, the Secretary of State for India, Spencer Cavendish, argued to Lord Ripon in 1882 that

> in the eastern districts of Bengal Proper, there were tendencies and circumstances at work which led to events demonstrating the great difficulties in the way of the determination of rents existing under the present law. Prosperity had been stimulated by the development of the jute trade; the Muhammadan element preponderated in the population; in extensive waste lands reclaiming settlers had obtained leases on favourable terms; and, in general, the ryots were strong and well-to-do, and were

yearly becoming better acquainted with their rights and better able to assert them. In these circumstances even legitimate demands [for enhancement] might not be met without a struggle; whilst exaction was likely to provoke the retaliation of outrage or tumult.[101]

And the Joint-Magistrate of Dhaka commented in 1873 on the success of the raiyats of that district in retaining a substantial portion of their surplus from superior landholding interests:

> I have been much struck with the large proportion of the gross produce which falls to the share of the cultivator of the soil in many parts of this district; and, although the condition of the Bengal ryot is generally supposed to be analogous to the miserable cottier tenants of Ireland, yet the result of my investigations shows that, far from any such analogy existing here, the peasantry of Eastern Bengal hold their lands on much more favourable terms than the Metayers [sharecroppers] of France and Italy; while in places where the tenantry have combined, from the increasing difficulty of enhancing rents, the status of ryots with rights of occupancy, is little removed from that of hereditary tenants holding their lands at easy and practically fixed rates.[102]

The "increasing independence" of the peasantry of eastern Bengal, invoked in almost every annual report of the 1870s, was surely just the colonial name for the politics of the free commodity producer.

Another prominent expression of this politics emerged in the 1870s in Pabna. Pabna was a jute-producing district where more than half of the cultivators had established occupancy rights under the Rent Act. Zamindars responded with aggressive attempts to consolidate illegal cesses into the base rental rate, and forcibly execute written agreements that made tenants "liable to ouster if they should quarrel with the zemindar," effectively reducing them to tenants at will. In response, raiyats formed agrarian leagues to resist these measures.[103] Once again, George Campbell, a well-known advocate of jute cultivation, and now appointed Lieutenant-Governor of Bengal, would provide a crucial impulse to this new peasant politics. In July 1873, he gave official sanction to peaceful peasant combinations: "Neither in India nor in Ireland have I ever sought to justify abuses of riots, leagues, or plans of campaign, intimidation, or even combination to withhold fair rents duly settled by legal process; but on the principle of the bundle of sticks, I do think that small men are justified in combining to obtain a settlement of unsettled questions in their dealings with a big man."[104]

In Pergunnah Isufshahye, the epicenter of revolt in Pabna, "the name of 'Rajah' Ishan Chunder Roy [was] in everyone's mouth," reported the commissioner of Rajshahye Division on the basis of a local magistrate's investigation; "and there is no doubt that he was generally looked up to as the inaugurator of a new *regime* in which zemindars were to be superseded."[105] Raiyats were called upon to declare "themselves to be ryots only of the Queen, whose mofussil representative was Raja

Ishan Chunder Roy," a "small landholder" who "possesses considerable means besides his property."[106] The Assistant Magistrate of Serajganj, Peter Nolan, was clear though that explanations of the unrest in terms of "the evil counsel of Isan Chunder Roy" were "obviously insufficient." He instead explained the "willingness of the ryots to listen" to Roy in terms of their desire "to defend their property, and the interest they possessed in their holdings, as occupying ryots, against present and future litigation." This was a desire that could only be effected through systematic combination since the law admitted "as a legitimate cause of enhancement, the fact that a higher rate than the one in question is paid by neighbouring ryots of the same class for similar lands."[107] Kalyan Kumar Sen Gupta was no doubt right to follow Campbell in arguing that the "root of the agrarian discontent seemed to be the tendency of the landlords to annihilate the tenants' newly acquired right of occupancy" on the basis of "the doctrine of high landlordism."[108] The zamindari offensive was aimed not merely at enhancing rents, but at eroding the foundations of the occupancy right itself. Sen Gupta argued, however, that raiyats were embracing an essentially reactive defense of customary rights against the initiatives of zamindars aspiring to the absolute landlordism of the British model.[109] It seems more plausible to see raiyats who "watch and intelligently follow the markets" as attempting to affirm their status as independent commodity producers in an area characterized by a precocious embrace of jute cultivation.[110]

Obviously, whatever the inchoate possibilities present in the archival residues of the Faraizi movement, agrarian political actors did not necessarily articulate their aspiration to an independence that linked property and commerce directly in terms of the liberal discourse of custom. But given the fit between such an aspiration and the Lockean conception of property, it should be no surprise to discover that many pro-raiyat advocates did come to adopt the general contours of the liberal discourse of custom in their advocacy of legislative reform in the lead-up to the 1885 Tenancy Act. This was not only true of liberals intervening at the highest levels of public debate, like Parbati Churn Roy.[111] In an 1884 petition, the self-described "cultivator-ryot," Rajkissore Mookerjee of Hooghly district, objected to the provisions in the proposed bill allowing for a right of rent enhancement on the basis of a rise in the "average prices of food crops." He argued that, since such a rise was never occasioned by landlord improvements, the raiyat was "entitled to its full benefit." "Your petitioners crave leave to submit that Zemindars have no claim to a proportionate increase of rent . . . .That rise in prices should be no ground of enhancement is a proposition which your petitioners deem to be justified not only by considerations of justice and economy but by the Permanent Settlement and the usages and traditions which have prevailed in Bengal."[112]

Mookerjee then went on to warrant this claim by drawing directly on the extensive appendices of Hollingbery's *Zemindary Settlement of Bengal* to claim that "enhancement ought not to be regarded as a matter of course but . . . [as] in reality an anomalous and unjustifiable proceeding" which should only be allowed strictly "on grounds of the most obvious considerations of justice. Historically speaking, all enhancements are illegal; and Act X of 1859 in so far as it allowed enhancements was *ultra vires* [without authority]."[113] The right of occupancy at permanently fixed rates ultimately rested, he argued (still following Hollingbery), on the fact that the "rent which the ryot pays is only a land-tax, and he cannot be ejected so long as he pays his determined rent."[114] Mookerjee was presumably a bhadralok raiyat, but his adoption of the conceptual resources available in the liberal discourse of custom is perhaps as clear an example as we can get in this period of the convergence of agrarian aspirations to a property-based commercial independence with an insistence on the property-constituting powers of labor. This was a convergence rooted ultimately in their commensurability as claims whose meaning was inextricably embedded in the practices of abstract interdependence constituted by commodity production and exchange.

The raiyat's "independence," far from being a model of subsistence-based autarchy rooted in timeless customary entitlements, expressed a deepening commitment to household-based commodity production.[115] Independent peasant production based on secure quasi-proprietary rights meant production for the market. The figure of the rights-bearing raiyat invoked a society of male householders, each exercising authority over households that were organized simultaneously as ethical and productive units of subsistence reproduction. But subsistence reproduction was, in this vision, premised not on household autarky but on a deepening commitment to commercial production. Under these circumstances, the insistent maleness of the raiyat represented something more than the gendered nature of legally defined property entitlements. It also expressed the privileged status of the implicitly male master of the household, the *karta* (literally: doer or maker). The *karta* was the subject of the household's productive activity, in the sense that it was his will that unified the household as an ethical and functional unit. At the same time, though, he was also the subject of exchange, in the sense that it was he who was the effective subject of the household's buying and selling of commodities. As members of the household subordinate to the *karta,* women and children were both normatively excluded from either of these modes of subjectivity. (This was despite the undeniable empirical fact that women did broadly engage in commerce, and could even, in the absence of a suitable male, serve in the role of *kartri,* or mistress of the household.) Thus the independence of the raiyat was fully complementary with the solidarity of the household and its gendered and generational hierarchies.[116]

Faced with the early assertion of raiyat independence during the indigo disturbances, even "Delta," the pamphleteering revenant of the anti-Company, anti-official cause of the private trader in Bengal, had to admit that the ruination of the indigo planter would not provoke a retreat into primordial autarchic production.

He foresaw merely an immiserating transfer of "both the ryot's share [in the profits from the crop], and that of the Planter, to the moneylender and the lawyer"—that is to say, to nonproductive exploitative classes.[117] The agrarian politics of "independence" of the 1860s and 1870s seemed to provoke no reaction that quite rose to the apocalyptic dread voiced by Thomas Carlyle in the aftermath of emancipation in Jamaica. Carlyle thought that the very existence of civil society as such was threatened by the emancipated slave's capacity, without labor and without exchange, to eke a bestial and slothful existence out of the spontaneous plenty produced by a natural bounty that had been made available in the first place through heroic European blood and toil. Carlyle was giving racial form to Edward Gibbon Wakefield's argument that the colonies needed labor if they were to be developed, but that labor would only be available if it were denied access to land on its own behalf.[118] Liberals insisted on solving the problem of labor through market mechanisms, notably by increasing the supply of laborers. But Carlyle dreaded the prospect of Jamaica being left to rot on the model of an overpopulated, rack-rented Ireland: "To have 'emancipated' the West Indies into a *Black Ireland;* 'free' indeed, but an Ireland, and Black!"

Compelling emancipated Africans, whose labor had hitherto been elicited effectively under the direct compulsion of the system of slavery, to work as wage laborers on plantations was the only means to resist the transformation of a previously valuable plantation system into an impoverished jumble of subsistence farms.[119] It was just such a jumble that Charles Trevelyan had invoked in 1848 (the year before Carlyle published *The Negro Question*) when he described a backward Ireland, trapped in coils of custom, ignorance and low productivity that were in turn compounded by the pressures of a Malthusian crunch. Ireland had been awaiting the providential depopulation that the Famine had finally brought as a means to consolidate larger holdings capable of improvement through the combined efforts of landlord and capitalist.

> The Irish small holder lives in a state of isolation, the type of which is to be sought for in the islands of the South Sea, rather than in the great civilized communities of the ancient world. A fortnight for planting, a week or ten days for digging, and another fortnight for turf-cutting, suffice for his subsistence; and during the rest of the year, he is at leisure to follow his own inclinations. . . . The excessive competition for land maintained rents at a level which left the Irish peasant the bare means of subsistence.[120]

If Ireland's pre-Famine smallholding society was thus still awaiting its emergence into civil society, Carlyle's Jamaica was on the contrary threatened with the destruction of civil society itself. In other words, a black Ireland.

I am not suggesting that Carlyle had a realistic grasp of the historical or social situation in Jamaica. Jamaican emancipated slaves were hardly abandoning, in any straightforward sense, either labor or commerce outright in their embrace of market gardening. But they did seem to be seeking in smallholding agriculture a means to offset their continued dependence on waged plantation labor under their former masters by carving out a space of autarkic autonomy. Smallholding was the basis for creating a "home," withdrawing family labor from the plantation system, and independently determining how to apply labor to various tasks (including whether and when to sell it for wages).[121] Smallholding could be construed, from this perspective, as a space of withdrawal from civil society, even if that withdrawal was a means to consolidate the standing of the former slave as an independent agent in civil society. No wonder, then, that the underlying impulse of Jamaican smallholding could be so easily painted (and not just by Carlyle) as African atavism, a "savage" repudiation of relations of social interdependence.

Bengal's politics of raiyat independence, in contrast, was consistently and explicitly articulated as an affirmation of commercial interdependence through commodity production. The raiyat complaint was precisely that their aspiration to a deeper form of commercial interdependence was constrained by their subordination to indigo planters and zamindars. The Bengal raiyat was positioned, in these terms, as the champion of civil society rather than its critic. The raiyat household seemed to have much more in common with the model of "family enterprise" that had been at the core of a nonconformist missionary discourse that had championed Jamaican emancipation and post-emancipation smallholding. This was itself a discourse rooted in petty-bourgeois artisanal society in the British Midlands, where the household remained a relevant unit of production well into the nineteenth century.[122] Indeed, the raiyat was so commonly understood, across the lines of colonial political debates, to be implicated in networks of credit and commerce that Carlyle's rhetoric of absolute social dissolution had to be moderated. The "independence" of the Bengal raiyat was already an independence based on social interdependence in commercial society.

AGRARIAN POLITICAL ECONOMY

The critique of planter coercion voiced in the indigo disturbances was thus a moment of an evolving agrarian politics that offered an implicit affirmation of the rationality of political economy. Such politics did not represent a repudiation of political economy, whether as a language of colonial exploitation or a technology of colonial governance, from the external standpoint of "subaltern" resistance. The raiyat politics of the 1860s and 1870s served first and foremost to develop and realize agrarian society's emergent potential as a "civil society." It was in no sense a project to qualify or resist that possibility. Peasant politics in the second half of the nineteenth century might not yet have had much access to the conceptual resources developed in the discourse of political economy. It was arguably already deeply political-economic, however, in its core presuppositions. The problem of property, posed in the context of an intensification of commercial interdependence, defined the practical space within which political-economic concepts could be received in agrarian Bengal. Of course, agrarian Bengalis could at any point have "used" the vocabulary and arguments available in the writings of political economists as strategic means to address the colonial state, assuming they could access them. But that kind of instrumental appropriation assumes that subaltern agents were seeking to achieve ends defined in relation to extrinsic normative concerns. Such a situation should not be confused with one in which subaltern agents came to construe their own aims, purposes and normative commitments in ways that constitutively presumed political-economic concepts. To understand the conditions of possibility of this trajectory requires understanding the fit between political-economic concepts and the social ecology of agrarian politics.

The ability of agrarian Bengalis to inhabit the normative space of political economy was thus at least partly premised on the degree to which fundamental Lockean claims about the property-constituting powers of labor provided a plausible framework for expressing raiyat political aspirations. To say this is not to imply that nineteenth-century agrarian Bengal was bound to reprise the history of the development of political economy in early-modern Western Europe by beginning from its simplest formulation. The reception of political-economic concepts in agrarian Bengal did not await the general subordination of labor to capital in the countryside. Capital was a fully developed social relationship in the imperial metropole, and political economy was already a highly elaborated discourse. Under such circumstances, agrarian Bengalis did not have to reinvent the categories of political-economic analysis from the ground up. Those categories became available to a nineteenth-century commercial society that still operated to a great extent on the basis of an exchange of surpluses. The reception of political economy was in terms of a relatively basic Lockean formulation of the normative structure of social obligations. This was not, however, because agrarian Bengal was "like" the seventeenth-century England that Locke knew. It was in the era of fully developed capitalism that exchange between independent agrarian producers could function as an imaginary redoubt for the maintenance of mutual recognition among property-owning and property-constituting liberal subjects. This is why Campbell could find in Bengal the independent propertied subjects that had, he feared, disappeared in Britain itself. It is also why the emphasis in peasant politics on the property-constituting powers of labor emerged in direct response to attempts to subordinate labor to capital.

Of course, to the extent that capital did take hold of the production process in the countryside, the embrace of a language of political economy by actors intent on extending its grasp is no mystery. But political economy also arrived in agrarian Bengal by a different path that outstripped and challenged those more visible mechanisms of transfer. It arrived as part of a package of claims about the normative entitlements and obligations implicit in the category of property. This was a package of claims that upheld the rights of the independent producer, even as it did so in ways that opened the path to the endorsement of the subordination of labor to capital. The development of capitalist social relations in the Bengal countryside posed challenges to broad-based aspirations to independent commodity production. Yet those aspirations were deeply encoded in capitalist practices of commodity exchange. As such, this development could only function to renew and intensify the relevance of Lockean concepts rather than to erode them.

None of this is to say that agrarian society could be adequately grasped, as early as the 1860s and 1870s, through political-economic categories that assumed the generalization of the commodity form. Yet the more peasant reproduction came to depend on production for commercial exchange, the more purchase the abstractions of political economy had on it. This was true even before this commercialization would assume the specifically capitalist forms that had been the historical presupposition for the development of those categories. Smallholding production was becoming sufficiently dependent on commodity production that exchange could constitute the normative standpoint for some kinds of agrarian mobilization. These kinds of mobilization sought to *extend* certain potentialities immanent within the logic of commodity exchange on the basis of an elaboration of adverse claims to the land as the basis for commodity production. The structure of political demands being voiced by agrarian leagues in the 1860s and 1870s was in turn what grounded the capacity of elite colonial society, British and Bengali, to find *plausible* its characterization of Bengali custom as intrinsically organized around the categories of political economy. What we are seeing in the transformation of the concept of custom into a political-economic category was not the violent imposition of alien Western abstractions. It was rather an intellectual reckoning with profound changes in an agrarian society coming to be more deeply mediated by the very forms of real abstraction that political economy had been developed to make sense of. The subalternists were right to argue that we need to take much more seriously the subjective agency of agrarian actors.[123] But they insisted that that subjectivity would necessarily express itself in forms of political agency that were radically incommensurable with the categories and the purposes of colonial discourse (i.e. as "resistance"). They thereby assumed that subaltern subjectivity finds its purposes and its meanings only in an anthropologized hermeneutic space of inherited cultural meaning, necessarily external to the history of capitalist social relations. Yet the raiyat politics of independence discussed in this chapter pressed for the extension and reinforcement of the primacy of commodity production in agrarian society.

This chapter has had to rely on the colonial archive to construe the contours of agrarian political discourse in the nineteenth century. A subalternist skeptic might reasonably doubt the ability to infer the nature of subaltern subjectivity from the official record, and I concede the difficulty. But as will become clear in chapter 5, when agrarian political actors did begin, in the early twentieth century, to articulate their concerns and demands in pamphlets and newspapers, they did so by emphasizing property as the foundation of independence. Furthermore, they frequently placed the property-constituting powers of labor at the core of such claims. This chapter serves as a prehistory of those more explicit political demands. I assume that the pervasiveness of discourses of property and labor in vernacular literature of that later period provides sufficient grounds to take the claims of the colonial archive seriously on these issues in relation to the nineteenth century, when no comparable body of evidence exists. At the very least, I would suggest, any challenge to the evidentiary basis of this argument would have to rest on the empirical grounds of an alternative account—and not on general theoretical or methodological objections to the epistemological standing of the colonial archive.

I do not mean to suggest, however, that the liberal discourse of custom therefore *adequately* grasped the nature of social relations in nineteenth-century agrarian Bengal. My argument operates at the level of the formal purchase of political-economic concepts, rather than at the level of a directly empirical reference. It therefore operates on a level quite different from earlier attempts to correlate colonial legislative classifications with sociological realities at the level of stratification, or even to reconstruct the history of agrarian social transformations out of the history of colonial agrarian legislation.[124] The legal abstractions that were drawn from the apparatus of revenue extraction were undoubtedly an impoverished and misleading taxonomy for the kinds of political-economic analysis that the liberal advocates of custom were trying to sketch. Furthermore, the central ideological impulse organizing the recovery of the political-economic logic of custom was one that drove these advocates to focus monodimensionally on the raiyat as a subject of market exchange to the exclusion of the dynamics of credit dependence and social differentiation on class, gender and generational axes that that market exchange entailed.

Situating social transformations at the regional level within ideological concerns generated by the social dynamics of the metropolitan-imperial scale opens up the possibility of a radical reconceptualization of the status of political-economic discourse in the context of colonial society. To the extent that we want to understand how political economy became available as a way of making sense of social relations, political economy cannot be seen as a transparent medium of analysis. But nor can we grasp its historicity adequately by narrating its emergence in terms of radical contingency or of the mechanisms of colonial governance.[125] In the course of the nineteenth and twentieth centuries, the deepening purchase of political economy on Bengali agrarian society was indexed by, among other things, the greater vulnerability of that society to the vagaries of international markets. It is true that already by the 1820s price levels and credit flows in the Bengali coun-tryside were susceptible to the effects of crises in the European-centered world economy. The drying up of credit in the wake of the financial crisis of 1847–48 might have had an indirect role in the emergence of the unrest around indigo planting in the 1850s. When the global economy slid into depression in 1929, how-ever, the result was a profound restructuring of landholding across the region.[126]

Under these circumstances, political economy became a historically relevant conceptual repertoire for grasping social relations in an ever *deeper* sense. As a language of abstraction, the adequacy of its purchase on any specific constellation of social relations depended upon the degree to which those abstractions were practically operative as real forms of social interdependence. "Custom" was a con-cept that had previously been used to grasp forms of normative and overt social relations that exceeded the arbitrary will of despotic masters. Its radical transfor-mation into a liberal category, as a mode of natural political-economic rationality that was also opposed to arbitrary political will, indexed the deepening mediation of agrarian social relations in Bengal by forms of abstract social interdependence. It was this that made possible the identification of agrarian Bengal as a social loca-tion where liberals might, under the banner of native custom, counterintuitively hope to preserve the property-bearing subject of Lockean liberalism, threatened by the dynamic of capitalist society in the metropole. But this hope was pinned to the aspirations of Bengali raiyats, responding to the tensions of commercialization with their own conception of independence grounded in the free exchange of the products of labor. The adequacy of political economy as a framework for under-standing agrarian society was thus inextricable from the history of an agrarian politics that demanded the extension of dynamics of commercialization in the countryside.

Intermezzo

The Forgetting of Liberal Custom

How did the liberal discourse of custom subsequently become so obscured that it has been essentially invisible to the rich historiography of both modern Bengal and British colonial policy? The authority of custom would certainly remain a fundamental reference point for colonial administrations throughout the British Empire, most famously in Africa. In the wake of the 1885 Tenancy Act, however, British administrators and public intellectuals in Bengal tended to be more muted about custom's capacity to serve as a model of how liberal norms might function in an agrarian civil society. There were, I would suggest, at least four reasons for this.

The first factor to be recognized is that colonial legislators began the process of rendering the legal standing of custom increasingly marginal to the terms of the legislative debate from the moment they formulated the 1859 Rent Act as declaratory legislation. By bringing the ostensible authority of custom *into* the domain of positive law, they established custom as the grounds for the new legislation's legitimacy and proper interpretation. At the same time though, they also began the process of displacing attention away from inquiries into the indeterminacies of actual usage, to the history of judicial precedent, legislative wording and intention, and jurisprudential and political principles of justice and expediency. In the end, it was primarily legislation and case law to which raiyats and zamindars (as regionally general rather than locally specified legal subjects) had most immediately to appeal if they were to assert their rights as proprietors. The law claimed to base its principles on customary usages, but it was as law that it had to be engaged.[1] In the lead-up to the 1885 act, custom would once again be invoked as the appropriate regulative principle of revised legislation, reiterating the logic of the 1859 act. But to the very extent that it was more successful in bringing about the sought-after transformation in agrarian relations, it was correlatively more effective in pushing custom to the margins of debate.[2] As the terrain of social contestation broadened in the twentieth century from debate over the status of the occupancy raiyat to that of the under-raiyat (almost universally regarded in the 1860s and 1870s as beyond the protections of custom), the authority of custom was increasingly replaced by a more direct appeal to a language of rights. The scope of that language far exceeded the narrower vision of the "occupancy ryot" that had been established under the banner of liberal custom. The pro-raiyat activists of the twentieth century would retain their commitment to the Lockean principles that had underwritten the liberal discourse of custom. They would retain the liberal discourse of custom's assumption that such norms had historically been authoritative *within* established agrarian social relations. They were also happy to appeal to the authority of specific customary usage when it seemed to authorize the limitation of zamindari entitlements. But they were far from consistent in identifying "custom" as the historical vehicle of the property-constituting capacities of labor. Thus in 1937 we find Tamizuddin Khan, a leading voice of raiyat politics who most certainly endorsed the property-constituting powers of labor, declaring that custom was the origin of many landlord prerogatives. In "the name of custom anything evil could be defended," but "evil custom" could not be allowed to grant "sanctity" to "the evil disposition of mankind."[3]

Secondly, the denial of coevality that was fundamental to Henry Maine's theoretical reconstruction of custom resonated profoundly, as a response to the crisis of liberal imperialism, with the racialized structure of colonial politics. This kind of intensified racism achieved an explosive explicitness right in the middle of the process of framing the Tenancy Act, in the form of the Ilbert Bill controversy of 1882–83.[4] While Maine's theoretical outlook was certainly different from James Fitzjames Stephen's, their alliance against aggressively universalistic liberalism was politically more coherent than Maine and Campbell's conjunctural common-cause against Wingfield, Peacock and the ahistorical application of political-economic doctrine in the colonial context.[5] Advocates of liberal custom were strikingly blind to the incommensurability of their own arguments with Maine's historicist proto-sociology. It is hardly surprising then that Maine's reputation would overshadow and ultimately subsume the competing liberal conceptions of custom, which had no comparably authoritative or sophisticated theoretical exponent. With an empire-wide tendency to identify liberalism ever more narrowly as a peculiarity of the West in the second half of the nineteenth century, Maine's theory represented a perfect combination of liberal universalism (Britain as the bearer of contract-cum-civilization) and sociology of colonial difference (India as a status-based society). It was increasingly hard to recall that there had been a liberal discourse of custom sandwiched between conceptions of custom as an irrational barrier to liberal reason, and conceptions of custom as the authorization for strategies of indirect rule.

Thirdly, the section of educated Hindus who had participated in defending the liberal discourse of custom were themselves grappling with a parallel crisis in the coherence of their own liberal commitments. Even defenders of the liberal project began to identify a tension between liberal values and the framework of imperial institutions to which liberalism had been largely bound earlier in the century. They increasingly viewed the realization of a liberal society in the future as contingent on self-sacrifice and coordinated effort through national ethical renewal in the present.[6] Like the liberal discourse of custom, the Bengali culturalism that emerged in the 1880s turned on a deep association of custom with labor. This was an association whose ready intellectual availability to this generation, it now seems to me, is in fact best understood in terms of the vibrancy of the liberal discourse of custom in the 1860s and 1870s.[7] Bengali culturalism, however, severed labor from its association with civil society, which it took as its primary target of critique. It instead invoked productive activity as a function of the social totality. The rationality of productive activity was thus defended as the logical negation of relations of free commercial exchange, where labor served as a mediation between independent individuals rather than as an expression of coordinated collective agency. Custom and labor were thus identified with the logics of production and of self-consciously ethical life *in contrast to* the irrationality of civil society.[8] With civil society now the object of a sustained ideological critique, custom was transmuted into "culture." It was thus integrated into the new Swadeshi nationalist imagination as the site of India's difference. There was little room for a liberal discourse of custom that identified indigenous society as a key site for the articulation of liberal norms.

Finally, the propensity of raiyats to demand their proprietary rights as laboring subjects could always potentially be associated with Muslimness instead of (or as well as) custom. The Faraizi movement of the 1840s had hitched deep local understandings of Islam as an agent of agricultural enterprise and the domestication of wildness to the claims of the raiyat to dominion over his holding. By the 1870s, the figure of the "Mahomedan ryot" as bearer of a dynamic propensity for independence and combination was beginning to crystallize in colonial discourse. The census of 1871 had demonstrated for the first time the demographic significance of Muslim Bengal. But the trope of the "Mahomedan ryot" indexed not just the loose religious correlates of social stratification in eastern Bengal's agrarian society (Muslim tenant and debtor, Hindu landlord and creditor), but also political demands for the consolidation of free commodity production emerging from agrarian society during the unrest of the 1870s.

During the indigo disturbances of 1859–60, we find very few references to Islam except in experienced indigo planters' memories of an earlier period of Faraizi mobilization. Ashley Eden would explain his apprehension of serious conflict over new efforts at land measurement as a result of the fact that "Charghat contains several thousand Mussulman inhabitants, all banded together to prevent any interference with their rights, real or supposed." The assertiveness of these raiyats of Barasat district had been proverbial since Titu Mir's rebellion of 1831. Eden further noted of these "Ferazees" (as they are labeled in the margin of the 1861 House of Commons parliamentary papers) that "[t]hey are nearly all rich men," voicing a prophetic association of Muslimness with material prosperity.[9] Nonetheless, the planter impulse to unearth a conspiracy was more generally satisfied by implicating zamindars, scheming Hindus, and government officials themselves. The very fact that Muslims were so "passionate" in their participation, the Magistrate of Nadia suggested in 1860, seemed to imply that "the real leadership must be in the hands of the Hindoos."[10]

Writing in the mid-1870s, Henry Beveridge would provide an account of the demography of Bakarganj district that would (rightly) reject forcible conversion as an explanation for the preponderance of Muslims in eastern Bengal. He first argued the classic case that Islam represented a historical escape for lower castes from ritual subordination. Observing, however, that much of Bakarganj had only recently been reclaimed from jungle, he then identified Muslim "colonization" of the deltaic churs as the most important factor. Not only was the soil especially rich in the delta, but its reclamation was less obviously bound by collective obligations in a landscape where homesteads tended to be spread out in amorphous patterns along higher ground to avoid flooding, rather than concentrated in village formations.[11] Unsurprisingly then, the raiyats of Bakarganj were not only generally affluent, Beveridge argued, but this "plenty, combined with the feeling of ownership and independence produced by the system of peasant properties, gives vigour and energy to the character."[12] The Muslims who predominated in the area, he noted, were generally hardier and more "enterprising" than Hindus. They were also less bound by joint family obligations, and more willing to move. It was these factors that accounted for their overwhelming preponderance among the colonizers of the jungle.[13] Muslim characteristics thus echoed the virtues of property and independence. Beveridge would never quite make explicit the connection between Muslimness and the independent raiyat, but its potential was already deeply embedded in his account.

George Campbell was known in his own time as a proponent of Muslim interests (and roundly reviled for it in some sections of the Hindu press). Thinking back on the 1870s in his memoirs, he would remark on the "independence and power of combination of the Mahomedan ryots of Bengal."[14] "In fact," he explained, "the Bengal Zemindars (apart from those of Behar) were not very pushing people . . . and they were generally content to take the customary rents, with such extra legal cesses and occasional benevolences as they could get. The ryots too, being in many districts largely Mahomedan, were not so subservient as low-caste Hindoos, and were much given to land leagues and such expedients to maintain their rights, both out of court and in court. And so it happened that the Bengal ryots held their own tolerably well."[15] Indeed, in 1873 Campbell even sent out a circular to district officers in Bengal to confirm, among other things, whether it was true that "the Mahomedan ryots [who form the great mass of the agricultural peasantry over a large part of Bengal proper] are a well-to-do class as ryots go . . . [and] the better placed and leading ryots generally?"[16]

Agrarian unrest in eastern Bengal in the 1870s further solidified an association between property-constituting cultivation and Muslimness. In his report of July 1, 1873, Peter Nolan, the Subdivisional Officer of Sirajganj, conceded that the newly formed agrarian leagues were utterly secular in their aims, and were even led symbolically by a Hindu ("Raja" Ishan Chunder Roy). Nonetheless, he noted, "I fear that the fact that most of the ryots are Mahomedans, and nearly all zemindars and their superior servants Hindus, may introduce a religious element, or an element of race antipathy into the conflict."[17] By 1876, the *Som Prakash* could offhandedly observe, in an article on "The Need for a Law for the Suppression of Refractory Ryots," that a "Mahomedan tenantry is a source of considerable annoyance to a zemindar. They do not readily pay the rents, and seek every pretext for evading payment." They were, the author noted, "a most unquiet, selfish, and hard-hearted people; and become furious when forming combinations among themselves. They are easily got up, as soon as their interests are touched. This power of unity in sympathy is a remarkable feature of the Mahomedans."[18] The Muslim raiyat was thus marked by his pursuit of material interests: "a Hindu landlord once described to me his Muslim tenants," Sir Arthur Dash would recall many years later, "as mindless combinations of stomachs and testicles," whose primal drives were only kept in check by "the actual social power system" through which they were subordinated to the higher wills of the gentry.[19] The propensity to selfish utility-maximization symbolized by the Muslim peasant's slavery to his stomach and his sexual appetites was thus opposed as an interruptive presence to the paternalistic structure of traditional zamindar-ryot relationships—and, only a little later, to the organic unity of (Hindu) nationhood.[20]

In the end then, the liberal discourse of custom would simply be overshadowed by rival discourses that would assume greater political significance. Nonetheless, it bequeathed a juridico-political framework through which liberal norms and political-economic rationality could be conceived as immanent to the organizing practices and institutions of Bengali agrarian society. Even when "custom" could no longer function as a persuasive vehicle for that constellation of claims, many forms of peasant politics in the region would come to rely crucially on the argument that labor's capacity to constitute property had been a fundamental premise governing the legitimate distribution of rights over environmental resources in agrarian Bengal. The authority of claims to property could be drawn from an account of indigenous social obligations whose binding force *preceded* the development of political life and positive law. Construed in this form, such obligations became available as a normative standard against which the legitimacy of political and legal institutions could be judged.

For this reason, long after its marginalization as an explicit political and legal paradigm, the liberal discourse of custom would continue to haunt political argument in and about agrarian Bengal. The liberal discourse of custom did not remain vibrant into the twentieth century. It did, however, bequeath a significant legacy of arguments concerning the immanence of the property-constituting powers of labor to the normative structure of rights and entitlements within indigenous agrarian society. Agrarian political agents could (and did) dip at their pleasure into an institutionalized political and judicial memory of nineteenth-century debates over property for authorities, precedents, and inspiration. The persistence of the core impulses underlying the liberal discourse of custom depended even more fundamentally, however, on the fact that the currents of nineteenth-century agrarian politics discussed in the previous chapter, while far from exhausting the range of political imaginations at work in the countryside, would nonetheless achieve only greater depth, breadth, organizational structure, and ideological articulateness in the first decades of the twentieth century.

5

Peasant Property and Muslim Freedom

If we consider the founding of Pakistan in 1947 as the single most consequential political expression of a self-identifiedly "Muslim" aspiration to collective self-determination in South Asia (whatever the ambiguities, contradictions and exclusions of that aspiration, and whatever the disappointments that the reality of Pakistan soon presented to those who had advocated for it), we will quickly arrive at a realization of the enormous historical significance of the apparently obscure Bengali agrarian politics of property. When Muhammad Ali Jinnah pressed his claims to be the "sole spokesman" for India's Muslims in the final negotiations of the terms of British withdrawal, his position turned crucially on his ability to demonstrate that there was strong support for the Muslim League in the 1945–46 provincial elections.[1] Bengal was home to the single biggest concentration of Muslims in the subcontinent, and without a good showing there, Jinnah risked being radically undermined. Yet Bengal had been a region that had rarely given Jinnah the occasion for much delight or comfort in the preceding decades. As a Muslim-majority region, the political concerns of its Muslim politicians were different from those of the central League leadership, whose center of gravity was firmly planted in the Muslim-minority regions of northern India.

In the first elections held under the 1935 Government of India Act, with an expanded franchise that reached much more deeply into the countryside, the Bengal Provincial Muslim League had won a smaller proportion of the Muslim vote than the Krishak Proja Party (KPP), a predominantly Muslim organization organized around the political demands of agricultural cultivators (*krishak*) and tenants (*praja*). Both won a smaller proportion of the vote than independent candidates. If the League won slightly more seats overall than the KPP (39 and 36 respectively), it was only because of a weighting in favor of urban electorates, where North Indian–identified Muslims predominated and where the League did very well (61.47% of the vote) in the face of an understandably weak KPP presence. Overall in fact, the League had garnered 27.1%, against the KPP's 31.51%. In the countryside, where Bengali-speaking Muslims predominated, the League had done best in the Muslim minority regions of western Bengal, but had managed to win only 26.52% of the overall rural vote. This was hardly a resounding affirmation in the face of the KPP's 31.78%, and its especially strong showing in the Muslim heartland of eastern Bengal.[2] Yet in 1946, the Muslim League succeeded in capturing all six of the Muslim seats reserved for Bengal at the center, 115 out of 117 Muslim seats in the Bengal Legislative Assembly, 95% of the urban Muslim vote in Bengal, and, crucially, 84.6% of the massive rural Muslim vote.[3] This victory established a necessary presupposition for Jinnah's credibility in negotiating for a sovereign Pakistan on behalf of India's Muslims.

There are many histories to this transformation in the fortunes of the Muslim League in Bengal. The KPP collapsed in the face of its inability to form a stable and effective ministry under Fazlul Haq's leadership, driving many leading figures from its ranks into the League. Abul Hashim's election as General Secretary of the Bengal Provincial Muslim League organization led for the first time to the development of a functional organizational apparatus in the districts, as well as to its democratization. Under these twin pressures, the provincial League seemed to many to have taken on a distinctly left-leaning political hue, mitigating its longstanding status in the region as a party of the westward-gazing gentry (*ashraf*), rather than the "Bengali Muslims."[4] At the same time, the increasing momentum towards the negotiation of a final settlement at the political center in Delhi—rather than at the level of the provinces—meant that Bengali Muslims were confronting an imminent transformation from majority to minority status as they passed from a political structure centered on regional autonomy to a Hindu-majority, pan-Indian state. Under these circumstances, Jinnah's insistence on establishing Indian Muslims as a separate sovereign nation rather than a minority began to take on increasing resonance even in this Muslim-majority region. And all of this was further compounded, no doubt, by Jinnah's insistent vagueness about just what the demand for Pakistan really meant. This was a pragmatic reticence that was necessary if he was to hold the allegiance of politically and regionally disparate constituencies. But it was also no doubt convenient for a figure who may have been using the demand for Pakistan as a bargaining chip all along, and who in any case seemed to have a remarkably abstract conception of the Pakistan he ultimately brought to fruition.[5] Certainly many in Bengal understood the Pakistan demand to imply a separate Muslim-majority state in eastern India, even if that project was openly contested by the urban *ashraf* who, for example, controlled the English-language Muslim daily, *The Star of India*. Jinnah did little to correct such ambiguities until the very last moment.[6]

Nonetheless, there is also (at least) one more crucial lineage to the ascendancy of the Muslim League in rural Bengal in the 1940s. This is the story of its success in identifying itself, and its demand for Pakistan, as the preeminent vehicle for the realization of agrarian aspirations to Muslim self-determination. These aspirations were, as we shall see, inextricably bound to claims about the property-constituting power of labor; and in this sense they represent the elaboration of the impulses in peasant politics discussed in chapter 4. The ability of the Muslim League to draw upon agrarian political energies that began to assume a new level of articulateness in the 1920s was crucial to the breadth of its rural political base in the mid-1940s. The confluence of the idea of Pakistan with the idea of agrarian self-determination goes a long way to explaining the genuine widespread enthusiasm of the Bengali Muslims for partition. But that confluence necessarily involved the interlocking of a discourse of Muslimness whose focus on property was fundamentally indifferent to the Hindu other with a discourse of Muslimness that was centrally concerned with negotiating a relationship (whether hostile or amicable) with the Hindu other. In this chapter, I will focus squarely on the conceptual terrain that that ideology inhabited—a terrain defined by claims about the property-constituting capacity of labor—to show how through the 1930s and early 1940s many of the advocates of raiyat politics came to see the Pakistan demand as the most promising vehicle for their aspirations.

As I hope will become clear, this narrative is not meant to imply a teleological narrative of the origins of Pakistan. On the contrary, the conception of labor as the natural foundation of property was one that could and did point in many different possible directions politically. The discourse of the Muslim cultivator was in no necessary or fundamental sense addressed to the problem of the relationship between religious communities. The convergence between Muslimness and Pakistanism, meanwhile, was as steeped in political contingencies as the Muslim League's embrace of the Pakistan demand itself. Still, the role of Lockean conceptions of property in underwriting the Pakistan demand is no less one of its most momentous impacts on the course of events in the subcontinent. As such, for my purposes here it will be sufficient if I can show how the Pakistan demand in Bengal was able to draw its vibrancy and energy in the countryside from a discourse of Muslimness that haunted raiyat politics in eastern Bengal. This was a raiyat politics that was most immediately concerned not with the relationship between religious communities but with the affirmation of a conception of property as grounded in labor.

The 1930s were, as many have recognized, a crucial period in the development of both rural political mobilization and rural communal violence. The 1932 Communal Award dramatically redistributed representation in the legislature between Hindus and Muslims in such a way as to shift legislative power into the latter's hands. This in turn served as the lead up to the 1935 Government of India Act, which dramatically expanded the Muslim franchise in the countryside.[7] Mean-while, and more pressingly for rural constituencies, the market crash of 1929 set in motion a long chain of consequences that led simultaneously to a prolonged depression in the price of jute and rice, as well as to a sudden drying up of the flow of credit on which many smallholders in the eastern districts had come to rely for their basic capacity for household reproduction. This calamity followed on a longer period of gradual rural immiseration. This process had begun in the later nineteenth century in many parts of eastern Bengal, but had become particularly acute in the wake of an earlier collapse of jute prices in 1914, followed in the post-war period by soaring rice prices. The rising tide of debt, coupled with the dimin-ishing productivity of ever-smaller holdings in a declining delta ecology, meant that raiyats were bound to cultivate high-value commercial crops, especially jute, as the only means to household reproduction. Yet that same dependence on com-mercial agriculture rendered agrarian households radically more vulnerable to the vagaries of the prices of both the jute they grew for sale and the rice that they needed to purchase for subsistence, making the impact of the 1930s Depression that much more brutal.[8]

As the consequences of the Depression unfolded in the Bengal countryside through the 1930s, rates of usufructurary mortgage and foreclosure continued to rise, the demesne lands of zamindars and talukdars expanded, and the incidence of sharecroppers and under-raiyats holding under noncultivating raiyats contin-ued to rise. It was increasingly difficult for small jotedars, already pauperized under the pressures of the 1920s, to retain possession of their property as they lost access to the continued flow of credit. (I do not use the term "jotedar" here in the sense of the rich peasants of Bengal historiography, but in the sense, common in eastern Bengal, of raiyats with permanent rights in their holdings.)[9] The fact that the interruption of the flow of capital into rural production was so disruptive to rural relations was itself an indication of the degree to which many smallholders had in fact become dependent on capital for their capacity to produce and repro-duce. In this sense, such jotedars had already been fundamentally proletarianized before their control over their holdings came under the more radical threat of the 1930s and 1940s. They did of course have a property in their holdings, and were not as such proletarianized in the classical sense of being rendered landless. Yet the retention of their status as jotedars, and with it the reproduction of the smallhold-ing system generally, had come to depend on inputs of capital that functioned, despite their appearance as usurious capital, as productive inputs into the agricul-tural household.[10] Their transition to a status of sharecropper or landless laborer was from this perspective a transition *internal* to the condition of proletarianiza-tion, not the process of proletarianization as such.

The crumbling of this system of credit-dependence in the course of the 1930s Depression led in turn, as Sugata Bose has argued, to a crisis in the relations between Hindus and Muslims in rural areas across eastern Bengal. In these districts the relationship of creditor/debtor had tended to overlap substantially with the relationship of Hindu/Muslim. The fracturing of the first relationship therefore also produced a correlative crisis in the latter relationship. Hindu creditors ceased to play a significant role in the countryside, and were in this sense rendered superfluous in agrarian society. To the extent that the Muslim was identified as the producer, a politics focused on the foundational virtues of productive labor might be taken to imply a correlative hostility to Hindus—at least to the Hindu gentry (the bhadralok).[11] It is of course true that communal violence itself operated as a polarizing engine that rendered communal relations more prominent in political discourse.[12] Even so, however, the ability to convert the economic crisis into a communal one depended on more than the crisis in the immediate relations of credit or outbreaks of violence that were interpreted as being motivated by communal hostilities. In the end, in a context where low-caste Hindu cultivators and prominent Muslim landlords were part of the agrarian landscape, the Hindu/Muslim divide never mapped more than roughly onto the creditor/debtor divide, requiring some supplement to complete the closure of the equation. While the "mobilisers of peasant discontent" could find in Islam "a powerful legitimizing ideology" that provided "an array of symbols to challenge existing disparities," and mosques were often "the only real institutional facilities available" for organizing, "the conflict in the East Bengal countryside did not, without external interference, flow easily into a communal mould."[13]

The trope of rent that appeared to have played so central a role in the proja movement's critique of zamindari seems oddly anomalous given the marginality of the role of rent extraction to the crisis in comparison to that of credit mechanisms. Writing a note of dissent to the Floud Commission's majority recommendation of the abolition of the zamindari system, Radha Kumud Mukherjee noted that "the ills of the peasantry are due to causes and circumstances for which the existing land system is not responsible."[14] He had a point. Insofar as the discourse of property implied that rent extraction was an important factor in producing agrarian misery, it was misleading. As Partha Chatterjee has persuasively argued, by the 1920s and 1930s rentier interests had become radically devalued (at least above the level of raiyati itself, which since the 1880s had become a new source of rentier income for the bhadralok, especially in eastern Bengal). This had been the condition of possibility for a radicalization of middle-class Hindu bhadralok that would shape first the radicalization of the Congress in the later 1930s, and later post-Independence West Bengal's vibrant leftism.[15] It seems hard then to understand why the rent-taker should have assumed such prominence in raiyat political discourse.

But attending more carefully to what might have been at stake for proja activists in the affirmation of property suggests something other than a wholesale confusion on the part of proja activists. Property entitlements had emerged over the course of the nineteenth century as a crucial issue in determining the agrarian producer's social status in relationships defined by commodity production and exchange. Property was thus at the very core of agrarian aspirations to self-determination. If the combination of credit crunch and depressed agricultural prices was what fundamentally drove agrarian discontent in the 1930s, then the threat that that combination posed to the viability of the smallholding "jotedar" was also a threat to the possibility of raiyat independence as such. The insistence in raiyat politics on demarcating the boundary between zamindar and jotedar claims to proprietorship functioned less as a direct means of struggling over the distribution of the rent fund than as a placeholder for the defense of the status of the beleaguered jotedar as a property owner.

It is in this context that we should understand the urgency of ubiquitous calls for a renewal of Muslim piety as the foundation for a reform of everyday habits that could render smallholding viable. If external agents of communal mobilization, from the towns or elsewhere, wanted to hang their appeals to the Muslimness of the peasantry on anything, this was surely their way in. And that in turn opened up the specific terms in which the conception of "otherness" on which the communalization of agrarian conflict turned could be framed. As Pradip Kumar Datta has so insightfully argued, vice was construed as symptomatic of the Muslim's own inner Hindu, whose corrupt presence was expressed outwardly in the form of extravagance and debt, and who stood as the obstacle between the proja and his property.[16] From this perspective, we might think of the conception of Muslimness in rural Bengal as *doubled*. It was a category belonging to the field of claims about property, and also to the field of claims about rival communal entitlements. Each of these discourses could be articulated independently of each other. The normative concerns about the independence of the Muslim jotedar, however, also established very specific ways in which they could be brought together. This chapter thus examines the ways in which the articulation of this duality was fundamental to the success of the Pakistan demand in the eastern Bengal countryside. In the process, it attempts to show how profoundly liberal norms entered into the fabric of agrarian political thought in early twentieth-century agrarian Bengal, even in a field of discourse that ostensibly had little intrinsically to do with either liberal political thought or political economy.

MUSLIM FREEDOM

When rural Muslims in Bengal (that is to say, the vast majority of Muslims in Bengal) committed themselves to a politics of Muslim emancipation, what did they imagine the substance of that envisaged freedom to be, and in what sense did they construe that freedom as "Muslim"? There was never, of course, one answer to this question. Nor were any of the answers offered necessarily bound to the promise of "Pakistan," to which so many of these various aspirations would ultimately come to be pinned in the final years of colonial rule. But without sustained work to understand the ways in which Bengali Muslims identified their Muslimness as a crucial element of the struggle for emancipation, we can make little sense of the broad-based resilience of mobilization under the banner of Islam in the Bengal countryside. Nor can we understand the vibrant enthusiasm with which the realization of Pakistan in 1947 was greeted, in the very districts where demands for regional autonomy would so soon begin proliferating after independence, and where a full-scale civil war over such issues of self-determination would be fought within a quarter of a century.[17]

One answer to these questions does immediately present itself. The connection between Muslimness and political self-determination was determined by practices of colonial representation. Since the colonial state's systems of representation were structured by communal identities (Hindu/Muslim), those identities constituted frameworks within which to mobilize constituencies around specific political aspirations. This was compounded by the fact that in the Muslim-majority districts of eastern Bengal, religion and class were broadly aligned. The majority (but never anywhere near the totality) of rent- and debt-payers were Muslim. The majority (but never anywhere near the totality) of rent- and interest-receivers were Hindu. So if one aspired to control a Local or District Board, Muslim religious associations (notably the rural anjumans) provided the primary basis for organization and mobilization. One sought to control the Board in the name of Muslims. Furthermore, one sought control over it in the name of a Muslim peasantry, thereby confounding the machinations of an unproductive Hindu gentry bent on exploitation. Through appealing to religious identity, an "ambitious Muslim elite" might further hope to blunt the awkwardness of their own social position, manipulating the "economic grievances of the Muslim peasantry against Hindu zamindars" in order to contain the internal fissures that separated *ashraf* (high-born, claiming foreign descent) from *atrap* (low-born, of local descent), and wealthy peasants from their less affluent neighbors.[18]

The plausibility of this account, however, rests on two presuppositions. First, it assumes that Muslim political ideology was elaborated primarily in response to competition between rival communities. This was a common enough assumption. Kamruddin Ahmad, himself a left-leaning Muslim Leaguer with strong pro-raiyat sympathies, nonetheless explained the success of the Muslim League primarily in terms of "competition and rivalry between the Hindu and Muslim middle classes" over limited "opportunities of employment in government, commerce, trade and industry."[19] But the primacy of these concerns cannot safely be taken as given once we move beyond the limited social space of battles over colonial representation. This remains true even if we acknowledge that such limits were far from narrow when seen in the context of struggles for control over Local and District Boards. Secondly, it assumes a purely contingent alignment of class and religion reliant on the demography of eastern Bengal. It therefore tells us almost nothing about the determinate associations that were forged ideologically between Muslimness and agrarian political aspirations. That is, it tells us almost nothing about why the appeals to Muslimness on the part of possibly manipulative and opportunistic political rhetoricians were so persuasive to so many. It certainly tells us nothing about how this connection between Muslimness and agrarian political aspirations could have been sincerely expounded, rather than cynically deployed. So here I want to focus on the core question of how it was possible to forge an *intrinsic logical connection* between Muslimness and the political aspiration to self-determination in a way that was broadly plausible to rural Muslims in Bengal.

I therefore examine the history of twentieth-century Bengali-Muslim agrarian politics in terms of an upward vector of how subaltern political commitments shaped the possibilities of politics at higher levels, rather than the downward vector of how political and cultural elites co-opted subaltern energies to their own fundamentally alien political projects. As such, I do not begin with the debates of high politics, but with the production of political discourse in the agrarian context. But I do not thereby intend to replicate the anthropological insistence on the autonomy of subaltern consciousness typical of Subaltern Studies. Rather, I aim to focus on the domain of ideology as the place where colonial institutional politics could be articulated with agrarian subaltern politics. It is impossible to understand the self-identified "progressive" currents in Bengali Muslim politics without understanding their responsiveness to political demands emanating from the agrarian constituencies that elite politicians claimed to represent. Such agrarian political demands cannot be properly grasped in turn without recognizing that broadly Lockean commitments to the normative centrality of the labor-property nexus were shared across a wide range of rural political actors. This was the case even when the "liberalism" of specific political projects, as in the case of the discourse of Muslim piety that will be the starting point of this chapter's discussion, was far from obvious. I do not mean to suggest that all Muslim politics in Bengal was liberal. Nor do I mean to imply that all liberal Muslim politics was liberal in the same way. Mohammad Ali Jinnah was a liberal insofar as he was committed to a political resolution in which the rights of minorities would be protected through the recognition of the right of Muslims to national self-determination. Yet he could find little common ground with Bengali left-leaning Muslim Leaguers. Nonetheless, I do want to suggest that liberal commitments were not limited to elite politics, and that the ideological positions assumed in elite politics remain opaque until we recognize that.

This chapter turns on a close reading of rural Muslim political texts, a reading that focuses more on their status as a constellation of claims than as a source for social-historical information. I focus in this section on a cluster of pamphlets produced in a mofussil town in a single district of eastern Bengal. Mymensingh was a district that possessed especially vibrant Muslim and proja political scenes. It produced prominent figures on both the right and the left of Muslim politics. It was the site of some of the earliest incidents of agrarian economic-cum-communal violence in 1930.[20] And it sat at the cusp of powerful currents of Bengali-Muslim mobilization in eastern Bengal and in the neighboring province of Assam. I want to begin with A. F. M. Abdul Hai Bhawali's enormously influential and widely circulating pamphlet, *Usman, adarsha krishak* (Usman, the Ideal Cultivator), published in Mymensingh town in 1920 and reissued in a second, enlarged and illustrated edition a year or so later. This is a pamphlet that belongs to the much broader genre that Pradip Kumar Datta has called "Muslim Improvement Literature," which focused on Islam as a means of improving the worldly condition of rural Muslims through a reform of everyday habits.[21]

The pamphlet describes the life and habits of Usman, whose real existence the author goes out of his way to insist on. Usman is a veritable "laboring hero" whose unremitting diligence "caused a revitalized current to flow within the dormant cultivating classes of the world."[22] Usman was not himself even remotely interested in politics. On the contrary, unlike those who "stand with heads high and hands on their hearts presenting new proposals to the world" (all the while, deep down, "selfish, deceitful, dissembling and hungry for reputation"), Usman's "honest heart and pure life was engrossed entirely by the call of his own duty" without regard to reputation.[23] Usman had no time for these frivolities. He was too busy working. And oh how he worked! He built himself a house and furniture. He dug himself a reservoir two spadefuls at a time. He planted his own trees. He worked his own fields. When he was exhausted from working those fields, he did not lie around smoking tobacco, gossiping, or arguing with his wife like a "lazy cultivator."[24] Rather, he weeded, tended and watered his garden. That garden had itself been born of Usman's irrepressible combination of diligence, calmness and austerity in the face of natural calamity. When a typhoon had torn through eastern Bengal, his own home had been spared because it was small and low, and his trees were, through "the grace of God," spared the worst.[25] Usman had secured the weakened roots of his trees by planting betel and pepper saplings at the base of each while enclosing the entire area with a fence to protect the garden from livestock intrusion. Then he secured the fence with more saplings. Between the *pan* (betel leaf) and the excess saplings that he took to market, Usman was able to save a lot of money, especially because "after the typhoon *pan* became very difficult to obtain and [therefore] very expensive."[26] He never spent this income on frivolities or luxuries, or indeed even on basic necessities if he could produce viable substitutes from local resources. But Usman's dedication to self-sufficiency was not a renunciation of commerce in the name of peasant autarchy. Its concern was rather, in keeping with the wider conventions of the genre of texts to which this pamphlet belonged, a savvier approach to commerce.[27] Whenever Usman did sit down, it was "after invoking the name of Allah after much labor, on a stool he made with his own hands, by the bank of a reservoir dug with his own hands."[28] However primitive such a life might appear to the educated reader, his "rough stool" was in reality "more noble than the jewel- and pearl-encrusted, gilded, noble throne of a world-conquering, independent [*svadhin*] emperor."[29]

Usman was presented explicitly as a model for emulation and for the improvement of one's wealth and standing. "Usman's financial position is very good, and he is free of debt."[30] So many cultivators, Bhawali explained, had tried to ape the ways of the rich. They had overextended themselves, relying on income they had fleetingly realized from jute cultivation. As a result, they were now being driven from the lands that they had themselves once won "like heroes." They were now forced to lead their families to almost certain death in the jungles of Assam. Here the author referred to the massive migration, beginning in the first years of the twentieth century, of predominantly Muslim eastern Bengali cultivators (and especially those from Mymensingh, which was the immediately adjoining district in Bengal) up the Brahmaputra Valley into Assam. "Remember, no one has defeated you; you have defeated yourselves. That is, greed, ignorance, delusion and folly are your eternal enemies. They have defeated you."[31] For the land in Mymensingh was as fertile as the land in Assam. Its soil was capable of supporting twice its current population. Its climate was superior, and civilization was more deeply entrenched. If the land was failing to support the people on it, it was only because cultivators were too lazy to work hard enough to extract its wealth-producing potential. "Slothfulness should be eliminated from within the cultivator at the root." Religion was clearly fundamental to the reform of personal habits (giving up tobacco and pan, hygiene, thriftiness, agricultural self-sufficiency, commercial savvy, unremitting diligence and, of course, religious discipline) that lay at the core of this program for realizing the "freedom" that would redeem the Mymensingh cultivator from his poverty and suffering.[32] "Oh Assam-bound cultivator brothers. . . . The words of the mullahs and maulvis have still not gone into your ears."[33] In contrast, the words of the mullahs and maulvis had most definitely gone into Usman's ears. His "moral strength," his thirst for religious education, his "deep devotion and faith," and his faultless performance of the call to prayer from a prayer tower he had himself built in the trees of his property, all signal the centrality of Usman's "religiosity" to his life of work.[34]

The deep commitment to the normative standing of the ideal of self-determination that Bhawali was articulating may have had a longer pedigree in nineteenth-century Faraizism. It seemed to have emerged explicitly as a widely articulated template of specifically Muslim agrarian political demands, however, only in the first decades of the twentieth century. In this sense, interpretations of twentieth-century

agrarian politics in terms either of *longue durée* structures of subaltern consciousness or of ongoing struggles over the apportionment of or control over environmental resources are both equally one-sided in their refusal to take seriously the
larger normative claims that structured these new political demands. I am not suggesting that the Muslim piety Bhawali invoked was itself directly a function of such
concerns. It was indisputably the ready availability of practices of Muslim piety in
the agrarian setting that made their invocation as a basis for self-cultivation so compelling. And no doubt, the satisfactions of piety could never be reduced to the political purposes to which Bhawali's tract was addressed. Nonetheless, the point at
which those practices of piety intersected with agrarian political aspirations was
specifically the desire to intensify the connection between the jotedar and his holding. Usman's dedication to his work as a cultivator is the basis of his independence—that is, his ability to produce his own needs with his own hands, his ability to
limit those needs to the truly necessary, his ability to withstand natural calamity, his
ability to accumulate wealth, and his ability to retain control of his holding. This is
why he is comparable to a "world-conquering, independent ruler." The core value
organizing Bhawali's discussion is not the aspiration to prosperity, but rather the
aspiration to freedom. That freedom is in turn premised on a cultivated capacity for
"moral strength" that underpins his worldly asceticism. Not only is Usman's Muslimness the foundation of his independence, but Usman's diligent practice of cultivating the soil becomes a model of Muslim self-determination generally. That
model would resonate in powerful ways with both the discourse of cultural self-
determination that would emerge so prominently among Bengali Muslim students
and intellectuals, and the discourse of national political economy those same Bengali Muslim intellectuals so often espoused.[35]

"What great kings are we Bangals [east Bengalis]," declared the epigraph on the
frontispiece of the first edition of *Usman,* "who are all by birth the descendants of
those who have worked at cultivating the earth since Adam and Eve!" The reference to Adam and Eve echoes the epigraph published in English at the head of the
postscript: "When Adam delved and Eve span, who was then the gentleman?" This
was a well-known couplet from the fourteenth-century English peasant wars. Its
availability to a Muslim pamphleteer in the eastern Bengal mofussil is to be attributed, most likely, to its use as an epigraph to the second volume of *Burir Suta* (The
Old Woman's Thread). This was a pamphlet by Mohammad Mohsen Ulla of the
eastern Bengali district of Rajshahi, first published in 1909, and circulated free of
charge in a second edition a year later under the sponsorship of the Naogaon
Mahomedan Association of the same district.[36] The pamphlet was largely a compi-
lation of articles and poems, most of which had been previously published in the
preceding several years in the *Mihir-o-Sudhakar,* an anti-Swadeshist, antinational-
ist newspaper owned by Syed Nawab Ali Chaudhuri. (Chaudhuri was himself a
major zamindar of Mymensingh, as well as one of the founders of the Muslim

League in 1906, and later a prominent old-guard dissenter from the 1916 Lucknow Pact that aligned the League with the Congress.) In this pamphlet, Mohsen Ulla had expressed sharp skepticism about Swadeshi nationalists' specious concern for Bengal's cultivators. He argued for stronger representation of Muslims in colonial institutions, but insisted that Muslims could only be better represented if cultivators were better represented. The "cultivator is your father, the cultivator is your brother, the cultivator is one of your own, you yourself are a cultivator, the flesh and blood that is in your body is the flesh and blood of a cultivator." And yet the Muslims disavowed "the stigma of the cultivator," judging "husbandry to be lowly and contemptible" while aspiring to salaried employment. "Fifteen and a half sixteenths of Muslims are cultivators. If the interests of the Muslims are to be protected, the interests of the cultivators must be protected. If the interests of the cultivators are to be protected, we must constantly fight the zamindars and other constituencies." As such, whenever they had the opportunity, the Muslims needed to choose legislative representatives who had "no connection with the zamindars," but rather possessed "independent minds and strength and who wish the cultivators well," without regard to the relative "prestige of their lineage."[37]

Mohsen Ulla was quite clear that the interests of the cultivator turned most fundamentally on the security of the cultivator's property in his holding. The cultivator had been "gradually dispossessed" of this property through rent enhancements, difficulties in the inheritance of privileged tenure statuses, obstacles to the free sale and purchase of holdings, and limitations on his right to use his land as he wished.[38] It was therefore crucial that cultivators organize themselves into "cultivators' associations" to press their interests on the basis of the "needs of the belly."[39]

> Muslims! You are beggars. You have no commerce and no trades, you have only a small land holding [jot] which you have nurtured through generations. Today you have been able to recognize yourselves as men—and it is only husbandry's rights to the soil that prevent you from being seen now as creatures of toil or mere laborers. Once you had full ownership over that holding, but today you no longer have those rights. Your duty is to protect that holding. And if you are to protect it, you must stand forth as cultivators.[40]

Under circumstances where the status of the community as a whole had degenerated, what established the full humanity of the Muslim was his practice of cultivating the soil. The labor of cultivation—the sacrifice of the cultivator's suffering body—constituted a form of "rightful property" that in turn provided the basis for his claim to self-determination.[41] Mohsen Ulla was thus insisting, first, that cultivator interests were predominantly Muslim interests in Bengal, and second, that Muslim interests were fundamentally cultivator interests. He further nested both these claims in turn within a broader narrative invoked directly by his choice of epigraphs for both parts of the book: "The history of civilization is nothing other than the history of the cultivator," attributed to Aristotle; and "The labor of the cultivator is the source of the wealth of a nation," attributed to Adam Smith. "The cultivator can say without presumption, 'I am not dependent on anyone—I shall not go to anyone—I shall not fall at anyone's feet—I shall not beg at anyone's door-step.'"[42]

As a political intervention, *Burir Suta* sat right at the intersection of agrarian organization in the name of Muslimness and early agrarian organization in the name of cultivators' interests. This was a duality mirrored in the Nator Cultivators Association, with whose efforts the text is explicitly aligned, and the Naogaon Mahomedan Association, whose members sponsored the free-of-charge second edition. This duality was already present in the first decade of the twentieth century, when the Mymensingh Raiyat Association, founded in 1903, was denouncing rent enhancements, illegal cesses, and exorbitant interest rates, while the so-called *Red Pamphlet* of 1907 was declaring: "In Bengal, consider, you [Muslims] form the majority, you are the peasant, from agriculture comes all wealth. Where did the Hindu get his wealth from? He had nothing, he has stolen it from you and become wealthy."[43] But the actual connection between Muslimness and cultivation in *Burir Suta* is left to the arbitrary accidents of demography. The Bangal (eastern Bengali) is Muslim only by default, as a question of numbers. The claims of the cultivator in no sense turn on his Muslimness. While Mohsen Ulla was virulently hostile to the Swadeshi movement, he also condemned communal competition as damaging to the aspirations of cultivators to press their demands politically.[44] The invocation of Adam as the original cultivator in the epigraph was repeated in the text of the pamphlet too. But that invocation occurred right alongside the claims that "many prophets have also cultivated with their own hands," and that "at one time the brahmans of India also used to engage in cultivation with their own hands," thus confirming the status of husbandry as the most "sanctified occupation" of all, regardless of religious affiliation.[45]

Unlike the *Burir Suta* of 1909/1910, however, the *Usman* of 1920/1921 took a crucial new step in the elaboration of a Muslim agrarian politics by positing an intrinsic connection between Muslimness and cultivation. Bhawali identified the cultivator, rather than the educated bhadralok, as the true Bengali: "When one says 'Bengali,' one must understand 'cultivator.'"[46] Seen in this light, though, Usman's Muslimness was precisely what rendered him the quintessential Bengali, because it was his piety as a Muslim that bound him most firmly to his occupation as a cultivator. In the rural context, the Bengaliness that differentiated the "Bengali Muslim" from Indian Muslims in general thus connoted the occupation of agriculture more radically than it did the question of mother tongue. Usman would never have to choose between an identity as Muslim, as a Bengali, and as a cultivator. Even though they were far from congruent categories, these were all mutually enforcing categories. The pious Muslim was the most successful and dedicated cultivator, and the cultivator was the truest Bengali. This logic never implied the exclusion of non-Muslims from either the peasantry or Bengaliness, for the connections between Muslimness, cultivation and Bengaliness were not premised on demographic congruence.[47]

Bhawali grounded the Muslim aspiration to self-determination in cultivation, like Mohsen Ulla. But he identified Muslim piety as the practical foundation of the *capacity* to render cultivation into an effective vehicle of that aspiration. Bhawali invoked piety as a practice of everyday moral discipline capable of ordering a proper relationship between man and nature. Implicit here was already a politics of Muslim self-determination fundamentally bound to property. The ideal of self-determination depended first on the "jote" itself, and secondarily on the capacity to accumulate that the diligent exploitation of its soil could make possible. This was a politics of Muslimness that had nothing to do with self-determination in competition with some rival Hindu constituency. The connections *Usman* makes between Muslimness, the labor of cultivation, and self-determination have nothing to do with communalism. In fact, the text does not mention Hindus or Hinduism at all. That is not to say that one cannot easily recognize where the figurative invocation of Hindus would fit into this text if they were to be invoked. As Pradip Kumar Datta has observed, the "eternal enemies" of the Muslim cultivator—"greed, ignorance, delusion and folly"—could easily be coded as "Hindu" vices. Moneylending was dominated by the Hindu gentry, Muslim tenants had long resented the demands of Hindu landlords for collections to fund religious ceremonies, and Hindu polytheism (conjoined with musical and colorfully processional popular religious practices) contrasted sharply with the austerity of Muslim practices.[48] Nonetheless, such a properly "communal" elaboration of Bhawali's ethical discourse was superfluous to his core concerns. These concerns centered on the viability of smallholding cultivation.

Not only was the text of *Usman* silent on the entire question of Hindu/Muslim rivalry or animosity, more surprisingly it failed even to discuss landlords and moneylenders except indirectly through allusions to peasant indebtedness and emigration. Where the issue of property comes up, it is in the form of Usman's immediate proprietorship over his holding. That proprietorship is not framed in colonial legal terms. It is not a claim that Usman is the "owner" of his holding in a way that a discussion of legal status might frame it. Rather, Usman's homestead is "his" because it was made "with his own hands."[49] "One must keep in mind that this is Usman's reservoir, and it really is his reservoir," and so too his stools and his hut and his cot, because he made all these things himself.[50] The conception of property at issue here is discussed as if it exists in an entirely separate dimension from the kind of property institutionalized by the colonial state. But it is also as if that property claims a primordiality that renders legal questions of property of such secondary significance that they disappear from immediate sight. The problem for Bhawali is to establish the right relationship between the cultivator and his holding. This was the basis on which his secure control over that holding, and his consequent independence, could be established.

That said, there are good reasons to think that Bhawali was far from blind to the wider implications that the establishment of the right relation between man and nature carried. These implications included the most urgent questions of competing legal claims to the control of land. When Bhawali asserted the primordiality of Usman's proprietorship over his homestead, the implicit juxtaposition was to property acquired by other means. Such other means could not, however, refer to commercial exchange, for Bhawali emphatically celebrated Usman's participation in commerce. That essentially leaves as the implicit contrast forms of acquisition that turn on parasitical dependence on the labor of others, expressed in zamindari and mahajani, as well as in the alien culture of the "Sahebs" and "Misters" who have abandoned the villages for the towns and the culture of Bengal for Western education and have in the process ceased to be "Bengali."[51] The very secondariness and marginality of political questions of property to the argument of *Usman* were themselves the logical expression of the kind of politics that Bhawali was voicing. Yet their real relevance to his concerns can be demonstrated relatively easily by turning to other contemporary pamphlets that he did not himself author, but with whose publication he was closely associated.

Krishak-bilap (The Cultivator's Lament) was published in 1922 in Mymensingh by Shah Abdul Hamid, and distributed through the "All Bengal Cultivators Association," which presumably either paralleled or subsumed the more local "Kishoreganj Proja Sova" (Kishorganj Tenant Association) of which Hamid was also Secretary. I do not invoke this pamphlet arbitrarily. Hamid specifically acknowledged Bhawali as a "dearer-than-life brother" who "spent day and night looking [*Krishak-bilap*] over and revising it from beginning to end." Bhawali, whose *Adarsha krishak* had "received the title of 'treasure of the heart' from the Bengal cultivator," had also "helped publish the book through financial assistance."[52] Clearly, Hamid wanted the reader to understand that there was a connection between his own writings and *Usman*. And in this pamphlet, the full-scale defense of proja property was elaborated quite clearly.

Bengal threatened to revert into a land of thick jungles in the absence of a viable class of cultivators. Moneylenders had grown rich on proja indebtedness. They had turned trifling advances to the projas into vast returns in interest. Projas were left unable to pay the rent on their holdings. They had been plunged into such despair that many of them had ultimately been forced to lead their families away into the jungles of Assam. There most of them proceeded to die from the ravages of disease. Without the proja, who would cultivate? Who would pay the rent? Who would clear the jungle and improve the land? Who would grow food? Without the proja, there could be no prosperity and certainly no landlords, and Bengal itself would be left a "graveyard, a playground for ghouls."[53] Even landlords had grudg-ingly begun to awaken to the need to defend the rights of cultivators both from their own arrogations and from the depredations of moneylenders. The only way to reverse this situation was to restore the rights that projas had once enjoyed over the soil. These rights extended to the right to transfer holdings freely, and the right to do as they pleased with their own lands, such as digging reservoirs and cutting trees. They did not require permission from the zamindar to do these things—and they certainly should not have to pay a fee to the zamindar to get such permission. Hamid was hardly a radical exponent of agrarian revolution. He framed the clos-ing passages of his pamphlet as a plea to zamindars and moneylenders for coop-eration. He harkened back to a time under the Mughals when "the projas used to be released from any obligation to their superiors once they had paid a fixed pro-portion of the crops grown in their fields as revenue." Agriculture was the founda-tion of government revenues. The zamindars, appointed as revenue agents, there-fore used to attend to augmenting fertility and productivity, and assisted in times of famine by offering rent remissions and throwing open the royal granaries. By thus uniting their interests with the projas, the zamindars had been invested in agricultural improvement and prosperity without infringing on the primordial rights of the projas. The resulting "relationship between landlord and proja was one of father and son." In contrast, the current landlords had become mere "rent-iers" (*khajanadar*), without interest in the welfare of their tenantry.[54] They had furthermore compounded their disgrace by turning to moneylending, advancing to tenants at high interest money that had been borrowed at low interest. What is more, they also tied the credit they advanced to mortgages on their tenants' hold-ings, threatening large-scale dispossession. As a result, the proja's rights over the soil now conflicted with landlord interests, giving rise to the necessity of the new kind of political organizations that the "All Bengal Cultivators Association" repre-sented.

Shah Abdul Hamid also wrote another pamphlet around the same time (this time with Bhawali serving as publisher), *Shasan-sanskare gramya mochalman* (The Rural Muslim in the Government Reforms). Here he elaborated on the theme of "self-rule" in the context of the opportunities offered by the Montagu-Chelmsford Reforms of 1919 and of the demands for immediate self-government being voiced by the Congress in the course of the Non-Cooperation campaign of 1920–22. Hamid declared outright that "in our Bengal the interests of the projas generally and the interests of the zamindar class are completely opposed, that is, contrary to each other in kind."[55] As such, "it was necessary for our self-interest that we, the party of the projas, refuse to desist from standing up actively against the zamindar class."[56] This did not, however, mean that projas should respond to irresponsible propaganda from the educated classes of Congress-allied activists who were incit-ing "ignorant raiyats, that is, the cultivator community, against the zamindars" in a spirit of anger and violence.[57] Instead, projas needed to "understand our own interests calmly and with disciplined emotions." If they did so, they might "acquire our just rights" through the voicing of demands in a newly constituted legislature in which projas for the first time were presented with the opportunity to find an effective political voice.[58] This was because the "village-dwelling middle class" had been admitted to the franchise. They could therefore direct their votes to village-based Muslim cultivators like themselves. Furthermore, such candidates could not be undercut by bad-faith competition because Muslims had been granted separate electorates.[59] The reformed legislature therefore represented the greatest opportunity for "self-rule" for the "village-dwelling Muslim," not the anti-government posturing of Non-Cooperation. In this same spirit, Hamid echoed the politics of anti-sophistication voiced by Bhawali. He contrasted the honest wants of food and work with the artificiality of "babuism" and "sahebism" and urban life more generally. He bemoaned the contempt in which rural Muslims were held by even the lowliest city dwellers, who saw the simplicity of their needs and their piety merely as the rusticity of "jungle dwellers" rather than the stern virtues fundamental to self-determination.[60] The "just rights" to which projas were to lay claim were quite clear. They sought to defend and restore "our ownership over the only resource we have, the land we cultivate (the property in our holding) [*chasher jamir svatva* (*jot svatva*)]."[61] Reading this pamphlet alongside *Usman*, the "self-rule" that Hamid had in mind was clearly the self-rule of the property-constituting cultivator. And reading *Usman* alongside this pamphlet, it seems clear that the orientation of the Muslim cultivator to worldly asceticism was itself a practice that reinforced the very connection between cultivator and soil on which the political demands of the proja rested. If any proja could claim a proprietary right over his holding, surely it was Usman. The strength of that claim rested ultimately on his Muslim piety. It was his piety that sustained the worldly asceticism of his commitment to labor, and it was labor that constituted his proprietary relationship to his homestead.

Hamid and Bhawali positioned themselves firmly in the broadly nationalist but anti-Non-Cooperation camp of the "never-to-be-forgotten" Fazlul Haq. Haq had been involved in proja politics in Mymensingh since (at least) 1914, and Hamid would go on to work closely with him in establishing an institutional framework for proja politics at the provincial level in the form of a Proja Party in the legislature in 1929.[62] Hamid's nationalist commitments combined a distinctly noncommunal embrace of religious pluralism (of the let-Hindus-be-Hindus-and-let-Muslims-be-Muslims variety) with an unequivocal voicing of the need for Muslim representation of Muslim interests and cultivator representation of cultivator interests. Hamid's writings never systematically aligned landlord with Hindu and proja with Muslim. For instance, he offered an example of a Muslim talukdar taking loans from a Hindu mahajan and then advancing that money to his tenants.[63] Still, that was itself an example that could cut both ways. The Hindu moneylender preceded the corruption of the Muslim landlord. The Muslim landlord's exploitation of the proja was dependent on the capital advanced by the Hindu moneylender. So the Muslim moneylending talukdar could well have been seen as an example of the Muslim corrupted by that eternal enemy, "greed." And greed could always be construed, in the context of eastern Bengal, as a Hindu vice, even when it was the vice of Muslims.[64] In this sense, a fundamentally noncommunal identification of the Muslim as cultivator *could* be communalized at any point. Furthermore, it could be communalized in a way that systematically identified the Hindu as the root of the problem of exploitation without relying on any correlative conflation of community and class. Crucially, however, it was not intrinsically communal, and did not have to be communalized. Indeed, it did not have to refer to the religious other at all.

It is worth observing, however, that the transition from Bhawali's text to Hamid's pamphlets does introduce an important terminological slide. "Cultivator" (*krishak*) becomes "proja," the Bengali equivalent of "raiyat." Hamid's argument very much presumed that the proja was himself a cultivator, and that the projas therefore formed a collective interest in opposition to the interests of rent- and interest-receivers. It was on this basis that Hamid could consider the enfranchisement of the "village-dwelling middle class" as sufficient to begin a process of proja self-representation, even though the qualifications (Rs. 2 per year in chaukidar tax or R. 1 per year in road cess) excluded the vast majority of projas. But neither Hamid nor Bhawali was blind to the relevance of fractures internal to agrarian society. Bhawali might if pressed have plausibly conceded the possibility that misfortune alone could sometimes account for foreclosure and emigration. The rhetorical force of his writing, though, pointed unambiguously towards the association of the viability of proja property with ethical self-cultivation, and correlatively towards condemning the landless as moral failures. In this sense, the image of the "Muslim cultivator" that Bhawali projected was already by default implicitly identified with the "jotedar." This was a term employed in these writings to refer to the proja who was in possession of a permanent interest in his "jote," or holding. Shah Abdul Hamid's submission, as Secretary of the Kishoreganj Proja Sova, to the Department of Revenue in response to proposals to reform the tenancy law of the province further reinforced this implicit identification of "Muslim" with "jotedar." There Hamid called for the recognition of the free transfer of raiyati holdings, the reduction and limitation of the transfer fee to be paid to the landlord in cases of such transfers, no rights for the zamindar to preempt such sales, and the raiyats' absolute proprietorship over all trees on his holding. These were version of all the basic demands of most proja organizations in the 1920s. At the same time though, Hamid specifically rejected calls for the extension of rights of occupancy to sharecroppers and under-raiyats, who in existing law enjoyed no legal protections beyond local custom.[65]

The rights of the cultivator were implicitly the rights of the jotedar—and the properly "Muslim" cultivator had to be a jotedar. The claim that Muslim piety could serve to intensify the connection between cultivator and jote implicitly assumed such an identification. But that logic only made sense in the context of a broader endorsement of labor's property-constituting capacities. It further assumed that the jotedar was the proper subject of a history of property-constituting labor. Hamid was far from unusual in his insistence that *praja svatva* (tenant right or proja property, depending on how it was construed) be limited to jotedars. This was a tendency shared across the boundaries that otherwise separated the politics of the (merely default Muslim) "raiyat" from the politics of the emphatically "Muslim" cultivator. It was also a tendency shared across the boundaries that otherwise separated both these positions from the politics of those sections of the bhadralok that had bought into raiyati rights. After all, the 1885 Tenancy Act had transformed raiyati holdings into highly desirable rental properties precisely because it denied all tenancies held under raiyats the kinds of legislative protections that raiyati holdings enjoyed.[66]

The Anjuman-i-Islamia of Netrokona subdistrict of Mymensingh described a "thrill of panic amongst all classes of tenants" at the thought that the value of occupancy raiyats' property could be suddenly annihilated by legislation in favor of their undertenants.[67] Such sentiments were echoed by raiyat organizations and conferences across eastern Bengal. *Prajasvatva ainer sanshodhan bishaye prajar jnatabya o kartabya* (Facts and Duties of Projas in the Matter of the Amendment of the Tenure Law), produced in 1923 by the Mymensingh Central Raiyat Association, articulated these same associations without any emphasis on the ethical role of Islam. Before the permanent settlement, "it was the proja who was the owner of the land. He used to cultivate the land, he used to work at improving the land, and he used to enjoy the grain that the land produced."[68] But the permanent settlement abolished this state of affairs, in which labor and property were united. It artificially raised the zamindars to proprietorship and condemned "those who were the real owners of the land" to live as "landless exiles on their own ancestral plots."[69] But now the proja was being threatened on a second front. A proposed new amendment to the tenancy law would allow under-raiyats (*korfa praja*) to bring suits before the court to commute rents in kind into cash equivalents. This would set in motion their transformation into projas under the law, ultimately entitling even sharecroppers to rights of occupancy. The consequence of these two proposals for the jotedar would be simple: "if you allow any person to cultivate on your land using their own plough and cattle, then that land will permanently pass out of your hands."[70]

This policy appeared to be in the interests of cultivators. But projas would simply refuse to sublet their lands. They would instead use hired labor when possible, and keep land fallow when necessary. As a result, those poor cultivators who had maintained their status as projas by supplementing their income through share-cropping on a neighbor's holding would now have "no choice but to work as laborers."[71] Meanwhile, the situation of the proja would also be rendered perilous. The author gives first the (highly conventional) example of a man named Izzatullah (*ijjat* itself means "honor"), who dies and leaves behind four young children and a wife whose only hope of providing for her family lies in the rents she receives from her sharecroppers. But under the proposed amendment, this arrangement threatens to dispossess her of her holding and thereby truly rob her and her family of *ijjat*, their standing as jotedars rather than landless laborers. "This is what the condition of the jotedar has come to."[72] Such provisions further threatened the proja's ability to access affordable credit by mortgaging his interest in the land. If his rights over the land were weakened, then his holding would become poor security, and the value of such land as collateral would depreciate. And meanwhile, uncultivated land produced no crops. Yet the zamindar would dun the proja for the same rent as always. Everyday proja holdings were being "put up for auction, their lands are passing from their hands into the zamindar's or the mahajan's hands, and they are moving to Assam with their families and there dying of the black fever."[73] Proja society was already at breaking point. Now it was proposed to give the zamindars new rights to take 25% of the sale price on all transfers of raiyati properties, and to incorporate the land into their own demesne through preemption. The jotedar was fighting on two fronts.

Speaking in the Legislative Council in 1923, Emdadul Haq, a prominent leader of proja political organization in the eastern districts, invoked Jaimini, Manu and the *Ain-i-Akbari,* to insist that historically "those who actually tilled the soil were virtually the owners of the land." This was a right qualified by the revenue demands of the state. Yet its moral claim was underwritten by the hardships and high rates of mortality suffered by those whose "indefatigable industry" had sowed the seed of agriculture in the jungles of Bengal.[74] The proja, the presumptive bearer of this waste-reclaiming ancestry, was presumed to be a cultivator. It did not necessarily follow, however, that the cultivator was therefore always a proja. This in turn opened up some complicated tensions.

It is true, as Sugata Bose and Partha Chatterjee have argued, that eastern Bengal had moved less far towards peasant differentiation than western Bengal. Nonetheless, Mymensingh had a more uneven distribution of holdings than, say, Faridpur—which in any case by this time had itself seen the rise of wealthy projas.[75] In Mymensingh, a class of substantial landholders enjoyed a net surplus on their holdings. To this section of the peasantry, the appeal of the insistence on the jotedar as proprietor is not hard to imagine. Nor is their affinity for the kind of ethical affirmation of prosperity that *Usman* offered. But Hamid, like his Faridpur-based ally Tamizuddin Khan, was himself from a more modest family of jotedars.[76] As the invocation of the new Assam-bound emigration in these texts makes clear, the first decades of the twentieth century were a period when the effects of peasant differentiation were beginning to be felt. Population continued to climb, and the agrarian frontier had reached its limit.[77] Mymensingh was the region's most intensive producer of jute, supplying as much as a fifth of Bengal's aggregate crop out of what by the late 1930s would be almost a quarter of the total area under cultivation in the district. It was a district where some had improved their fortunes through such commercial agriculture. Yet it was also one where the degree to which cultivators dedicated potential paddy land to jute reflected a turn to higher-value commercial crops in the face of rising population pressure on fragmented holdings. It correlatively implied a greater reliance on rice imports for subsistence. On the one hand, this allowed cultivators generally to increase the value of crops from eversmaller average holdings. On the other hand, it also rendered cultivators more vulnerable to price fluctuations in either commodity. While jute cultivation was nominally independent, in practice involvement in jute production bound all but the most affluent cultivators in complicated and inescapable relations of credit dependency with agents (whether landlords or moneylenders) who employed capital often provided by Calcutta-based purchasing companies and who used advances to purchase jute at below-market prices.[78] The trajectories of agrarian commercialization discussed in chapter 4 had thus by 1920 in Mymensingh arrived at a distinctly capitalist telos. A polarization of landlords and landless labor had not occurred in any decisive sense. But the lower end of smallholding reproduction was only being sustained by capital inputs in the form of advances and credit. That same dependence on capital had rendered smallholding reproduction vulnerable in new, historically determinate ways. These smallholders were the very projas who needed a secure proprietary interest in their land to maintain their access to credit. They were also the ones most vulnerable to foreclosure in times of crisis, such as when jute prices plummeted during the First World War. So we should not rush to identify the discourse of the Muslim cultivator too closely with the sectional interest of affluent peasants. It was an ideological framework with comprehensive appeal across the spectrum of jotedar cultivators, from the affluent to the barely subsisting.

An emphatic insistence on the Muslimness of the proja was intended to cement the connection between the jotedar and his property. That discourse of Muslimness, however, was itself only an attempt at a supplementary intervention within a much wider field of political discourse. That broader ideological framework, whose normative commitments the discourse of the Muslim jotedar took as its point of departure, grounded proprietary rights in property-constituting labor. The embrace of labor as the foundation of the interests of jotedars was an effective weapon against landlord interests. But despite the attempt to consolidate the association between property-constituting labor and the jotedar, this was nonetheless a form of political discourse that inevitably opened new fields of social contestation. If the primacy of proja property turned on labor, then the proja had to be a cultivator. But "raiyat" was a legal status that was not always bound to the person who actually tilled the soil. This was ever more true under the twin pressures of peasant differentiation and bhadralok investment in raiyati tenures.

Consequently, this proja politics was inescapably haunted by a *krishak* politics. This was the politics of the "cultivator" that it sought simultaneously to subsume and to foreclose through the insistent identification of the jotedar as the agent of property-constituting labor. Closing the door to the moral claims of cultivators who were not jotedars, but who were nonetheless the actual tillers of the soil, presented intractable difficulties. So just a month after his submission on behalf of the Kishoreganj Proja Sova demanding that under-raiyats be denied rights of occupancy, we find Shah Abdul Hamid personally seconding a motion at the Mymensingh Raiyat Conference of 1923 to grant under-raiyats occupancy rights. "[W]hereas the *bhag-chasis* or *bargadars* [sharecroppers] have not the same status as the *corpadars* (under-raiyats) in this country, this Conference think it quite undesirable to bring them under the same class." The motion proposed instead "that *corpadars* (under-raiyats) be given the right of occupancy, but *bargadars* should not be deemed as tenants."[79] Unsurprisingly, claims on behalf of sharecroppers would indeed come to be formulated on the basis of the same basic appeal to the normative force of labor's property-constituting powers. Even more forcefully, so too would claims on behalf of those Mymensingh cultivators who migrated up the Brahmaputra Valley into Assam, and who rallied behind Maulana Bhashani in the 1940s to demand inclusion in Pakistan.

The centrality of the "jote" to the figure of the "Muslim cultivator" involved the projection of a normative class position. This vision of a society of independent producers did not, however, express anything like an actual homogeneous class interest shared by "jotedars." The jotedar's proprietary claim to an interest in the soil might superficially seem to render jotedari into the basis of a class position defined by small property. In reality though, "jotedari" extended across a broad social spectrum. Farmers with substantial holdings and often considerable interests in grain trading and moneylending (i.e. those who have featured so prominently under the name "jotedar" in agrarian historiography) were jotedars. So too were the increasingly squeezed middle peasants. And so too were the indebted smallholders whose objective relation to the credit that sustained the reproduction of household life was essentially crypto-proletarian (i.e. not essentially distinct in logic from the relationship between labor and capital).[80] The power of the discourse of the "Muslim cultivator" lay precisely in its ability to provide an ideological framework through which the really quite diverse political and social interests that the term jotedar encompassed could be articulated. The appeal to the property-constituting powers of labor, however, also opened a door to appropriations that extended beyond the lower limits even of the jotedars—into the world of "cultivators" more generally. Thus we find already in 1923 the Cultivator Associations of Lakhipur and Raipur in Noakhali district railing against the Tenancy Act of 1885 for its fixation of heritable raiyati rights in perpetuity in a single link in the chain of landholding. "In this part of the province the word 'raiyat' was synonymous with the term [*cashat praja*], and whenever a raiyat would sublet his land to another cultivating tenant, the former would be treated as [*manib*] (landlord or rent-receiver) and from that time the latter would be treated as [*rayat*] (cultivating tenant)." This system maintained the appropriate ongoing unity of raiyati rights with the rights of the cultivator. In the wake of the fracturing of this unity in 1885, the "poor *ex*-raiyats, who were *bona fide* cultivators of the soil, were compelled to take under-raiyati leases under those so-called raiyati-holders [many of whom were nonagriculturists and/or bhadralok] who wrongly usurped the occupancy rights of the *ex*-raiyats."[81]

In this flexibility to articulate so wide a range of political claims lay the fundamental power of the conception of the property-constituting power of labor as a template for visions of agrarian, and Muslim, emancipation. To say this is not to deny the processes through which more privileged sections of rural society co-opted the political energies of less privileged sections under the banner of "Muslim self-determination." That is a story well known from the works of Rafiuddin Ahmed, Partha Chatterjee and Taj ul-Islam Hashmi. Rather, it is to provide a way of making sense of the "co-optability" of diverse agrarian interests under the banner of "Muslim interests." It explains how "Muslimness" could have been broadly understood as a plausible vehicle for diverse social interests, when those interests were seemingly incommensurable among themselves, and when the interests of the wealthiest segment (who, after all, were typically the authors of the kinds of pamphlet-literature I have been discussing) were so clearly in conflict with the interests of the lowest segments. What the Muslimness of the Bengal cultivator in fact highlights, when properly examined, is the centrality of labor to the constitution of property.

THE MUSLIM BLOC

The Bengal Tenancy (Amendment) Bill had had to trudge a tortuous path to the Legislative Council before finally coming up for detailed discussion, amendment and passage in 1928. Following initial canvassing of opinion, an attempt at amendment had first been introduced in the Council in 1923. This was the moment that had elicited the responses of the various proja organizations mentioned in the previous section. The proposed measure would have extended rights of occupancy to under-raiyats. It would also have deemed sharecroppers to be tenants, so that they would henceforth have been entitled to correlative legislative protections including the ability to accrue occupancy rights. That proposal was promptly withdrawn from the Council in the face of resounding hostility from the Hindu press, moderates in the Council under the leadership of Surendranath Banerjea, zamindar interests organized preeminently under the banner of the British Indian Association, those Congressites boycotting the Council in line with the Civil Disobedience strategy of the orthodox Gandhian Congress, and the newly vocal raiyat organizations of the mofussil.

In 1925, a bill came before the Council again. "The widespread practice of subdivision and subinfeudation of rights in land has necessitated the revision of the fundamental provision of the Act, by which the occupancy tenant right is limited to one person in the chain of those interested in the land," explained its statement of purpose. "A common result of this limitation has been that the cultivating tenant, for whom this occupancy right was intended, has become a tenant-at-will under the holder of the occupancy right." The bill thus proposed to extend a right of occupancy to "persons holding land under the tenant who enjoys the legal status of raiyat." The Council before which this new bill was presented had been significantly transformed in membership. In the elections held at the end of 1923, the newly formed Swarajya Party had swept the old moderates aside. The Swarajya Party had been formed in 1922 at the initiative of Chittaranjan Das and Motilal Nehru to end the Congress boycott of the new Councils established under the Montagu-Chelmsford reforms. The Swarajists sought to revitalize the Congress in the wake of the termination of the Non-Cooperation Movement by directing its energies into the new strategy of wrecking the system of dyarchy through systematic obstruction from within the Councils. This was an approach grudgingly permitted by the central Congress leadership as the necessary cost of retaining the loyalty of two such prominent national leaders. By the end of 1923, Das's Swarajya Party had not only captured the machinery of the Bengal Provincial Congress, but had also succeeded on that basis in taking the largest bloc of seats in the Legislative Council (47 out of 139), almost half of which (21) were taken by Muslim candidates.

Das's success in bringing nationalist Muslims into the fold of his new political organization built on the already existing alliance between the Congress and the Khilafat Committee that had been the basis of their joint mobilization in 1920–22. But his ability to overcome both the tensions that had developed in the wake of Gandhi's decision to call off Non-Cooperation after the Chauri Chaura incident in 1922, and the resistance of the Bengal Khilafat Committee to Council entry, rested in no small part on the Bengal Pact, ratified by Swarajists and Khilafatists at a joint meeting in December 1923. The pact conceded to Muslims (1) representation in the Legislative Council on the basis of population and through separate electorates immediately upon attainment of self-rule; (2) 80% of all new government appointments until Muslims had 55% of all positions; (3) representation in municipal bodies in the proportion of 60/40 in favor of the majority community; (4) the voluntary banning of musical processions before mosques; and (5) a guarantee not to interfere in the practice of ritual cow-slaughter.

But by the time the Tenancy (Amendment) Bill came before the Legislative Council in 1925, much water had passed under the bridge. By 1925, the coalition that Das had put together was coming apart at the seams. So too was Das himself: he fell ill and died that same year. While Das had succeeded in forging a coalition between Hindu and Muslim nationalists across Bengal, his actual control of the Congress machinery rested on a much tighter network of alliances centered firmly on Calcutta. Das had never shown much interest in prioritizing the village reconstruction projects he had promised to undertake. He simply could not countenance any serious effort at agrarian reform. To do so would jeopardize his support from the tight circle of people he had himself promoted to control over the Bengal Congress's financial and electoral machinery (the so-called Big Five of Nirmal Chandra Chandra, Sarat Chandra Bose, Nalini Ranjan Sarkar, Bidhan Chandra Roy and Tulsi Goswami). It would also cost him the support of the Hindu bhadralok membership of the Swarajya Party more generally, which was permeated with minor landed interests whose value (with the exception of raiyati holdings) had been subject to a more or less continuous squeeze since the consequences of the 1859 and 1885 acts had begun to be felt in the later nineteenth century.[82] In the context of these pressures, and despite support from the left wing of their own party, the Swarajists blocked discussion of the bill again in 1925. They referred it on to a Select Committee while at the same time obstructing efforts to include more pro-tenant voices in that committee's composition. In doing so, the Bengal Swarajists took their first steps toward defining themselves irreversibly as a party representing the interests of rent-receivers.

Relations between the Swarajya Party and its Muslim members were entering a period of precipitous decline. The Khilafat Movement had been highly effective in mobilizing the rural ulema, whose energies intersected with the rising tide of proja politics. The subsequent collapse of the Khilafat/Non-Cooperation movement left behind a residue of disappointment and ill will. 1926 and 1927 would turn out to be years of intense communal violence in both Calcutta and mofussil towns. This was violence mostly set off by conflicts over the playing of music before mosques and cow-killing. Hindu and Muslim politicians were polarized around these kinds of conflicts. Meanwhile, the impulse to organize politically around specifically "Muslim" interests found a refreshed impulse also in the threat posed in northern India by the *shuddhi* movement, which worked under the leadership of the Arya Samajist Swami Shraddhanand to "reconvert" Muslims to Hinduism in the mid-1920s. This was a threat brought close to home by a series of Arya Samajist public meetings held in Calcutta late in 1925; and further reinforced again when Shraddhanand's murder at the hands of a Muslim assassin in 1926 provoked a tirade of anti-Muslim vilification in Calcutta's Hindu press.

As far as the top-heavy political unity that Das had managed to forge in Bengal went, by 1926 most Muslim nationalists in the Bengal Legislative Council had lost all faith in the Swarajya Party. The Indian National Congress had immediately rejected the Bengal Pact in 1923. Das had, however, managed to keep it alive as the basis for intercommunal goodwill at the level of the Bengal Provincial Congress. In 1924, he had been forced to oppose a deliberately mischievous resolution to give immediate effect to the pact introduced in the Legislative Council by Khan Bahadur Musharraf Hussain. Even then though, Das had been able to mobilize the trust and support of nationalist Muslims to survive the crisis through an appeal to the pact's stipulation that its provisions would be given effect only on the attainment of self-government. But in the wake of his death, the Bengal Provincial Congress hastened to rescind the pact officially at its Krishnagar meeting in 1926—reinforcing the perceived need for a politically organized defense of Muslim interests in the region. Already in 1925, Sir Abdur Rahim, speaking as president of a Muslim League that had, since the 1916 Lucknow Pact, held its meetings in conjunction with the Congress, denounced Hindu communalism from the podium and called for Muslims to draw together to defend themselves. He thereby set in motion a series of political maneuverings that would result in the League and the Congress holding their meetings in separate cities for the first time in 1927.[83] At the national level, Jinnah would continue to attempt to renew the solidarity between the Indian National Congress and the All India Muslim League. He sought to use the 1927 announcement of the all-white Simon Commission as just such an opportunity to push back at a rival faction, backed in Bengal by Sir Abdur Rahim, that sought to cooperate with the commission as a means to further Muslim interests. But by 1928 Jinnah's effort had collapsed in the face of Congress intransigence.

It was under such unpropitious circumstances that in 1928 a new tenancy bill, drafted in accordance with the recommendations of the Select Committee appointed in 1925, finally arrived for discussion on the floor of the Legislative Council. Sir Provash Chunder Mitter, the Executive Council member in charge of the Department of Revenue, introduced the legislation in the Council on behalf of the government. The bill, he declared, represented "the results of a compromise between conflicting interests," extending the rights of raiyats and under-raiyats while securing crucial powers and privileges to rent-receivers.[84] The next four months of Council meetings were substantially given over to debating the specific provisions of the legislation and a long list of amendments moved by the Council members.

The pattern of this debate was clear enough: a sharp divide between the already sharply divided Hindu and Muslim members of the Council. Only the zamindar bloc, elected on the basis of a special electorate and including several Muslims in its ranks, partly bucked this trend. The "Muslim bloc," traversing a number of factions including the disaffected nationalist Muslims, lined up consistently behind the rent-payer. Thus they supported amendments furthering the raiyat's interest when the raiyat was being discussed as a rent-payer, but also supported amendments that infringed upon the interests of raiyats when the raiyat was being discussed as a rent-receiver. They supported the right of under-raiyats to accrue occupancy rights, and the rights of sharecroppers to be recognized as tenants and, as such, accrue rights of occupancy as under-raiyats insofar as they met the criteria laid out in the draft bill. They supported the right of raiyats to freely transfer their occupancy holdings, and as such they objected to the zamindar's entitlement to a percentage of the purchase price (salami) and the right of preemption according to which zamindars could veto any sale by paying 110% of the agreed purchase price and thereby incorporating the holding into their demesne lands. Meanwhile, despite the Swarajya Party's foundational commitment to oppose the government as part of its program of wrecking dyarchy from within, the (now exclusively Hindu) Swarajist members of the Council generally backed the government bill at every opportunity. They overwhelmingly supported amendments that strengthened the position of rent-receivers. They identified their general embrace of the bill's moderate extension of the rights of raiyats and under-raiyats, alongside the preservation of the privileges of zamindars and other rent-receivers, with a general commitment to furthering the national interest without class partiality. After all, it was axiomatic to the nationalist position that the various social interests in the country were ultimately (at least in principle) commensurable within the larger framework of the national interest. Sir Provash Chunder Mitter, a loyalist zamindar, had introduced the bill with an invocation of the hope that settling "the conflicting class interests with justice and fairness to all" would lay "deep the foundations of true nationalism in this province." He was echoed almost exactly by J. M. Sengupta, the Swarajist mayor of Calcutta and party leader, who declared his party's position as attentive both to "the reasonable interests of the tenants and also to the reasonable interests of the zamindars so far as they are consistent with the interests of the nation," so that "neither the one nor the other was in the slightest way injured."[85]

Zamindars were of course vocal in the course of the 1928 Council debates in defending their proprietary claims. They held up the Permanent Settlement as a quasi-constitutional document that established a rule of property in Bengal.[86] Satyendranath Roy Choudhuri declared that "the right to the soil was given to the zamindars by the Permanent Settlement. . . . [R]aiyats neither had nor have any right to it save and except that of permanent occupation and enjoyment."[87] But it was not only zamindars who took this position. Even Sarat Chandra Bose, one of the most important Swarajists and a self-declared enemy of zamindars, affirmed the "right of property given to the zamindars at the time of the permanent settlement."[88] Nalini Ranjan Sarkar—businessman, President of the Bengal National Chamber of Commerce, and another member of the Big Five—was quite explicit in declaring that "the permanent settlement invested the landlords" with an "absolute proprietary right" over the soil, reserving to the state only the "right of ensuring the protection and welfare of the raiyats and other cultivators." Since the raiyats and cultivators could claim no proprietary right in the soil, he argued in an exact inversion of the liberal discourse of custom, any rights invested in the raiyats or cultivators could only be derived from the state's authority. As such, the transfer of occupancy rights between tenants, which had been permitted subject to local custom in 1885 but was now to be generalized (subject to the landlord's fee and right of preemption), "does not detract from the proprietary right of the zamindar over the occupancy holding." Such a transaction was not properly a sale. Rather, the outgoing tenant was abandoning the holding in favor of an incoming tenant, receiving a fee to compensate him for his abandonment of the holding. The fee was notionally paid by the zamindar even if received from the incoming tenant.[89] For Sarkar, the defense of the proprietary rights of the zamindar was part and parcel of the defense of property itself. Since 1793, most zamindari estates had exchanged hands for money, on the expectation that those estates would be appropriately remunerative. To suddenly deprive zamindars of that income "by legislative fiat would amount to the confiscation of a vested right."[90] These were more than idle invocations of general principle. In deriving the occupancy raiyat's right of transfer from the provisions in the Permanent Settlement for protection of raiyats and cultivators, Swarajists were providing a theoretical and legal foundation for the landlord's rights to transfer fees and preemption. Indeed, for Jogesh Chandra Gupta, a successful Swarajist lawyer, the fee to be paid to the landlord on transfer (salami) was nothing less than compensation for the partial abrogation of his absolute proprietary rights in the land.[91]

The members of the Muslim bloc rejected the zamindar's rights to transfer fees and preemption by attacking these kinds of claims at their roots. In doing so, they drew on the well-established battery of arguments outlined in chapters 2 and 3. Syed Nausher Ali, a left-leaning nationalist lawyer, would "not accept for a moment that the proprietary right in the land was ever given by the Permanent Settlement to the zamindars."[92] Abdur Rahim, a right-leaning lawyer and himself a zamindar, thought that Lord Cornwallis had been under the impress of "ideas of mediaeval England" when he unjustly raised zamindars from the status of "bailiffs for the collection of rent" to that of landlords. But even with the Permanent Settlement in place, he insisted, the zamindar could have no claim on either transfer fees or preemption when they possessed no interest in what was being transferred.[93] Fazlul Huq accused the zamindars of attempting to deprive tenants of "the most elementary proprietary right in the land." He reminded the Council that a full bench of the High Court had determined in 1865 that "the zamindars were not really the proprietors of the soil."[94] Kader Baksh attacked the very idea that rents should be subject to enhancement just because the price of grain might increase.

"Has the zamindar ever helped the raiyat in advancing the fertility of the soil? The rise, if any, is not due to any act undertaken by the landlord; why then should he get a share of it?" Azizul Haque, a lawyer with substantial landed interests of his own—and hardly a political firebrand—declared that "the proposition that the land belongs to the zamindars is entirely erroneous." It was "a legal myth, a historical myth, a fact which has no basis whatsoever."[95] He accepted that rent was legally subject to enhancement, but echoed Hollingbery in arguing that it had only become so in 1859.[96] Zamindars were "proprietors only to the extent of paying the revenue and not to the extent of extinguishing the rights of the people, who are actually the tillers of the soil."[97] As a result, if the land "belongs to the landlord, it also belongs to the tenant. . . . The tenants have as much right as the landlords, and anyone who wants to be the absolute proprietor of the soil is either a fool or does not know the history of this controversy."[98] He denounced the "present tenancy law" for taxing villages so hard that "the entire unearned increment goes to the landlords."[99] There can be little doubt that what he had in mind by "the history of the controversy" was precisely the debate that began with the Great Rent Case and culminated in the 1885 Tenancy Act.

The attack on zamindari could point in two quite different directions. The raiyat could be defended either as a rent-receiver or as a rent-payer. Where the Swarajists defended the raiyat's interest in the soil, it was primarily as a rent-receiver. Jogindra Chandra Chakravarti was quite clear that "raiyats as a class may not necessarily actually cultivate the soil, because we know that some raiyats have their lands cultivated by bhagchasis and bargadars [sharecroppers]." He went on to observe that, if it were argued as a consequence that, as the actual cultivators, sharecroppers were entitled to be recognized as the proprietors of the soil, "the raiyats would consider it to be disastrous to their interests."[100] Satyendranath Roy Choudhuri noted that the impulse to extend raiyat rights to include alienation of their holdings was in contradiction with the impulse to restrict their rights to resumption and reentry by extending rights of occupancy to under-raiyats.[101] As Jitendralal Bannerjee noted, to give under-raiyats occupancy rights was necessarily to deprive the raiyat of his preexisting occupancy right. That could only be a "barefaced measure of spoliation and expropriation."[102] Akhil Chandra Datta argued (dubiously, given the importance of sharecropping on demesne lands) that the question of the legal status of sharecroppers had little to do with the relations between zamindars and raiyats, but was essentially a question of a conflict of interest between raiyats and the sharecroppers who worked their lands. He denounced the recognition of sharecroppers as tenants as a flagrant disregard for "private property." In effect it represented "a confiscation of the property of the raiyats," who had invested their money in raiyati land on the "assurance that the law is there and that the bargadar is a mere labourer."[103]

The Swarajist radical, Jitendralal Bannerjee, did cross the floor to join the Muslim bloc in opposing the zamindar's right to preemption and to receive a fee on the transfer of occupancy holdings. When he denounced his own party for failing to live up to its own stated principles, however, he did so in the name of the right of the raiyat to the full value of his property. From this perspective, it was entirely consistent for him to oppose both the claims of sharecroppers *and* the claims of zamindars.[104] This becomes clearer still once one recognizes the kind of raiyat Bannerjee, and most other Swarajists, had in mind. The rent-receiving raiyat whose interest they defended was for them not primarily the "peasant" but the bhadralok. Thus Bannerjee declared himself sympathetic to the notion that the actual cultivator of the soil should be given the primary right in the soil. He was unable to understand though why, in the course of debates over the legal status of sharecroppers, "some of my friends should put an unduly narrow construction on what is meant by the expression 'cultivator of the soil.' Is only the cultivator of the soil the man who tills the soil with his own hands? Has the bhadralok agriculturist who invests money in land no place in the economy of things? And should not his rights be recognized as much as the right of the man who actually tills the soil?"[105] This was a point that had already been forcefully articulated by Akhil Chandra Datta, who had also taken it for granted that raiyati interests were generally acquired through purchase.[106] Amarendranath Ghose explained with some care that the term "landlord" should not be conflated with "zamindar," nor "tenant" with "peasant." Between "the opulent landlord and the poor peasant" stood "the middle class, which makes up the bulk of the nation."[107] Nalini Ranjan Sarkar would similarly call for the protection of "the landholding class which constitute the middle class" and which, despite their "pitiable condition," were responsible for holding "up the banner of culture in the villages."[108]

In contrast, the Muslim bloc sided overwhelmingly in all questions with the rent-payer, whether the rent-payer was the raiyat, the under-raiyat or the sharecropper. They did so on the basis of the oft-cited principle that the proprietary interest in the soil lay with the person who tilled it. In the debates of 1928, this principle was widely voiced by the Muslim bloc members. Abul Kasem, one of the earliest Muslim members of Congress and a founder in 1906 of the pro-Swadeshi and pro-Congress Bengal Presidency Mahommedan Association, complained that the discussion had so far been in terms "of zamindars, of tenants, of raiyats and under-raiyats." But he stood "only for the class of men who are the actual cultivators of the land. He is the man who earns, he is the man who produces wealth, and the rest live upon him. . . . I do not understand the intricacies of revenue law but I am interested in the actual tillers of the land. . . . You must remember the actual cultivators are the real people of Bengal and others are mere, if not interlopers, middlemen."[109] The policy of the Muslim bloc, Nurul Huq Choudhuri said, was "to give as much as possible to the actual cultivators," so that "there should be nothing in the Amending Bill which would prevent the actual and bona fide cultivator from acquiring land. . . . What we object to is that the land should be . . . in the hands of persons who will not cultivate with plough but want to cultivate with quill pen" and "want to cultivate through the bargadars."[110] Huq Chaudhuri was, like Kasem, objecting to the identification of raiyati as a tenure status attaching to the person, as a property in perpetuity, rather than as a status bound to actual cultivation.[111] Sir Abdur Rahim hitched this same impulse to the history of colonial legislation. He argued that the "principle underlying the whole Act [of 1885] is that the actual cultivator should have an interest in the land."[112] Azizul Haque made the same point more forcefully when he identified the Swarajist offensive against sharecroppers as the inauguration "of a new phase in the economic history of this country, namely, that the cultivator of the soil is not the actual owner of the soil."[113] In future, Haque prophesied, cultivation would more and more be in the hands of under-raiyats. He proposed to limit the power of raiyats to evict their tenants with a view to replacing them with sharecroppers, who had earlier in the debate been deprived of any status as tenants.[114] Ekramul Huq argued that the combination of the exclusion of sharecroppers from tenant status and the provision for landlord preemption guaranteed that sharecroppers would be the "real tillers of the soil" and "the actual producers of the wealth of the country." Yet they would perform this function as "serfs" and "slaves" rather than yeomen, "left to starve in their own country while they produce enough for themselves and many."[115] A proprietor of private lands was certainly entitled to cultivate them using hired labor. But he was not entitled to settle the land with cultivators who, because they sharecropped, lacked the status of tenants while the landlord himself sported the title of raiyat.[116]

Jogindranath Ray, a zamindar, was concerned that "the Communist spirit has been slowly creeping into our society." He took comfort in the belief that that "outlandish spirit" would find no home in Bengal.[117] To the Swarajist, Akhil Chandra Datta, the Muslim bloc proposal to establish the sharecropper in the legal status of a tenant amounted to "a revolution," though in his case it was the raiyats who stood to be effectively stripped of their proprietary rights. "If you want a Bolshevik legislation, have it by all means. . . . But if you want to have any regard for private property, you cannot rob people of their property."[118] In direct riposte to Datta, Asimuddin Ahamad charged, "on the contrary, that the present move to take away some sort of right to land which bargadars have obtained in some parts, is Bolshevik legislation."[119] Kasiruddin Ahamad would warn that a measure so baldly pro-landlord as the bill under discussion threatened "to bring about revolution among the tenants and will pave the way of Bolshevism in the near future."[120] Thus Nalini Ranjan Sarkar was clearly onto something when he noted that the Muslim bloc's endeavor to deprive the landlord of his interest in the unearned increment was something less than the nationalization of land "on the principle that there should be no property in land." Sarkar (presumably disingenuously) expressed sympathy for the proposition that expropriation of the unearned increment could be justified where "the benefit accrues to the entire nation." In the amendments under debate in 1928, however, "the zamindar is to be deprived of his rights, not on the ground that there should be no property in land but because another section of the people wants that right."[121]

It was clearly misleading of Sarkar to characterize the Muslim bloc as fixated on the interests of the "occupancy raiyats, comprising 30 per cent. of the population." He nonetheless put his finger on a more fundamental issue: they were mounting a *defense of property*. That defense was not, as Sarkar phrased it, simply one class's property claim being favored over another's. It was one *kind* of property claim being privileged over another. Whether phrased moderately or radically, the Muslim bloc's ostensible commitment to the rights of the actual tiller of the soil linked up to a set of usually implicit assumptions about the natural constitution of property. Abul Kasem complained that the zamindar "received the benefit of unearned increments," yet failed in their duty to provide "irrigation, embankments, and other things," and even harmed the fertility of the land by destroying irrigation reservoirs and obstructing drainage.[122] Asimuddin Ahamad declared that "the tenants are the true owners of the land because it is very often they who reclaim forests and render land fit for cultivation."[123] Kasiruddin Ahamad would reinforce the same point: "the lands belong to the tenants. It is the tenant who improves the land, manures it and irrigates it and does everything in fact for the improvement of the same. The zamindars have nothing to do with it. It escapes my imagination why a zamindar has been made a sharer of the value of the land."[124] That the property constituted through such productivity was more than either derivative or merely notional was demonstrated most strikingly and powerfully by Tamizuddin Khan. He noted that the value of a zamindar's interest in a bigha of raiyati land when sold at auction was likely to be considerably less than the amount he would receive in the form of his 25% salami in the event of that bigha being transferred between occupancy raiyats.[125] The value of the land as a source of zamindari rental income was considerably less than the value of the land as a productive instrument in the hands of capital and labor. This demonstrated that the raiyat's interest in the soil vastly exceeded any claim the zamindar could legitimately make to a property in it.

It was Abdul Karim Ghuznavi, another Mymensingh zamindar, who first introduced the figure of the moneylender as a device to defend the privileges of zamindari. "A wise and benevolent zamindar . . . can save [the tenantry] from the clutches and the cupidity of the ever devouring monsters in human shape, viz., the usurious mahajans." For this reason, he argued, giving raiyats power to freely transfer their holdings was ill advised. Such transfers would "gradually tend to reduce the raiyats into landless labourers," as the zamindar would no longer be able to act as a "safeguard for the raiyats vis-à-vis the money-lender and the land-grabber."[126] Provash Chunder Mitter defended the proposed right of preemption on the same basis. Since the future purchasers of raiyat holdings would probably be mostly moneylenders, the zamindar was far more likely to exercise his right of preemption against moneylenders and in favor of the raiyat, who would generally be resettled on the very land his debts had cost him.[127] The Swarajists also invoked the threat of the alien nonagriculturalist seizing land and reducing the peasantry to proletarian labor. Akhil Chandra Datta wanted to exclude "foreign capital" from "the domain of agriculture" by stipulating that "the tranferee must be a bona fide cultivator and not a capitalist or a company who invest money for the purpose of earning dividends and utilize hired or imported labour." He further wanted to require that the transferee be "a bona fide man of the locality."[128] Satyendranath Roy Choudhuri sought to limit the raiyat's right of free transfer to preclude the possibility of the raiyat being reduced to a landless laborer when such holdings fell gradually but inevitably into the hands of "non-agriculturalists, capitalist[s] and companies."[129]

Abul Kasem repudiated the charge that raiyats, who were the real producers of the nation's wealth, were incapable of managing their own affairs: "they have better sense" than to lose their lands to predatory moneylenders, and "can protect themselves." The right of transfer promised not that "the cultivators will be deprived of their lands," but that "the cultivator will get a better price than what he gets today."[130] Abdur Rahim identified the right of preemption as a mechanism for the gradual transfer of raiyati lands into the demesne of absentee landlords. It was preemption that would turn the "peasants of Bengal" into "mere serfs" and "day-labourers—mere coolies."[131] Yet the Muslim bloc were not unmoved by the Swarajist vision of moneylender predation. Syed Muhammad Atiqullah moved a motion to limit the transfer of occupancy rights to "bona fide agriculturists only," to protect credit-dependent cultivators from conniving moneylenders. He cited the Punjab Land Alienation Act of 1900 as an exemplary precedent.[132] Abul Kasem himself immediately seconded this proposal in the name of his interest in "our national wealth, in the productive powers of the land, and in the wellbeing of the tillers of the soil," which the Punjab act had so successfully promoted despite the opposition to it from "influential and educated" quarters. Besides the zamindar, Kasem noted, there was the "capitalist" and the "money-lender," who will be drawn by the simplification of the process for transferring occupancy rights to invest more heavily in them. "I would rather prefer the actual agriculturists remained under the zamindars than that they would be a tenant or a hireling or a serf of any money-lender."[133] Ekramul Huq identified a "conspiracy among the capitalists of this country to place all lands with zamindars and capitalists." These latter were possessed by a "land-hunger or earth-hunger" the result of whose free play would be that "lands will gradually pass away from the hands of the actual producers of the wealth of the country and will vest in persons who have absolutely nothing to do with it."[134] Tamizuddin Khan went further, arguing that far from exercising a "salutary check upon the transfer of occupancy holdings to non-agriculturists like

Marwaris, speculators and money-lenders," landlords preferred such tenants. Unlike poor raiyats, "the money-lender can and does invariably supply what alone the landlord cares for."[135] The right of preemption would encourage usufructuary mortgages to moneylenders who would cultivate holdings "by hired labourers." Upon the inevitable foreclosure of the mortgage, these creditors would then stand as "absolute masters of the lands."[136]

This concern about the threat of proletarianization mirrored the earlier elaboration of the liberal discourse of custom. As before it was an element in a larger civic discourse that continued the nineteenth-century liberal concern to ground liberal subjectivity in property. Abul Kasem insisted that it was "the actual cultivators" who were "the real people of Bengal," and not the rent-receiving classes, whom Amarendranath Ghose had identified as "the bulk of the nation" but whom Kasem identified merely as "middlemen."[137] Syed Nausher Ali identified the origins of "salami" in the ancient worship of the landlord "as a deity," and denounced it as such as "degrading," while Abdur Rahim called for those who "advocate the cause of freedom" in the Swarajya Party to "fight shy of any such mediaeval and barbarous custom as salami to the landlords."[138] "In every country in the world," Tamizuddin Khan noted, "labour is asserting itself and its star is on the ascension." Yet in Bengal, the extension of a right of preemption to landlords represented first and foremost the tightening of a "halter round the neck of sleeping, innocent and unsuspecting labour" that could culminate only in "the enslavement of the raiyat."[139] Azizul Haque linked the extension of the rights of cultivators to "the spirit of democracy which has come into the country. . . . The people are coming to know bit by bit their responsibilities and rights. . . . I believe we will find soon that the representatives of the people in this Council will be people looking after the interests of the tenantry in Bengal and not the interests of the zamindars, unlike as we find in the Swaraj Party which is composed to-day of a majority of landlords."[140] Tenancy legislation should be guided by the principle that "a free man ought not to be at the mercy of anybody, a free man should owe no master, but the law of his country and depend on nothing but his industry."[141] What all this clearly implied, in the context of the larger push that the Muslim bloc was making, was that such modern freedoms and rights could only exist in the context of recognizing the kind of property that "industry" constituted. The raiyat's interest in the soil was constituted outside of the political structure of revenue obligation through a history of labor invested in the soil. As such, it was the proper normative foundation of legitimate political and legal principles.

"The deputies of the peasants, who are in this House at this moment," Amarendranath Ghose noted of the Muslim bloc, "have, unfortunately, interests that differ from and sometimes clash with the interests of the people whom they represent. I am sure there is not one who has ever handled a sickle in his life."[142] The claim could hardly be gainsaid. Ekramul Huq noted that "out of 300 bighas [about 100

acres] 200 bighas of my best lands are with bargadars [sharecroppers]."[143] Fazlul
Huq put the point more sharply still:

> Not one of us is a cultivator or a son of a cultivator or a grandson of a cultivator. We
> are also small landlords, and although I do not like personal references, I do not use
> the language of vanity when I say that I myself am one of the voters in the landhold-
> ers' constituency of the Dacca Division for election of members to the Legislative
> Council. We have got our own rights at stake, and we understand our own responsi-
> bilities, but, Sir, our position is a most difficult one. We have come to this Council on
> the votes of the people, 95 per cent. of whom are raiyats and the position is this: that
> we must either take up their cause or we must resign our seats in this Council. We
> have got absolutely no business to remain here if we do not take up the cause of the
> countless millions who have trusted us with their votes in the hope that we shall put
> forward their point of view before this Council.[144]

We need not get stuck on the invocation of "countless millions" when just over
half a million Muslims province-wide had been eligible to vote in the Legislative
Council elections of 1926—that is, less than 2% of the Muslim population of Bengal.[145] The more important point is the recognition that the Muslim bloc was itself
composed of interests not so radically different from large sections of the Swarajya
Party. In other words, it was composed of rent-receivers. So the fact that the former
articulated a relatively consistent defense of the rent-payer, and claimed in doing
so to be representing the interests of a larger agrarian constituency, must surely
leave us wondering about their motivations for doing so.

One can isolate several plausible explanations, all of which might indeed have
purchase in different cases. Muslim members of the Council, like Fazlul Huq in the
above quote, might have been appealing to an alternative source of political legitimacy as a means of circumventing the stranglehold on institutional and organizational power held by a small number of Muslim families of aristocratic or quasi-
aristocratic standing, and by Calcutta itself as a closed shop of political networks.[146]
But to represent those mofussil districts in 1928 still meant to represent a very narrow electorate whose franchise was based on a property qualification. Thus we
might conclude that in turning their attention to the districts, Muslim members
were in effect trying to hitch their political aspirations to the rising star of the more
substantial and affluent jotedars, many of whom were indeed Muslim (even in
western Bengal). They might have embraced such jotedar interests for narrowly
instrumental reasons. They represented, after all, a formidable base with which to
combat the stranglehold on political, public and cultural influence possessed by a
common enemy, the respectable Hindu classes with deep ties to rent-receiving
interests. Such instrumentality might in turn often have been rooted in a politics
of self-interest, in which the primary goal was to consolidate one's own political
standing and to maximize one's share in the state's loaves and fishes. But it might
also have been rooted in other commitments of a more ethical nature. They might

have seen this as a means to defend Islam, whatever that might have meant to them. They might have seen it as a means to further the rightful interests of a "backward" community. They might have seen the rich jotedars as the dynamic engines of Muslim self-improvement, or of the region's economic renewal more generally. All of these are plausible, and none of them necessarily precludes the others.

What is more difficult to account for in such explanations, however, is the Muslim bloc's insistent defense, not merely of the raiyat, but of the rent-payer more generally. This defense embraced the under-raiyat and the sharecropper, two constituencies whose interests were at unambiguous odds with the interests of jotedars (and especially of rich jotedars), and whose electoral presence was nonexistent. In fact, the voting behavior of the renegade Swarajist, Jatindralal Bannerjee—against the rights of sharecroppers, but in favor of the rights of raiyats—would seem to have been far more consistent with this kind of interpretation than the voting pattern of the Muslim bloc itself.

Partha Chatterjee seems to have been one of the few advocates of an explanation in terms of jotedar interests who recognized this problem and offered a solution:

> Of the 21 members in the Muhammadan bloc, 17 were from the east and north Bengal districts. Their consistency in supporting the raiyat against the landlord is easily explained, for in eastern Bengal this meant supporting a relatively undifferentiated peasantry, predominantly Muslim, against the Hindu zamindar. And their support for the cause of sharecroppers and undertenants is also not difficult to explain, for given the agrarian structures in much of eastern Bengal such peasants with inferior tenancy rights, constituting in any case a very small part of the agricultural population, were mainly employed by zamindars and tenureholders on their *khas* [demesne] lands. The principal target of attack of the Muslim legislators was always the zamindar, and their support or opposition to various motions indicate an attempt to rally the entire peasantry against the zamindar. Indeed, these compulsions of electoral politics were so clear that even such illustrious members of the Anglo-Muslim social scene of Calcutta as Sir Abdur Rahim and Khwaja Nazimuddin spoke and voted on behalf of Bengal's oppressed tenantry.[147]

Chatterjee argued that the Muslim bloc's stand on agrarian issues fundamentally expressed the interests of rich jotedars in their struggle for control over agrarian society against zamindars. He further argued that this account of jotedar/zamindar conflict, as well as arguments about eastern Bengal's more homogeneous peasantry and their hostility to zamindar exactions, needed to be supplemented with a recognition of the dynamics specific to peasant structures of communal power. The crucial distinction between a jotedar moneylender and a Saha, Marwari or bhadralok moneylender was that the former was recognized as a member of the peasant community while the latter was not. Since the jotedar tended to be

Muslim, especially in eastern and northern Bengal, the specific form of such peasant consciousness functioned as a mechanism to convert peasant grievances into communal ones relatively blind to the internal class fractures of the village. When the "communal mode of power" was brought into articulation with the institutional dynamics of the colonial state, the result was the creation of a communalized politics.[148]

This explanation, however, has its own difficulties. To begin with, the "eastern Bengal" invoked in his calculation of subregional representation in the Council elides key distinctions. In the heartland of eastern Bengal, the cultivator-raiyat still predominated. In the southern and northern districts, however, jotedar-raiyats cultivating with sharecropping labor were common, and the contradiction between jotedar interests and the broader pro-rent-payer stance assumed by the Muslim bloc in the debates was most acute. (This remains a contradiction regardless of whether hired laborers were landless or merely possessed inadequate holdings, and of whether the substantial raiyat of the Sunderbans was like or unlike the jotedar of northern Bengal.) Consequently, we begin to see the force of Chatterjee's explanation significantly attenuated once we exclude the four members from Rangpur, Backarganj, and Khulna from his calculations, bringing the count down to thirteen out of twenty-one. It is attenuated again if we acknowledge the rise of affluent peasants deploying sharecroppers and hired laborers in places like Pabna, Bogra, Noakhali, Mymensingh and even Faridpur in the eastern Bengal heartland, and factor in their disproportionate political significance in a property-based rural franchise. And it is attenuated yet again if we give due weight to the energetic intellectual and rhetorical leadership in the debates provided by Azizul Haque from Nadia, Ekramul Huq from Mushidabad, and Abul Kasem from Burdwan, all three prominent advocates of the rent-payer rooted in central and western districts. It is far from clear why the Muslim bloc's strategy should have been thought capable of mobilizing "the entire peasantry against the zamindar" if its appeal was pitched directly at the level of the specific interests of the wealthiest segment of the peasantry, while their actual amendments specifically threatened to compromise the interests of the very jotedar-raiyats who apparently stood at the core of their political strategy. After all, these jotedars had proven perfectly articulate in their denunciation of the rights of under-raiyats and sharecroppers as contrary to their interests.

Still, I think that Chatterjee was fundamentally right to identify the Muslim bloc's efforts as "an attempt to rally the entire peasantry against the zamindar." He was also right to think that the larger agrarian political strategy to which the Muslim bloc was committing itself turned in part on cultivating the support of the wealthy jotedars. But the Muslim bloc appealed to wealthy jotedars through the invocation of an ideological framework that had emerged from agrarian society itself. They articulated jotedar interests in the much broader terms of a discourse of proprietary right, or *praja svatva*. The appeal to the property-constituting capacity of labor implicit in this drew on a political language that focused on a specific axis around which the affluent jotedar could distinguish the substantiality of his proprietary claim from the fictive claims of the zamindar. This was a politics that was no doubt rife with contradictions, insofar as it appealed to quite incompatible social interests. But all those interests were being championed in terms of a single and more or less consistent set of ideological premises. The Muslim bloc was therefore capable of articulating a remarkably univocal and formally consistent ideological framework as the basis for representing that multiplicity of interests. From this perspective, we cannot afford to ignore the fact that there was no chance of any substantial amendment from the Muslim side of the house actually being passed in the course of the 1928 session. As a result, once the party lines on the legislation had been established (that is, before anyone had even entered the chamber), the Muslim bloc actually was not jeopardizing any actual agrarian interests at all in championing the rent-payer. It was engaging in a pure act of political self-representation. In this sense, ideological consistency was far more important, practically speaking, than the contradictions among the interests being so championed.

The invocation of particular social interests in the demands of the Muslim bloc in 1928 turned crucially on ideological form rather than transparent representation. What mattered in the Muslim bloc's attempt to represent agrarian interests was not just the constituencies to which it was appealing, but also the fact that they construed those diverse interests consistently in terms of the property-constituting powers of labor. The ways in which the Muslim bloc construed the interests it claimed to represent did not achieve political purchase over constituencies merely because they appealed to specific interests. The sheer self-evidentness of the contradictions between these interests would render this a dubious strategy. The political purchase of this discourse depended rather on the fact that those constituencies were representing their own interests through appeals to the same sets of ideological presuppositions. The Muslim bloc members never explicitly identified the diverse rural interests it championed as "Muslim." This was an identification that operated only implicitly, insofar as the representation of those interests was itself communalized in the Council itself. But if we are to account for the identification of agrarian interests as "Muslim," this can be done from within the logic of the discourse of the Muslim cultivator. Whatever associations were set in motion by the broad correlation of Muslimness with the interests of rent-payers in the legislative debates of the 1920s could only have redounded upon associations already firmly established outside of that rarified forum—including by figures like Bhawali.

The arguments of the Muslim bloc thus sat at the intersection of two mutually reinforcing currents flowing since the nineteenth century: first, a colonial legal and political discourse of raiyat property; and second, an agrarian political mobilization in the name of the right of the cultivator-tenant to an interest in their holding. This was an intersection constituted by claims for the property-constituting capacity of labor. In this moment, we see the potential for both the major impulses of Muslim political mobilization that would develop in the subsequent decade. On the one hand, the identification of the property-constituting power of labor as the foundation of the rights of the rent-payer would lead directly into the organization of the Krishak-Praja Party. On the other hand, the alignment of Muslim representatives with the cause of the rent-payer amplified the power of the discourse of the Muslim cultivator to constantly pull the noncommunal politics of that organization in an identitarian direction. By the early 1940s, these two impulses in Bengali Muslim politics would ultimately resolve themselves into the leftist project of Pakistanism.

THE PROJA PARTY

The new impulse to orient Muslim political activity around agrarian issues emerged at a crucial moment in 1928. The defeat of the Muslim bloc in the legislative debates over the Bengal Tenancy Amendment bill of 1928 was soon followed by a similar, though less dramatically polarized, routing over the Bengal (Rural) Primary Education Bill the following year, with Abul Kasem arguing that it was appropriate for universal and compulsory primary education to be funded by zamindars, merchants and professionals "so long as the poor cultivators and day labourers have to pay for the higher education of the middle and higher classes" through their land taxes.[149] Such predictable defeats were not unproductive. Abdur Rahim had been working hard to produce a united Muslim front in the Council since 1925. The freedom given to the Muslim representatives by the overwhelming futility of their advocacy in the Council allowed them to develop for the first time a fully articulated, broadly shared ideological commitment whose relevance extended beyond the towns, where communal violence remained confined for the most part and where educated middle-class and upper-class Muslims were locked in competition with the Hindu bhadralok over the distribution of jobs, educational opportunities and political representation. On July 1, 1929, Muslim members of the Bengal Legislative Council, newly elected after a fresh round of elections, convened at the initiative of Abdur Rahim. At the suggestion of Azizul Haque, they formed the Bengal Muslim Council Association to represent Muslim interests generally. They also agreed, however, that membership of this organization would not preclude membership in other parties. At the same meeting, Fazlul Huq, Tamizuddin Khan and Shah Abdul Hamid led the charge for the foundation of a non-communal Proja Party. Fazlul Huq proposed a resolution that a Council Proja Party (soon renamed the Nikhil Banga Praja Samiti, or All Bengal Tenant

Association) be established as an organization to defend "the interests of tenants and labouring classes of the province." This party would be distinct from the Bengal Muslim Council Association, and would sit separately in the Council chamber. But it would be open to any of its members. Two-thirds of the newly elected Muslim representatives signed the Proja Party pledge to vote in accordance with the party majority in Council.[150]

These two overlapping organizations, and the increasing tensions between them, were the seeds from which the great currents of Bengali Muslim politics in the 1930s would flow. The rump of the Council ultimately transformed in the lead-up to the 1937 elections into the United Muslim Party (UMP). It was then quickly subsumed under the umbrella of the All India Muslim League in an act of self-abolition facilitated by Jinnah's allies in the non-Bengali business community in Calcutta. Meanwhile, the Proja Party developed its standing through annual proja conferences, rallying support through a platform of the abolition of zamindari without compensation and the mitigation of indebtedness. It successfully convinced all district-level proja organizations but one to enroll themselves as its local affiliates. It then transformed itself in the lead up to the 1937 elections into the Krishak Proja Party (KPP), campaigning on a platform of the abolition of zamindari, rent reduction, abolition of landlords' transfer fees and rights of preemption, regulation of interest rates, establishment of debt arbitration boards, river renewal, free and compulsory primary education, and Bengal's political independence.[151] The incorporation of the term *krishak* in the organization's name itself signified the extension of its political ambitions to incorporate sections of the peasantry beyond the pale of jotedari. This was a concession to the more radical voices in Tippera, Noakhali and Comilla who demanded that the unity of raiyati and the real "tiller of the soil" be maintained.[152]

In the context of an electoral system in which they were competing for votes in a separate Muslim electorate, the two parties turned their rhetoric not on the Congress, but on each other. Those from the Muslim bloc who moved rightward into the UMP dismissed the KPP as something less than "a purely Muslim organization" because it articulated its political agenda in economic terms. They sometimes even suggested that its efforts to set Muslims against each other on a class basis were secretly sponsored by Hindus in the Congress. Those who moved leftward into the KPP dismissed the UMP as a party ruled by a combination of provincial zamindari interests (symbolized by the Khawaja clan of Dhaka), and the interests of the non-Bengali Muslim business communities of Calcutta (symbolized by M. A. H. Ispahani, Jinnah's man in Bengal) who functioned as the link between the UMP and the central League organization.[153]

It would be easy enough, on the basis of these kinds of rhetoric, to see the UMP group as the expression of mobilization on the basis of community, and the KPP group as the expression of mobilization on the basis of class. But this short-circuits some of the complexities of the political dynamics involved. It is of course reasonable to be skeptical of the Muslim League's proclaimed commitment to proja interests in the 1937 campaign when it at the same time foreswore any interference in established property rights. Indeed, it allowed its deep commitment to precisely that principle to stand in the way of an electoral alliance with the KPP.[154] Yet already by 1937 several prominent advocates of proja interests had moved into the ranks of the UMP/Muslim League. Azizul Haque, the leading voice calling for Muslim unity in the Council in 1929, was also one of the most articulate and consistent advocates of agrarian reform in the legislatures of the 1920s and 1930s. Once elected to the Legislative Assembly, he quickly gave up his status as an independent and joined the Muslim League. Haque's interest in questions of communal representation, education and placement were decades old. "If ever a people stood in need of human sympathies and co-operation, of Government aid and patronage, it is we, the Musulmans of Bengal," he had declared in 1917. "Poor in education, shut out from all legitimate and noble vocations of life by force of circumstances and stress of competition and lastly reduced to the lowest stage of penury, we find ourselves hopelessly lost in the battle of life."[155] Yet when it came to agrarian issues, his voice was as consistently noncommunal as that of any representative in the KPP. In 1939, we find him observing that the "problem of 'Dal-Bhat,'" the key term of Fazlul Huq's election campaign as leader of the KPP in 1937 (referring to the supply of basic food needs), "is not a mere political phraseology; it is *the* problem for the Province."[156] Of course, Haque said this in the context of the ultimate formation of a KPP–Muslim League coalition ministry. But as we have seen, his commitment to the principles on which this sentiment was founded long preceded that conjuncture. Upon the formation of that coalition, he would play a crucial role as Speaker in shepherding the Bengal Tenancy Amendment Bill through the Legislative Assembly in 1937–38. Haque valued the jotedar as a smallholder who combined a primary reliance on family labor with "a species of ownership" that had gradually developed out an older occupancy right. It was that combination that had successfully (at least until the ravages of the Depression decade of the 1930s) kept at bay a collapse of rural society into "two distinct classes—the capitalist-farmer and the landless labourer."[157] This activation of the proletarianization anxiety as the basis of an anti-class language no doubt served to blunt the force of any contradiction between his espousal of agrarian reform and his alignment with an alliance for cross-class Muslim unity. That in turn left his dual commitment to both proja and Muslim causes as simply two distinct political fronts. If they could be confounded at all, that could surely only happen because of a sense that the Congress was acting as an instrument of landed interests, and that therefore Muslim solidarity was a condition for the effective championing of the agrarian cause. It was not on the basis of a conception of any more profound linkage between Muslimness and cultivation.

Conversely, the KPP's insistence on mounting a noncommunal case for agrarian reform should not be assumed to preclude a politics centered on the figure of the Muslim cultivator. The early role of Shah Abdul Hamid in the formation of the Proja Party in 1929, and his fidelity to the cause through the 1930s as a KPP legislator, should already sufficiently suggest as much. As we have seen, Hamid's commitments to the Muslim cultivator never entailed an exhaustive identification of Hindus as rent- and interest-receivers and Muslims as rent- and interest-payers. The secular language of rights at the core of this politics had its own intrinsic capacity to resonate with a politics of Muslimness in the countryside. The KPP was throughout its career overwhelmingly Muslim in both personnel and constituency: "We have kept the door open for Hindus to come in, because the problems with which we deal are all of provincial concern where united action by all sections seems to be essentially necessary," noted Fazlul Huq in 1936. "But as facts stand, the Hindus are practically non-existent in the Council of the Praja Party."[158] There was nothing in the party's program that would have failed to resonate and reinforce commitments to the Muslim cultivator. Even the very composition of its personnel, especially *despite* its noncommunal constitution, seemed to underline the profound association between cultivation and Muslimness. An assumption that the noncommunal stance of the KPP was somehow intrinsically in tension with Muslim politics is one that seems commonsensical in the context of the kind of attacks from the right that the KPP experienced. But that common sense only holds up when one assumes that the politics of Muslimness was coextensive with a politics of communal representation. This assumption of coextensivity, however, elides the "doubleness" of the concept of Muslimness available in the countryside. As a category operating primarily in the context of relationships between Muslim and non-Muslim communities, Muslimness did indeed stand in tension with the KPP's secular agenda. But as a category operating primarily in the context of a discourse of property, Muslimness was entirely commensurable with that secular agenda.

In 1929, Abul Mansur Ahmad had been one of those Muslim nationalists who had "abandoned the Congress and formed the Nikhil Banga Praja Samiti."[159] Having qualified as a pleader in 1929, Ahmad left his job as a journalist at a leading Muslim newspaper in Calcutta to set up a practice back in his home district of Mymensingh. There he launched himself into political activity. Having abandoned the Congress at the provincial level, he nonetheless remained active as vice-president of the district Congress. He was also secretary of the vibrant district proja society, and was involved in producing its weekly newssheet, *Chashi* (The Cultivator). Alongside these activities, he had risen rapidly in the ranks of the district Anjuman Islamia (Islamic Association), whose activity had been enormously enlivened by the realization that its "leaders would in the future wield greatly increased political power and stand the chance of gaining political prizes."[160] His difficulties resolving these multiple roles are suggestive.

Although there were many Muslim zamindars in the anjuman, most members were projas, and as such also more or less supported the proja movement. But all were uniformly hostile to the Congress. Having seen the popularity of the proja movement a number of Congress activists were backing the proja association. I called a conference of activists with the aim of organizing the proja association. The members of the anjuman advised me to call a conference of the Muslim activists. I tried to make them understand that in effect only Muslim activists would respond to my call. Even though the proja society was a non-communal organization, it was mainly made up of Muslims. It wasn't necessary to call a solely communal conference. Otherwise the proja association and the proja movement would be given a communal form. The anjumanis were not persuaded by this reasoning. They said, when the majority of projas are Muslim, and when the Hindus will not join the proja movement, then is it still necessary for the proja association to be non-communal in name? The simplest way to accomplish my goal would be to call a Muslim conference.[161]

The Muslim composition of the proja association was taken by those allied explicitly with a politics of Muslim unity to imply the futility and undesirability of maintaining the organization's communal neutrality. This very neutrality seemed to implicate proja activists as "agents of the Hindus" (*hindur dalal*) through their unsavory association with the Congress.[162] Advocates of Muslim unity thus sought to collapse the politics of the proja into the politics of Muslimness in a manner that subsumed the former into the framework of communal competition.

But for a proja activist like Ahmad, the Muslimness of the organization's composition, which its overt secularism only served to highlight, did not conflict with its noncommunal politics. What it did conflict with, though, was the (perceived) politics of the provincial Congress. For even after the Bengal Congress was captured in the later 1930s by its left wing, led by Sarat Chandra Bose, the memory of the 1928 debates would remain firmly in place. Bose's role in defending zamindari in 1928 could hardly have been forgotten. In any case, the leftists were deemed incapable of carrying their party with them on issues of agrarian reform. When the Huq ministry introduced the Bengal Tenancy Amendment Bill into the new Legislative Assembly in 1937, Sarat Bose's Congress criticized it from the left. They claimed it was overly wedded to the interests of the jotedar rentier, at the expense of the actual cultivator. That response seems to have been a strategy for containing the deepening tensions between the leftist and pro-rentier voices in the Congress.[163] As Amhad put it:

> Inevitably among the activists in the Congress of this district it was the Muslims who openly joined the proja movement. But those who were opposed to zamindari among the Hindu Congressites joined in establishing krishak and kishan [cultivator] associations instead of joining the proja association. Many of them condemned the proja movement of Bengal as a jotedar movement. As a simple fact there was much

truth in their accusation. But in my opinion their position was, for that time, ultra-leftism. Even if the ultra-leftism was not, in the communist language of the day, manifestly infantile leftism, they could indirectly harm the movement against the zamindars. My more serious concern was that some zamindar-supporting Congress leaders instigated this ultra-leftism with precisely this aim. I believe that the proja movement of that time was in its demands the popular movement appropriate to its time. . . . For this reason I was shunning the left wing and leading the proja movement. As a result the proja association of our district was in appearance a unanimously Muslim organization. From this perspective what my anjumani friends were saying was correct.[164]

Ahmad interpreted the Hindu (provincial) Congress, which "in practice and in principle was hostile to the proja movement," as a threat to his efforts on two fronts. Firstly, it was an instrument of rentier interests. Secondly, it was an instrument of political disruption from the left, a nefarious extension of those same rentier interests who advanced the claims of the sharecropper in order to delegitimize the claims of the proja.[165] If it became more difficult for Ahmad to maintain the compatibility of his politics of Muslimness with his commitment to a noncommunal organization espousing agrarian reform, it was in the face of his perception of the provincial Congress as a redoubt of hostile interests that were simultaneously rentier and Hindu. He would have entirely disassociated himself from the district Congress had his superior in the district proja association not forbidden it. When the anjuman called a rival conference on the same day as the proja conference, "I thought to myself, good. If the people from the mofussil come to their conference, then motions will be passed about the demands of the projas there too. As a result the two conferences will both effectively be proja conferences."[166] Ahmad thus anticipatorily drew the reader's attention to the vector of his own political trajectory in the early 1940s, when the two forms of politics would be synthesized under the banner of a left-leaning Muslim League.

Unsurprisingly given their role as vehicles of jotedar political organization, there can be little doubt that the anjumans of the Muslim-majority districts of Bengal had indeed assimilated the broad impulses of proja politics to a very large extent. In their submissions to the 1938 Bengal Land Revenue Commission (the so-called Floud Commission), the Dhaka District Muslim Federation, the Rajshahi Muhammadan Association, the Anjuman-i-Islamia of Mymensingh and the Anjuman Ettefaque-i-Islam of Nadia all broadly concurred on several of the basic presuppositions of proja politics: firstly, that the zamindars had been illegitimately raised to proprietorship from their proper station as revenue collectors by the permanent settlement; secondly, that before the permanent settlement, the cultivating raiyat was recognized as the true proprietor of the land; thirdly, that the zamindars had never contributed anything substantial to the improvement or extension of cultivation; fourthly, that such improvement and extension of cultivation was entirely to be attributed to the enterprise of raiyats; and fifthly, that the raiyat was therefore the only proper and legitimate claimant to a property in the soil.[167] At the more conservative end of the spectrum, the Dhaka District Muslim Federation made clear that its commitment to raiyat property precluded claims to state ownership. They rejected a proposal for the state to purchase zamindaris as a way to achieve a raiyatwari system as a dangerous expression of "[s]ocialistic ideas." In the same spirit, they also rejected restricting "occupancy rights to the tenants actually cultivating the soil" as detrimental to the "better class of tenants who are the backbone of the society."[168] At the more radical end of the spectrum, the same Mymensingh anjuman that had expelled Abul Mansur Ahmad was calling for the abolition of zamindari and of all intermediate tenures without compensation, the transfer of the zamindar's interest in the "unearned increment" to the state's coffers, the narrow restriction of occupancy rights to the "tenants actually cultivating the soil" (including sharecroppers), the forfeiture of occupancy rights when lands were sublet, and the reduction of rents to the levels that pertained in 1793 without any possibility of future enhancement.[169]

There was nothing to distinguish these kinds of positions from those enunciated by krishak-proja activists more generally. "History says . . . that the tillers of the soil are the proprietors of the soil, and even Governments are not declared by the law to have any proprietary rights in the soil," declared the KPP assemblyman, Abdul Latif Biswas, in the course of the protracted debates over the Bengal Tenancy Amendment Bill in 1937–38.[170] Shamsuddin Ahmed, leader of the dissident KPP representatives in the Legislative Assembly, called for an abolition of all mechanisms for rent enhancement and a further reduction of existing rates by 50%.[171] Tamizuddin Khan, another prominent dissident, complained of the bill that it gave "some valuable rights to raiyats with occupancy rights," but ignored the "under-raiyats who are also tillers of the soil."[172]

"We wholly disapprove of the substitution of the system of the temporary settlements in the place of the Permanent Settlement," declared the submission from the Bakarganj District Krishak Proja Party, a dissident branch of the KPP that, like so many others, had by 1938 "revolted" against Huq's official party and established itself as "an independent body." "We advocate the transference of permanency from the landlords to the tenants, real owners of the soil," whose "industry and hard labour and reclamation of waste and jungle lands" was solely responsible for the "increase in the rent roll of the permanently settled areas" since 1793.[173] They thus set themselves up in direct opposition to the conclusions that the majority of the Floud Commission would ultimately embrace. On a theoretical basis indistinguishable from that which had grounded the majority position articulated by Dampier and Field in the Rent Law Commission report of 1880, the Commission's majority report endorsed the fundamental raiyatwari commitment to the politically constituted nature of peasant property, expressed most succinctly in the claim that there "is no essential difference between land revenue and rent."[174] Only by maintaining the political nature of the chain of claims to the land, the report argued, was it possible to maintain the ongoing connection between cultivation and *praja svatva,* as prescribed by custom in Bengal.[175] In contrast, the Bakarganj Proja Party seemed to follow a Lockean impulse in insisting that that amounted to no recognition of property at all.

THE PROBLEM OF THE KRISHAK

But the Bakarganj Proja Party had its own instructive internal tensions. On the one hand, its spokesmen maintained that "cultivators may cultivate their own lands or may sublet them as they like partly or entirely having permanent unfettered rights to lands." On the other hand, they held that trade in lands was abhorrent because it led to the passing of lands into the hands of "non-agriculturists" and the gradual degeneration of the Bengal raiyats into a class of "landless labourers" and share-croppers deprived of rights.[176] That seemed confusing enough. Surely the cultivator who sublet all his lands was no longer an agriculturist? But the submission went a step further, recommending also the system of "nationalization of property and wealth of the country based on equal distribution on the co-operative principles."[177] This seemed to suggest that the only viable mechanism for guaranteeing an equitable distribution of access to environmental resources was through centralized state action. Without that state regulation, the labor-property nexus would seem destined to collapse just as the first contradiction seemed to imply. But to bring the state forward as the agent for maintaining this labor-property nexus seemed to bring one back to at least the essentials of a raiyatwari model—and then one was left with the question of what remained of property itself as a pre-political form grounded in labor. The simplest explanation for these kinds of contradictions is indeed the most likely: the document was the result of a compromise between different voices within the organization. Yet the dilemmas here were real and intransigent. In order to articulate a broad platform for the defense of property, the proja movement had to commensurate the claims of differently positioned claimants through the endorsement of labor's property-constituting powers. Yet in order to stand as a defense of property, in the face of land scarcity and rural immiseration, the proja movement had to reestablish a limitation on universal access to the soil, and so was inevitably faced with the impossibility of valuing all such claimants equally. At this point, the impulse to formally commensurate through an appeal to the property-constituting powers of labor necessarily confronted the substantial incommensurability of the interests thereby formally commensurated.

This was all made painfully clear in the course of the oral evidence presented by Syed Habibur Rahman and Syed Abdur Sattar on behalf of the Bakarganj Proja Party. Rahman "did not approve of State landlordism and would not have the whole province as a khas mahal [government estate]." He recommended the grant-ing of full rights of heritable property to the actual tiller, regardless of their status as raiyat or bargadar, and the permanent fixing of rent. He did this on the basis of an affirmation of the role of the "tenants" as the agents of jungle reclamation "by the sacrifice of their lives and labour." He sidestepped, however, the more basic problem of how a heritable property in land could stand as a solution to the ten-dency for property and labor to diverge. At the same time, he admitted that he himself held land as a zamindar, as an intermediary tenure holder, and as a raiyat. He further admitted that he "sometimes employs bargadars to cultivate his land. They pay him three-quarters of the crop and receive one-fourth. He would not propose that his own bargadars should be given occupancy rights." When the glar-ing inconsistency of his position was pointed out to him, he retreated to the varie-ties of custom in the countryside. Even though his own bargadars were cultivators who supplied their own seed and cattle, bargadars were only customarily entitled to rights in "western Bengal," not in Bakarganj.[178] To compound the embarrass-ment, Maulvi Abdus Sattar then confessed that he also "cultivates through barga-dars who receive one-fourth of the produce," who sometimes "supply seed and cattle," and who do "all the work of cultivation." He further admitted that such a bargadar "might not be able to live on" his quarter share.[179] The impulse to com-mensurate agrarian interests *formally* ran sharply up against the impossibility of commensurating those interests *substantially*. And at that point, the advocates of the Lockean discourse of property were faced with a sharp dilemma. They could either stand with the jotedar, or they could take a leap into radicalism.

The politics that was overtly "Muslim" in its identification tended to stick more closely to the claims of the jotedar. This should be no surprise. Firstly, the more affluent jotedars substantially expanded their power over agrarian relations over the course of the Depression decade, as the viability of more modest smallholdings (along with the bhadralok-led credit mechanisms that had underpinned them) began falling apart. In the process, they seized firm control over anjumans and proja associations, using them as vehicles for furthering their own political inter-ests. Secondly, the level of anxiety that was pervasive among less fortunate jotedars in the face of a prolonged collapse of prices and credit availability cannot have disposed them well to any threat to the market value of their holdings. Finally, the jotedar had already emerged in the 1920s as the quintessential embodiment of the Muslim cultivator in agrarian political discourse in eastern Bengal, providing pre-cisely the normative relationship between man and land that Muslim piety could intensify.

The hostility to socialism expressed by the Dhaka District Muslim Federation was also echoed by Azizul Haque, without implying any correlative hostility to "planned production and distribution."[180] This resonated in turn with the dynam-ics of representative politics. Sarat Chandra Bose had led a radicalization of the

Bengal Congress. This was the Congress's last hope of appealing to a constituency broader than the hopelessly outnumbered bhadralok, on the narrowness of whose interests the Congress (and he with it) had taken its stand in 1928. In the process, the left of the Congress undertook to assimilate wholesale the claims about the property-constituting powers of labor into Congress agrarian political discourse. Yet this strategy also served, as Abul Mansur Ahmad's recollections make clear, to reinforce the sense among Muslim activists that the Hindu Congress was implacably hostile to the proja movement. This reinforced not just the well-known opposition between Muslim rent- and interest-payer and Hindu rent- and interest-receiver, but also the perception of a double front (above and below) for the Muslim jotedar-proja.[181] The forces at work in the domain of a communalized representative politics thus tended to redound upon the narrowing of the identification of the Muslim cultivator with the jotedar. It also amplified a correlative hostility to the more radical trajectories of liberal discourses of property.

Those who embraced these more radical trajectories tended to be much less interested in a politics of Muslimness. The structure of this politics, under circumstances of land scarcity, simply had less room for the specific intervention that Muslimness offered. Its promise to intensify the proprietary relationship between the jotedar and his holding, and thereby produce affluence and independence, stood in sharp tension with the aspirations of cultivators who had no claim to a jote. If the claim of the krishak working under a proja was as important as the claim of the proja himself, then the political solution had to involve at least a partial critique of jotedari, the central organizing trope of the discourse of the Muslim cultivator.

Nonetheless, even the espousal of socialist transformation cannot be understood outside the larger framework of the discourse of property generally prevalent in agrarian society. We can see this quite clearly in the Memorandum submitted to the Floud Commission in 1939 by the Bengal Provincial Kisan Sabha, the communist-backed peasant organization that had established a foothold in Mymensingh in the course of sharecroppers' agitations in the later 1930s.[182] The Memorandum undertook what by now we must recognize as the rather conventional task of reconstructing the historical contours of proprietorship in Bengal. It argued that "the zamindars were not the original proprietors of land." It was the East India Company that had "set aside the immemorial custom of peasant proprietorship" and "substituted this custom by the theory of State-ownership," on which was implicitly founded the state's proclaimed right to recognize the zamindars as proprietors of the soil. Here, it should be noted, the zamindari system was portrayed as merely a variant on the raiyatwari model of politically constituted property, to which "a confusion . . . between *revenue* and *rent*" was fundamental. Against both was juxtaposed a pre-political peasant proprietorship grounded in custom.[183] The Kisan Sabha's suggestions proceeded from the normative standpoint of the latter—

that is, from the standpoint of the liberal discourse of custom. And when I say the liberal discourse of custom here, I mean it quite specifically. The Memorandum relied fundamentally on the authority of R. H. Hollingbery's *Zemindary Settlement of Bengal* to warrant its case. It cited Hollingbery extensively to establish its fundamental historical claims that "under Indian Tenurial Law, the soil belonged neither to the 'landlord' nor to the State; and it is therefore hard to see how either of these parties could have acquired a right to bestow the soil on the other."[184] Its fidelity to Hollingbery extended even to his argument that the Permanent Settlement was intended "to stabilize rents for ever, not merely to limit their growth;" and to his critique of the Rent Act of 1859 (to which was added a correlative critique of the Tenancy Act of 1885) for having given "legal sanction to relations and practices which had come into being extra-legally."[185]

Yet that was all largely background to the Kisan Sabha's most important criticism of colonial legislation:

> the most serious criticism of the Tenancy Act as a check upon enhancement is that it seeks to protect the occupancy raiyat as such. It gives virtually no protection to the non-occupancy raiyat nor does it provide any check on a raiyat losing his status of occupancy. In other words, the person whom the Act protects is a creature of status; the Act does not protect as such, the men who tills the soil [sic]. What has happened to-day in Bengal is that the man who has an occupancy right in the land no longer tills the land. He sublets it to a sub-raiyat, but he retains (to his advantage) all the rights of an occupancy raiyat. The sections of the Act which were meant to protect the cultivating peasant are now being used to protect a new type of landlord; the right of occupancy which were meant to save cultivator [sic] from unfair enhancements actually serve to enable petty landlord to rack-rent some one below him . . . The vital blunder was to choose a legal personality for protection under the Act.[186]

Here, of course, the Memorandum veered sharply away from Hollingbery. Yet it did so by insisting that the terms in which the liberal discourse of custom had been articulated had been inverted in their practical significance. If the raiyat was now the landlord, then labor was being robbed of its property-constituting capacity. This problem had become ever more urgent as rates of sharecropping continued to rise through the 1920s and 1930s. The sharecropper had "no rights or title in the land he tills" and so must be considered an example of a peasant who has been "to all intents and purposes driven from the land." Indeed, he had often lost to foreclosure rights over the very land he now cultivated as a sharecropper.[187] The problem, the Kisan Sabha effectively argued, was that singling out any particular class of persons for privileged terms of tenancy amounted to the creation of a property divide. Under circumstance of agrarian stress in the face of an intersection of economic crisis with population pressure on the land, that meant the extinction of the unity of labor and property through the law's inevitable reproduction of the very class division that the law was meant to mitigate.

The only viable path, the Kisan Sabha suggested, was a new and radical departure, a departure so dramatic that it would effectively abolish rent entirely. Proprietary rights would have to be extended to *all* tillers. "Rent must go. In place of rent we must have the agricultural tax," which would only be leviable "above a minimum income."[188] The Kisan Sabha was not, however, recommending the assertion of state proprietorship. It rather called for a "transfer of full rights of property to the individual cultivators," a restoration of peasant proprietorship that was in keeping with "the opinion of the overwhelming majority of the cultivators themselves."[189] Rent-receivers would be entitled to no compensation; subletting would imply an immediate loss of occupancy rights to the lessee; and sharecroppers would have to be recognized as tenants.[190] With this universal restitution of the unity of labor and property, peasants would in the face of their poverty readily allow themselves to be collectivized without any need for political coercion.[191] Only, in other words, by *universalizing* labor-constituted property would the *impossibility* of property be practically realized in the form of collectivization.

There was, needless to say, absolutely no room whatsoever in a vision of this kind for the discourse of Muslimness. The fundamental point of Muslimness in *Usman* had been to secure and intensify the proprietary relationship between jotedar and jote, a relationship constituted by labor. The entire point of the Kisan Sabha's program of extending proprietary rights to all tillers of the soil, and thereby strictly maintaining the unity of labor and property, was ultimately to abolish property. Property in the soil was now to be contingent on continued personal cultivation. Hence, in some fundamental sense, it was to become something more like the old Roman prescriptive right of occupation rather than a fully proprietary interest. Furthermore, if property was really constituted by labor, then property, under circumstances of the finite availability of land, was unfeasible. The property so constituted could not support the lives of those who cultivated it. Under such circumstances, the cultivator would have to turn to a higher form of collective farming.

SETTLER COLONIALISM?

The conflict between the politics of the Muslim jotedar and the politics of the krishak was driven by a conflict over entitlements to scarce land and resources. Correlatively, where natural barriers to the appropriation of land could be overcome, those tensions faded. Where the scarcity of land was imposed by directly political mechanisms, the conception of the Muslim cultivator could actually become a powerful element in krishak politics. For the clearest instance of this, we need merely follow the tracks of the Mymensingh peasants who followed the Brahmaputra Valley up into Assam. There uncultivated land was plentiful and cheap. Abdul Hai Bhawali had offered these emigrants as a monitory counterexample to the virtues and prosperity of Usman. But the entire constellation of ideologies of property-constituting labor and Muslimness would be rearticulated by these same land-hungry migrants themselves in the course of their politicization under the leadership of Maulana Abdul Hamid Khan Bhashani in the 1930s and 1940s.

Bhashani had been born in Sirajganj, a subdistrict of Pabna on the western shore of the Brahmaputra River that had been the center of the agrarian disturbances of the 1870s and would develop into a major node in the jute trade. After a brief stint at the famous Deoband madrasah, he began teaching primary school in Tangail, Mymensingh, just across the river from Sirajganj. There he apparently became involved in Congress nationalist politics, the Khilafat-Non-Cooperation agitation, and the early proja movements. By 1930, like many others, he had become sufficiently disillusioned with the Bengal Congress to switch his affiliation to the Muslim League. By the early 1930s, he had acquired a considerable reputation as an agrarian agitator. Without awaiting the sanction of the leaders of the Proja Party, he organized a stunningly successful proja conference in Sirajganj in December 1932. There proposals were passed representing "all the conventional demands of the cultivators and debtors' interests," including "the abolition of zamindari, the reduction of the rental rate, the prohibition of the landlord's transfer fee, the revocation of the zamindar's right of preemption, the fixation of the rate of mahajani interest, the proclamation of the illegality of compound interest, and so on."[192] But his reputation had also brought him enough unwelcome harassment from zamindars and the police that he followed the flow of migration out of Mymensingh upriver into Assam.[193]

The "Mymensinghias," as the Bengali immigrants were generally known (because of the notable prevalence of immigrants from Mymensingh), had not awaited Bhashani's permanent migration to become politicized. Proja meetings had been going on throughout the 1920s. It was apparently during an earlier visit to one of these, on Bhashanchar in 1924, that Abdul Hamid Khan had earned the nickname by which he would come to be generally known.[194] But Bhashani's career as one of the most important Bengali political leaders of post-Independence Pakistan, whose leadership was crucial both in toppling the government of Ayub Khan and in opening the political space for the emergence of Bangladesh, began with his rise as the foremost leader of these Mymensinghia colonists in Assam.

Having shifted his base to Assam, Bhashani settled on the char-lands of the Brahmaputra River. These were the shifting alluvial islands (chars) on which the Bengali colonies in Assam were centered. There he began working as a contracting agent organizing further settlement and reclamation of the still-extensive char wastelands. As Layli Uddin has noted, in doing so Bhashani was slotting himself into a role that was well established for an eastern-Bengali Muslim holy man, effectively reinstituting the very forms of social relationship that had given rise to the ax-and-plow associations of Islam in the deltaic regions in the first place.[195] Bengali immigrants had already by the 1930s transformed Assam through the extension of jute cultivation and the massive expansion of rice cultivation. But with the growth of their numbers compounding the difficulties posed by the endless mutability of the chars, they began pushing further up the valley and also inland.

Their early colonization of the char-lands had already brought the immigrants into (sometimes violent) conflict with the tribal groups that had previously inhabited them.[196] Their movement onto the mainland inhabited by Assamese, however, provoked a fully articulated political response. At a public meeting held in Guwahati in 1920, a resolution was passed that "this meeting views with alarm the grant of huge areas of wastelands to foreign capitalists and adventurers indiscriminately in different parts of Assam which has been detrimental to the interests of the *children of the soil* and strongly urges the government to grant lands to the bonafide Assamese applicants."[197] Soon after, in order to contain emerging conflicts over land control, the colonial government of Assam introduced the Line System to the large portion of Assam managed as *khas mahal* (government estates administered on raiyatwari principles). The Line System sought to delimit zones in which "the advancing hordes of the Mymensinghia army," the thousands of landless immigrants who flocked like "vultures" to wherever the "carcass" of "waste land" was to be found, could and could not hold land as tenants.[198] With the Line System firmly in place, though, the growth of the immigrant population outstripped the rate at which the government was making land available for settlement. This rendered the Line System an increasingly tangible obstacle to the aspirations of Mymensinghias. It became the object of enormous conflict as a result of its infringement and of its enforcement (notably in the form of evictions). This was the central theme of the Bengali-Muslim politics to which Bhashani lent his voice.[199]

Bhashani compared the exclusion of Bengali immigrants through the Line System to Hindu caste exclusion. But the exclusion invoked here was immediately linked not only to a problem of dignity and recognition, but also to the subsistence entitlements of those who labored as sharecroppers. "It will not do merely to open the door of the temple [i.e. to the Untouchable]—men need food, and clothing too."[200] The Bengali immigrant was deprived of means to fulfill these subsistence requirements adequately because the state had disallowed him from acquiring land. It thereby condemned him to labor on the land of Assamese projas as sharecroppers. Even as he thereby produced the wealth on which the state's revenues depended, he remained deprived of any right or even aspiration to property in the soil he cultivated. "The lease will be in the name of the Assamese; but the Bengali sharecroppers will be doing the cultivation. The sharecroppers are the ones who must pay the revenues. When the sharecroppers have purchased all this land [in proscribed transactions with Assamese] and established residences on it, then the government removes them by force." Yet, Bhashani noted, if the sharecroppers ceased to cultivate for the Assamese projas who held leases from the government, it would be impossible "for a handful of Assamese people to cultivate all these hundreds of thousands of acres."[201] The Bengalis were trapped in an insuperable dependence, whether on the Assamese projas or on fellow Muslim immigrants who sheltered them in their homes. "If the Bengali Hindu and Muslim cultivators still had land in Bengal, if they still had money—if they had any basis whatsoever for remaining in their own country, they would never have abandoned Bengal to come to the jungles of Assam." But having migrated to Assam, they found that even though "within the Line [i.e. on the Assamese side] much land has fallen into jungle," they were still not permitted to work it. The Bengali cultivator had already through his industry transformed the agriculture of the province. "If today they were able to get land and cultivate freely—if they could have land of their own," then Assam's revenues would be plentiful and the people would be prosperous. "If land were given to all the cultivators who had no land, they would be able to improve the condition of Assam."[202]

Debating a bill modeled on the 1938 Bengal Tenancy Amendment Bill and pertaining to Goalpara, a heavily colonized Assamese district under zamindari settlement, Bhashani sharpened the claims of labor to the soil. "[I]n an age where people all over the world long for freedom, the zamindars have bound hundreds of thousands of projas in the chains of slavery in such a way that they cannot present themselves as worthy of the name of man. Who is the real owner of the soil? Who freed this soil from the jungle? The cultivator, the proja. So the owner of the soil is the cultivator and the proja." Zamindars had been mere revenue collectors before the Permanent Settlement, but under colonial rule they were given proprietorship over the soil, the rights to enhance rents, even a right to a fee when the proja sold his holding. Yet it was the proja who had "provided for the improvement of the land through great hardship and toil" while the zamindar himself spent "not so much as a cowrie to increase the fertility of the soil."[203] Today's absentee zamindars no longer possessed even the paternalistic kindness of their forebears. "So I say they will have to give the proja complete independence. The proja has improved the soil through back-breaking labor. It is the proja who is the real owner and he should have full rights over the soil."[204] Such entitlements should not be limited only to "occupancy projas." Bhashani sought to radically extend the property-constituting claims of labor by arguing that "the government should show the same compassion towards all projas, whatever rights they may have, that is, whether they have occupancy rights or are korfas without occupancy rights, and so on. If the government really wants to help the projas at all, then they will have to give proprietary rights and every other kind of right alike to every class of proja."[205] Against the privileged claim of the "children of the soil," not merely to land already under cultivation, but also to future reclamations and extensive grazing lands,

Bhashani thus pitched a by now entirely familiar Lockeanism as the foundation for the claims of the Mymensinghia immigrants. In the process, he produced an uncanny subaltern echo of the ideology of settler colonialism. As Abul Kalam Shamsuddin, a prominent journalist and Muslim League activist from Mymensingh who had been invited to preside over a massive rally organized by Bhashani in 1946, would recall of the Mymensinghias years later: "As a result of their back-breaking labor, they cleared jungles that had been home to ferocious beasts and transformed them into places of human habitation. . . . Through their labor much of the uncultivated land in Assam became cultivable, and as a result revenues increased greatly. . . . Through backbreaking labor the migrants transformed this area from a great wasteland into land fit for cultivation"—until, that is, greedy Assamese landlords had conspired to use the colonial state to deprive them of the property they had thereby constituted.[206]

While speaking on behalf of Bengali colonists irrespective of religion, Bhashani nonetheless linked the politics of property to an invocation of the Bengali immigrant's Muslimness. Already in 1939 we find him reportedly declaring, in response to a government decision to begin evicting Bengalis without compensation from lands located within zones reserved for Assamese,

> I have lost my patience on account of the inhuman oppression carried on [against] the lakhs of poor Muhammadans of Assam by the Congress Government. Not only do I kick at the law by means of which the houses of the lakhs of people have been burnt down, I declare *Jehad* in the name of Allah. . . . It is not possible for the minority Mussalmans of Assam to end this oppression. It is not possible to solve this problem without resorting to *Jehad* for the sake of Allah. . . . The days have come now to get your demands fulfilled by becoming *Sahids* [martyrs] in the Path of Allah.[207]

By 1944, newly elected as President of the Assam Provincial Muslim League, he was publicly aligning the claims of settler colonialism with the demand for Pakistan. "The Muslim brethren of the twelve districts of Assam will assemble together in a grand conference and will adopt a resolution to establish Pakistan based on full independence. Except Pakistan there is no other means by which we can achieve our advancement."[208] In the face of the strength of Bhashani's following within the Assam Muslim League, Sir Saadullah, the patrician leader of the Assamese Muslims and the Chief Minister of a precarious League Ministry, was obliged to accommodate his vision of Pakistan as a homeland for the Muslim cultivator: "Let Assamese people learn the art of cultivation from you [Mymensinghias] and you too should learn what the Assamese people possess and in this way let us make Assam bigger."[209]

Bhashani's articulation of the property-constituting capacity of labor no more depended on an identification of the Bengali immigrant as Muslim than the wider discourse on which it was based. A minority of Bengali immigrants were low-caste

Hindus. In the end, Bhashani's invocation of the Muslimness of the immigrant never turned on the complete congruence of the categories "Muslim" and "immigrant." The invocation of Muslimness served only to reinforce rights of property that had already been constituted fundamentally on universal principles of natural law. Bhashani's embrace of the Pakistan demand emerged most urgently in the course of controversies over the eviction of Bengali immigrants from lands on the wrong side of the Line but on which they had already established homesteads. These evictions were themselves premised on a distinction between the rights of immigrants who had arrived before and after 1938, a distinction clearly intended to hinder the flow of further immigration into Assam.[210] Bhashani exhorted the evicted to return to their lands. "They will not abandon so much as an inch of the land that is their property."[211] It was not in his general claims for immigrants to have access to waste land that Bhashani most emphasized the Muslimness of the immigrants. It was rather at the moment when the connection between the cultivator and the land he had appropriated was under threat. That threat was not, as in Mymensingh itself, primarily manifested in terms of the threat of population density and uneconomical holdings, unsustainable levels of indebtedness, fluctuations in commodity prices and the availability of credit, or the precariousness of shifting deltaic islands and monsoon ecology. The impact of the Depression certainly registered among jute- and rice-growing cultivators in Assam, and the environment in Assam was hardly less unpredictable. But it was the *political* restriction of access to new lands that exacerbated the impact of these problems on the char-dwelling immigrants by concentrating a dense and vulnerable population. So the threat to the connection between the cultivator and the soil was posed by the colonial state itself, and by the Assamese governments that determined its policies.

That the obverse of restricting access to land was the potential availability of land for further appropriation meant, though, that Bhashani could mount a form of Muslim politics that was unriven by the internal tensions of its equivalent in eastern Bengal. In Mymensingh, the Muslimness of the jotedar implied a tension with the propertyless cultivator. On the contrary, Bhashani's sharecroppers were being deprived of their property-constituting capacities not by the property of other claimants to a natural property in the soil, but most immediately by the state. Of course, Assamese also appealed to proprietorship as children of the soil. But such claims did not depend on cultivation, and extended over lands left uncultivated. They therefore did not provoke the same kinds of contradictions. In this situation, the Muslimness of the immigrant cultivator could be activated in its long-standing function of intensifying and sustaining the connection between the cultivator and the soil without recourse to demarcating the limits of its primary constituency to the jotedar. Furthermore, it could do so in a directly political context where that connection was to be maintained in the face of a state policy of exclusion that was associated simultaneously with British colonialism, with the (allegedly) anti-Muslim policies of the Congress, and with Assamese nativism.[212] These were all understood to be instances of the same kind of politically consti- tuted property based on the expropriation of natural property that the figure of the zamindar had represented in the liberal discourse of custom since the 1860s and in the discourse of the Muslim cultivator since the 1920s. Bhashani fought hard for the inclusion of Assam in an envisaged eastern Pakistan. Assam's expanding fron- tier of reclaimable land was a crucial precondition for his peculiar combination of Muslim and leftist-agrarian politics, in which a form of self-determination based on the property-constituting powers of labor was identified with a peculiarly Mus- lim inability "to accept servitude."[213] The radicalism of Bhashani's articulation of an agrarian politics that was nonetheless Muslim would have been much harder to articulate back in Mymensingh, where for Bhawali landlessness and emigration had been the quintessential indices of Muslim moral failure.

Many years later, Bhashani would recall a meeting in 1946 with the chain-smok- ing radical North Indian alim, Azad Subhani. Subhani had asked Bhashani to take an oath that "you will struggle for the foundation of government by human beings acting as God's agents [*hukumate rabbaniya kayemer laksye*]." Bhashani would embrace Subhani's conception of *rabbaniya* as those spiritual qualities whose culti- vation would allow men to serve as the delegated agents of God's will. It was God's divine qualities (*rabbiyyat* or *rububiyyat*) that underpinned the preservation and evolution of the world through a natural law that moved creation gradually towards perfection. Man assumed this role according to Subhani when he lived in harmony with the laws of nature, through which God manifested the perfection of his will.[214] Bhashani of course took the oath as invited. "I have held to that path since 1921." For Bhashani as for Subhani, the doctrine of *rabbaniya* implied the equality of all men. That equality in turn presumed the need to subordinate selfishness to the common good. "I keep saying, the ownership of all wealth belongs only to Allah. Man is merely its custodian. Therefore all the wealth of the state must be distributed pro- portionately on the basis of need, and private property must be abolished, in the name of Allah."[215] The evidentiary force of a recollection composed twenty-seven years later and in the context of Bhashani founding the Hukumat-e-Rabbaniya Society is hardly overwhelming. But what this story does indicate is the general trajectory of Bhashani's movement towards self-conscious socialism. It thus high- lights its profound similarities with the intellectual trajectory charted by the Kisan Sabha's radicalization of the discourse of property into a program for the abolition of property. Bhashani was able to keep together the radicalizing impulse of the unity of labor and property with an explicitly Islamist politics. "When I talk about God's governance [*hukumate rabbubiya*] not only do the communist and leftist political thinkers oppose me, but at the same time the right-wing ulema and big- oted political thinkers [he clearly means his right-wing Islamist nemesis, Maududi[216]] bring forth furious objections . . . The communists do indeed want to abolish private property, but in their opinion this must happen not in the name of Allah but in the name of the state. The ulema do indeed respect Allah's ownership over everything, but they don't want to abolish private property."[217] The basic trajectory of this kind of leftist Islamism was forged in the peculiar political context of Assam.

THE MUSLIM LEAGUE LEFT

Bhashani was not Subhani's only prominent disciple in Bengal. The other was Abul Hashim, the son of the famous Swadeshist and Khilafatist, Abul Kasem of Burdwan. Hashim had been raised out of obscurity by his unexpected election as General Secretary of the Bengal Provincial Muslim League in 1943. By his own account, it had been Subhani who had urged him to stand for the position.[218] Hashim had immediately begun transforming the party organization. First, he established functional local branches. Second, he instituted on the basis of these branches an effective electoral process for determining office-holding within the League. Third, he used this process of democratization to fracture the stranglehold that notable families, especially the Khawajas of Dhaka, had had over the organization. Fourth, he thereby opened the space for leftist voices in the League to assert themselves more strongly. Those left-leaning voices had been steadily drifting into the League over the course of the late 1930s and early 1940s. As the provincial Congress drifted into crisis, Fazlul Huq formed a ministry that produced a coalition between the KPP and the Muslim League. Huq formally joined the League in 1937, assumed the presidency of its Provincial organization, and personally moved the Pakistan Resolution at the Lahore annual meeting in 1940. He thus lent the League legitimacy among Bengal's rural voters. At the same time, Huq's political maneuvering had generated considerable disaffection, and gradual defection, among those with more radical aspirations for agrarian reforms. He also alienated those without the stomach for the audacious compromises he embraced in order to stay in power. The most unpalatable of these was no doubt the inclusion of Shyam Prasad Mukherjee, leader of the Hindu Mahasabha, in his cabinet in 1941. The Bengal Congress took a sharp turn to the right after the expulsion of the Bose faction in 1939. Jinnah's efforts to negotiate a final political settlement at the center began assuming increasing importance. The Muslim League began to seem like an increasingly attractive redoubt for Muslim leftists set adrift by the collapse of their own movement.[219] In this sense, Abul Hashim's rise in the party organization reflected a broader shift in the constituency of the provincial League. This shift was indisputably crucial to the broad-based enthusiasm in agrarian areas for the League's Pakistan demand in the 1940s.

But unlike Bhashani, and despite his father's deep involvement in the 1928 legislative debates, there is little reason to think that Hashim's leftism was deeply rooted in agrarian struggles over property. He was a lawyer from a landholding family in the western district of Burdwan whose Khilafatist connections to the North Indian ulema were seemingly grounded in much older connections that had also underpinned the spread of the Mahommadi movement in that district in the nineteenth century.[220] In 1937 he was elected to the new Legislative Assembly as an independent—which is as much as to say, on the basis of his father's reputation. He soon affiliated himself, however, with the Muslim League. Proja political organization was taking place in Burdwan at this time. He himself later recalled "a conference of the peasantry of Burdwan" in 1937. When the gentry of the district argued over the responsibilities of landholders at "a conference of the Muslim leaders of the district" that same year, a debate ensued over whether the costs for canal construction should fall on zamindars as a consequence of their responsibilities under the terms of the Permanent Settlement, or on tenants.[221] Whatever sympathies Hashim may have had for peasant aspirations at this time, however, they seem to have been framed in a distinctly paternalistic form. In that same year, we find Hashim completely deaf to the politics of proja property in the course of the legislative debates over the Bengal Tenancy Amendment Bill. He declared himself convinced in principle of the justice of rental enhancements. If he supported a moratorium on enhancement, it was not because "there is no just cause for it, but on the ground of hardship. . . . [W]e propose to stop the enhancement as a temporary measure."[222] These were hardly words to fire any proja activist with enthusiasm. "There is a good deal of difference between caste Hindu landlords and Muhammadan landlords like the Nawab Bahadur of Dacca," he argued (an example he no doubt would have least cared to reminisce about in his reminiscences). Throughout British rule it had been "the caste Hindus who have been exploiting the Muhammadan masses," not the good Muslim landlords who ran the League.[223] He declared that "the landlords cannot think of anything else except taking as much money as they can . . . from the tenants. . . . [T]he landlords have completely lost their social utility," which had depended on their paternalistic care for their projas. Apparently confusing the politics of raiyatwari for the peasant politics of property, he called for "a new order of things under which the tenants may be under the direct control of the Government themselves."[224]

Nonetheless, it was in the end Abul Hashim who effected the most dramatic opening of the Bengal League to the aspirations of peasant politics. He drafted a manifesto with the help of "a very efficient young [Hindu] communist," and published it in the *Star of India* in 1945 under the title, "Free Pakistan in Free India." There he boldly announced the Bengal Provincial Muslim League's commitment to the "realization of complete independence for the whole of India together with the achievement of Pakistan for the Muslims in the country." Pakistan would be a "democratic state in areas where the Muslims constitute the majority." He also announced its "complete solidarity," as a part of the global "struggle for freedom," with "the freedom movements of the oppressed peoples all over the world." In the quest for a "democratic reconstruction of society," he acknowledged that "vested interests whether on land or in capital have to be rigidly controlled." Meanwhile, the state would have to "guarantee work for all able-bodied persons," to which was added the provocative proposition that "[a]ll toilers shall have the right to the enjoyment of the full fruits of their labour." In the context of the colonial politics of the 1940s, this apparently implied in more pragmatic terms mainly basic progressive commitments such as "guaranteed minimum living wages," eight-hour workdays, unemployment insurance, and the right to organize. But writing in the immediate shadow of the massive famine of the early 1940s, Hashim went much further in relation to the peasants:

> All rent receiving interest in land shall be abolished. . . . All existing monopolies particularly in jute shall be forthwith abolished. . . . The interest of the peasants shall be protected and all rents shall be standardized and all forms of inequitous [sic] impositions and levies shall be abolished. The State shall encourage co-operative farming and co-operative marketing, so that the peasant may be guaranteed fair price for agricultural produce. . . . [T]he resuscitation of dying rivers . . . will help to bring large tracts under cultivation. . . . Permanent Zamindary settlement shall be forthwith abolished and agriculture rescued from being an uneconomic occupation.[225]

This was an agenda that was certainly far from anything that Jinnah had in mind! It is not hard to see how it could be interpreted to mean that the Muslim League's demand for Pakistan, inspired as it was by "the gospel of Freedom and Equality that Islam preaches to all its followers," represented a promise to fulfill the demands voiced by the agrarian politics of property. And it is also not hard to see that the plausibility of its subsumption of these demands to the concern for Muslim self-determination required little additional elaboration in the context of the agrarian discourse of the Muslim cultivator. If Pakistan was the completion of the Muslim demand for self-determination, in agrarian Bengal this could not help but imply the intensification of the labor-property nexus. By the time Hashim was writing these word with the help of his "very efficient young communist," he was merely incorporating a well-established constellation of associations between Muslimness and peasant property into a broad progressive platform. In the process, he made a major contribution to the realization of a partition settlement that he ultimately abhorred for its division of Bengal. Furthermore, he did so on the basis of policies and principles that Jinnah, the architect of the Pakistan demand, abhorred.

Still, Hashim's ambivalence towards the "Bengali Muslim," as a figure that united laboring activity with property, remained to the end. If we think back to Bhawali, the truest Bengali was a proja, and the truest proja was a Muslim, because it was the Muslim who most successfully united labor and property. From this perspective, his championing of the Islamic reform of everyday practices turned on an attempt to fulfill the Bengali Muslimness of the Bengali Muslim. Hashim is nothing if not famous for his regional patriotism as a Bengali. He was a key supporter of the futile last-minute United Bengal scheme of 1947.[226] Nonetheless, his Islamism assumed no such mutually reinforcing intimacy between Islamic reform and Bengali Muslimness. Abul Mansur Ahmad would recall years later a conversation he had had with Hashim, whom he admired enormously and with whom he felt a close intellectual bond. "Although we agree on almost everything, where we differ slightly is over a certain basic principle, as a result of which you and I will never be able to agree. Do you know what it is? . . . . You love Islam, I love Muslims." Hashim reportedly thought about this for a few days before answering: "It's not just that I don't love Muslims, I hate them." Ahmad replied: "Then that means that you love the medicine, but you hate the patient." To this Hashim responded: "How shall I not hate a patient who adulterates a medicine as valuable as Islam?" Ahmad pressed his point: "The sign of whether a medicine is valuable or not is whether it cures the disease." After a brief pause, Hashim asked, "Is it the fault of the medicine if it does not cure the disease of a crazy patient who takes adulterated medicine?"[227]

This conception of the sick Muslim of Bengal was a notion with a long pedigree among the ashraf Muslims of the cities and of North India. But it sits in very strange juxtaposition with the Bengali nationalism that he inherited from his Swadeshist father, and that rested on memories of the Bengal Pact and on the celebration of syncretism. "Hindus and Muslims of Bengal," he declared in 1947, in futile protest against the impending partition of the province, "preserving their respective entities had by their joint efforts, in perfect harmony with the nature and climatic influence of their soil developed a wonderful common culture and tradition."[228] Judging from the way in which Hashim would go on to invoke parallels with Vedantic philosophy in his major theological work of 1950, *The Creed of Islam*, the "common culture" invoked here seems to have been pointing to a much more rarified domain of cultural production, against which the syncretic "culture" of the Bengali-Muslim peasant (as indeed the idolatrous polytheism of the Hindu peasant) could only have been found disappointing. Indeed, there is much in that work that mirrors developments in post-Swadeshi thought in ways that seem strikingly atypical of the major currents of Bengali Muslim thought.[229] Whatever the sources and motivations of Hashim's Bengali nationalism and of his Islamic reformism, neither seems to have been closely bound to the discourses of either proja property or the Muslim cultivator. Yet these were the ideological frameworks that provided the popular energy fueling the rural popularity of the Pakistan demand as the vehicle of peasant aspirations. No wonder his moment of political prominence was so brief. No wonder he was not to share the enormous political significance that Bhashani would enjoy in the post-Independence era.

LIBERALISM?

I began this chapter with a detailed discussion of the discourse of the Muslim cultivator. Read in terms of its immediate content, the combined emphasis on practices of everyday piety and savvy commerce that characterized this discourse has little to do with the history of liberalism. Indeed, in some very real sense it would be absurd to characterize it as a form of liberalism. It speaks not primarily to the value or meaning of liberal norms, but rather to a set of normatively extraneous practices centered on the cultivation of a worldly asceticism. Yet if what I have argued is correct, then we must recognize that a crucial context for the ubiquitous invocation of the pious reform of everyday habits was a claim to property founded on labor. While the content of this discourse was in no obvious sense liberal, it was only in its relationship to broadly liberal commitments to the pre-political normative status of property constituted by labor that the urgency of piety assumed its force and meaning. The purpose of piety, from the perspective of this discourse, was participation in liberal social institutions in a period of increasing vulnerability. What that means, among other things, is that the practical entailments of liberal commitments do not *necessarily* have to be very liberal at all, without being for that reason any the less entailments of such commitments.

In the introduction to this book, I invoked the idea that political economic abstractions take their force not merely from an elision of concrete institutional entailments, but also from the capacity of those abstractions to grasp social relationships of interdependence that in modern capitalist society are themselves abstract.[230] The figure of the Muslim cultivator discussed in this chapter in some sense undoes the very distinction posed there. The invocation of Muslim piety as the ethical grounding for viable participation in a society of property holders represents the elaboration of a set of concrete practical entailments acting as a necessary supplement to abstract social relationships. Yet the figure of the Bengali Muslim that emerges from this discourse is incomprehensible outside of the kinds of abstraction that political economy names, even if it is irreducible to them. One cannot properly say what a Bengali Muslim is in the context of the political arguments of the 1930s and 1940s without invoking political economic abstractions. We should recognize just how strange that is. After all, it is very easy, in the abstract, to grasp the meaning of the identitarian category, "Bengali Muslim," simply as the intersection of linguistic and religious identifications. Yet such a general characterization would leave us far short of the full range of determinations necessary to grasp the specific meaning of that category in the discourse of the Muslim cultivator or in the discourse of Pakistanism that prevailed in rural Bengal. What this shows us is that the history of political economic abstractions, and the political theoretical abstractions with which they are so intimately connected (the property holding subject of civil society), can saturate fields of discourse that seem to have very little to do with them, including abstractions like "Bengali Muslim" that are not in any obvious sense "political-economic" abstractions.

Uday Mehta has argued that liberal abstractions are premised on the erasure of concrete institutional entailments fundamentally indifferent to liberal norms. Yet in the case discussed in this chapter, the relationship between concrete and abstract would appear to be inverted. Muslim piety involves a set of everyday practices that is foregrounded, while the abstract social relationships that render those practices meaningful (in the terms of this particular discourse) are taken for granted. It would seem in this case that the practices of piety were the concrete entailments of liberal abstraction rather than vice versa, as in Mehta's account. Indeed, concrete practices did not seem to function primarily as a limit to the exorbitant freedoms threatened by liberal abstractions. They appear to have been offered as the means to make possible an aspiration to participate in liberal normative institutions, especially under conditions of deepening social crisis. To the extent that we can understand the discourse of the Muslim cultivator as inhabiting the space of liberal norms, we would have to say that the specific power that this concept of Muslimness carried was dependent on political-economic and political-theoretical abstractions rather than vice versa.

Finally, what that in turn implies is that the history of liberal thought is expansive in a way that few political theorists and intellectual historians have really contemplated. It is of course expansive in terms of a fuzzily bounded aggregation of discrete arguments capable of coming together in mutually exclusionary constellations. This is the specific kind of expansiveness with which political theorists and historians have been much preoccupied. It is also expansive, as C. A. Bayly has recently argued, in the sense that specific liberal texts and arguments have traveled across wide geographies, so that liberalism came to be rooted in diverse social and cultural contexts. But it is *also* expansive insofar as the basic conceptual terrain that liberalism has occupied was always potentially one that was lived practically in the forms of abstract interdependence characteristic of modern capitalist society. That means that the history of liberalism must be imagined on a vastly greater scale. It means that the history of liberalism exceeds even the more ambitious undertakings of historians of traveling concepts and non-Western intellectual histories. If the potentialities, the pragmatics, the historicity and the normative structure of liberalism are to be grasped, and perhaps even judged, that can only be done after we have recognized and overcome the narrowness of what we currently construe as the history of liberal thought. In this sense, the history of a vernacular liberalism of the kind I have described in nineteenth- and twentieth-century Bengal should not be mistaken for a secondary supplement to the history of liberalism. It is this very history that challenges us to rethink just what a history of liberalism needs to be. And what that history needs to be is a global intellectual history. I don't mean this primarily in the sense of global connectedness, but in the sense that liberal ideas have been bound inextricably to practices of social abstraction. This is not to say that social abstraction (let alone liberal thought!) is evenly or identically significant always and everywhere, even in the epoch of modern capitalism. It is to say, however, that the problem of liberal abstraction—its irreducibility to ecologies of concrete institutional entailments—means that the history of liberal thought might be found in many more archives than those in which we are accustomed to searching, and in many more political imaginations than we might easily anticipate.[231]

Conclusion

Political Economy, Liberalism, and
the History of Capital

Why focus on the history of arguments about labor's capacity to create property in a place like colonial rural Bengal? There is little reason to think that this was in any sense the most pressing preoccupation of those we generally identify as liberal thinkers in the later nineteenth or early twentieth centuries. Indeed, stated in that bald form, it is a proposition that many of the best-known liberal thinkers of that period would have repudiated. Approaching the history of liberalism primarily in terms of this one theme may seem capricious given the remarkable diversity of arguments that have traveled under the mantle of "liberalism," as well as the apparent marginality of Locke's argument about property to political thought in the very century when liberalism emerged as a self-conscious political position. Yet if the normative force of liberal arguments is bound to practices of commodity exchange, then the theory of labor's property-constituting capacity is not so easily banished from liberal thought.

It has never been my intention to treat liberalism as necessarily characterized or motivated by a commitment to the property-constituting capacity of labor. Liberalism, as a bundle of arguments whose normative premises are bound to practices of abstract interdependence in capitalist society, was generative of contradictory trajectories. These different vectors were bound inextricably to each other in ways that rendered it exceedingly difficult even for forms of liberalism intent on shedding or forgetting claims about the property-constituting powers of labor to banish entirely the specter of Lockeanism. In this sense, I have treated liberalism as something more than a single coherent body of theoretical doctrine, and something less than a diversity of discrete arguments bound together by loose family resemblances. I approach liberalism as contradictory in a generative way, a field of irresolvable contestation rather than one of peaceable consensus. This has allowed me to treat fields of political discourse that normally fall to the margins of histories of liberalism as in fact crucial to the unfolding of liberal arguments in the nine-teenth- and twentieth-century British imperial world. And while I have treated the history of liberalism as bound to the history of capitalism, I have argued that liberal thought *for this very reason* has been generative of critiques of both capital-ism and empire, albeit in crucially ambivalent ways. These are dimensions of the history of liberalism that do not come easily to presentist historians anxious to narrate the prehistories of neoliberalism. Yet, I contend, recognizing these dimen-sions is key not only to a richer understanding of the history of the agrarian question in twentieth-century Bengal (and beyond), but also to a more reflexive approach to both the epistemological and normative foundations of historical inquiries into these issues.

The Victorian-era experience of nonwhite empire has most often been under-stood as generative of metropolitan reaction. Such accounts certainly capture an unquestionably consequential dynamic of later nineteenth-century British impe-rial rule. This is also the dynamic that is most immediately visible in the canonical literature of Victorian political thought about empire. Yet it does not exhaust the dynamics of that period of crisis in liberal thinking. The intersection of proletari-anization and democratization in the metropole presented an irresolvable dilemma to a political theory that posited individual property as a foundation of political personality. One simple resolution of this problem might seem to have been to embrace the universal self-ownership implicit in the commodification of labor. But how to do that without endorsing the forms of collective politics characteristic of the labor organizations through which the recognition of such self-ownership had been demanded and whose compatibility with liberal polity seemed unclear? Many possible paths forward were charted in this generative period of crisis, many rightward but some also leftward.

Not least significant among arguments that sought to renew liberalism through radicalization was an impulse to extend rights of property more broadly through-out society, thereby undoing the polarization of capital and labor and renewing the foundations of liberal political personality. In the metropole itself, such arguments were mostly fanciful, like the idea of providing industrial workers with garden plots. In those colonies where peasant agriculture still predominated, however, these arguments could find more plausible traction—although always in the face of formidable alternative liberal arguments in favor of the developmental desira-bility of proletarian labor and the sanctity of existing proprietary claims. In India and Ireland, liberals committed to broadening the base of property holding could focus their energies on the restoration and extension of the rights of smallholders. They understood smallholding property to be grounded in the natural rights of labor. These rights were in turn construed through the discourse of political economy, the heir of the Lockean theory of property. Seen from this perspective, the political vector represented by the liberal discourse of custom is best understood in terms of an expansively radicalizing impulse in later nineteenth-century liberalism, rather than in terms of the kind of contractive reaction represented most famously by Henry Maine. Furthermore, the politics of this liberal political project cannot be adequately understood through a conventional and limited sociology of colonial power. The liberal discourse of custom was no doubt a project linked to the consolidation and extension of colonial state power in the 1860s, 1870s and 1880s. The occasion for political intervention was provided by concerns about securing government revenue streams and consolidating a post-Mutiny political order in the face of rural unrest and legal unclarity. Yet the ideological impulse that drove this liberal project forward was not directly constituted at the interface of colonizer and colonized, ruler and ruled, European and other. From this perspective it is significant that, while endorsing British rule over India, exponents of the liberal discourse of custom nonetheless radically undermined what Partha Chatterjee calls "the rule of colonial difference."

The liberal discourse of custom did not merely reprise James Mill's project of creating a rational society out of native unreason. Its identification of the colonial peasant as the proper recipient of liberal favor turned on the claim that the peasant's property was itself, as a property constituted by labor, an expression of natural reason. When Campbell and Hollingbery stepped forward to defend Bengal's peasantry from the illegitimate exactions of the zamindar and the arbitrary expropriation effected historically by colonial law, they did so because they identified rural Bengal as a civil society founded on liberal norms. The plausibility of this characterization turned on the development of an agrarian politics in nineteenth-century Bengal that used claims to autonomous rights over environmental resources as a basis for participation, as independent commodity producers, in relationships of expanding and deepening commercial interdependence. This pro-commercial politics of property did not consistently articulate proprietary rights in terms of the property-constituting powers of labor. The connection that it forged between commodity exchange, property and independence represented, however, a fertile ground for the reception of the kind of Lockeanism that exponents of the liberal discourse of custom articulated through the languages of law and political economy. This suggests that liberal norms were embraced in Bengali agrarian society on a footing that goes beyond instrumental and strategic modes of discursive engagement with colonial law or the colonial state.

This is not to say that liberal norms became the primary (let alone the only) norms to which agrarian actors could and did appeal as authoritative. Indeed, even merely insofar as they were embraced, as we have seen in the previous chapter, we might expect the result to have been generative of an agonistic dissensus whose liberal underpinnings are in any case far from obvious. The point is that liberal norms did ultimately become sufficiently intelligible *as norms* (i.e. not merely as means) to agrarian Bengalis in the course of the nineteenth and twentieth centuries that they began to assume authority in political argument. They became so intelligible not merely because British colonial institutions imposed them through legal institutions, but because those norms resonated with the kinds of practices of social interdependence that agrarian Bengalis increasingly inhabited. The history of agrarian political thought about property therefore cannot be satisfactorily conceived in terms either of the articulation and performance of inherited cultural codes, or of the rational pursuit of objective interests. As arguments premised on practices of social interdependence, yet framed in the context of a multitude of alternative arguments (as well as generative in turn of a multitude of incompatible claims), agrarian discourses of property need to be treated as ideology.

The appeal to liberal norms in political argument by agrarian Bengalis matters not only in terms of an account of Bengali or South Asian or British imperial history. It has even broader implications for questions of epistemological and normative reflexivity.

If political economy represents, as Marx thought it did, its own time apprehended in thought, then certain epistemological uncertainties about the status of political economic concepts in relation to noncapitalist societies immediately arise. Marx himself offered a brief but subtle account of the ways in which concepts that were bound to the abstract interdependencies of capitalist social relations were peculiarly able, because of their abstractness, to grasp aspects of other social formations. Yet he also argued that, in so doing, those abstractions tended to generate a misapprehension of their transhistorical transparency and of their linear unfolding over time.[1] This raises a fundamental question about the status of political-economic concepts in relation to agrarian societies, insofar as such societies are deemed to stand outside of capitalist social forms. One response to the insistence on the historical specificity of political economy as a form of thought has been to treat its concepts as intrinsically allied to the coercive extension of capital and empire. A classic instance of this model would be James Mill's scheme to cultivate social rationality by instituting a revenue system that would simulate market effects in the absence (as he saw it) of any germ of such rationality being already present in Indian society (beyond the level of universal human capacities).[2] But the epistemic condition in which political economy arrived in India was not necessarily the epistemic condition in which it remained through all subsequent developments.

The history that I have sketched in the preceding chapters seems to suggest a more complicated set of trajectories in the history of political economy. The coercive imposition of political-economic categories came in time to be mirrored by an agrarian politics premised on an insistence on the applicability of political economic categories to rural social relations. The fact that Bengali agrarian social actors began to appeal to political-economic concepts in order to frame claims over environmental resources (an appeal implicit, as I have suggested, in the argument that property is constituted by labor) functions as a basis at least for the *suspicion* that political-economic concepts might have been emerging as appropriate ways of talking about agrarian social relations—even if they remained something less that the only way to talk about them. If then it is now difficult (indeed, obtuse) for historians to give an account of Bengali agrarian society without appealing to political economy, we need to recognize both sides of the epistemological problem this represents: first, the more familiar projective dimension (that is, that our own epistemological norms make it difficult to imagine social analysis without appealing to such concepts); and second, the referential dimension (that is, that it may be something about how agrarian society presents itself that makes it difficult to talk about it without appealing to such concepts). To stress this second dimension implies neither a naïve objectivism nor a dogmatic universalism. It simply assumes that the historical conditions that render the conceptual categories that historians use meaningful and plausible bear directly on the question of the epistemological status of those categories in relation to particular objects of analysis.[3]

The implications of this epistemological reflexivity are also normative. To approach the history of political economy through claims about the property-constituting powers of labor is to treat political economy as a deeply normative discourse. Subalternist scholarship developed a stringent critique of the violence of liberal norms in relation to other forms of life. That scholarship was much less eloquent, however, in grappling with the question of the normative *standpoint* of such a critique. When subalternists denounce liberalism for its complicity with colonial racism, for example, what normative commitments underwrite that critique? What are the historical conditions of possibility for that critique's implicit endorsement of equality and freedom? How did such norms become available (*as norms*, not merely as discourses) in South Asia? And how is that history related to the history of liberalism? Of course, one might say that liberalism construes both equality and freedom in very particular, narrow, and even self-contradictory ways. Even so, we are left with the task of explaining the historical possibility of the authority of such norms, and the historical availability of more adequate conceptions of those norms to the subalternist critic. That task seems to sit at considerable odds with the insistence on the autonomy of subaltern consciousness and the consequent availability of subalternity as an external standpoint for the critique of capitalism and colonialism.[4]

There is little question that liberalism arrived in agrarian Bengal as an import bound to coercive political and economic institutions, or that it was complicit with a regime of hierarchical subordination on the basis of race. Yet I have argued that agrarian Bengalis came to recognize the authority of liberal norms under historically specific circumstances that cannot be reduced to the epistemic violence effected by colonial institutions. If that is right, then judgments in terms of liberal norms, like epistemological judgments in terms of political-economic concepts, can no longer be conceptualized as extrinsically imposed by colonial institutions. To say this is not to endorse the adequacy of liberal norms. It is to point towards a form of critique that emphasizes the contradictions and inadequacies of liberal norms (as played out in the dynamics explored in chapters 3 and 5 of this book), rather than one that searches for a secure standpoint outside of those norms.

A history of the kind of Lockeanism I have been examining in this book can thus open new avenues for the interpretation of imperial and agrarian political thought, and it can also provide a catalyst for historical reflexivity. It can at the same time provide us with ways of thinking about both of these in nonreductive relation to the historical specificity of capitalist social forms. This book is clearly inspired by Marxian social theory. But it also requires some rethinking of how Marx's theoretical categories are relevant to the agrarian question in the colonial world. At the very moment one might have expected *Capital* to be providing us with a theoretical blueprint of how to think about the relationship between Lockeanism and capitalism, Marx turns out to have been an unreliable guide to the implications of his own arguments. Indeed, Marx himself becomes a kind of Lockean, a natural law moralist of the very kind he denounced in his many polemics against Proudhon. A Lockean by definition can have little to say about the historical conditions under which conceptions of the natural rights of labor have assumed their normative significance. In the final paragraphs of this conclusion, I want to briefly outline both the problematic nature of Marx's discussion of the relationship between smallholding and capitalism, and point towards the more complex approach that his own theoretical categories implied. In the process, I seek to restate the premises of the argument made in the preceding chapters in directly theoretical terms.

Marx argued in the final chapters of the first volume of *Capital* that the "primitive accumulation of capital, i.e. its historical genesis," rested ultimately on "the expropriation of the immediate producers, i.e. the dissolution of private property based on the labour of its owner," as the basis for the consolidation of a "socially concentrated means of production."[5] As a history of property relations in Britain at the dawn of capitalism, this might be unproblematic. Marx went on to explain, however, that "political economy confuses, on principle, two different kinds of private property, one which rests on the labour of the producer himself, and the other on the exploitation of the labour of others. It forgets that the latter is not only the direct antithesis of the former, but grows on the former's tomb and nowhere else."[6] Marx here casually assimilated the contradiction between the property-constituting powers of labor and the self-positing dynamic of capital to a language of historical transition. This effectively implied a juxtaposition between the substantiality of labor and the insubstantiality of capital (wealth versus value), and a straightforward conflict between natural rights and coercive exploitation. From this perspective, if liberalism was the ideological expression of commodity exchange (as Marx told us earlier in *Capital*), then it must correlatively have functioned as an expression of capital and empire in their exploitative assault on a productive peasantry. This was an assumption ultimately shared by subalternists.[7] Correlatively, a leftist critique of capital would necessarily entail a repudiation of liberalism as such, and any popular history of liberalism could only be a history of collaboration or false consciousness. The availability to both the populist right and the radical left of common normative grounds for a defense of small property, as in the opposition to Special Economic Zones in West Bengal, becomes difficult to understand historically.

Marx himself had already elaborated an analysis in *Capital* that refused these very oppositions, insisting instead on their antinomic condition of mutual entailment. In fact, Marx showed us that the contradiction between the two forms of property (and correlatively between the horizontal relationships characterizing civil society and the vertical relationships characterizing capitalist society) cannot be adequately grasped as a sequential transition. After all, where the conflict between the two modes of private property became evident, even in the final chapter on colonialism, was not in the relation of past and present, but rather in the contemporaneous relation of Old World and New. It was in the settler colonies that "the capitalist regime constantly comes up against the obstacle presented by the producer, who, as owner of his own conditions of labour, employs that labour to enrich himself instead of the capitalist." This is because in settler colonies (that is, in Locke's "America") the "bulk of the soil is still public property, and every settler on it can therefore" (following the logic of Locke) "turn part of it into his private property and his individual means of production, without preventing later settlers from performing the same operations."[8] Confronted with this situation, the political economist is compelled to admit the contradiction in his own conception of private property, and to "proclaim aloud the antagonism between the two modes of production. To this end he demonstrates that the development of the social productivity of labour, co-operation, division of labour, application of machinery on a large scale, and so on, are impossible without the expropriation of the workers and the corresponding transformation of their means of production into capital."[9]

The notion of the property-constituting powers of labor necessarily assumes, as I suggested in the introduction, labor's power as a social mediation. According to Marx's theory, then, the normative authority of labor's property-constituting powers would surely vary directly with the degree to which commodity exchange was the basis of social interdependence. That implies that the normative force of the property-constituting powers of labor would be at their height in a capitalist society, where the commodity is the general form of the product. But that in turn also means that such normative force is *strongest* under circumstances where labor does *not* in fact generally create property, because it is subordinated to capital. Marx himself had provided grounds to think that the practices of social interdependence that generate this contradiction also posit the conditions under which the property-constituting powers of labor can be misrecognized as the historical antecedent of capitalist property. That is to say, the figure of the independent producer as the prehistory from which capital emerged is a trope generated from within capitalist society.

In the penultimate section of *Capital,* just before the turn to primitive accumulation, Marx had outlined an argument that at once showed the fundamental role of exchange of quantities of materialized labor between independent individuals in capitalist reproduction, and the substantive negation of such exchange by the very practices that posited the generalized role of exchange. Marx argued that the production of surplus value out of capital can be resolved into two notionally distinct moments: firstly, the moment when an original fund of capital was invested to produce surplus value; and secondly, the subsequent moment when the additional value of that fund is in turn used to generate more surplus value. The first moment already takes as its point of departure the existence of an original accumulation available to be advanced into the production process: "Where did its owner get it from? 'From his own labour and that of his forefathers,' is the unanimous answer of the spokesmen of political economy. And, in fact, their assumption appears to be the only one consonant with the laws of commodity production."[10] Marx's skepticism about the premise of this original equal exchange, posited conjecturally by political economy itself, indexes a correlative skepticism about the condition of free proprietorship based on labor that "must" have preceded capitalism. In other words, the first moment of exchange is posited only retrospectively—it is not a real historical event or phase.[11] In this first moment, the purchase of labor power represented a regular exchange of magnitudes of labor between free contractors. It is a horizontal relation that conforms to the model of commodity exchange in civil society. In the second moment, however, there has been an additional accumulation of surplus value generated out of the surplus of the value of labor's product beyond the value of the labor power that produced it. While there appears to be a continuity with "the laws of commodity exchange" (i.e. the free exchange of equal values), in reality there is no actual exchange at all. This is because "the capital which is exchanged for labour-power is itself merely a portion of the product of the labour of others which has been appropriated without an equivalent." Furthermore, this capital is itself necessarily employed not only with a view to replacing its own value, but to eliciting a further quantity of surplus value. As a result, Marx observes, "the laws of appropriation or of private property, laws based on the production and circulation of commodities, become changed into their direct opposite through their own internal and inexorable dialectic."[12] It is this second moment that produces the historical conditions under which the commodity becomes the general form of the product, and correlatively the conditions under which the practice of free exchange is posited as a normative social relationship.

Formally, the capitalist and the worker exchange equivalents in the sphere of circulation. Substantively, however, capital constantly appropriates "without equivalent . . . a portion of the labour of others which has already been objectified." It repeatedly exchanges "this labour for a greater quantity of the living labour of others." Originally, "the rights of property *seemed to us* to be grounded in a man's own labour." This was the necessary starting assumption for a state of affairs where "only commodity-owners with equal rights confronted each other" in the sphere of circulation. In fact though, the tendency of capitalist appropriation was to transform private property into the "right, on the part of the capitalist, to appropriate the unpaid labour of others or its product, and the impossibility, on the part of the worker, of appropriating his own product. The separation of property from labour thus becomes the necessary consequence of a law that apparently originated in their identity."[13] Here then, Marx recognized that commodity exchange ("the productive, real basis of all *equality* and *freedom*") in the sphere of circulation (that "very Eden of the innate rights of man" that forms the logical starting point from which the analysis of *Capital* sets out) generates, as part and parcel of the liberal conception of universal rights, a natural and originary state in which labor is constitutive of, and the true measure of, property. This in turn is the foundation for the fantasy that the original accumulation advanced into circulation was itself necessarily the result of prior labor.[14] As he had put it so sharply in the *Grundrisse*: "Thus there should be no longer any ground for astonishment that the system of exchange values—exchange of equivalents measured through labour—turns into, or rather reveals as its hidden background, the *appropriation of alien labour without exchange*, complete separation of labour and property. For the domination of exchange value itself, and of exchange-value-producing production, *presupposes* alien labour capacity itself as an exchange value—i.e. the separation of living labour capacity from its objective conditions; a relation to them—or to its own objectivity—as alien property; a relation to them, in a word, as *capital*."[15] The temporal sequentiality of the passage from Locke to Wakefield is posited internally in capitalist social relations. It cannot function as an account of the transition from precapitalist to capitalist social relations.

There is much more at stake here than the (irresolvable) question of how to read Marx correctly. It is rather a question of whether the concept of "primitive accumulation," that ubiquitous trope of Marxist analysis of the agrarian question, is an adequate point of departure for thinking about the relationship of metropolitan capitalism in the nineteenth and twentieth centuries to the far-flung and diverse worlds with which it interacted. Roman Rosdolsky noted long ago that Marx's discussion of primitive accumulation was never meant to refer only to a process completed with the transition to capitalism. He insisted that Marx thought it told us something about the ongoing expansionary and expropriative dynamic of capitalism.[16] That I think is correct; but it does not mean that the resulting theoretical hybrid is viable or coherent. Marx's resort to the concept of primitive accumulation stemmed most fundamentally from his insight that one cannot explain capitalist society on the basis of its own categories, once one has taken the Hegelian leap of grounding concepts in historical forms of life.[17]

The dynamic of expropriation under circumstances where capital is already fully constituted is necessarily a theoretical problem different from that of the origins of capital itself. This remains true even when capital enters into new social spaces organized around different (noncapitalist) norms and practices. Only a naïve methodological nationalism could lead us to think that the question of the transformation of a particular social space by capital is the same as the question of the creation of capital in the first place—as if the history of capitalist social transformation is an iterative process that takes place in one national space at a time. Not every transition to capitalism is an instance of primitive accumulation. But the historical context described in this book is even further removed from primitive accumulation. In agrarian Bengal, commodity exchange had become a plausible foundation for normative claims. To invoke the concept of primitive accumulation could only begin to be coherent if Marx's characterization of the property-constituting powers of labor as precapitalist at the end of the first volume of *Capital* is taken at face value. In fact, when agrarian actors organized politically to defend a right to property grounded in labor, they articulated a critique of capital that was imaginable only in relation to commodity exchange. This does not necessarily mean that "capitalist transformation" had already occurred in rural Bengal. It does mean, however, that such actors were no more assuming an external standpoint in relation to capitalism than were the Lockean smallholders of the New World. It also means that the "accumulation by dispossession" that has occurred periodically in the course of the colonial and postcolonial periods in Bengal (most recently in the form of the SEZs with which this book began) should not automatically be assumed to correlate with a "primitive accumulation" through which precapitalist agrarian society transitions to capitalism.[18] To critique the one-sidedness of Marx's account of the fate of smallholding property under capital, and correlatively of the fate of the property-constituting powers of labor, is thus the necessary first step towards recovering the capacity of Marx's analysis of capital to speak to these issues.

NOTES

1. HOW TO WRITE A HISTORY OF LIBERALISM?

1. Shepard Daniel with Anuradha Mittal, *The Great Land Grab: Rush for World's Farmland Threatens Food Security for the Poor* (Oakland, CA: Oakland Institute, 2009); Lorenzo Cotula, Sonja Vermeulen, Rebeca Leonard and James Keeley, *Land Grab or Development Opportunity: Agricultural Investment and International Land Deals in Africa* (London and Rome: IIED/FAO/IFAD, 2009); Joachim von Braun and Ruth Meinzen-Dick, *"Land-Grabbing" by Foreign Investors in Developing Countries: Risks and Opportunities* (IFPRI Policy Brief 13, April 2009); "Ethiopia at Center of Global Farmland Rush," *The Guardian,* March 21, 2011; W. Anseeuw, L. Alden Wily, L. Cotula and M. Taylor, *Land Rights and the Rush for Land: Findings of the Global Commercial Pressures on Land Research Project* (Rome: International Land Coalition, 2012); W. Anseeuw, M. Boche, T. Breu, M. Giger, J. Lay, P. Messerli and K. Nolte, *Transnational Land Deals for Agriculture in the Global South: Analytical Report Based on the Land Matrix Database* (Bern/Montpellier/Hamburg: CDE/CIRAD/GIGA, 2013).

2. See for example Kheya Bag, "Red Bengal's Rise and Fall," *New Left Review* 70 (July–August 2011): 69–98.

3. See classically J. G. A. Pocock, *The Machiavellian Moment: Florentine Political Thought and the Atlantic Republican Tradition* (Princeton, NJ: Princeton University Press, 2003), ch. 13.

4. Major interventions in the history of liberalism in relation to the British Empire include David Armitage, *Foundations of Modern International Thought* (Cambridge: Cambridge University Press, 2013); Barbara Arneil, *John Locke and America: The Defense of English Colonialism* (Oxford: Oxford University Press, 1996); C. A. Bayly, *Recovering Liberties: Indian Thought in the Age of Liberalism and Empire* (Cambridge: Cambridge University Press, 2012); Duncan Bell, *The Idea of Greater Britain: Empire and the Future*

of World Order, 1860–1900 (Princeton, NJ: Princeton University Press, 2007); P. J. Cain, *Hobson and Imperialism: Radicalism, New Liberalism, and Finance, 1887–1938* (Oxford: Oxford University Press, 2002); Simon Gunn and James Vernon (eds.), *The Peculiarities of Liberal Modernity in Imperial Britain* (Berkeley: GAIA and University of California Press, 2011); Catherine Hall, *Civilising Subjects: Metropole and Colony in the English Imagination, 1830–1867* (Chicago: University of Chicago Press, 2002); Thomas C. Holt, *The Problem of Freedom: Race, Labor, and Politics in Jamaica and Britain, 1832–1938* (Baltimore: Johns Hopkins University Press, 1992); Theodore Koditschek, *Liberalism, Imperialism, and the Historical Imagination: Nineteenth-Century Visions of Greater Britain* (Cambridge: Cambridge University Press, 2011); Domenico Losurdo, *Liberalism: A Counter-History* (London: Verso, 2011); Karuna Mantena, *Alibis of Empire: Henry Maine and the Ends of Liberal Imperialism* (Princeton, NJ: Princeton University Press, 2010); Thomas McCarthy, *Race, Empire, and the Idea of Human Development* (Cambridge: Cambridge University Press, 2009); Uday Singh Mehta, *Liberalism and Empire: A Study in Nineteenth-Century British Liberal Thought* (Chicago: University of Chicago Press, 1999); Thomas R. Metcalf, *Ideologies of the Raj* (Cambridge: Cambridge University Press, 1995); Steve Pincus, *1688: The First Modern Revolution* (New Haven, CT: Yale University Press, 2009); Jennifer Pitts, *A Turn to Empire: The Rise of Imperial Liberalism in Britain and France* (Princeton, NJ: Princeton University Press, 2005); Lynn Zastoupil, *John Stuart Mill and India* (Stanford, CA: Stanford University Press, 1994). For a survey of recent literature in political theory, see Jennifer Pitts, "Political Theory of Empire and Imperialism," *Annual Review of Political Science* 13, no. 2 (2010): 211–35.

5. Bayly, *Recovering Liberties*, 343–44.

6. See for classic but otherwise very diverse examples of such accounts: Anil Seal, *The Emergence of Indian Nationalism: Competition and Collaboration in the Later Nineteenth Century* (Cambridge: Cambridge University Press, 1971); Eric Stokes, *The English Utilitarians and India* (Delhi: Oxford University Press, 1989); Ranajit Guha, "Neel-darpan: The Image of a Peasant Revolt in a Liberal Mirror," *Journal of Peasant Studies* 2, no. 1 (1974): 1–46; Sudipta Sen, *Empire of Free Trade: The East India Company and the Making of the Colonial Marketplace* (Philadelphia: University of Pennsylvania Press, 1998).

7. For powerful examples of these kinds of approaches, see Anupama Rao, *The Caste Question: Dalits and the Politics of Modern India* (Berkeley: University of California Press, 2009); Rachel Sturman, *The Government of Social Life in Colonial India: Liberalism, Religious Law, and Women's Rights* (Cambridge: Cambridge University Press, 2012); and Jon E. Wilson, *The Domination of Strangers: Modern Governance in Eastern India, 1780–1835* (Basingstoke, UK: Palgrave Macmillan, 2008).

8. Wilson, *Domination of Strangers*, chapter 7, makes the same point, though it speaks mainly to the constitution of an elite Bengali liberalism. I believe, however, that the Bengali discourse of civil society he characterizes broadly as "liberal" was in fact a much more conflictive ideological terrain involving liberal, nonliberal and antiliberal political arguments.

9. On the new imperial Toryism of this period, see David Cannadine, *Ornamentalism: How the British Saw Their Empire* (Oxford: Oxford University Press, 2001); David Cannadine, "The Context, Performance and Meaning of Ritual: The British Monarchy and the 'Invention of Tradition,' c. 1820–1977," in Eric Hobsbawm and Terence Ranger (eds.), *The Invention of Tradition* (Cambridge: Cambridge University Press, 1992), 101–64; Bernard Cohn, "Representing Authority in Victorian India," in Hobsbawm and Ranger (eds.), *Inven-*

tion of Tradition, 165-210; C. C. Eldridge, *England's Mission: The Imperial Idea in the Age of Gladstone and Disraeli* (Chapel Hill: University of North Carolina Press, 1974); Hall, *Civilising Subjects;* Holt, *The Problem of Freedom;* Mantena, *Alibis of Empire;* Thomas R. Metcalf, *The Aftermath of Revolt: India, 1857–1870* (Princeton, NJ: Princeton University Press, 1964); Metcalf, *Ideologies of the Raj*. For the same process viewed from the other side of the colonial divide in Bengal, see Andrew Sartori, *Bengal in Global Concept History: Culturalism in the Age of Capital* (Chicago: University of Chicago Press 2008), esp. ch. 3. While that book sought to elucidate the structure of a specifically postliberal ideological formation (culturalism), it also recognized that "[l]iberalism did not simply die in 1848: the categories of liberal thought would go on to enjoy a long and eminent ideological career in the second half of the nineteenth century" (99). On the persistence of liberal argument in India throughout its period of retrenchment in the British imperial context, see Bayly, *Recovering Liberties,* and Koditschek, *Liberalism, Imperialism, and the Historical Imagination,* ch. 6.

10. This alienness was a fundamental presupposition that lay at the core of Ranajit Guha's classic, *Elementary Apects of Peasant Insurgency in Colonial India* (Oxford: Oxford University Press, 1983).

11. Indeed, there are suggestive resonances, for example, with the South Indian case examined in Sharad Chari, *Fraternal Capital: Peasant-Workers, Self-Made Men, and Globalization in Provincial India* (Stanford, CA: Stanford University Press, 2004).

12. Michael Freeden, *The New Liberalism: An Ideology of Social Reform* (Oxford: Clarendon Press, 1978), 246.

13. The importance of popular liberalism in Britain has been emphasized most recently by Eugenio F. Biagini, *Liberty, Retrenchment and Reform: Popular Liberalism in the Age of Gladstone, 1860–1880* (Cambridge: Cambridge University Press, 1992); but its significance is rarely contemplated in discussions of political theory or intellectual history.

14. Peter Laslett first demonstrated that Locke's treatises had been written much earlier, in 1679–80 during the exclusion crisis, rather than in the immediate wake of the Glorious Revolution as its publication in 1689 suggested: see his introduction to the *Two Treatises of Government* (Cambridge: Cambridge University Press, 1988). This suggested that the text expressed not the consensus view of an ascendant Whiggism, but the contentiousness of a period of profound dissensus. Richard Ashcraft, pursuing this insight, contended that the treatises were composed a little later at a more radical political conjuncture in early 1680s: see his *Revolutionary Politics and Locke's Two Treatises of Government* (Princeton, NJ: Princeton University Press, 1986). The specific political purposes of Locke's intervention are of less importance here than the normative principles to which Locke appealed in elaborating his arguments.

15. This construction of "Lockeanism" builds on the approach to intellectual history more broadly outlined in Sartori, *Bengal in Global Concept History,* ch. 2.

16. On early-modern political debates over claims to imperium versus dominion, see David Armitage, *The Ideological Origins of the British Empire* (Cambridge: Cambridge University Press, 2000), ch. 3.

17. On the patriarchal underpinnings of Locke's thought, see Carole Pateman's classic, *The Sexual Contract* (Oxford: Blackwell, 1988).

18. For my purposes, it doesn't really matter whether Locke composed the chapter on property concurrently with, before or after the composition of the rest of the text; for the

chapter serves to fill a crucial explanatory function in the argument as a whole. For a recent discussion of the dating of this chapter and the significance of its pervasive references to America, see Armitage, *Foundations of Modern International Thought,* ch. 6.

19. John Locke, *An Essay Concerning the True Original and Extent of Civil Government* (Dublin: George Bonham, 1798), 34.

20. John Dunn, "The Contemporary Political Significance of John Locke's Conception of Civil Society," in Sudipta Kaviraj and Sunil Khilnani (eds.), *Civil Society: History and Possibilities* (Cambridge: Cambridge University Press, 2001), 39–57.

21. James Mill, *The Article Government: Reprinted from the Supplement to the Encyclopædia Britannica* (London: Traveller Office, 1821), 5.

22. John Stuart Mill, *Principles of Political Economy* (Amherst, NY: Prometheus, 2004), 224, 234–36.

23. From this perspective, Richard Bellamy's attempt to appeal to the history of British new liberalism to disentangle what he calls "ethical [i.e. rights-based] liberalism," an ideology of early capitalism, from "democratic liberalism," an ideology suited to the complexity of developed capitalist society, restates the temporal fetish that is one of the central concerns of this book. Richard Bellamy, *Liberalism and Modern Society: A Historical Argument* (University Park: Pennsylvania State University Press, 1992).

24. Roger Woolhouse, *Locke: A Biography* (Cambridge: Cambridge University Press, 2007), esp. 275–76.

25. Donald Winch, *Riches and Poverty: An Intellectual History of Political Economy in Britain, 1750–1834* (Cambridge: Cambridge University Press, 1996), ch. 6.

26. Mill, *Article Government.*

27. C. B. Macpherson, *The Political Theory of Possessive Individualism: Hobbes to Locke* (Oxford: Oxford University Press, 2011), 3.

28. Macpherson, *Political Theory of Possessive Individualism,* 221.

29. Karen I. Vaughn, "John Locke and the Labor Theory of Value," *Journal of Libertarian Studies* 2, no. 4 (1978): 311–26.

30. Locke, *Civil Government,* 36.

31. For further discussion of this point, see Andrew Sartori, "Global Intellectual History and the History of Political Economy," in Samuel Moyn and Andrew Sartori (eds.), *Global Intellectual History* (New York: Columbia University Press, 2013), 110–33.

32. Locke, *Civil Government,* 37.

33. Ibid., 38.

34. John Ramsay McCulloch, *Outlines of Political Economy: Being a Republication of the Article upon that Subject Contained in the Edinburgh Supplement to the Encyclopedia Brittanica* (New York: Wilder and Campbell, 1825), 54. See also Karl Marx, *Theories of Surplus Value* (Amherst, NY: Prometheus Books, 2000), vol. 1, 367. Joyce Appleby presents an insightful discussion of this issue in "Locke, Liberalism and the Natural Law of Money," *Liberalism and Republicanism in the Historical Imagination* (Cambridge, MA: Harvard University Press, 1992), 58–89.

35. Neal Wood, *John Locke and Agrarian Capitalism* (Berkeley: University of California Press, 1984), 38–39, 113.

36. See Steve Pincus, "Neither Machiavellian Moment nor Possessive Individualism: Commercial Society and the Defenders of the English Commonwealth," *American Histori-*

cal Review 103, no. 3 (1998): 705–36; Pincus, *1688*; and Wood, *John Locke and Agrarian Capitalism.*

37. See especially John Dunn, *The Political Thought of John Locke: An Historical Account of the Argument of the "Two Treatises on Government"* (Cambridge: Cambridge University Press, 1969); and James Tully, *A Discourse on Property: John Locke and his Adversaries* (Cambridge: Cambridge University Press, 1980).

38. See the introduction to Istvan Hont and Michael Ignatieff (eds.), *Wealth and Virtue: The Shaping of Political Economy in the Scottish Enlightenment* (Cambridge: Cambridge University Press, 1983), 39–40.

39. Hont and Ignatieff (eds.), *Wealth and Virtue*, 37–39.

40. Locke, *Civil Government*, 39.

41. Karl Marx, *Grundrisse: Foundations of the Critique of Political Economy (Rough Draft)* (Harmondsworth, UK: Penguin, 1973), 103–05.

42. This characterization of Marx's argument is elaborated rigorously in Moishe Postone, *Time, Labor and Social Domination: A Reinterpretation of Marx's Critical Theory* (Cambridge: Cambridge University Press, 1996).

43. A point I discuss in detail in Sartori, "Global Intellectual History and the History of Political Economy."

44. Karl Marx, *Capital: A Critique of Political Economy*, trans. Ben Fowkes (London: Penguin, 1976), 280; see also Marx, *Grundrisse*, 83–85, 240–45.

45. Neal, *John Locke and Agrarian Capitalism;* Vaughn, "John Locke and the Labor Theory of Value."

46. Hont and Ignatieff (eds.), *Wealth and Virtue*, 39. This Grotian argument for the reliance of property itself on a social contract was one that Locke had himself espoused only a few years before composing the Second Treatise: see Armitage, *Foundations of Modern International Thought*, 109.

47. Thus Smith argued in *Wealth of Nations* that labor was an adequate measure of value only in an "early and rude state of society which precedes both the accumulation of stock and the appropriation of land." We find him only a few pages later, however, describing rent and profit as *deductions* from the product of labor, implying that, bracketing the self-correcting fluctuations of market price, the aggregate value of the product might still ultimately correlate with "real price." Smith was thus as bound to the antinomic logic of the practices he was analyzing as Locke had been. Adam Smith, *An Inquiry into the Nature and Causes of the Wealth of Nations* (Chicago: University of Chicago Press, 1976), vol. 1, 53, 72–73.

48. Richard Ashcraft, "Liberal Political Theory and Working-Class Radicalism in Nineteenth-Century England," *Political Theory* 21, no. 2 (1993): 249–72.

49. James Tully, "The Framework of Natural Rights in Locke's Analysis of Property," in his *An Approach to Political Philosophy: Locke in Contexts* (Cambridge: Cambridge University Press, 1993), 99.

50. See also Andrew Sartori, "The British Empire and Its Liberal Mission," *Journal of Modern History* 78, no. 3 (2006): 623–42.

51. Mehta, *Liberalism and Empire*, 47, 49, 57.

52. Ibid., 11–13.

53. Ibid., 1.

54. Ibid., 21.

55. Ibid., 58.

56. Smith, *Wealth of Nations,* vol. 1, 18.

57. Ibid., vol. 1, 15–16.

58. Pincus, "Neither Machiavellian Moment nor Possessive Individualism," 707–08, 716.

59. Pincus, *1688,* ch. 12.

60. Smith, *Wealth of Nations,* vol. 1, 26.

61. See Marx, *Capital,* vol. I, 470–80.

62. For further discussion of the historical relationship between liberal abstraction, social abstraction and modern capitalism, see Sartori, "Global Intellectual History and the History of Political Economy."

63. Javed Majeed, *Ungoverned Imaginings: James Mill's History of British India and Orientalism* (Oxford: Clarendon, 1992).

64. A broadly parallel argument has been made in Jennifer Pitts's account of British liberalism in *A Turn to Empire.* For Pitts, liberal commitments, being diffuse in both historical content and contextual significance, could have no necessary relationship to imperial projects. This she demonstrates primarily by means of a historicization of the relationship between the liberalism of sentiment and the liberalism of reason, whereby eighteenth-century liberal thought was sensitized to issues of diversity through its attention to the relativity of reason to context and sentiment, whereas it was precisely this crucial resource of which nineteenth-century liberals, armed with imperial and modernizing hubris, lost sight. This approach is further echoed in Sankar Muthu's work on continental "Enlightenment anti-imperialism," the peculiarity of whose arguments turned fundamentally on the elaboration of a view of human beings as universally endowed with "cultural agency"; that is, with "a range of rational, emotive, aesthetic, and imaginative capacities that create, sustain, and transform diverse practices and institutions over time." Sankar Muthu, *Enlightenment Against Empire* (Princeton, NJ: Princeton University Press, 2003), 7–8.

65. For Burke's conception of India as a society organized around a great landed aristocracy, and his endorsement of Philip Francis (ideological architect of a permanent zamindari settlement, in the name of the restoration of the ancient rights of an indigenous gentry) as the defender of Indian constitutional rights and liberties against the corrupt greed of Company servants, see Edmund Burke, *On Empire, Liberty, and Reform: Speeches and Letters,* ed. David Bromwich (New Haven, CT, and London: Yale University Press, 2000), 296, 350; and the discussion in Robert Travers, *Ideology and Empire in Eighteenth-Century India: The British in Bengal* (Cambridge: Cambridge University Press, 2007), 217–23. On the centrality of landed families to Burke's understanding of the British and French ancient constitutions, see Edmund Burke, *Reflections on the Revolution in France* (Indianapolis: Hackett, 1987), 38, 44–45, 96.

66. See Mehta, *Liberalism and Empire,* 186. On the role of popular politics in shaping the emergence of a new conservatism, see Kathleen Wilson, *The Sense of the People: Politics, Culture and Imperialism in England, 1715-1785* (Cambridge: Cambridge University Press, 1998); and James Vaughn, "The Politics of Empire: Metropolitan Socio-Political Development and the Imperial Transformation of the British East India Company, 1675-1775" (PhD dissertation, University of Chicago, 2008).

67. See Nicholas Dirks, *The Scandal of Empire: India and the Creation of Imperial Britain* (Cambridge, MA: Belknap Press, 2006).

68. Winch, *Riches and Poverty*, part II; Iain Hampsher-Monk, "Edmund Burke and Empire," in Duncan Kelly (ed.), *Lineages of Empire: The Historical Roots of British Imperial Thought* (Oxford: Oxford University Press for the British Academy, 2009), 117–36; Emma Rothschild, *Economic Sentiments: Adam Smith, Condorcet, and the Enlightenment* (Cambridge, MA: Harvard University Press, 2001), ch. 2.

69. The classic critique of the colonial archive in South Asian scholarship was Ranajit Guha, "The Prose of Counter-Insurgency," in Ranajit Guha (ed.), *Subaltern Studies II: Writings on South Asian History and Society* (Delhi: Oxford University Press, 1983), 1–42.

2. THE GREAT RENT CASE

1. J.G.A. Pocock, *The Machiavellian Moment: Florentine Political Thought and the Atlantic Republican Tradition* (Princeton, NJ: Princeton University Press, 2003), 11–16; J.G.A. Pocock, *The Ancient Constitution and the Feudal Law*, 2nd ed. (Cambridge: Cambridge University Press, 1987).

2. Pocock, *Machiavellian Moment*, 340–41, 404–05.

3. Sir William Blackstone, *Commentaries on the Laws of England* (San Francisco: Bancroft-Whitney, 1915), vol. I, 107, 113, 116.

4. Blackstone, *Commentaries*, vol. I, 120–21. On the conservatism implicit in Blackstone's emphasis on prescription and landed property, see David Lieberman, "Property, Commerce, and the Common Law: Attitudes to Legal Change in the Eighteenth Century," in John Brewer and Susan Staves (eds.), *Early Modern Conceptions of Property* (London: Routledge, 1996), 144–58.

5. Edmund Burke, *Reflections on the Revolution in France* (Indianapolis: Hackett, 1987), 27–28, emphasis in original; cf. Blackstone, *Commentaries*, vol. I, 4, 132–33.

6. Burke, *Reflections*, 29, 96–97.

7. Ibid., 84–85.

8. Mary Wollstonecraft, *A Vindication of the Rights of Men, in a Letter to the Right Honourable Edmund Burke* (London: J. Johnson, 1790), 22. See also Wollstonecraft, *A Vindication of the Rights of Woman, with Strictures on Political and Moral Subjects* (London: T. Fisher Unwin, 1891), 39–40.

9. Thomas Paine, *The Rights of Man, for the Benefit of All Mankind* (Philadelphia: D. Webster, 1797), 1, emphasis in original.

10. Paine, *Rights of Man*, 2, 5, 18.

11. Jeremy Bentham, *Works* (Edinburgh: William Tait, 1843), vol. II, 501.

12. Cited from Javed Majeed, *Ungoverned Imaginings: James Mill's History of British India and Orientalism* (Oxford: Clarendon, 1992), 146; and see also David Lieberman, "From Bentham to Benthamism," *Historical Journal* 28, no. 1 (1985): 199–224; and J.H. Burns, "Bentham and Blackstone: A Lifetime's Dialectic," *Utilitas: A Journal of Utilitarian Studies* 1, no. 1 (1989): 22–40.

13. Cited from Clive Dewey, "Celtic Agrarian Legislation and the Celtic Revival: Historicist Implications of Gladstone's Irish and Scottish Land Acts, 1870–1886," *Past and Present* 64 (1974), 30–70, on 40 n.33. For similar arguments by Mill and Bentham, see Majeed, *Ungoverned Imaginings*, 145–47.

14. Walter Bagehot, *Physics and Politics* (New York: D. Appleton, 1873), 53.

15. John Stuart Mill, *On Liberty and Other Essays* (Oxford: Oxford University Press, 1991), 487–90.

16. Mill, *On Liberty,* 78.

17. Ibid., 14–15, 74, 78.

18. John Stuart Mill, *Principles of Political Economy* (Amherst, NY: Prometheus, 2004), 245.

19. Mill, *Principles of Political Economy,* 244.

20. Ibid., 249.

21. Ibid., 245.

22. Ibid., 311.

23. Ibid., 313; Clive Dewey, "The Rehabilitation of the Peasant Proprietor in Nineteenth-Century Economic Thought," *History of Political Economy* 6, no. 1 (1974): 17–47. For more detailed discussion of Mill's positions on land reform in Ireland and India, see Bruce Kinzer, *England's Disgrace? J. S. Mill and the Irish Question* (Toronto: University of Toronto Press, 2001), chs. 3 and 5; Samuel Hollander, *The Economics of John Stuart Mill* (Toronto: University of Toronto Press, 1985), vol. 2, ch. 11; E. D. Steele, "J. S. Mill and the Irish Question: The Principles of Political Economy, 1848–65," *Historical Journal* 13 (1970): 216–36; E. D. Steele, "J. S. Mill and the Irish Question: Reform and the Integrity of Empire," *Historical Journal* 13 (1970): 419–50; and Lynn Zastoupil, *John Stuart Mill and India* (Stanford, CA: Stanford University Press, 1994), ch. 5.

24. See for example Terence Ranger, "The Invention of Tradition in Colonial Africa," in E. Hobsbawm and T. Ranger (eds.), *The Invention of Tradition* (Cambridge: Cambridge University Press, 1992), 211–62; Mahmood Mamdani, *Citizen and Subject: Contemporary Africa and the Legacy of Late Colonialism* (Princeton, NJ: Princeton University Press, 1996).

25. Neeladri Bhattacharya, "Remaking Custom: The Discourse and Practice of Colonial Codification," in R. Champakalakshmi and S. Gopal (eds.), *Tradition, Dissent and Ideology: Essays in Honour of Romila Thapar* (Delhi: Oxford University Press, 1996), 20–51.

26. Eric Stokes, *The English Utilitarians and India* (Delhi: Oxford University Press, 1989), 18; Burton Stein, *Thomas Munro: The Origins of the Colonial State and His Vision of Empire* (Delhi: Oxford University Press, 1989); Martha McLaren, *British India and British Scotland, 1780–1830: Career Building, Empire Building, and a Scottish School of Thought on Indian Governance* (Akron, OH: University of Akron Press, 2001).

27. Mamdani, *Citizen and Subject,* 49–52; and Karuna Mantena, *Alibis of Empire: Henry Maine and the Ends of Liberal Imperialism* (Princeton, NJ: Princeton University Press, 2010), 171–76.

28. Mantena, *Alibis of Empire.*

29. Thomas R. Metcalf, *The Aftermath of Revolt: India, 1857–1870* (Princeton, NJ: Princeton University Press, 1964); Thomas R. Metcalf, *Ideologies of the Raj* (Cambridge: Cambridge University Press, 1995), 43–65.

30. Metcalf, *Aftermath of Revolt,* ch. 4.

31. Cited from S. Gopal, *British Policy in India, 1858–1905* (Cambridge: Cambridge University Press, 1965), 33.

32. S. Ambirajan, *Classical Political Economy and British Policy in India* (Cambridge: Cambridge University Press, 1978), 110–29; G. R. G. Hambly, "Richard Temple and the Punjab Tenancy Act of 1868," *English Historical Review* 79, no. 310 (1964): 47–66; Clive Dewey,

"Images of the Village Community: A Study in Anglo-Indian Ideology," *Modern Asian Studies* 6, no. 3 (1972): 291–328.

33. Metcalf, *Ideologies of the Raj.*

34. Cf. Zastoupil, *Mill and India*, 186–87.

35. Ratnalekha Ray, "The Bengal Zamindars: Local Magnates and the State before the Permanent Settlement," *Indian Economic and Social History Review* 12, no. 3 (1975): 263–92; Rajat Datta, *Society, Economy and the Market: Commercialization in Rural Bengal, c. 1760–1800* (New Delhi: Manohar, 2000), 134–38; Richard Eaton, *The Rise of Islam and the Bengal Frontier, 1204–1760* (Berkeley: University of California Press, 1993), 248–57; B. R. Grover, "Evolution of the Zamindari and Taluqdari System in Bengal," *Tritiya barshik itihas sammelan: abhibhashan, prabandhabali, o karja bibarani* (Dhaka: Bangladesh Itihas Parishad, 1975), 86–113.

36. Ranajit Guha, *A Rule of Property for Bengal: An Essay on the Idea of Permanent Settlement* (Durham, NC: Duke University Press, 1996); Robert Travers, *Ideology and Empire in Eighteenth-Century India: The British in Bengal* (Cambridge: Cambridge University Press, 2007), chs. 4–6; and Jon E. Wilson, *The Domination of Strangers: Modern Governance in Eastern India, 1780–1835* (New York: Palgrave Macmillan, 2008), ch. 5.

37. See Guha, *Rule of Property*; Travers, *Ideology and Empire in Eighteenth-Century India*, chs. 4–6; and Wilson, *Domination of Strangers*, ch. 5.

38. John William Kaye, *The Administration of the East India Company: A History of Indian Progress* (London: Richard Bentley, 1853), 140.

39. Kaye, *Administration*, 140–41, 159.

40. Ibid., 174, 176–77.

41. Ibid., 181.

42. Ibid., 185.

43. Ibid., 192–93.

44. Ibid., 209, 224, 227, 232.

45. Cited from *Memorandum Respecting the Operation of the Law for the Recovery of Revenue by the Sale of the Lands Permanently Settled in Bengal* (London, 1835), 42, emphasis in original.

46. Lord Argyll to George Campbell, Feb. 4, 1873, *Campbell of Edenwood Papers* (IOL Euro. Mss. E349/11). While serving as Under-Secretary of State for India in 1865, the future Viceroy and powerful Ulster landlord, Lord Dufferin, made a complementary observation about the inverse relationship between the rental rate and the customary right of a tenant to a payment upon vacation of a tenancy. He would be happy, he noted, to "let his land at a far lower rate than the rackrent or competition price, in order that, by leaving them a more ample margin, his tenantry may live better," but saw such moderation in practice "entirely neutralized by a surreptitious sale of nominal improvements, which abstracts from the pocket of his future tenant perhaps forty years' purchase of the difference between the fair rent he is content to take and the exorbitant rent he might have had from a dozen people, had he been so minded." Cited from W. E. Vaughn, *Landlords and Tenants in Mid-Victorian Ireland* (Oxford: Clarendon, 1994), 72. See also Barbara Lewis Solow, *The Land Question and the Irish Economy, 1870–1903* (Cambridge, MA: Harvard University Press, 1971), 26–29.

47. See David Washbrook, "Law, State and Agrarian Society in Colonial India," *Modern Asian Studies* 15, no. 3 (1981): 662–63; Wilson, *Domination of Strangers*, 119–20.

48. Since landlord abuses could themselves be seen as illegitimate, defenders of market rationality could sometimes suggest that the solution was to strengthen rights of property. In practice, zamindaris "are mortgaged to the Government, the mortgage being liable to be foreclosed, as soon as they fail to make their quarterly payments." More security of property could encourage the flow of capital to the land in ways that would improve conditions for everyone—especially if the oppression of raiyats was partly driven by the insecurity of zamindari under the Permanent Settlement. See "Petition of Protestant Missionaries Residing in or near Calcutta, to the Honourable Legislative Council of India," *Fourth Report from the Select Committee on Colonization and Settlement (India), Parliamentary Papers,* 1857–58 (461-I), 290–96.

49. "Capital and Land," *Calcutta Review* 38 (1863), 321–22, 345.

50. Ibid., 324–26.

51. Ibid., 328, 332.

52. Ibid., 334–36.

53. Ibid., 337–38.

54. Ibid., 338.

55. Ibid., 338–40.

56. Ibid., 342.

57. Ibid., 344.

58. Kaye, *Administration,* 198–99.

59. *Memorandum Respecting the Operation of the Law for the Recovery of Revenue,* 41, 44–45.

60. Eric Stokes, *The English Utilitarians and India* (Delhi: Oxford University Press, 1989), chs. 1–2.

61. Iftekhar Iqbal, *The Bengal Delta: Ecology, State and Social Change, 1840–1943* (Houndsmills, UK, and New York: Palgrave Macmillan, 2010), ch. 2.

62. W.S. Seton-Karr, *Rulers of India: The Marquess Cornwallis* (Oxford: Clarendon, 1898), 32.

63. J.H. Harington, *Extracts from Harington's Analysis of the Bengal Regulations* (Calcutta: Office of Superintendent of Government Printing, 1866), 222–23.

64. J.H. Harington, "A Regulation for Maintaining the Rights of *Khoodkasht, Chupperbund,* and Other Resident Ryots, who by Prescriptive Usage are Entitled, on Certain Conditions, to the Permanent Occupancy of the Lands Cultivated by Them, within the Limits of the Village in which they Reside," *Report from the Select Committee on the Affairs of the East India Company, Parliamentary Papers,* 1831–32 (735-III), Appendix 21, 117–23.

65. Opinions of W. Leycester and A. Ross, Judges of the Sudder Dewany Adawlut, *Parliamentary Papers,* 1831–32 (735-III), Appendix 21, 123–26.

66. "[T]he Ejectment Act [of 1852] . . . destroys the last remaining vestige of the independent right of the tenant in his land. . . . The ryot had originally a right in the soil. This right Lord Cornwallis first attacked, and the irresistible course of events has compelled the Government more and more to raise the zemindar into the position of a proprietor in fee simple, and to depress the ryot into a labourer. This last Act consummates the work. . . . [I]n the year 1852, the last vestige of the ryot's claim to be proprietor of his own land, disappeared from Bengal." [Anonymous,] "Annals of the Bengal Presidency for 1852," *Calcutta Review* 19, no. 37 (1853): 207–08.

67. *Papers Relating to the Passing of Act X of 1859 (an Act to Amend the Law Relating to the Recovery of Rent in the Presidency of Fort William in Bengal)* (Calcutta: Office of the Superintendent of Government Printing, India, 1883), vol. I, 206–07.

68. *Papers of Act X of 1859*, vol. I, 1.

69. *Decisions of the High Court of Judicature, at Fort William in Bengal, during the Years 1864 and 1865, Illustrating the Rent-Laws, and Bearing upon the General Duties of the Officers of the Revenue Department* (Calcutta: Calcutta Central Press, 1866), vol. II, 578.

70. Cf. P. G. Robb, *Ancient Rights and Future Comfort: Bihar, the Bengal Tenancy Act of 1885, and British Rule in India* (Richmond, UK: Curzon, 1997), 81–82.

71. *Papers of Act X of 1859*, vol. I, 120–32, on 121.

72. Ibid., vol. I, 49.

73. Ibid., vol. I, 82–83.

74. Ibid., vol. I, 44.

75. Ibid., vol. I, 47.

76. Ibid., vol. I, 143.

77. See Ishwar Ghose (Defendant) Appellant *versus* Hills (Plaintiff) Respondent, September 24, 1862, *Decisions under the Rent Laws of the Court of Sadr Dewani Adalat, and of the High Court of Judicature, at Fort William in Bengal (from the Passing of Act X. of 1859)* (Calcutta: George Wyman, 1865), vol. I, 77–84; Mr. James Hills (Plaintiff) Appellant *versus* Ishwar Ghose (Defendant) Respondent, September 2, 1863, *Decisions*, vol. I, 180–200; and Ishur Ghose, Petitioner, *versus* Mr. James Hills, Opposite Party, March 17, 1864, *Decisions*, vol. II, 30–49.

78. J. Hills, Esq., to L. B. Bowring, Private Secretary to the Governor General, Sept. 14th, 1860, *Parliamentary Papers*, 1861 (72-II), 57.

79. *Decisions*, vol. I, 79–80.

80. *Decisions*, vol. I, 82–83.

81. *Decisions*, vol. II, 41.

82. *Decisions*, vol. II, 42.

83. *Decisions*, vol. II, 43.

84. *Papers of Act X of 1859*, vol. I, 36–42, 145–52, 201–03; *Decisions*, vol. II, 127–28.

85. *Decisions*, vol. II, 130.

86. *Decisions*, vol. II, 127–34.

87. Indeed, Henry Maine, then Law Member of the Viceroy's Council, had initially expressed suspicion to Sir Charles Wood, Secretary of State for India, that Peacock had abused his powers as Chief Justice to secure the precedent he wanted against Pandit's reservations, but quickly retracted the accusation. Henry Maine to Sir Charles Wood, Sept. 11, 1863, *Sir Charles Wood Papers* (IOL Euro. Mss., F78/114/1).

88. *Decisions*, vol. II, 134.

89. *Decisions*, vol. II, 48–49.

90. *Selections from the Records of the Bengal Government, No. XVI: General Report of a Tour of Inspection, by W. B. Jackson, Esq., C.S., Judge of the Sudder Court; also Report of the District of Singbhoom, by H. Ricketts, Esq., S.C., Member of the Board of Revenue* (Calcutta: F. Carbery, Bengal Military Orphan Press, 1854), 4, 13–14. On the development of the system of patni leases, see Wilson, *Domination of Strangers*, ch. 5.

91. *Papers of Act X of 1859*, vol. I, 31–32; Chittabrata Palit, *Tensions in Bengal Rural Society: Landlords, Planters and Colonial Rule, 1830–1860* (Calcutta: Progressive, 1975), 179.

92. *Decisions,* vol. II, 44.

93. Harish Chandra Kundu *versus* Alexander, May 12, 1863, *Decisions,* vol. I, 140–43.

94. Bindrabund Chunder Chowdree *versus* Issur Chunder Biswas and others, January 4, 1864, *Decisions,* vol. II, 1–2.

95. Baboo Dhunpat Singh *versus* Baboo Gooman Singh and others, May 5, 1864, *Decisions,* vol. II, 81–82. Ultimately, the size of holdings would be a key criterion for the determination of raiyat status: see *Report of the Rent Law Commission, with the Draft of a Bill to Consolidate and Amend the Law of Landlord and Tenant within the Territories of the Lieutenant-Governor of Bengal* (Calcutta: Bengal Secretariat Press, 1880), vol. 1, 6–7, 10–11.

96. Minutes on the Rent Laws by the Judges of the High Court and Members of the Board of Revenue, *Decisions,* submitted August 5 through December 28, 1864, vol. II, 400–86.

97. See John Murdoch, *A Letter to the Right Honorable the Earl of Elgin, Governor General of India, on the Rent Question in Bengal* (Calcutta: Baptist Mission Press, 1863), 10–14.

98. *Papers of Act X of 1859,* vol. II, 106.

99. Henry Maine to Sir Charles Wood, June 7th, 1863, *Sir Charles Wood Papers* (IOL Euro. Mss., F78/114/1).

100. Minute by Hon. H. S. Maine, July 10th, 1864, §20–23, *Sir Charles Wood Papers* (IOL Euro. Mss., F78/114/3a).

101. *Papers Relating to the Working and Amendment of Act X of 1859 (An Act to Amend the Law Relating to the Recovery of Rent in the Presidency of Fort William in Bengal)* (Calcutta: Office of the Superintendent of Government Publishing, 1883), vol. II, 1–3; and see also T. H. B., "The Right of Occupancy in Oude and Bengal: The Rent Case—Hills v. Issar Ghos," *Fraser's Magazine* 72 (July 1865): 77–91.

102. R. T. Larmour, *Notes on the Rent Difficulties in Lower Bengal, and on the Proposed Amendment of Act X. of 1859* (Calcutta: Savielle and Cranenburgh, 1862), 5, 8.

103. See for example Delta, *Indigo and its Enemies; or, Facts on Both Sides* (London: James Ridgway, 1861), 4, 42, 51, 85; H. R., *The Rent Difficulties in Bengal, and How to Remedy Them; The Rent Facilities in Cuttack, and How Best to Preserve Them* (London: Smith Elder, 1863), 8.

104. Henry Maine to Sir Charles Wood, Sept. 11th, 1863, *Sir Charles Wood Papers* (IOL Euro. Mss., F78/114/1), emphasis in original.

105. *Papers of Act X of 1859,* vol. II, 4, 47, 81–82, 128–33.

106. *Decisions,* vol. II, 244.

107. *Decisions,* vol. II, 549–670.

108. *Decisions,* vol. II, 550.

109. *Decisions,* vol. II, 553, emphasis in original.

110. *Decisions,* vol. II, 555, emphasis in original.

111. *Decisions,* vol. II, 555.

112. *Decisions,* vol. II, 556.

113. *Decisions,* vol. II, 559.

114. *Decisions,* vol. II, 561, emphasis in original.

115. *Decisions,* vol. II, 563, 565.

116. *Decisions,* vol. II, 565.

117. *Decisions*, vol. II, 567.

118. *Decisions*, vol. II, 448; see also Justice Seton-Karr, *Decisions*, vol. II, 408.

119. *Decisions*, vol. II, 400, 408–10, 450, 462, 474.

120. *Decisions*, vol. II, 450.

121. *Decisions*, vol. II, 406; see also Justice Trevor, *Decisions*, vol. II, 441.

122. *Decisions*, vol. II, 474, emphasis in original.

123. *Decisions*, vol. II, 402, 409, 424, 452, 464–65.

124. *Decisions*, vol. II, 412, 450.

125. *Decisions*, vol. II, 418, 448.

126. *Decisions*, vol. II, 626–28; see also Justice Norman, *Decisions*, vol. II, 636.

127. *Decisions*, vol. II, 457.

128. *Decisions*, vol. II, 418.

129. *Decisions*, vol. II, 420.

130. *Decisions*, vol. II, 573–74.

131. *Decisions*, vol. II, 458–59.

132. *Decisions*, vol. II, 447, 471.

133. *Decisions*, vol. II, 454; and see also 403, 416, 474, 580, 608.

134. *Decisions*, vol. II, 402–03, 440, 485–86.

135. *Decisions*, vol. II, 419, 465–66.

136. Ambirajan, *Classical Political Economy and British Policy in India,* 125.

137. Metcalf, *Ideologies of the Raj.*

138. "The Relations of Landlord and Tenant in India," *Calcutta Review* 39 (1864): 111.

139. *Decisions*, vol. II, 453.

140. *Decisions*, vol. II, 420, 452–53, 459.

141. *Decisions*, vol. II, 414.

142. *Decisions*, vol. II, 455.

143. *Decisions*, vol. II, 370.

144. *Decisions*, vol. II, 411, emphasis in original.

145. *Decisions*, vol. II, 460–61.

146. *Decisions*, vol. II, 407, 427, 451–52, 464–65.

147. Sir Henry Sumner Maine, *Village-Communities in the East and West* (London: John Murray, 1913), 224, 233.

148. Henry Maine to Sir Charles Wood, July 3rd, 1864, *Sir Charles Wood Papers* (IOL Euro. Mss., F78/114/3a). See also Zastoupil, *Mill and India,* 186–90; George Feaver, *From Status to Contract: A Biography of Sir Henry Maine, 1822–1888* (London: Longmans, Green, 1969), 119–22.

149. Henry Maine to Sir Charles Wood, August 19th, 1865, *Sir Charles Wood Papers* (IOL Euro. Mss., F78/114/4).

150. That Campbell and Maine were blind to their substantial differences is suggested by Maine's comment, in his preface to the first edition of *Village-Communities,* that the "principal statements made in the text about the Indian Village-Communities have been submitted to Sir George Campbell, now Lieut.-Governor of Bengal, who has been good enough to say that they coincide in the main with the results of his own experience and observation, which have been very extensive" (viii).

151. Lal-Behari Day, *Bengal Peasant Life* (London: Macmillan, 1908), 364.

152. Cited from *Memorandum respecting Law for Recovery of Arrears of Rent,* 40. See also his note on "Proprietary Tenures" and "Proprietary Rights," in John William Kaye (ed.), *Selections from the Papers of Lord Metcalfe* (London: Smith, Elder, 1855), 253, 255–63.

153. Wilson, *Domination of Strangers.* Contrast this to a distinctly political conception of custom that had predominated in the mid-eighteenth century: Travers, *Ideology and Empire.*

3. CUSTOM AND THE CRISIS OF VICTORIAN LIBERALISM

1. Sir George Campbell, *Memoirs of My Indian Career* (London: Macmillan, 1893), vol. I, 6; vol. II, 96.

2. Campbell, *Memoirs,* vol. II, 186–87.

3. "Views on Social Reform as Distinguished from Political Freedom in India, and on Progress from Village Communities," Presidential Address to Bengal Social Science Association, Jan. 10th, 1874, in Campbell, *Memoirs,* vol. II, 404, 410.

4. Clive Dewey, "Images of the Village Community: A Study in Anglo-Indian Ideology," *Modern Asian Studies* 6, no. 3 (1972): 319; C. E. Buckland, *Bengal under the Lieutenant-Governors; Being a Narrative of the Principal Events and Public Measures during their Periods of Office, from 1854–1898* (Calcutta: S. K. Lahiri, 1901), vol. I, 571.

5. George Campbell, *Modern India: A Sketch of the System of Civil Government, to which is Prefixed Some Account of the Natives and Native Institutions* (London: John Murray, 1852), 11.

6. Campbell, *Modern India,* 83.

7. Campbell, *Memoirs,* vol. I, 11, 15; vol. II, 39.

8. T. M. Devine, *The Great Highland Famine: Hunger, Emigration and the Scottish Highlands in the Nineteenth Century* (Edinburgh: John Donald, 1988), 181–82.

9. On Wingfield's policies in Awadh, see Thomas R. Metcalf, *The Aftermath of Revolt: India, 1857–1870* (Princeton, NJ: Princeton University Press, 1964), chs. 4–5.

10. During his two years at Haileybury, Campbell had focused on political economy and law for his special subjects. Campbell, *Memoirs,* vol. I, 9. Campbell had also held the position of Associate of the Court of Queen's Bench in the early 1850s, while on furlough. This was not a position that required any expertise in questions of law, but it did provide him with some knowledge of legal procedure. See Campbell, *Memoirs,* vol. I, 133–37.

11. Campbell, *Memoirs,* vol. II, 39–40, 51–52.

12. Ibid., vol. II, 54.

13. George Campbell, "Property in Land," *Westminster Review* 133 (January–June, 1890): 181–83.

14. Campbell, "Property in Land," 188.

15. Ibid., 183, 188.

16. *Addresses of Sir George Campbell, M.P., to his Constituents, November 1883* (Kirkcaldy: Strachan and Livingstone, 1883), 4, 6, 8, 16 (included in *Campbell of Edenwood Papers* [IOL Euro. Mss. E349/18]).

17. Campbell, "Property in Land," 184, 189; *Addresses of Sir George Campbell, M.P., to his Constituents,* 15; George Campbell, "Address on Economy and Trade" (Glasgow, 1874), 115 (included in *Campbell of Edenwood Papers* [IOL Euro. Mss. E349/18]).

18. Campbell, "Property in Land," 189.

19. George Campbell, "Some Current Politics by an Outsider" (unpublished paper included in *Campbell of Edenwood Papers* [IOL Euro. Mss. E349/18]), 6.

20. Campbell, "Address on Economy and Trade," 103.

21. *Addresses of Sir George Campbell, M.P., to his Constituents,* 4; Sir George Campbell, *The American People, or the Relations between the White and the Black. An Outcome of a Visit to the United States* (New York: Worthington, 1889), 119–20.

22. *Addresses of Sir George Campbell, M.P., to his Constituents,* 15.

23. Campbell, "Address on Economy and Trade," 113–14.

24. Campbell, "Some Current Politics by an Outsider," 18.

25. Campbell, *Memoirs,* vol. II, 154.

26. Ibid., vol. II, 156.

27. Ibid., vol. II, 174, 205, 279.

28. Dewey, "Images of the Village Community," 293–94.

29. A point emphasized in Dewey, "Images of the Village Community," 319–20.

30. My reading of Campbell is radically different from the "historicist" one offered by Dewey in "Celtic Agrarian Legislation," 56–57, and replicated by Peter Gray, "The Peculiarities of Irish Land Tenure, 1800–1914: From Agent of Improvement to Agent of Pacification," in Donald Winch and Patrick K. O'Brien (eds), *The Political Economy of British Historical Experience, 1688–1914* (Oxford: Oxford University Press, 2002), 154–56.

31. See Boyd Hilton, *A Mad, Bad and Dangerous People? England, 1783–1846* (Oxford: Clarendon, 2006), 350–53.

32. Cited from Hilton, *A Mad, Bad and Dangerous People,* 350.

33. G. Poulett Scrope, *Principles of Political Economy, Deduced from the Natural Laws of Social Welfare, and Applied to the Present State of Britain* (London: Longman, Rees, Orme, Brown, Green and Longman, 1833), 164–69.

34. Scrope, *Principles of Political Economy,* 14–19, emphasis in original.

35. Ibid., 21.

36. Ibid., 25–26.

37. Ibid., 99.

38. Ibid., 102.

39. Ibid., 103–06.

40. Bernard Semmel, *The Rise of Free Trade Imperialism: Classical Political Economy, the Empire of Free Trade and Imperialism, 1750–1850* (Cambridge: Cambridge University Press, 1970), 75 n.4, 97–98, 117–18.

41. Scrope, *Principles of Political Economy,* 178–79.

42. James Mill, *The Article Government: Reprinted from the Supplement to the Encyclopædia Britannica* (London: The Traveller Office, 1821), 5.

43. Mill, *Article Government,* 9; and cf. J.S. Mill, *Principles of Political Economy,* 224.

44. Mill, *Article Government,* 4.

45. Thomas Babington Macaulay: "Mill's *Essay on Government:* Utilitarian Logic and Politics," *Edinburgh Review* 49 (March 1829): 159–89.

46. See the selections in Mark Goldie (ed.), *The Reception of Locke's Politics* (London: Pickering and Chatto, 1999), vol. 6.

47. Thomas A. Horne, *Property Rights and Poverty: Political Argument in Britain, 1605–1834* (Chapel Hill and London: University of North Carolina Press, 1990), 123–26.

48. See Goldie, *Reception of Locke's Politics,* vol. 1, xxx–xxxix.

49. On Blackstone, see Horne, *Property Rights and Poverty,* 126–31.

50. Ibid., 202–09, 211–12.

51. Thomas Paine, *Agrarian Justice, Opposed to Agrarian Law, and to Agrarian Monopoly* (London: T. G. Ballard, [1797]), 4, 7.

52. Malcolm Chase, *"The People's Farm": English Radical Agrarianism, 1775–1840* (Oxford: Clarendon, 1988), ch. 2.

53. Horne, *Property Rights and Poverty,* 237–42; Chase, *"The People's Farm,"* ch. 7; Ashcraft, "Liberal Political Theory and Working-Class Radicalism;" Trygve R. Tholfsen, *Working-Class Radicalism in Mid-Victorian England* (New York: Columbia University Press, 1977). The same impulse was arguably also manifested in the Chartist Land Plan project spearheaded by Feargus O'Connor in the mid-1840s: see Joy MacAskill, "The Chartist Land Plan," in Asa Briggs (ed.), *Chartist Studies* (London: MacMillan, 1965), 304–41. On the role of Hodgskin in naming "capitalism," see Raymond Williams, *Keywords: A Vocabulary of Culture and Society* (New York: Oxford University Press, 1983), 50.

54. In relation to Ireland, even Scrope's reluctant Lockeanism found full-throated expression in a precocious advocacy, during the Famine years, of the universal legal recognition of tenant right in Ireland. Gray, "The Peculiarities of Irish Land Tenure," 145–46.

55. William Conner, *The True Political Economy of Ireland: or, Rack-Rent, the One Great Cause of All Her Evils: with its Remedy. Being a Speech Delivered at a Meeting of the Farming and Laboring Classes, at Inch, in the Queen's County* (Dublin: W. F. Wakeman, 1835).

56. Conner, *True Political Economy of Ireland,* vi.

57. Ibid., vi–vii.

58. Ibid., vii.

59. Ibid., iii.

60. Ibid., iii–iv.

61. Ibid., viii–ix, 31–32.

62. Peary Chand Mittra, "The Zemindar and the Ryot," *Calcutta Review* 6 (1846): 305–53. For a discussion of Mittra's essay in the wider context of early nineteenth-century Bengali liberalism, see Sartori, *Bengal in Global Concept History,* ch. 3.

63. Mittra, "Zemindar and Ryot," 305.

64. Ibid., 305–06.

65. Ibid., 307.

66. *Institutes of Hindu Law: or the Ordinances of Menu, according to the Gloss of Culluca. Comprising the Hindu System of Duties, Religious and Civil,* trans. by Sir William Jones (London: Sewell and Debrett, 1796), 250.

67. David Ludden links this idea of a right of first possession (reiterated by Aurangzeb in the seventeenth century) to practices of royal authority and conquest-colonization in premodern South Asia: see *An Agrarian History of South Asia* (Cambridge: Cambridge University Press, 1999), 79, 96ff.

68. Mittra, "Zemindar and Ryot," 310.

69. Ibid., 311–12.

70. Ibid., 313–14.

71. Ibid., 316, emphasis in original.

72. Ibid., 316, 318, 325, 328, 351.

73. Cf. William Sharman Crawfurd, *A Defense of the Small Farmers of Ireland* (Dublin: Joshua Porter, 1839).

74. W. Neilson Hancock, *The Tenant-Right of Ulster, Considered Economically, Being an Essay Read before the Dublin University Philosophical Society; with an Appendix, Containing the Evidence of John Hancock, Esq., Taken before the Landlord and Tenant Commissioners* (Dublin: Hodges and Smith, 1845). On the Devon Commission, see R. D. Collison Black, *Economic Thought and the Irish Question, 1817–1870* (Cambridge: Cambridge University Press, 1960), 27–28.

75. Black, *Economic Thought and the Irish Question,* 34, 46, 63–64.

76. Gray, "Peculiarities of Irish Land Tenure," 151–52.

77. Hancock, *Tenant-Right of Ulster,* 7.

78. Ibid., 9.

79. David Ricardo, *On the Principles of Political Economy and Taxation* (London: Empiricus Books, 2002), 34–35.

80. Hancock, *Tenant-Right of Ulster,* 19–27, 29–30.

81. Ibid., 33–34, emphasis in original.

82. Ibid., 46.

83. "Sharman Crawfurd on Ulster Tenant Right, 1846," *Irish Historical Studies* 13, no. 53 (1963): 246–53, on 247.

84. Clive Dewey, "The Rehabilitation of the Peasant Proprietor in Nineteenth-Century Economic Thought," *History of Political Economy* 6, no. 1 (1974): 17–47, on 21–22; Philip Pusey, *The Poor in Scotland* (London: James Burns, 1844). He was, incidentally, the brother of the prominent Tractarian, Edward Pusey.

85. *Report from the Select Committee on Agricultural Customs; together with the Minutes of Evidence and Index* (1848), *Parliamentary Papers* 1847–48 (461), iii–iv.

86. *Report on Agricultural Customs,* iv.

87. Ibid., xii.

88. Sunjeeb Chunder Chatterjee, *Bengal Ryots: Their Rights and Liabilities, Being an Elementary Treatise on the Law of Landlord and Tenant* (Calcutta: D'Rozario, 1864), 13.

89. Chatterjee, *Bengal Ryots,* 15–20.

90. Bankimchandra Chattopadhyay, *Bankim racanabali: sahitya samagra,* ed. Bishnu Basu (Calcutta: Tuli-Kalam, c. 1986), 290–91.

91. *Bankim racanabali,* 305.

92. Ibid., 306.

93. Ibid., 310.

94. Ibid., 314.

95. Robb, *Ancient Rights and Future Comfort,* 116.

96. [R. H. Hollingbery], *The Zemindary Settlement of Bengal* (Calcutta: Brown, 1879), vol. I, 2.

97. *Zemindary Settlement of Bengal,* vol. I, 3.

98. Sir Richard Temple, Administrative Report for 1875–1876, cited in *Report of the Government of Bengal on the Proposed Amendment of the Law of Landlord and Tenant in that Province* (Calcutta: Office of the Superintendent of Government Printing, India, 1881), Appendix I (Alexander Mackenzie, "Memorandum on the History of the Rent Question in Bengal Since the Passing of Act X of 1859"), vol. I, 116–17.

99. Sir Richard Temple, Minute of May 25, 1875, cited in *Report on the Proposed Amendment of the Law of Landlord and Tenant*, vol. I, 118, emphasis added.

100. *Zemindary Settlement of Bengal*, vol. I, 3.

101. Ibid., vol. I, 4.

102. Ibid., vol. I, 5.

103. Ibid., vol. I, 6–7.

104. Ibid., vol. I, 7.

105. Ibid., vol. I, 8; vol. II, 22.

106. Ibid., vol. I, 9.

107. Ibid., vol. I, 8; vol. 2, 92–95.

108. Ibid., vol. I, 13.

109. Ibid., vol. I, 12.

110. Ibid., vol. I, 9.

111. Ibid., vol. I, 19.

112. Ibid., vol. I, 38–39, emphasis in original.

113. Ibid., vol. II, 18.

114. Ibid., vol. II, 38–39.

115. Ibid., vol. I, 16.

116. Ibid., vol. I, 17.

117. Ibid., vol. I, 19; vol. II, 7–14.

118. Ibid., vol. I, 46–47; vol. II, 117.

119. Ibid., vol. I, 42, 46; vol. II, 43.

120. Ibid., vol. I, 49, 51; vol. II, 172.

121. Ibid., vol. I, 86.

122. Ibid., vol. I, 109.

123. [R. H. Hollingbery], *A Handbook of Gold and Silver, by an Indian Official* (London: Longmans, Green, 1878), x.

124. Hollingbery's commitment to the constitutive function of labor as the measure of wealth—and the basis of a critique of the silver standard to which the depreciating rupee was tied—is elaborated further in [R. H. Hollingbery], *The Silver Question Reviewed, by an Indian Official* (London: Longmans, Green, 1878), ch. 5.

125. For the key distinction between the inheritance of republicanism as a set of rhetorical tools and its substantial continuance as an ideological framework, see Pincus, "Neither Machiavellian Moment nor Possessive Individualism." On Tory Romanticism in relation to smallholding, see Karen O'Brien, "Colonial Emigration, Public Policy, and Tory Romanticism, 1783–1830," in Duncan Kelly (ed.), *Lineages of Empire: The Historical Roots of British Imperial Thought* (Oxford: Oxford University Press for the British Academy, 2009), 161–80.

126. On the "rule of colonial difference," see Partha Chatterjee, *The Nation and Its Fragments: Colonial and Postcolonial Histories* (Princeton, NJ: Princeton University Press, 1993), ch. 2.

127. See for example R. C. Dutt, *The Peasantry of Bengal, Being a View of their Condition under the Hindu, Mahomedan, and the English Rule, and a Consideration of the Means Calculated to Improve their Future Prospects* (Calcutta: Thacker and Spink, 1874), 55, 57, 76–83.

128. W. W. Hunter, *Seven Years of Indian Legislation* (Calcutta: Truebner, 1870), 11.

129. George Campbell, "Views on Social Reform as Distinguished from Political Freedom in India," in Campbell, *Memoirs*, vol. II, 403–04, 409–10.

130. Andrew Sartori, *Bengal in Global Concept History: Culturalism in the Age of Capital* (Chicago: University of Chicago Press, 2008), chs. 4–5.

131. See Partha Chatterjee, "A Modern Science of Politics for the Colonized," in Partha Chatterjee (ed.), *Texts of Power: Emerging Disciplines in Colonial Bengal* (Minneapolis: University of Minnesota Press, 1995), 101–02.

132. Secretary of State for India to Government of India, Aug. 17th, 1882, *Correspondence regarding the Proposed Amendment of the Law of Landlord and Tenant*, 54–55. The history of the emerging argument that a new act was needed to reform the 1859 Rent Act is recounted in Alexander Mackenzie's rather tedious "Memorandum on the History of the Rent Question in Bengal Since the Passing of Act X of 1859," *Report on the Proposed Amendment of the Law of Landlord and Tenant*, Appendix I. Robb, *Ancient Custom and Future Comfort*, provides an extensive and detailed analysis of the debates surrounding the 1885 Act; S. B. Cook, *Imperial Affinities: Nineteenth Century Analogies and Exchanges between India and Ireland* (New Delhi: Sage, 1993), chs. 4 and 5, gives a good summary of the central role of Irish civilians in driving pro-raiyat policy and the role of the Irish analogy in framing the debates; and Kedar Nath Roy gives a detailed commentary on the legislation itself in *The Bengal Tenancy Act, Being Act VIII of 1885, as Amended up to Date, with Notes, Judicial Rulings, Rules, and Notifications, &c, &c* (Calcutta: Majumdar Press, 1906).

133. Government of India to Secretary of State for India, March 21, 1882, *Papers Relating to the Bengal Tenancy Act of 1885* (IOL W5803), vol. 1, 8, 15, 18, 37.

134. *Papers Relating to the Bengal Tenancy Act*, vol. 1, 16.

135. Sugata Bose, *Peasant Labour and Colonial Capital: Rural Bengal since 1770* (Cambridge: Cambridge University Press, 1993), chs. 3–4.

136. Robb, *Ancient Rights and Future Comfort*.

137. Stokes, *English Utilitarians and India*, 254–55.

138. A District Officer, "The Policy of the New Rent Law for Bengal and Behar," *Calcutta Review* 72, no. 143 (1881): 161.

139. On the composition of the commission, see Kedar Nath Roy, *The Rent Law of Bengal* (Calcutta: Calcutta Central Press, 1886), 1–2; and Robb, *Ancient Rights and Future Comfort*, ch. 4.

140. *Report of the Rent Law Commission, with the Draft of a Bill to Consolidate and Amend the Law of Landlord and Tenant within the Territories of the Lieutenant-Governor of Bengal* (Calcutta: Bengal Secretariat Press, 1880), vol. 1, 19–20.

141. *Report of the Rent Law Commission*, vol. 1, 24.

142. Ibid., vol. 1, 64.

143. Ibid., vol. 1, 19–20; vol. 2, 427.

144. Sir Thomas Munro, "On the State of the Country and the Condition of the People," in Sir Arthur J. Arbuthnot (ed.), *Major-General Sir Thomas Munro, Governor of Madras* (London: C. Kegan Paul, 1881), vol. I, 240–43, 246–47, 252–56. Cf. Rachel Sturman, *The Government of Social Life in Colonial India: Liberalism, Religious Law, and Women's Rights* (Cambridge: Cambridge University Press, 2012), 42–45. Martha McLaren's argument that Munro should be understood as a progressive product of the Scottish Enlightenment does not imply that liberalism (a category she specifically disavows) was the basic impulse of the

Enlightenment. Certainly, in the wider context of British political argument, there is little reason to see Munro's insistence on the priority of the political over the social as anything more than a highly qualified liberalism, if it was a liberalism at all. See her *British India and British Scotland, 1780–1830: Career Building, Empire Building, and a Scottish School of Thought on Indian Governance* (Akron, OH: University of Akron Press, 2001), esp. ch. 11.

145. *Report of the Rent Law Commission*, vol. 1, 24.

146. Ibid., vol. 1, 96.

147. Ibid., vol. 1, 110.

148. Ibid., vol. 1, 111.

149. Ibid., vol. 1, 112.

150. Ibid., vol. 2, 467.

151. Ibid., vol. 2, 468.

152. Ibid., vol. 2, 444.

153. Cook, *Imperial Affinities*, 85; see also Robb, *Ancient Rights and Future Comfort*, (sing.) 214.

154. See Dewey, "Rehabilitation of the Peasant Proprietor;" and F.M.L. Thompson, "Changing Perceptions of Land Tenures in Britain, 1750–1914," in Winch and O'Brien (eds.), *Political Economy of British Historical Experience*, 119–38.

155. John Bright, *Mr. Bright's Speech on Ireland. Meeting of Irish Residents in Manchester. Presentation of an Address to J. Bright Esq., M.P.* (Manchester: A. Ireland, 1850), 4.

156. *Bright's Speech on Ireland*, 6.

157. Richard Cobden, *Cobden on the Land Question: A Plea for Small Holdings* (London: Cassell, 1907), 3–4.

158. Thompson, "Changing Perceptions of Land Tenures in Britain," 128–32.

159. Codben, *Land Question*, 5.

160. J.E. Cairnes, "Political Economy and Land," *Essays in Political Economy, Theoretical and Applied* (London: Macmillan, 1873), 187–231, on 187. Cf. William Neilson Hancock, *Three Lectures on the Questions, Should the Principles of Political Economy be Disregarded at the Present Crisis, and If Not, How Can They be Applied towards the Discovery of Measures of Relief* (Dublin: Hodges and Smith, 1847).

161. Cairnes, "Political Economy and Land," 187–88.

162. Ibid., 196–202.

163. Ibid., 190, 191n.

164. Ibid., 196.

165. Ibid., 207–08, 212–13.

166. George Campbell, *The Irish Land* (London: Truebner, 1869), 5–6.

167. Campbell, *Irish Land*, 24.

168. Cairnes, "Political Economy and Land," 220–24; E.D. Steele, "Ireland and the Empire: Imperial Precedents for Gladstone's First Irish Land Act," *Historical Journal* 11 (1968): 64–83; E.D. Steele, *Irish Land and Irish Politics: Tenant-Right and Nationality, 1865–1870* (Cambridge: Cambridge University Press, 1974), 104–08; Dewey, "Celtic Agrarian Legislation," 56–61; Black, *Economic Thought and the Irish Question*, 62–69; Cook, *Imperial Affinities*; Kinzer, *England's Disgrace?*, 200–08.

169. Hilton, *Mad, Bad and Dangerous People*, 554; Semmel, *Rise of Free Trade Imperialism*, 144–45.

170. E. J. Hobsbawm, *The Age of Empire, 1875–1914* (New York: Pantheon, 1987), ch. 2 (Marshall quotation cited on p. 36); E. J. Hobsbawm, *Industry and Empire: From 1750 to the Present Day* (Harmondsworth: Penguin, 1969), 237–44; Ronald Hyam, *Britain's Imperial Century, 1815–1914: A Study of Empire and Expansion* (Houndmills, UK: Palgrave Macmillan, 2002), 189–202.

171. Duncan Bell, *The Idea of Greater Britain: Empire and the Future of World Order, 1860–1900* (Princeton, NJ, and Oxford: Princeton University Press, 2007), 56–58, 143–49.

172. Thomas Carlyle, *Past and Present* (London: J. M. Dent, 1905), 190, 211; Bell, *Idea of Greater Britain,* 147.

173. Joseph Chamberlain, *The Radical Programme* (London: Chapman and Hall, 1885), 53.

174. Semmel, *Rise of Free Trade Imperialism,* ch. 6; Chamberlain, *Radical Programme,* 53–57, 92–125.

175. Mantena, *Alibis of Empire;* Sartori, *Bengal in Global Concept History.*

176. Chamberlain, *Radical Programme,* 59.

177. Ben Jackson, "Property-Owning Democracy: A Short History," in Martin O'Neill and Thad Williamson (eds.), *Property-Owning Democracy: Rawls and Beyond* (Oxford: Blackwell, 2012), 36–40.

178. For a brief statement of this argument, see Michael Freeden, "Liberal Community: An Essay in Retrieval," in Avital Simhony and D. Weinstein (eds.), *The New Liberalism: Reconciling Liberty and Community* (Cambridge: Cambridge University Press, 2001), 26–48.

179. Sartori, *Bengal in Global Concept History,* 99–101.

180. Metcalf, *Aftermath of Revolt,* 185; Steele, *Irish Land and Irish Politics,* 104.

181. Herbert Gladstone cited from Eugenio Biagini, *Gladstone* (New York: St. Martin's, 2000), 107.

182. John Morrow, "Private Property, Liberal Subjects, and the State," in Simhony and Weinstein (eds.), *The New Liberalism,* 92–93. See also P. J. Cain, *Hobson and Imperialism: Radicalism, New Liberalism, and Finance, 1887–1938* (Oxford: Oxford University Press, 2002), esp. chs. 2–3; Stefan Collini, *Liberalism and Sociology: L. T. Hobhouse and Political Argument in England, 1880–1914* (Cambridge: Cambridge University Press, 1979); Michael Freeden, *The New Liberalism: An Ideology of Social Reform* (Oxford: Clarendon, 1978); and Jackson, "Property-Owning Democracy," 40–44.

183. See P. F. Clarke, *Lancashire and the New Liberalism* (Cambridge: Cambridge University Press, 1971).

184. Bayly, *Birth of the Modern World,* 310.

185. Herbert Spencer, *The Man versus the State* (New York: D. Appleton, 1885), 1.

186. Stokes, *English Utilitarians and India,* 122.

4. AN AGRARIAN CIVIL SOCIETY?

1. P. G. Robb, *Ancient Rights and Future Comfort: Bihar, the Bengal Tenancy Act of 1885, and British Rule in India* (Richmond, UK: Curzon, 1997), 313.

2. On indigo cultivation in Bengal generally, see Sugata Bose, *Peasant Labour and Colonial Capital: Rural Bengal since 1770* (Cambridge: Cambridge University Press, 1993), 45–52; Benoy Chowdhury, *Growth of Commercial Agriculture in Bengal, 1757–1900* (Calcutta:

Indian Studies Past and Present, 1964), vol. I, 73–203; Blair B. Kling, *The Blue Mutiny: The Indigo Disturbances in Bengal, 1859–1862* (Philadelphia: University of Pennsylvania Press, 1966); Chittabrata Palit, *Tensions in Bengal Rural Society: Landlords, Planters and Colonial Rule, 1830–1860* (Calcutta: Progressive, 1975), chs 4–5; and Tirthankar Roy, "Indigo and Law in Colonial India," *Economic History Review* 64, Suppl. 1 (2011): 60–75. On the monopolization of grain stores by accepting payment of rents in kind as an additional means of extortion of raiyats (already pointing forward to the expansion of sharecropping), see F. Platts, Deputy Magistrate of Kurreempore to the Magistrate of Nadia, April 2nd, 1860, *Papers Relating to Indigo Production in Bengal, preliminary to Appointment of Commission, 1854–60, Parliamentary Papers* 1861 (72), 266.

3. A. Sconce to Secretary to the Government of Bengal, April 20th, 1854, and Minute by the Lieutenant-Governor, June 5th, 1854, *Parliamentary Papers* 1861 (72), 3–7.

4. F. Beaufort to the Commissioner of Rajshahye Division, Oct. 26th, 1854, *Parliamentary Papers* 1861 (72), 17–20.

5. A.C. Bidwell to Secretary to the Government of Bengal, Jan. 4th, 1855, *Parliamentary Papers* 1861 (72), 20.

6. A. Sconce to W. Grey, Secretary to Government of Bengal, *Parliamentary Papers* 1861 (72), 30–33.

7. H.B. Lawford to Undersecretary to Government of Bengal, Jan. 12th, 1855, *Parliamentary Papers* 1861 (72), 45–46.

8. *Parliamentary Papers* 1861 (72), 32–33.

9. G.U. Yule to A.W. Russell, Undersecretary to Government of Bengal, Jan. 20th, 1855, *Parliamentary Papers* 1861 (72), 36.

10. *Parliamentary Papers* 1861 (72), 37.

11. [G. Graham], *Life in the Mofussil, or the Civilian in Lower Bengal. By an Ex-Civilian* (London: C. Kegan Paul, 1878), vol. 2, 5.

12. J.H. Mangles, Officiating Joint Magistrate of Barasat, to Commissioner of Nadia Division, May 19th, 1856, *Parliamentary Papers* 1861 (72), 59–60.

13. See for example Graham, *Life in the Mofussil*, 5–6; W.H. Elliott, Officiating Commissioner of the Burdwan Division, to Secretary to Government of Bengal, March 22nd, 1855; and W. Luke, Civil and Sessions Judge of Midnapur, to Undersecretary to Government of Bengal, Jan. 4th, 1855; C. Steer, Judge of Backergunge, to Secretary to Government of Bengal, Feb. 7th, 1855, *Parliamentary Papers* 1861 (72), 25, 28, 41.

14. See for example, Henry Maine to Sir Charles Wood, Dec. 4th, 1862, *Sir Charles Wood Papers* (IOL Euro. Mss., F78/114/1); Henry Maine to Sir Charles Wood, Feb. 13th, 1863, *Sir Charles Wood Papers* (IOL Euro. Mss., F78/114/1); and Henry Maine to Sir Charles Wood, Nov. 5th, 1863, *Sir Charles Wood Papers* (IOL Euro. Mss., F78/114/2). See also S.N. den Otter, "The Political Economy of Empire: Freedom of Contract and 'Commercial Civilization' in Colonial India," in Martin Daunton and Frank Trentmann (eds.), *Worlds of Political Economy: Knowledge and Power in the Nineteenth and Twentieth Centuries* (Houndmills, UK, and New York: Palgrave MacMillan, 2004), 69–94.

15. Henry Maine to Sir Charles Wood, July 3rd, 1864, *Sir Charles Wood Papers* (IOL Euro. Mss., F78/114/3a).

16. See for example the Humble Petition of the Indigo Planters' Association in Bengal to the Honourable Lieutenant-Governor of Bengal, *Parliamentary Papers* 1861 (72), 196; Peti-

tion of the Bengal Indigo Planters' Association to the Right Honourable His Excellency the Viceroy and Governor General of India in Council, *Papers Relating to Indigo Cultivation in Bengal, Parliamentary Papers* 1861 (72-II), 7.

17. Minute by the Lieutenant Governor of Bengal on the Report of the Indigo Commission, Dec. 17, 1860, *Parliamentary Papers* 1861 (72-II), 83.

18. A. Grote to Secretary to Government of Bengal, June 6th, 1859, *Parliamentary Papers* 1861 (72), 107.

19. F. R. Cockerell, late Magistrate of Nadia, to A. Grote, Nov. 17, 1859, *Parliamentary Papers* 1861 (72), 151; *Parliamentary Papers* 1861 (72-II), 7.

20. *Parliamentary Papers* 1861 (72), 198.

21. A. R. Young, Secretary to Government of Bengal, to the Officiating Commissioner of Nadia Division, July 21st, 1859; and Lieutenant Governor of Bengal to A. Sconce, Legislative Member for Bengal, March 23rd, 1860, *Parliamentary Papers* 1861 (72), 111–114, 201–202.

22. A. Eden, Joint Magistrate of Barasat, to the Commissioner of the Nadia Division, June 19, 1858, *Parliamentary Papers* 1861 (72), 126.

23. A. Eden to Secretary to Government of Bengal, March 28th, 1860, *Parliamentary Papers* 1861 (72), 329.

24. A. Eden to Baboo Hemchunder Kur, Deputy Magistrate, Kalarooah Subdivision, *Parliamentary Papers* 1861 (72), 330.

25. *Report of the Indigo Commission 1860, Parliamentary Papers* 1861 (72-I), Minutes of Evidence, 237.

26. *Parliamentary Papers* 1861 (72), 202.

27. Ibid., (72-II), 7.

28. Minute of the Lieutenant Governor, August 22nd, 1860, *Parliamentary Papers* 1861 (72-II), 11–12, emphasis added.

29. *Parliamentary Papers* 1861 (72-II), 13–14.

30. Delta, *Indigo and its Enemies; or, Facts on Both Sides* (London: James Ridgway, 1861), 29.

31. Secretary, Indigo Planters' Association, to W. Grey, Secretary to Government of Bengal, Oct. 13, 1860, *Parliamentary Papers* 1861 (72-II), 31.

32. J. Hills to L. B. Bowring, Private Secretary to the Governor General, Sept. 14, 1860, *Parliamentary Papers* 1861 (72-II), 58.

33. *Parliamentary Papers* 1861 (72-II), 77.

34. Binay Bhushan Chaudhuri, "Growth of Commercial Agriculture in Bengal—1859–1885," *Indian Economic and Social History Review* 7, nos. 1–2 (1970): 45–47.

35. Graham, *Life in the Mofussil*, 50.

36. *Decisions*, vol. I, 193.

37. Ibid., vol. I, 198.

38. Ibid., vol. I, 195.

39. Richard M. Eaton, *The Rise of Islam and the Bengal Frontier, 1204–1760* (Berkeley: University of California Press, 1993), 96–97, 204–07; Frank Perlin, "Protoindustrialization and Precolonial South Asia," *Past and Present* 98 (Feb. 1983): 30–95; David L. Curley, *Poetry and History: Bengali Mangal-kabya and Social Change in Precolonial Bengal* (New Delhi: Chronicle Books, 2008), ch. 2; Ludden, *Agrarian History of South Asia*, 144–53.

40. Rajat Datta, *Society, Economy and the Market: Commercialization in Rural Bengal, c. 1760–1800* (New Delhi: Manohar, 2000), emphasis in original.

41. For a discussion of the differences between subregions in relation to early-modern commercialization, see Tirthankar Roy, "Where Is Bengal? Situating an Indian Region in the Early Modern World Economy," *Past and Present* 213 (Nov. 2011): 115–46.

42. The fact that rice was also the main subsistence crop renders estimates of its proportional significance as a commercial crop in general (i.e. including intraregional and interregional commerce) especially difficult to generate. Chaudhuri does note, however, that the value of Bengal's rice exports from the Calcutta port rose from £200,000 in the mid-1830s to £4 million in 1864–65 (Chaudhuri, "Growth of Commercial Agriculture," 34). With regards to jute, Chaudhuri notes that by 1900–01 "jute cultivation in the districts of Rangpur, Tripura, Mymensingh and Dacca occupied nearly 30%, 27%, 18% and 13.5% respectively of the net cropped area" (Chaudhuri, "Growth of Commercial Agriculture," 57). See also Bose, *Peasant Labour and Colonial Capital*, 52–63; Sugata Bose, *Agrarian Bengal: Economy, Social Structure and Politics, 1919–1947* (Cambridge: Cambridge University Press, 1986), 83–87; David Ludden, "World Economy and Village India, 1600–1900: Exploring the Agrarian History of Capitalism," in Sugata Bose (ed.), *South Asia and World Capitalism* (Delhi: Oxford University Press, 1990), 159–77.

43. Roy, "Where Is Bengal?" 127.

44. Eaton, *Rise of Islam and the Bengal Frontier*, ch. 8, on 221.

45. Roy, "Where Is Bengal?"

46. Datta, *Society, Economy and the Market*, 71, 90–91, 102–07.

47. Cf. Tilottoma Mukherjee, "Markets in Eighteenth Century Bengal Economy," *Indian Economic and Social History Review* 48, no. 2 (2011): 143–76.

48. Datta, *Society, Economy and the Market*, 56–66.

49. Roy, "Where Is Bengal?" 127.

50. Jairus Banaji, *Theory as History: Essays on Modes of Production and Exploitation* (Leiden: Brill, 2010), has much to say on the complex relationship between mercantile and modern capital.

51. Curley, *Poetry and History*, 49.

52. Bose, *Agrarian Bengal*; Partha Chatterjee, *Bengal 1920–1947: The Land Question* (Calcutta: K.P. Bagchi, 1984); Iftekhar Iqbal, *The Bengal Delta: Ecology, State and Social Change, 1840–1943* (Houndmills, UK, and New York: Palgrave Macmillan, 2010), ch. 5.

53. Iqbal, *Bengal Delta*, ch. 4.

54. Cited from Sartori, *Bengal in Global Concept History*, 206.

55. Bose, *Peasant Labour and Colonial Capital*, 148–51; Muin-ud-din Ahmad Khan, *History of the Fara'idi Movement in Bengal (1818–1906)* (Karachi: Pakistan Historical Society, 1965); James Wise, "The Muhammadans of Eastern Bengal," *Journal of the Asiatic Society of Bengal* 63, no. 1 (1894): 28–63; Ranajit Guha, *Elementary Aspects of Peasant Insurgency in Colonial India* (Delhi: Oxford University Press, 1983), 172–73; Kalyan Kumar Sen Gupta, "Agrarian Disturbances in Eastern and Central Bengal in the Late Nineteenth Century," *Indian Economic and Social History Review* 8, no. 2 (1971): 201, 204–05.

56. Iqbal, *Bengal Delta*, 73–74.

57. Baber Johansen, *The Islamic Law on Land Tax and Rent: The Peasant's Loss of Property Rights as Interpreted in the Hanafite Legal Literature of the Mamluk and Ottoman Period* (London: Croom Helm, 1988); Martha Mundy and Richard Saumarez Smith, *Governing Property, Making the Modern State: Law, Administration and Production in Ottoman Syria*

(London: I. B. Tauris, 2007), ch. 2; Zafarul Islam, *Socio-Economic Dimension of Fiqh Litera-ture in Medieval India* (Lahore: Research Cell, Dyal Singh Trust Library, 1990); Irfan Habib, *The Agrarian System of Mughal India, 1556–1707*, 2nd ed. (New Delhi: Oxford University Press, 1999), 123–24.

58. Mundy and Smith, *Governing Property*, ch. 3; Kenneth Cuno, "Was the Land of Ottoman Syria Miri or Milk? An Examination of Juridical Differences within the Hanafi School," *Studia Islamica*, 81 (1995), 121–52; Kenneth Cuno, *The Pasha's Peasants: Land, Society, and Economy in Lower Egypt, 1740–1858* (Cambridge: Cambridge University Press, 1992), 76–81.

59. Eaton, *Rise of Islam and the Bengal Frontier*, 308.

60. For a strong version of the claim that such Lockeanism was central to Faraizism, see Ahmad Khan, *History of the Faraidi*, 114–15. See also Eaton, *Rise of Islam and the Bengal Frontier*, 282–83, 308–09.

61. James Westland, *A Report on the District of Jessore: Its Antiquities, its History and its Commerce* (Calcutta: Bengal Secretariat Office, 1871), 199; and see also Ramshunker Sen, *Report on the Agricultural Statistics of Jhenidah, Magurah, Bagirhat, and Sunderbans Sub-Divisions, District Jessore, 1872–73* (Calcutta: Bengal Board of Revenue, 1874), part II, 24.

62. Sen, *Report on the Agricultural Statistics of Jessore*, part II, 4–5.

63. Westland, *Report on the District of Jessore*, 198–99, 228; and cf. Sen, *Report on the Agricultural Statistics Jessore*, part II, 18–19.

64. Sen, *Report on the Agricultural Statistics of Jessore*, part II, 5.

65. A. P. MacDonnell, Sec'y to the Government of Bengal, Revenue Department, to H. J. S. Cotton, Sec'y to the Bengal Board of Revenue, May 12, 1884, Land Revenue Department, A Proceedings, Series 22, Batch 22, List 17, National Archives of Bangladesh.

66. Cited from Iqbal, *Bengal Delta*, 31.

67. Westland, *Report on the District of Jessore*, 226, 234, 235; Sen, *Report on the Agricultural Statistics of Jessore*, part II, 30.

68. Westland, *Report on the District of Jessore*, 225.

69. Ibid., 236.

70. Ibid., 174, emphasis in original.

71. Bose, *Peasant Labour and Colonial Capital*, ch. 3; Datta, *Society, Economy and the Market*, 200–20.

72. Chatterjee, *Land Question*, 36–59; B. C. Prance, *Final Report on the Survey and Settlement Operations in the Riparian Areas of District Pabna, Surveyed in the Course of the Faridpur District Settlement* (Calcutta: Bengal Secretariat Book Depot, 1916), 6–7.

73. Sen, *Report on the Agricultural Statistics of Jessore*, part I, 76–77, 86–87, 89.

74. J. B. P., "Rustic Bengal," *Calcutta Review* 59, no. 117 (1874): 180–214. See also Graham, *Life in the Mofussil*, 77.

75. Sen, *Report on the Agricultural Statistics of Jessore*, part I, 86.

76. P. Nolan, Sec'y to the Government of Bengal, to the Sec'y of the Government of India, Revenue and Agricultural Department, 30th June 1888, *Report on the Condition of the Lower Classes of Population in Bengal* (Calcutta: Bengal Secretariat Press, 1888), 3.

77. Bose, *Peasant Labour and Colonial Capital*, ch. 4.

78. Sen, *Report on the Agricultural Statistics of Jessore*, part I, 9, 10 13,

79. Ibid., part I, 65.

80. A. Smith, Commissioner of the Presidency Division, to the Sec'y of the Government of Bengal, Revenue Department, 17th May 1888, *Report on the Condition of the Lower Classes of Population in Bengal.*

81. Westland, *Report on the District of Jessore,* 207.

82. Sen, *Report on the Agricultural Statistics of Jessore,* part I, 24.

83. Cf. Datta, *Society, Economy and the Market,* 64–66.

84. Hugh B. Urban, *Songs of Ecstasy: Tantric and Devotional Songs from Colonial Bengal* (New York: Oxford University Press, 2001), 137.

85. Translation of a petition from Muneroodeen Mundle and others, 1859, *Parliamentary Papers* 1861 (72), 109.

86. Petition from Sreemunt Holdar and others, inhabitants of Collinga, Thannah Handrah, Zillah Nuddea, to the Honourable Lieutenant Governor of Bengal, dated 12 August 1859, *Parliamentary Papers* 1861 (72), 136.

87. Petition of Ram Gopaul Biswas and others, inhabitants of Poragatcha, Thannah Hanshkhally, Zilla Nuddea, to the Honourable Lieutenant Governor of Bengal, dated 12 August 1859, *Parliamentary Papers* 1861 (72), 139.

88. Gantidars were, from the perspective of colonial land law, an ambiguous category of intermediate tenureholder whom the authors of the Indigo Commission defined as "supposed to be a middleman, but, in reality, a tenant proprietor" who sometimes "holds half or a whole village" farmed by raiyats. See *Report of the Indigo Commission,* lxi; and for a more detailed explanation of the category "gantidar," Westland, *Report on the District of Jessore,* 99, 115–17, 191–200. For the classic discussion of the role of the "jotedar" in agrarian society, see Ratna Lekha Ray, *Change in Bengal Agrarian Society, 1760–1850* (Delhi: Manohar, 1979).

89. *Report of the Indigo Commission,* xvii–xviii, emphasis added.

90. Urban, *Songs of Ecstacy,* 139.

91. *Report of the Indigo Commission,* Minutes of Evidence, 64–70, 77, 80–81, 89, 94, 109–10, 141–42, 150–51, 178, 204–05.

92. E.g., ibid., 150, 208.

93. Ibid., 34, 44, 74, 100, 208; see also *Parliamentary Papers* 1861 (72), 186.

94. *Report of the Indigo Commission,* Minutes of Evidence, 77, 94, 151, 205, 241.

95. Ibid., 150, 178, 203, 208.

96. Ibid., 207; see also *Parliamentary Papers* 1861 (72), 187.

97. Petition from the inhabitants of Zillah Nuddea to the Lieutenant Governor of Bengal, dated Joyrampore, 16 February 1860, *Parliamentary Papers* 1861 (72), 187.

98. *Report of the Indigo Commission,* Minutes of Evidence, 95, 110.

99. Ibid., 62–63.

100. Lowis, "Annual General Administrative Report of the Chittagong Division, 1874–75," 7.

101. Secretary of State to Government of India, March 21st, 1882, *Correspondence between the Government of India and the Secretary of State regarding the Proposed Amendment of the Law of Landlord and Tenant in Bengal* (Calcutta: Office of the Superintendent of Government Printing, 1883), 4–5; and see also *Report on the Proposed Amendment to the Law of Landlord and Tenant,* Appendix 1, 85–86.

102. Cited from *Report on the Proposed Amendment to the Law of Landlord and Tenant,* Appendix 1, 97.

103. See E. W. Molony, Commissioner of Rajshahi Division, "Riots in the Pabna District," July 16th, 1873, *Proceedings of the Government of Bengal in the Police Department* (IOL P/258), 1; Kalyan Kumar Sen Gupta, *Pabna Disturbances and the Politics of Rent, 1873–1885* (New Delhi: People's Publishing, 1974), 14; Tariq Omar Ali, *The Envelope of Global Trade: The Political Economy and Intellectual History of Jute in the Bengal Delta, 1850s to 1950s* (unpublished dissertation, Harvard University, 2012), 48–53.

104. Sir George Campbell, *Memoirs of My Indian Career* (London: Macmillan, 1893), vol. II, 292.

105. Molony, "Riots in the Pabna District," 3, italics in original.

106. Ibid., 6, 12.

107. Ibid., 8–10.

108. Sen Gupta, *Pabna Disturbances,* 30–31.

109. Ibid., 124–32.

110. The quotation is from Ashley Eden in the late 1870s, cited from Binay Chaudhuri, "Agricultural Production in Bengal, 1850–1900: Coexistence of Decline and Growth," *Bengal Past and Present* 70 (1969): 196. See also Bose, *Peasant Labour and Colonial Capitalism,* 156–57.

111. See for example Parbati Churn Roy, *The Rent Question in Bengal* (Calcutta: Sadharan Brahmo Samaj Press, 1883).

112. "[Petition] from Babu Rajkissore Mookerjee, cultivator-ryot, Utterpara, to Secretary to Government of India, Legislative Department (dated 24th November, 1884)," *Papers Relating to the Bengal Tenancy Act,* vol. 4, appendix A47, 1840.

113. *Papers Relating to the Bengal Tenancy Act,* vol. 4, 1845.

114. "[Petition] from Babu Rajkissore Mukerjea, cultivator-ryot, Utterpara, to Secretary to Government of India, Legislative Department (dated 8th Janurary, 1885)," *Papers Relating to the Bengal Tenancy Act,* vol. 4, 2068.

115. For a classic statement of the "cultural" orientation of the Bengal peasant towards a subsistence ethic—and the subsequent crisis of this culture in the face of a crisis of subsistence in twentieth-century Bengal—see Paul R. Greenough, *Prosperity and Misery in Modern Bengal: The Famine of 1943–1944* (New York and Oxford: Oxford University Press, 1982), ch. 2.

116. Greenough, *Prosperity and Misery in Bengal,* 14, 215–16; Sartori, *Bengal in Global Concept History,* 58–59.

117. Delta, *Indigo and its Enemies,* 57.

118. See Marx's discussion of Wakefield in *Capital,* vol. 1, ch. 33.

119. Thomas Carlyle, *The Nigger Question* (1849), in Eugene R. August (ed.), *Thomas Carlyle, The Nigger Question, and John Stuart Mill, The Negro Question* (New York: Appleton-Century-Crofts, 1971), 1–37, on 7. See also Thomas C. Holt, *The Problem of Freedom: Race, Labor, and Politics in Jamaica and Britain, 1832–1938* (Baltimore and London: Johns Hopkins University Press, 1992), 42–46, 73–75, 166–67, 281–82; and Catherine Hall, *Civilising Subjects: Metropole and Colony in the English Imagination, 1830–1867* (Chicago and London: University of Chicago Press, 2002), esp. 101–10, 350–51.

120. Charles E. Trevelyan, *The Irish Crisis* (London: Longman, Brown, Green and Longmans, 1848), 5–6.

121. On the growth of Jamaican smallholding, see Holt, *Problem of Freedom,* ch. 5.

122. Hall, *Civilising Subjects*, 93–94, 109, 119–39.

123. The most relevant formulation of this claim from the perspective of this book is probably Chatterjee, *Land Question*.

124. See for example Sirajul Islam, *Rent and Raiyat: Society and Economy of Eastern Bengal, 1859–1928* (Dhaka: Asiatic Society of Bangladesh, 1989), esp. 7–26; and Dietmar Rothermund, *Government, Landlord and Peasant in India: Agrarian Relations under British Rule, 1865–1935* (Wiesbaden: Franz Steiner, 1978).

125. Cf. Sartori, "Global Intellectual History and the History of Political Economy."

126. Bose, *Peasant Labour and Colonial Capital*; Bose, *Agrarian Bengal*.

INTERMEZZO

1. On the "legalistic" impulse of the Pabna agrarian leagues, see Kalyan Kumar Sen Gupta, *Pabna Disturbances and the Politics of Rent, 1873–1885* (New Delhi: People's Publishing, 1974).

2. See for example *Correspondence between the Government of India and the Secretary of State regarding the Proposed Amendment of the Law of Landlord and Tenant in Bengal* (Calcutta: Office of the Superintendent of Government Printing, India, 1883), 54–62.

3. *Bengal Legislative Assembly Proceedings* 51, no. 4 (1937): 1379–80.

4. Karuna Mantena, *Alibis of Empire: Henry Maine and the Ends of Liberal Imperialism* (Princeton, NJ: Princeton University Press, 2010); Andrew Sartori, *Bengal in Global Concept History: Culturalism in the Age of Capital* (Chicago: University of Chicago Press, 2008), ch. 3. For a detailed account of the Ilbert Bill controversy, see Edwin Hirschmann, *'White Mutiny': The Ilbert Bill Crisis in India and Genesis of the Indian National Congress* (Columbia, MO: South Asia Books, 1980). The phrase "denial of coevalness" derives from Johannes Fabian, *Time and the Other: How Anthropology Makes its Object* (New York: Columbia University Press, 1983).

5. On Maine and Stephen, see George Feaver, *From Status to Contract: A Biography of Sir Henry Maine, 1822–1888* (London: Longmans, Green, 1969), ch. 15.

6. I do not dispute Bayly's contention that liberal ideas always remained prominent in Bengali political thought; but to treat classical and communitarian liberalisms as simply parallel species of a single ideological genus is to ignore the dynamic and historically sequential relationship between them. See C. A. Bayly, *Recovering Liberties: Indian Thought in the Age of Liberalism and Empire* (Cambridge: Cambridge University Press, 2012); Sartori, *Bengal in Global Concept History*, 99–101.

7. This would entail at once a supplementary refinement, and a deeper grounding, of the argument elaborated in Sartori, *Bengal in Global Concept History*, ch. 3.

8. See Sartori, *Bengal in Global Concept History*, chs. 4–6.

9. *Report of the Indigo Commission*, Minutes of Evidence, 97.

10. Ibid., 241.

11. Cf. Richard M. Eaton, *The Rise of Islam and the Bengal Frontier, 1204–1760* (Berkeley: University of California Press, 1993), 231–32.

12. Henry Beveridge, *The District of Bakarganj: Its History and Statistics* (London: Truebner, 1876), 215–16, 219.

13. Beveridge, *District of Bakarganj*, 254.

14. Sir George Campbell, *Memoirs of My Indian Career* (London: Macmillan, 1893), vol. 2, 293.

15. Campbell, *Memoirs*, vol. 2, 102.

16. "Condition and Social Life of the Mahomedans of Bengal Proper," *Proceedings of the Government of Bengal in the General Department (Miscellaneous)*, June 1873, 161 (IOL P/158).

17. "Riots in the Pabna District," 11.

18. Cited from Sartori, *Bengal in Global Concept History*, 205–06.

19. Sir Arthur J. Dash, *A Bengal Diary*, vol. 6, "The Fourth District," p. 8, in Box III of the Dash Papers, Cambridge South Asia Centre, Cambridge University.

20. Cf. Sartori, *Bengal in Global Concept History*, ch. 6.

5. PEASANT PROPERTY AND MUSLIM FREEDOM

1. Ayesha Jalal, *The Sole Spokesman: Jinnah, the Muslim League and the Demand for Pakistan* (Cambridge: Cambridge University Press, 1994), ch. 4.

2. Humaira Momen, *Muslim Politics in Bengal: A Study of the Krishak Praja Party and the Elections of 1937* (Dacca: Sunny House, 1972), ch. 7; see also Harun-or-Rashid, *The Foreshadowing of Bangladesh: Bengal Muslim League and Muslim Politics, 1906–1947* (Dhaka: University Press, 2003), 74–82.

3. Jalal, *Sole Spokesman*, 159–61.

4. For further discussion of the distinctions between *ashraf* and *atrap*, and non-Bengali and Bengali Muslims, see Rafiuddin Ahmed, *The Bengal Muslims, 1871–1906: A Quest for Identity* (Delhi: Oxford University Press, 1981).

5. Jalal, *Sole Spokesman*; Faisal Devji, "The Minority as Political Form," in Dipesh Chakrabary, Rochona Majumdar and Andrew Sartori (eds.), *From the Colonial to the Postcolonial: India and Pakistan in Transition* (Delhi: Oxford University Press, 2007), 85–95.

6. For histories of these developments more generally, see Jalal, *Sole Spokesman*; Shila Sen, *Muslim Politics in Bengal, 1937–1947* (New Delhi: Impex, 1976); Rashid, *Foreshadowing of Bangladesh*; and Thierry di Costanzo, *L'idée séparatiste dans la presse anglomusulmane du Bengale: Le cas du Star of India, 1937–1947* (Frankfurt: Peter Lang, 2011), chs. 4–5.

7. The best overall account of these developments is Joya Chatterji, *Bengal Divided: Hindu Communalism and Partition, 1932–1947* (Cambridge: Cambridge University Press, 1994), chs. 1–2.

8. Tariq Omar Ali, *The Envelope of Global Trade: The Political Economy and Intellectual History of Jute in the Bengal Delta, 1850s to 1950s* (unpublished dissertation, Harvard University, 2012); Sugata Bose, *Agrarian Bengal: Economy, Social Structure and Politics, 1919–1947* (Cambridge: Cambridge University Press, 1986); and Omkar Goswami, "Agriculture in Slump: The Peasant Economy of East and North Bengal in the 1930s," *Indian Economic and Social History Review* 21, no. 3 (1984): 335–64.

9. See Bose, *Agrarian Bengal*, 23, 26.

10. Jairus Banaji, *Theory as History: Essays on Modes of Production and Exploitation* (Leiden, Neth.: Brill, 2010), ch. 10.

11. Bose, *Agrarian Bengal*, ch. 6.

12. Partha Chatterjee, *Bengal 1920–1947: The Land Question* (Calcutta: K.P. Bagchi, 1984), 67–80; Pradip Kumar Datta, *Carving Blocs: Communal Ideology in Early Twentieth-Century Bengal* (Delhi: Oxford University Press, 1999).

13. Bose, *Agrarian Bengal*, 185, 187, 199.

14. *Report of the Land Revenue Commission, Bengal*, 6 vols. (Alipore: Bengal Government Press, 1940), vol. I, 311.

15. Chatterjee, *Land Question*, 172–82; but cf. Iftekhar Iqbal, *The Bengal Delta: Ecology, State and Social Change, 1840–1943* (Basingstoke, UK: Palgrave Macmillan, 2010), ch. 5.

16. Datta, *Carving Blocs*, ch. 2.

17. See A.H. Ahmed Kamal, "Peasant Rebellions and the Muslim League Government in Bengal, 1947–54," in Chakrabarty, Majumdar and Sartori (eds.), *From the Colonial to the Postcolonial*; A.H. Ahmed Kamal, *State Against the Nation: Decline of the Muslim League in Pre-Independence Bangladesh, 1947–54* (Dhaka: University Press, 2009).

18. See Ahmed, *Bengal Muslims*, on 161–62. See also Bose, *Agrarian Bengal*; Chatterjee, *Land Question*; Taj ul-Islam Hashmi, *Pakistan as a Peasant Utopia: The Communalization of Class Politics in East Bengal, 1920–1947* (Boulder, CO: Westview, 1992); Tazeen M. Murshid, *The Sacred and the Secular: Bengal Muslim Discourses, 1871–1977* (Calcutta: Oxford University Press, 1995), 186, 204.

19. Kamruddin Ahmad, *The Social History of East Pakistan* (Dhaka: Mrs. Raushan Ara Ahmed, 1967), 38, 46.

20. Of the Kishoreganj riots of 1930, a government report noted that "the latest report from the District Magistrate shows that the motive behind it is economic. Only money lenders were attacked and many Mahomedan money lenders were threatened or looted. . . . The outbreak seems to have been instigated by Maulvis and others from Bhowal [the neighboring subdistrict to the south] and Dacca, who told people that Government had ordered them to recover their documents from money lenders." Report on the Political Situation in Bengal, 1st half of July, 1930 (IOL L/PJ/12/697). On the Kishoreganj riots more generally, see Bose, "The Roots of Communal Violence in Rural Bengal: A Study of the Kishoreganj Riots, 1930," *Modern Asian Studies* 16, no. 3 (1982): 463–91; and Chatterjee, *Land Question*, 135–39. This chapter is *not* intended to explain such violence; it attempts only to contribute to our understanding of the terms on which the apparent conflation of "economic" and "communal" concerns, on which this kind of "communal violence" turned, might have been constituted.

21. See the excellent analysis of "Muslim Improvement Literature," including this text, in Datta, *Carving Blocs*, ch. 2.

22. A.F.M. Abdul Hai Bhawali, *Usman, adarsha krishak* (Mymensingh, 1920), 1. A second expanded edition incorporating this text was issued as *Adarsha krishak* (Dhaka, b.s. 1328 [1921/1922]).

23. Bhawali, *Usman*, 2.

24. Ibid., 10–11; postscript: p. 1.

25. Ibid., 5.

26. Ibid., 7.

27. Tariq Ali, *Envelope of Global Trade*, ch. 3.

28. Bhawali, *Usman*, 16–17.

29. Ibid., 17.

30. Ibid., 18.

31. Ibid., 12.

32. Ibid., postscript: p. 1; and see especially the chapter where Bhawali outlined these reforms in more detail, and which he significantly entitled "*Mukti*" (Freedom), included in the second edition: Bhawali, *Adarsha krishak,* 203–24.

33. Bhawali, *Usman,* 13–14.

34. Ibid., 17, 19.

35. See Andrew Sartori, "Abul Mansur Ahmad and the Cultural Politics of Bengali Pakistanism," in Dipesh Chakrabary, Rochona Majumdar and Andrew Sartori (eds.), *From the Colonial to the Postcolonial: India and Pakistan in Transition* (Delhi: Oxford University Press, 2007), 119–36; and Sartori, *Bengal in Global Concept History: Culturalism in the Age of Capital* (Chicago: University of Chicago Press, 2008), 219–23. For examples of the impulse to national political economy in this strand of Bengali Muslim political thought, see Abul Hosen, "*Fridrik list o tatkalin jarmmani,*" *Bangiya musalman sahitya pattrika* 3, no. 4 (b.s. 1327 [1921]): 265–73; and later, Abdus Sadek, "*Arthabijnan-shakhar sabhapatir abhibhashan,*" *Masik mohammadi* 17, nos. 10–11 (b.s. 1351 [1944]): 509–19.

36. This pamphlet is also discussed, from a different perspective, in Sumit Sarkar, "Two Muslim Tracts for Peasants: Bengal, 1909–1910," in *Beyond Nationalist Frames: Postmodernism, Hindu Fundamentalism, History* (Bloomington: Indiana University Press, 2002), 96–111.

37. Mohammad Mohsen Ulla, *Burir suta* (Calcutta, b.s. 1316 [1909/1910]), vol. 2, 30–33.

38. Mohsen Ulla, *Burir suta,* vol. 2, 23.

39. Ibid., vol. 2, 36.

40. Ibid., vol. 2, 31.

41. Ibid., vol. 1, 14.

42. Ibid., vol. 2, 10.

43. Cited from Sumit Sarkar, *The Swadeshi Movement in Bengal, 1903–1908* (New Delhi: People's Publishing, 1973), 457–58. As Sekandar Ali Mian put it in his 1917 rhyming tract, "*Banga deshe hindu gan ki janya prabal tahar bayan*" (An account of why the Hindus are dominant in Bengal), while the Hindus controlled almost all the professional, clerical and commercial occupations, and especially the trade in usury, "Muslims earn their living through cultivation and the plough, and all the money they get they give to Hindu households." Muslims had once been affluent but were now poor; meanwhile, the Hindus became the mahajans (moneylenders, wealthy merchants, the rich). Sekandar Ali Mian, *Musalman samaj tattva o beshara phakirer brittanta* (An Account of the Muslim Social Order and the Heterodox Fakir [or Baul], Tripura, 1917).

44. Mohsen Ulla, *Burir suta,* vol. 2, 39.

45. Ibid., vol. 2, 10.

46. Bhawali, *Usman,* foreword.

47. In this sense, I think Datta overstates the tension between these three possible modes of identification in *Carving Blocs,* 78–87.

48. Datta, *Carving Blocs,* 73–78 and 97–99.

49. Bhawali, *Usman,* 16.

50. Ibid., 3. *Bastabik-i* is rendered here "really"—but it also connotes "materially."

51. Ibid., foreword.

52. Shah Abdul Hamid, *Krishak-bilap* (Mymensingh, 1922), *nibedan.*

53. Hamid, *Krishak-bilap,* 13.

54. Ibid., 34–35 (fn.).

55. Shah Abdul Hamid, *Shasan-sanskare gramya mochalman* (Mymensingh, b.s. 1328 [1921/1922]), 29.

56. Hamid, *Gramya mochalman,* 32.

57. Ibid., 31.

58. Ibid., 32–33.

59. Ibid., 17.

60. Ibid., 9–11.

61. Ibid., 25.

62. Abul Mansur Ahmad, *Amar dekha rajnitir panchash bachar,* in *Abul mansur ahmad racanabali* (Dhaka: Bangla Academy, 2001), vol. 3, 11–12.

63. Hamid, *Krishak-bilap,* 16 (fn.).

64. See Datta, *Carving Blocs,* 76–78.

65. Shah Abdul Hamid, Secretary, Kishoreganj Proja Sova, to Secretary of the Government of Bengal Board of Revenue, March 22, 1923, *Opinions on the Bengal Tenancy Amendment Bill,* May 1927, p. 309, Department of Revenue, Land Revenue Branch, A Proceedings, Serial No. 76, Batch No. 76, List #17, National Archives of Bangladesh.

66. Iqbal, *Bengal Delta,* ch. 5.

67. Maulvi Elah Nawaz Khan, B. L., Secretary, Anjuman-i-Islamia, Netrakona, to the Secretary, Government of Bengal Revenue Department, April 28, 1923, *Opinions on the Bengal Tenancy Amendment Bill,* May 1927, p. 274.

68. Mymensingh Central Raiyat Association, *Prajasvatva ainer sanshodhan bishaye prajar jnatabya o kartabya* (Mymensingh, 1923), 1–2.

69. *Prajar jnatabya o kartabya,* 2.

70. Ibid., 7.

71. Ibid., 10.

72. Ibid., 9.

73. Ibid., 20–21.

74. *Proceedings of the Bengal Legislative Council* (hereafter PBLC), vol. 12 (1923): 72–73. Haq, who represented Tippera, referred that same year to his role in presiding over a "Raiyat Conference held in *Baisak* last at Fuljhuri in the district of Bakarganj," vol. 13 (1923): 51.

75. A point noted by Chatterji, *Bengal Divided,* 59.

76. Ibid., 74.

77. Indeed, the agrarian frontier might even have been beginning to recede under the environmental pressures generated by railway construction and the water hyacinth. See Iqbal, *Bengal Delta,* chs. 6–7.

78. F. A. Sachse, *Final Report on the Survey and Settlement Operations in the District of Mymensingh, 1908–1919* (Calcutta: Bengal Secretariat Book Depot, 1920), esp. 23–29; M. Azizul Haque, *The Man behind the Plough* (Calcutta: Book Co., 1939), 59. On jute, debt, and smallholding property in Bengal, see Bose, *Agrarian Bengal,* and Tariq Ali, *Envelope of Global Trade.*

79. Maulvi Afaz Uddin Ahmed, B. L., Secretary of the Reception Committee, Mymensingh Raiyat Conference, Gafargaon, to Secretary, Government of Bengal Revenue

Department, April 27, 1923, *Opinions on the Bengal Tenancy Amendment Bill*, May 1927, p. 312; and see also the submission of the Eastern Bengal Raiyat's Conference, Tippera, Ashuganj, 21st and 22nd Jyaishtha, b.s. 1330 [1923], which upheld similar resolutions and in which Hamid also prominently participated.

80. For the detailed elaboration of this last characterization of the smallholder, see Banaji, *Theory as History*, ch. 10; and cf. the discussion of debt in Bose, *Agrarian Bengal*.

81. *Opinions on the Bengal Tenancy Amendment Bill*, May 1927, 353–54. Bangla words in square bracket mark words transcribed from original Bangla script.

82. Chatterji, *Bengal Divided*, 91; Rajat Kanta Ray, *Social Conflict and Political Unrest* (Delhi: Oxford University Press, 1984), 59–68.

83. Ahmad, *Amar dekha rajnitir panchas bachar*, 34–35.

84. PBLC, vol. 30, part 1 (1928), 382.

85. Ibid., part 2 (1928), 154–55.

86. E.g., ibid., part 2 (1928), 431–32.

87. Ibid., part 1 (1928), 421.

88. Ibid., part 2 (1928), 503, 504.

89. Ibid., part 2 (1928), 427–28.

90. Ibid., part 2 (1928), 511.

91. Ibid., part 2 (1928), 595.

92. Ibid., part 2 (1928), 548.

93. Ibid., part 1 (1928), 400.

94. Ibid., part 1 (1928), 402–03.

95. Ibid., part 2 (1928), 456, 506.

96. Ibid., part 2 (1928), 325.

97. Ibid., part 2 (1928), 507.

98. Ibid., part 2 (1928), 668.

99. Ibid., part 1 (1928), 390.

100. Ibid., part 1 (1928), 420. See also part 2 (1928), 25.

101. Ibid., part 1 (1928), 421.

102. Ibid., part 2 (1928), 401.

103. Ibid., part 2 (1928), 21–22.

104. Ibid., part 2 (1928), 424–25, 559.

105. Ibid., part 2 (1928), 30.

106. Ibid., part 1 (1928), 424–25; part 2 (1928), 22–23.

107. Ibid., part 1 (1928), 453–54.

108. Ibid., part 1 (1928), 416.

109. Ibid., part 1 (1928), 396–97.

110. Ibid., part 2 (1928), 379–80.

111. Cf. the comments of F. A. Sachse, ibid., part 2 (1928), 101–02.

112. Ibid., part 2 (1928), 24

113. Ibid., part 2 (1928), 27.

114. Ibid., part 2 (1928), 342, 375.

115. Ibid., part 2 (1928), 41, 43.

116. Ibid., part 2 (1928), 887.

117. Ibid., part 1 (1928), 460.

118. Ibid., part 2 (1928), 22.

119. Ibid., part 2 (1928), 45–46.

120. Ibid., part 2 (1928), 665.

121. Ibid., part 2 (1928), 430.

122. Ibid., part 1 (1928), 397.

123. Ibid., part 1 (1928), 458.

124. Ibid., part 2 (1928), 516.

125. Ibid., part 2 (1928), 436.

126. Ibid., part 1 (1928), 387.

127. Ibid., part 2 (1928), 681.

128. Ibid., part 1 (1928), 426.

129. Ibid., part 1 (1928), 422.

130. Ibid., part 1 (1928), 396.

131. Ibid., part 1 (1928), 400–01.

132. Ibid., part 2 (1928), 441.

133. Ibid., part 2 (1928), 442.

134. Ibid., part 2 (1928), 225, 244.

135. Ibid., part 2 (1928), 535.

136. Ibid., part 2 (1928), 679.

137. Ibid., part 1 (1928), 397, 454.

138. Ibid., part 2 (1928), 548–49, 1006.

139. Ibid., part 2 (1928), 678.

140. Ibid., part 1 (1928), 389.

141. Ibid., part 1 (1928), 390.

142. Ibid., part 1 (1928), 454.

143. Ibid., part 2 (1928), 43.

144. Ibid., part 2 (1928), 484.

145. Murshid, *Sacred and the Secular,* 191–92.

146. Kenneth McPherson, *Muslim Microcosm: Calcutta, 1918–1935* (Wiesbaden: Steiner, 1974), 59.

147. Chatterjee, *Land Question,* 91–94; this argument is echoed, with qualifications, in Chatterji, *Bengal Divided,* ch. 2.

148. Chatterjee, *Land Question,* 126–29. Richard Eaton arguably provides a more plausible and simpler account of the inclusion of jotedar moneylenders within communal life than Chatterjee's recourse to the anthropological abstraction of a "communal mode of power," through his account of the centrality to property relations of families descended from founding pirs in Muslim Bengal. See his *The Rise of Islam and the Bengal Frontier, 1204–1760* (Berkeley: University of California Press, 1993), ch. 8.

149. PBLC, vol. 33 (1929), 108.

150. Momen, *Muslim Politics in Bengal,* 75–76; Rashid, *Foreshadowing of Bangladesh,* 28–30.

151. Ahmad, *Amar dekha rajnitir panchash bachar,* 67.

152. Abul Mansur Ahmad explained that it was because "the praja movement in Comilla and Noakhali was known as the 'krishak movement'" that the name of the party had to be changed to facilitate unity; though he did not then go on to draw out the political implica-

tions of this name change, or dwell on the discomfort it produced on the right of the party (centered in western Bengal): see Ahmad, *Amar dekha rajnitir panchash bachar,* 67–68. For an example of the kind of political rhetoric that traveled under the label of "krishak movement," see the passages discussed above, in *Opinions on the Bengal Tenancy Amendment Bill,* May 1927, 353–54. And see also Bose, *Agrarian Bengal,* 194–214; and Ahmad, *Social History of East Pakistan,* 26. The KPP was never able to articulate a program radical enough to hold the Tippera Krishak Samiti within its fold; the latter instead allied itself consistently with the left wing of the Congress.

153. Sen, *Muslim Politics in Bengal,* 75, 78, 83–85; Rashid, *Foreshadowing of Bangladesh,* 54–59, 68–74.

154. See for example the polyphonous equivocations voiced by Abdur Rahman Siddiqi, representative of the Muslim Chamber of Commerce in the assembly, *Bengal Legislative Assembly Proceedings* 52, no. 6 (1938): 279.

155. M. Azizul Haque, *History and Problems of Moslem Education in Bengal* (Calcutta: Thacker, Spink, 1917), 2–3.

156. Haque, *Man behind the Plough,* 343.

157. Haque, *Man behind the Plough,* 27–28.

158. Cited from Rashid, *Foreshadowing of Bangladesh,* 61.

159. Ahmad, *Amar dekha rajnitir panchash bachar,* 37.

160. Report on the Political Situation in Bengal, 1st half of April, 1932 (IOL L/PJ/12/720)

161. Ahmad, *Amar dekha rajnitir panchas bachar,* 38–39.

162. Ibid., 41.

163. For Bose's position on the bill, see *Bengal Legislative Assembly Proceedings* 51, no. 4 (1937): 2291–93. Compare the denunciation of the bill by T. C. Goswami (a zamindar and a member of the now defunct Big Five), *Bengal Legislative Assembly Proceedings* 51, no. 4 (1937): 1325. For a persuasive interpretation of Bose's difficult position, see Chatterji, *Bengal Divided,* 119–22.

164. Ahmad, *Amar dekha rajnitir panchas bachar,* 39.

165. Ibid., 42.

166. Ibid., 40.

167. *Report of the Land Revenue Commission,* vol. VI, 73–76, 92–93, 331–335, 342–45.

168. Ibid., vol. VI, 75–76.

169. Ibid., vol. VI, 332–35, 339.

170. *Bengal Legislative Assembly Proceedings* 51, no. 4 (1937): 1387–88.

171. Ibid., 2204.

172. Ibid., 2278.

173. *Report of the Land Revenue Commission,* vol. VI, 351–53, 369.

174. Ibid., vol. I, 5.

175. Ibid., vol. I, 41, 50–51, 67.

176. Ibid., vol. VI, 354–55.

177. Ibid., vol. VI, 353, 360.

178. Ibid., vol. VI, 362–63, 364.

179. Ibid., vol. VI, 363.

180. Haque, *Man behind the Plough,* 150–52, 346, 348–49.

181. Chatterji, *Bengal Divided,* 103–24.

182. For a discussion of the Bengal Provincial Kisan Sabha, see Adrienne Cooper, *Share-cropping and Sharecroppers' Struggles in Bengal, 1930–1950* (Calcutta: K. P. Bagchi 1988), ch. 4.

183. *Report of the Land Revenue Commission,* vol. VI, 4–5, 8.

184. *Report of the Land Revenue Commission,* vol. VI, 15.

185. Ibid., vol. VI, 17, 26.

186. Ibid., vol. VI, 33.

187. Ibid., vol. VI, 29–30, 46.

188. Ibid., vol. VI, 55.

189. Ibid., vol. VI, 57.

190. Ibid., vol. VI, 61, 63, 68.

191. Ibid., vol. VI, 58.

192. Ahmad, *Amar dekha rajnitir panchas bachar,* 50.

193. On Bhashani's rise to prominence in this period more generally, as well as further (but still scanty) biographical details of his pre-Assam career, see Ahmad, *Amar dekha rajnitir panchas bachar,* 49–50; F. O. Bell Papers, Cambridge South Asia Centre, "Record of Life in the Indian Civil Service, 1930–1947," 22; *Report on the Political Situation in Bengal,* 2nd half of December, 1932 (IOL L/PJ/12/720); Amalendu Guha, *Planter-Raj to Swaraj: Freedom Struggle and Electoral Politics in Assam, 1826–1947* (New Delhi: Indian Council of Historical Research, 1977), 214–15; Saiyad Abul Maksud, *Maulana Abdul Hamid Khan Bhashani* (Bangla, Dhaka: Bangla Academy, 1994), 1–33; and Peter Custers, "Maulana Bhashani and the Transition to Secular Politics in East Bengal," *Indian Economic and Social History Review* 47, no. 2 (2010): 231–59.

194. Maksud, *Maulana Abdul Hamid Khan Bhashani,* 24.

195. Layli Uddin, "Pir, Politician and Peasant Leader: The Making of Maulana Bhashani in Colonial Assam, c. 1930–1947" (unpublished M.Phil. thesis, Oriental Institute, Oxford University, 2011); and more generally, Eaton, *Rise of Islam and the Bengal Frontier.*

196. Anindita Dasgupta, "'Char'red for a lifetime: Internal Displacement in Assam Plains in India," *SARWATCH* 3–4 (2001–02): 6.

197. Cited from Anindita Dasgupta, *The Emergence of a Community: Muslims of East Bengal Origin in Assam in the Colonial and Postcolonial Period* (unpublished dissertation, Guwahati University, 2001), 199 (emphasis added).

198. Dasgupta, *Emergence of a Community,* ch. 5, on 184; and Guha, *Planter-Raj to Swaraj,* 212.

199. Dasgupta, *Emergence of a Community,* ch. 6.

200. *Assam Legislative Assembly Debates,* 1937 (IOL V/9/1410), 243. Bhashani's speeches in the assembly were all in Bangla. All translations are my own.

201. Ibid., 1937 (IOL V/9/1410), 246.

202. Ibid., 1937 (IOL V/9/1410), 245.

203. Ibid., 1938, vol. 2 (IOL V/9/1413), 298–99.

204. Ibid., 1938, vol. 2 (IOL V/9/1413), 299.

205. Ibid., 1938, vol. 2 (IOL V/9/1413), 301.

206. Abul Kalam Shamsuddin, *Atit diner smriti* (Reminiscences, Dhaka: Naoroj, 1968), 284.

207. Cited from Bimal J. Dev and Dilip K. Lahiri, *Assam Muslims: Politics and Cohesion* (Delhi: Mittal, 1985), 33.

208. Cited from Dev and Lahiri, *Assam Muslims,* 74.

209. Ibid.

210. See Dasgupta, *Emergence of a Community,* 247–52; Dev and Lahiri, *Assam Muslims,* ch. 3.

211. Cited from Maksud, *Maulana Abdul Hamid Khan Bhashani,* 50.

212. See for example Dev and Lahiri, *Assam Muslims,* 85, 92.

213. *Assam Legislative Assembly Debates,* 1944 (IOL V/9/1419), 88.

214. Azad Subhani, *The Teachings of Islam in Light of the Philosophy of Rabbaniyyat, for Beginners: First Series, Book I, "Allah and Alam" (God and the Universe)* (New York: Academy of Islam International, 1947), an English-language text Subhani published while visiting the United States in 1946–47, included as an appendix in Nabi Bakhshu Khanu Balocu, *Maulana Azad Subhani: tahrik-i azadi ke ek muqtadir rahnuma* (Lahore: Research Society of Pakistan, 1989).

215. Bhashani, *"Rabubiyater bhumika"* (An Introduction to Rabubiyat), in Maksud, *Maulana Abdul Hamid Khan Bhashani,* 698–702, on 699, 701.

216. See Seyyed Vali Reza Nasr, *The Vanguard of the Islamic Revolution: The Jama'at-i Islami of Pakistan* (Berkeley: University of California Press, 1994), 155–69.

217. Bhashani, *"Rabubiyater bhumika."*

218. Abul Hashim, *In Retrospection* (Dhaka: Subarna, 1974), 30–32. For his fuller elaboration of the rabbaniyat doctrine, see Abul Hashim, *The Creed of Islam, or the Revolutionary Character of Kalima* (Dhaka: Umar Brothers, 1950), which also included a foreword by Subhani.

219. For a more detailed discussion of the political shifts of this period, see Chatterji, *Bengal Divided,* ch. 3; Jalal, *Sole Spokesman,* ch. 3; Rashid, *Foreshadowing of Bangladesh,* chs. 3–4; and Sen, *Muslim Politics in Bengal.* See also Sartori, "Abul Mansur Ahmad."

220. See the map of the distribution of the Tariqah-i-Muhammadiyah movement in nineteenth-century Bengal in Iqbal, *Bengal Delta,* 71.

221. Abul Hashim, *In Retrospection,* 18.

222. *Bengal Legislative Assembly Proceedings* 51, no. 4 (1937): 2199.

223. Ibid., 1954.

224. Ibid., 2199–200.

225. "Free Pakistan in Free India," *Star of India,* March 23, 1945, 3; Abul Hashim, *In Retrospection,* 79–80.

226. For a sympathetic account of the United Bengal scheme, see Rashid, *Foreshadowing of Bengal;* for a more rigorous analysis, see Chatterji, *Bengal Divided,* 259–66.

227. Abul Mansur Ahmad, *Atmakatha* (Dhaka: Khoshroz Kitab Mahal, 1978), 222–23.

228. Hashim, *In Retrospection,* 141–42.

229. See the regular invocation of Vedantic ideas, and crucial figures in the development of Swadeshi Vedantism like Vivekananda, throughout Hashim, *Creed of Islam*—and especially the centrality of the interpretation given to the Kalima on pp. 43–48. On post-Swadeshi "rarification," see Sartori, *Bengal in Global Concept History,* ch. 6.

230. See also Andrew Sartori, "Global Intellectual History and the History of Political Economy," in Samuel Moyn and Andrew Sartori (eds.), *Global Intellectual History* (New York: Columbia University Press, 2013).

231. See Sartori, "Global Intellectual History and the History of Political Economy."

CONCLUSION

1. Karl Marx, *Grundrisse: Foundations of the Critique of Political Economy (Rough Draft)* (Harmondsworth, UK: Penguin, 1973), 100–108.

2. Eric Stokes, *The English Utilitarians and India* (Delhi: Oxford University Press, 1989), ch. 2.

3. See also Andrew Sartori, "Global Intellectual History and the History of Political Economy," in Samuel Moyn and Andrew Sartori (eds.), *Global Intellectual History* (New York: Columbia University Press, 2013), 110–33. Moishe Postone elaborates the outlines of a reflexive immanent critique of capitalist society in *Time, Labor, and Social Domination: A Reinterpretation of Marx's Critical Theory* (Cambridge: Cambridge University Press, 1996).

4. See also Andrew Sartori, *Bengal in Global Concept History: Culturalism in the Age of Capital* (Chicago: University of Chicago Press, 2008), 15, 20.

5. Karl Marx, *Capital: A Critique of Political Economy* (New York: Vintage Books, 1977), vol. 1, 927–28.

6. Marx, *Capital*, vol. I, 931.

7. This commonality is most immediately rooted, probably, in the debt Subaltern Studies owed to both Maoist and Thompsonian strands of Marxism. But that in this case Marxism merely participates in a more general set of assumptions is indicated by the degree to which this approach has become common sense in a range of scholarship that does not share the kind of early immersion in Marxism characteristic of the subalternists.

8. Marx, *Capital*, vol. I, 931, 934.

9. Ibid., vol. I, 932.

10. Ibid., vol. I, 728.

11. Cf. Postone, *Time, Labor and Social Domination*, 131–32.

12. Marx, *Capital*, vol. I, 729; and see also Marx, *Grundrisse*, 456–58.

13. Marx, *Capital*, vol. I, 730, emphasis added.

14. Marx, *Grundrisse*, 245; Marx, *Capital*, vol. I, 280.

15. Marx, *Grundrisse*, 509–10, emphases in original.

16. Roman Rosdolsky, *The Making of Marx's 'Capital'* (London: Pluto, 1977), vol. 1, 279–81.

17. Marx, *Capital*, vol. I, 873.

18. Cf. David Harvey, *The New Imperialism* (Oxford: Oxford University Press, 2003), ch. 4.

BIBLIOGRAPHY

OFFICIAL SOURCES

Assam Legislative Assembly Debates.

Correspondence between the Government of India and the Secretary of State regarding the Proposed Amendment of the Law of Landlord and Tenant in Bengal.

Correspondence between the Viceroy the Earl of Mayo and the Secretary of State for India the Duke of Argyll.

Decisions of the High Court of Judicature, at Fort William in Bengal, during the Years 1864 and 1865, Illustrating the Rent-Laws, and Bearing upon the General Duties of the Officers of the Revenue Department.

Decisions under the Rent Laws of the Court of Sadr Dewani Adalat, and of the High Court of Judicature, at Fort William in Bengal (from the Passing of Act X. of 1859).

Final Report on the Survey and Settlement Operations in the District of Mymensingh, 1908–19.

Final Report on the Survey and Settlement Operations in the Riparian Areas of District Pabna, Surveyed in the Course of the Faridpur District Settlement.

Fourth Report from the Select Committee on Colonization and Settlement (India), Parliamentary Papers, 1857–58 (461-I).

Memorandum Respecting the Operation of the Law for the Recovery of Revenue by the Sale of the Lands Permanently Settled in Bengal.

Opinions on the Bengal Tenancy Amendment Bill.

Papers Relating to Indigo Cultivation in Bengal, Parliamentary Papers, 1861 (72-II).

Papers Relating to Indigo Cultivation in Bengal, Preliminary to Appointment of Commission, 1854–60, Parliamentary Papers, 1861 (72).

Papers Relating to the Passing of Act X of 1859 (An Act to Amend the Law Relating to the Recovery of Rent in the Presidency of Fort William in Bengal).

Papers Relating to the Working and Amendment of Act X of 1859 (An Act to Amend the Law Relating to the Recovery of Rent in the Presidency of Fort William in Bengal).
Proceedings of the Bengal Legislative Assembly.
Proceedings of the Bengal Legislative Council.
Proceedings of the Government of Bengal, General Department (Miscellaneous).
Proceedings of the Government of Bengal in the Police Department.
Proceedings of the Land Revenue Department.
Report from the Select Committee on the Affairs of the East India Company, Parliamentary Papers, 1831–32 (735-III).
Report from the Select Committee on Agricultural Customs, Parliamentary Papers, 1847–48 (461).
Report of the Government of Bengal on the Proposed Amendment of the Law of Landlord and Tenant in that Province.
Report of the Indigo Commission, 1860, Parliamentary Papers, 1861 (72-I).
Report of the Land Revenue Commission, Bengal.
Report of the Rent Law Commission, with the Draft of a Bill to Consolidate and Amend the Law of Landlord and Tenant within the Territories of the Lieutenant-Governor of Bengal.
Report on the Administration of Bengal, 1872–73, with a Statistical Summary.
Report on the Agricultural Statistics of Jhenidah, Magurah, Bagirhat, and Sunderbans Sub-Divisions, District Jessore, 1872–73.
Report on the Condition of the Lower Classes of Population in Bengal.
A Report on the District of Jessore: Its Antiquities, its History and its Commerce.
Reports on the Political Situation in Bengal.
Selections from the Records of the Bengal Government, No. XVI: General Report of a Tour of Inspection, by W. B. Jackson, Esq., C.S., Judge of the Sudder Court; also Report of the District of Singbhoom, by H. Ricketts, Esq., S.C., Member of the Board of Revenue.

PRIVATE PAPERS

F. O. Bell Papers (Cambridge South Asia Centre).
Campbell of Edenwood Papers (IOL Euro. Mss.).
Dash Papers (Cambridge South Asia Centre).
Sir Charles Wood Papers (IOL Euro. Mss.).

PRIMARY SOURCE PUBLICATIONS

Ahmad, Abul Mansur. *Amar-dœkha rajnitir panchas bachar.* Dhaka: Naoroj Kitabistan, 1970.
———. *Atmakatha.* Dhaka: Khoshroz Kitab Mahal, 1978.
Ahmad, Kamruddin. *The Social History of East Pakistan.* Dhaka: Mrs. Raushan Ara Ahmed, 1967.
Anonymous. "Annals of the Bengal Presidency for 1852." *Calcutta Review* 19, no. 37 (1853): 156–209.
———. "The Land System of India." *Calcutta Review* 38 (1863): 109–58.

———. "Capital and Land." *Calcutta Review* 38 (1863): 321–46.

———. "The Relations of Landlord and Tenant in India." *Calcutta Review* 39 (1864): 97–124.

———. *Opinions of the Press in India, (I) on the Tenant Right Controversy in the Punjab, (II) the Action Taken by the Government of India, (III) the Legislative Measure Called "The Punjab Tenancy Act (Act XXVIII. of 1968)," as Collected from Newspapers.* Lahore: *Indian Public Opinion* Press, 1869.

B., T. H. "The Right of Occupancy in Oude and Bengal: The Rent Case—Hills v. Issar Ghos." *Fraser's Magazine* 72 (July 1865): 77–91.

Beveridge, Henry. *The District of Bakarganj: Its History and Statistics.* London: Truebner, 1876.

Bhawali, A. F. M. Abdul Hai. *Usman, adarsha krishak.* Mymensingh, 1920.

———. *Adarsha krishak.* Dhaka, b.s. 1328 [1921/1922].

Blackstone, William. *Commentaries on the Laws of England.* San Francisco: Bancroft-Whitney, 1915.

Bright, John. *Mr. Bright's Speech on Ireland. Meeting of Irish Residents in Manchester. Presentation of an Address to J. Bright Esq., M.P.* Manchester: A. Ireland, 1850.

Burke, Edmund. *Reflections on the Revolution in France.* Indianapolis: Hackett, 1987.

———. *On Empire, Liberty, and Reform: Speeches and Letters.* Edited by David Bromwich. New Haven, CT, and London: Yale University Press, 2000.

Cairnes, J. E. *Essays in Political Economy, Theoretical and Applied.* London: Macmillan, 1873.

Campbell, George. *Modern India: A Sketch of the System of Civil Government, to which is Prefixed Some Account of the Natives and Native Institutions.* London: John Murray, 1852.

———. *The Irish Land.* London: Truebner, 1869.

———. *The American People, or the Relations between the White and the Black. An Outcome of a Visit to the United States.* New York: Worthington, 1889.

———. "Property in Land." *Westminster Review* 133 (January–June 1890): 181–91.

———. *Memoirs of My Indian Career.* London: Macmillan, 1893.

Carlyle, Thomas. *Past and Present.* London: J. M. Dent, 1905.

———. *The Nigger Question.* In *Thomas Carlyle, The Nigger Question and John Stuart Mill, The Negro Question,* edited by Eugene R. August, 1–37. New York: Appleton-Century-Crifts, 1971.

Chamberlain, Joseph. *The Radical Programme.* London: Chapman and Hall, 1885.

Chatterjee, Sunjeeb Chunder. *Bengal Ryots: Their Rights and Liabilities, Being an Elementary Treatise on the Law of Landlord and Tenant.* Calcutta: D'Rozario, 1864.

Chattopadhyay, Bankimchandra. *Bankim racanabali: sahitya samagra.* Edited by Bishnu Basu. Calcutta: Tuli-Kalam, c. 1986.

Cobden, Richard. *Cobden on the Land Question: A Plea for Small Holdings.* London: Cassell, 1907.

Conner, William. *The True Political Economy of Ireland: or, Rack-Rent, the One Great Cause of All Her Evils: with its Remedy. Being a Speech Delivered at a Meeting of the Farming and Laboring Classes, at Inch, in the Queen's County.* Dublin: W. F. Wakeman, 1835.

Crawfurd, William Sharman. *A Defense of the Small Farmers of Ireland.* Dublin: Joshua Porter, 1839.

———. "Sharman Crawfurd on Ulster Tenant Right, 1846." *Irish Historical Studies* 13, no. 53 (1963): 246–53.

Day, Lal-Behari. *Bengal Peasant Life.* London: Macmillan, 1908.

Delta. *Indigo and its Enemies; or, Facts on Both Sides.* London: James Ridgway, 1861.

A District Officer, "The Policy of the New Rent Law for Bengal and Behar." *Calcutta Review* 72, no. 143 (1881): 161–95.

Dutt, R.C. *The Peasantry of Bengal, Being a View of their Condition under the Hindu, Mahomedan, and the English Rule, and a Consideration of the Means Calculated to Improve their Future Prospects.* Calcutta: Thacker and Spink, 1874.

[Graham, G.], *Life in the Mofussil, or the Civilian in Lower Bengal. By an Ex-Civilian.* London: C. Kegan Paul, 1878.

Hamid, Shah Abdul. *Shasan-sanskare gramya mosalman.* Mymensingh, b.s. 1328 [1921/1922].

———. *Krishak-bilap.* Mymensingh, 1922.

Hancock, W. Neilson. *The Tenant-Right of Ulster, Considered Economically, Being an Essay Read before the Dublin University Philosophical Society; with an Appendix, Containing the Evidence of John Hancock, Esq., Taken before the Landlord and Tenant Commissioners.* Dublin: Hodges and Smith, 1845.

———. *Three Lectures on the Questions, Should the Principles of Political Economy be Disregarded at the Present Crisis, and If Not, How Can They be Applied towards the Discovery of Measures of Relief.* Dublin: Hodges and Smith, 1847.

Haque, M. Azizul. *History and Problems of Moslem Education in Bengal.* Calcutta: Thacker, Spink, 1917.

———. *The Man behind the Plough.* Calcutta: Book Co., 1939.

Harington, J.H. *Extracts from Harington's Analysis of the Bengal Regulations.* Calcutta: Office of Superintendent Government Printing, 1866.

Hashim, Abul. "Free Pakistan in Free India." *Star of India,* March 23, 1945.

———. *In Retrospection.* Dhaka: Subarna, 1974.

———. *The Creed of Islam, or the Revolutionary Character of Kalima.* Dhaka: Umar Brothers, 1950.

[Hollingbery, R.H.], *A Handbook of Gold and Silver, by an Indian Official.* London: Longmans, Green, 1878.

———. *The Silver Question Reviewed, by an Indian Official.* London: Longmans, Green, 1878.

———. *The Zemindary Settlement of Bengal.* Calcutta: Brown, 1879.

Hosen, Abul. "*Fridrik list o tatkalin jarmmani,*" *Bangiya musalman sahitya pattrika* 3, no. 4 (b.s. 1327 [1921]): 265–73.

Hunter, W.W. *Seven Years of Indian Legislation.* Calcutta: Truebner, 1870.

Kaye, John William. *The Administration of the East India Company: A History of Indian Progress.* London: Richard Bentley, 1853.

———, ed. *Selections from the Papers of Lord Metcalfe.* London: Smith, Elder, 1855.

Larmour, R.T. *Notes on the Rent Difficulties in Lower Bengal, and on the Proposed Amendment of Act X. of 1859.* Calcutta: Savielle and Cranenburgh, 1862.

Locke, John. *An Essay Concerning the True Original and Extent of Civil Government.* Dublin: George Bonham, 1798.

Macaulay, Thomas Babington. "Mill's *Essay on Government:* Utilitarian Logic and Politics." *Edinburgh Review* 49 (March 1829): 159–89.

Maine, Sir Henry Sumner. *Village-Communities in the East and West*. London: John Murray, 1913.

Manu. *Institutes of Hindu Law: or the Ordinances of Menu, according to the Gloss of Culluca. Comprising the Hindu System of Duties, Religious and Civil*. Translated by Sir William Jones. London: Sewell and Debrett, 1796.

McCulloch, John Ramsay. *Outlines of Political Economy: Being a Republication of the Article upon that Subject Contained in the Edinburgh Supplement to the Encyclopedia Brittanica*. New York: Wilder and Campbell, 1925.

Mian, Sekandar Ali. *Musalman samaj tattva o beshara phakirer brittanta*. Tripura, 1917.

Mill, James. *The Article Government: Reprinted from the Supplement to the Encyclopædia Britannica*. London: Traveller Office, 1821.

Mill, John Stuart. *On Liberty and Other Essays*. Oxford: Oxford University Press, 1991.

———. *Principles of Political Economy*. Amherst, NY: Prometheus, 2004.

Mittra, Peary Chand. "The Zemindar and the Ryot." *Calcutta Review* 6 (1846): 305–53.

Munro, Sir Thomas. "On the State of the Country and the Condition of the People." In *Major-General Sir Thomas Munro, Governor of Madras*, edited by Sir Arthur J. Arbuthnot, vol. I, 237–75. London: C. Kegan Paul, 1881.

Murdoch, John. *A Letter to the Right Honorable the Earl of Elgin, Governor General of India, on the Rent Question in Bengal*. Calcutta: Baptist Mission Press, 1863.

Mymensingh Central Raiyat Association. *Prajasvatva ainer sanshodhan bishaye prajar jnatabya o kartabya*. Mymensingh, 1923.

P., J. B. "Rustic Bengal." *Calcutta Review* 59, no. 117 (1874): 180–214.

P., N. "Free Trade in Land." *Calcutta Review* 59 (1874): 273–84.

Paine, Thomas. *The Rights of Man, for the Benefit of All Mankind*. Philadelphia: D. Webster, 1797.

———. *Agrarian Justice, Opposed to Agrarian Law, and to Agrarian Monopoly*. London: T. G. Ballard, [1797].

Pusey, Philip. *The Poor in Scotland*. London: James Burns, 1844.

R., H. *The Rent Difficulties in Bengal, and How to Remedy Them; The Rent Facilities in Cuttack, and How Best to Preserve Them*. London: Smith Elder, 1863.

Ricardo, David. *On the Principles of Political Economy and Taxation*. London: Empiricus Books, 2002.

Roy, Kedar Nath. *The Rent Law of Bengal*. Calcutta: Calcutta Central Press, 1886.

———. *The Bengal Tenancy Act, Being Act VIII of 1885, as Amended up to Date, with Notes, Judicial Rulings, Rules, and Notifications, &c, &c*. Calcutta: Majumdar Press, 1906.

Roy, Parbati Churn. *The Rent Question in Bengal*. Calcutta: Sadharan Brahmo Samaj Press, 1883.

Sadek, Abdus. "*Arthabijnan-shakhar sabhapatir abhibhashan*." *Masik mohammadi* 17, nos. 10–11 (b.s. 1351 [1944]): 509–19.

Scrope, G. Poulett. *Principles of Political Economy, Deduced from the Natural Laws of Social Welfare, and Applied to the Present State of Britain*. London: Longman, Rees, Orme, Brown, Green and Longman, 1833.

Seton-Karr, W. S. *Rulers of India: The Marquess Cornwallis*. Oxford: Clarendon, 1898.

Shamsuddin, Abul Kalam. *Atit diner smriti*. Dhaka: Naoroj, 1968.

Smith, Adam. *An Inquiry into the Nature and Causes of the Wealth of Nations*. Chicago: University of Chicago Press, 1976.

Spencer, Herbert. *The Man versus the State*. New York: D. Appleton, 1885.

Subhani, Azad. *The Teaching of Islam in Light of the Philosophy of Rabbaniyyat, for Beginners: First Series, Book I, "Allah and Alam" (God and the Universe)*. New York: Academy of Islam International, 1947. In *Maulana Azad Subhani: tarik-I azadi ke ek muqtadir rahnuma*, by Nabi Bakshu Khanu Balocu. Lahore: Research Society of Pakistan, 1989.

Trevelyan, Charles E. *The Irish Crisis*. London: Longman, Brown, Green and Longmans, 1848.

Ulla, Mohammad Mohsen. *Burir suta*. Calcutta, b.s. 1316 [1909/1910].

Wise, James. "The Muhammadans of Eastern Bengal." *Journal of the Asiatic Society of Bengal* 63, no. 1 (1894): 28–63.

Wollstonescraft, Mary. *A Vindication of the Rights of Men, in a Letter to the Right Honourable Edmund Burke*. London: J. Johnson, 1790.

———. *A Vindication of the Rights of Woman, with Strictures on Political and Moral Subjects*. London: T. Fisher Unwin, 1891.

SECONDARY SOURCE PUBLICATIONS

Ahmad Khan, Muin-ud-din. *History of the Fara'idi Movement in Bengal (1818–1906)*. Karachi: Pakistan Historical Society, 1965.

Ahmed, Rafiuddin. *Bengal Muslims 1871–1906: A Quest for Identity*. New Delhi: Oxford University Press, 1988.

Ali, Tariq Omar. *The Envelope of Global Trade: The Political Economy and Intellectual History of Jute in the Bengal Delta, 1850s to 1950s*. Unpublished dissertation, Harvard University, 2012.

Ambirajan, S. *Classical Political Economy and British Policy in India*. Cambridge: Cambridge University Press, 1978.

Anseeuw, W., L. Alden Wily, L. Cotula and M. Taylor. *Land Rights and the Rush for Land: Findings of the Global Commercial Pressures on Land Research Project*. Rome: International Land Coalition, 2012.

Anseeuw, W., M. Boche, T. Breu, M. Giger, J. Lay, P. Messerli and K. Nolte. *Transnational Land Deals for Agriculture in the Global South: Analytical Report Based on the Land Matrix Database*. Bern/Montpellier/Hamburg: CDE/CIRAD/GIGA, 2013.

Appleby, Joyce. *Liberalism and Republicanism in the Historical Imagination*. Cambridge, MA: Harvard University Press, 1992.

Armitage, David. *The Ideological Origins of the British Empire*. Cambridge: Cambridge University Press, 2000.

———. *Foundations of Modern International Thought*. Cambridge: Cambridge University Press, 2013.

Arneil, Barbara. *John Locke and America: The Defense of English Colonialism*. Oxford: Oxford University Press, 1996.

Ashcraft, Richard. *Revolutionary Politics and Locke's Two Treatises of Government*. Princeton, NJ: Princeton University Press, 1986.

———. "Liberal Political Theory and Working-Class Radicalism in Nineteenth-Century England." *Political Theory* 21, no. 2 (1993): 249–72.

Bag, Kheya. "Red Bengal's Rise and Fall." *New Left Review* 70 (July–August 2011): 69–98.

Bagehot, Walter. *Physics and Politics*. New York: D. Appleton, 1873.

Banaji, Jairus. *Theory as History: Essays on Modes of Production and Exploitation.* Leiden, Neth.: Brill, 2010.

Bayly, C. A. *Recovering Liberties: Indian Thought in the Age of Liberalism and Empire.* Cambridge: Cambridge University Press, 2012.

Bell, Duncan. *The Idea of Greater Britain: Empire and the Future of World Order, 1860–1900.* Princeton, NJ, and Oxford: Princeton University Press, 2007.

Bellamy, Richard. *Liberalism and Modern Society: A Historical Argument.* University Park: Pennsylvania State University Press, 1992.

Bentham, Jeremy. *Works.* Edinburgh: William Tait, 1843.

Bhattacharya, Neeladri. "Remaking Custom: The Discourse and Practice of Colonial Codification." In *Tradition, Dissent and Ideology: Essays in Honour of Romila Thapar,* edited by R. Champakalakshmi and S. Gopal, 20–51. Delhi: Oxford University Press, 1996.

Biagini, Eugenio F. *Liberty, Retrenchment and Reform: Popular Liberalism in the Age of Gladstone, 1860–1880.* Cambridge: Cambridge University Press, 1992.

———. *Gladstone.* New York: St. Martin's, 2000.

Black, R. D. Collison. *Economic Thought and the Irish Question, 1817–1870.* Cambridge: Cambridge University Press, 1960.

Bose, Sugata. "The Roots of Communal Violence in Rural Bengal: A Study of the Kishoreganj Riots, 1930." *Modern Asian Studies* 16, no. 3 (1982): 463–91.

———. *Agrarian Bengal: Economy, Social Structure and Politics, 1919–1947.* Cambridge: Cambridge University Press, 1986.

———, ed. *South Asia and World Capitalism.* Delhi: Oxford University Press, 1990.

———. *Peasant Labour and Colonial Capital: Rural Bengal since 1770.* Cambridge: Cambridge University Press, 1993.

von Braun, Joachim, and Ruth Meinzen-Dick. *"Land-Grabbing" by Foreign Investors in Developing Countries: Risks and Opportunities.* IFPRI Policy Brief 13, April 2009.

Buckland, C. E. *Bengal under the Lieutenant-Governors; Being a Narrative of the Principal Events and Public Measures during their Periods of Office, from 1854–1898.* Calcutta: S. K. Lahiri, 1901.

Burns, J. H. "Bentham and Blackstone: A Lifetime's Dialectic." *Utilitas: A Journal of Utilitarian Studies* 1, no. 1 (1989): 22–40.

Cain, P. J. *Hobson and Imperialism: Radicalism, New Liberalism, and Finance, 1887–1938.* Oxford: Oxford University Press, 2002.

Cannadine, David. *Ornamentalism: How the British Saw Their Empire.* Oxford: Oxford University Press, 2001.

Chari, Sharad. *Fraternal Capital: Peasant-Workers, Self-Made Men, and Globalization in Provincial India.* Stanford, CA: Stanford University Press, 2004.

Chase, Malcolm. *"The People's Farm": English Radical Agrarianism, 1775–1840.* Oxford: Clarendon, 1988.

Chatterjee, Partha. *Bengal 1920–1947: The Land Question.* Calcutta: K. P. Bagchi, 1984.

———. *The Nation and Its Fragments: Colonial and Postcolonial Histories.* Princeton, NJ: Princeton University Press, 1993.

———. "A Modern Science of Politics for the Colonized." In *Texts of Power: Emerging Disciplines in Colonial Bengal,* edited by Partha Chatterjee, 93–117. Minneapolis: University of Minnesota Press, 1995.

Chatterji, Joya. *Bengal Divided: Hindu Communalism and Partition, 1932–1947*. Cambridge: Cambridge University Press, 1994.

Chaudhuri, Binay. "Agricultural Production in Bengal, 1850–1900: Coexistence of Decline and Growth." *Bengal Past and Present* 70 (1969): 152–206.

Chaudhuri, Binay Bhushan. "Growth of Commercial Agriculture in Bengal—1859–1885." *Indian Economic and Social History Review* 7, nos. 1–2 (1970): 25–60, 211–51.

Chowdhury, Benoy. *Growth of Commercial Agriculture in Bengal, 1757–1900*. Calcutta: Indian Studies Past and Present, 1964.

Clarke, P. F. *Lancashire and the New Liberalism*. Cambridge: Cambridge University Press, 1971.

Cobden, Richard. *Cobden on the Land Question: A Plea for Small Holdings*. London: Cassell, 1907.

Collini, Stefan. *Liberalism and Sociology: L. T. Hobhouse and Political Argument in England, 1880–1914*. Cambridge: Cambridge University Press, 1979.

Cook, S. B. *Imperial Affinities: Nineteenth Century Analogies and Exchanges between India and Ireland*. New Delhi: Sage, 1993.

Cooper, Adrienne. *Sharecropping and Sharecroppers' Struggles in Bengal, 1930–1950*. Calcutta: K. P. Bagchi 1988.

di Costanzo, Thierry. *L'idée séparatiste dans la presse anglo-musulmane du Bengale: Le cas du Star of India, 1937–1947*. Frankfurt: Peter Lang, 2011.

Cotula, Lorenzo, Sonja Vermeulen, Rebeca Leonard and James Keeley. *Land Grab or Development Opportunity: Agricultural Investment and International Land Deals in Africa*. London and Rome: IIED/FAO/IFAD, 2009.

Cuno, Kenneth. *The Pasha's Peasants: Land, Society, and Economy in Lower Egypt, 1740–1858*. Cambridge: Cambridge University Press, 1992.

———. "Was the Land of Ottoman Syria Miri or Milk? An Examination of Juridical Differences within the Hanafi School." *Studia Islamica* 81 (1995): 121–52.

David L. Curley, *Poetry and History: Bengali Magal-kabya and Social Change in Precolonial Bengal* (New Delhi: Chronicle Books, 2008).

Custers, Peter. "Maulana Bhashani and the Transition to Secular Politics in East Bengal." *Indian Economic and Social History Review* 47, no. 2 (2010): 231–59.

Daniel, Shepard, with Anuradha Mittal. *The Great Land Grab: Rush for World's Farmland Threatens Food Security for the Poor*. Oakland, CA: Oakland Institute, 2009.

Dasgupta, Anindita. *The Emergence of a Community: Muslims of East Bengal Origin in Assam in the Colonial and Postcolonial Period*. Unpublished dissertation, Guwahati University, 2001.

———. "'Char'red for a Lifetime: Internal Displacement in Assam Plains in India." *SARWATCH* 3–4 (2001–2002).

Datta, Pradip Kumar. *Carving Blocs: Communal Ideology in Early Twentieth-Century Bengal*. New Delhi: Oxford University Press, 1999.

Datta, Rajat. *Society, Economy and the Market: Commercialization in Rural Bengal, c. 1760–1800*. New Delhi: Manohar, 2000.

Dev, Bimal J., and Dilip K. Lahiri. *Assam Muslims: Politics and Cohesion*. Delhi: Mittal, 1985.

Devine, T. M. *The Great Highland Famine: Hunger, Emigration and the Scottish Highlands in the Nineteenth Century*. Edinburgh: John Donald, 1988.

Devji, Faisal. "The Minority as Political Form." In *From the Colonial to the Postcolonial: India and Pakistan in Transition,* edited by Dipesh Chakrabarty, Rochona Majumdar and Andrew Sartori, 85–95. Delhi: Oxford University Press, 2007.

Dewey, Clive. "Images of the Village Community: A Study in Anglo-Indian Ideology." *Modern Asian Studies* 6, no. 3 (1972): 291–328.

———. "Celtic Agrarian Legislation and the Celtic Revival: Historicist Implications of Gladstone's Irish and Scottish Land Acts, 1870–1886." *Past and Present* 64 (1974): 30–70.

———. "The Rehabilitation of the Peasant Proprietor in Nineteenth-Century Economic Thought." *History of Political Economy* 6, no. 1 (1974): 17–47.

Dirks, Nicholas. *The Scandal of Empire: India and the Creation of Imperial Britain.* Cambridge, MA: Belknap Press, 2006.

Dunn, John. *The Political Thought of John Locke: An Historical Account of the Argument of the "Two Treatises on Government."* Cambridge: Cambridge University Press, 1969.

———. "The Contemporary Political Significance of John Locke's Conception of Civil Society." In *Civil Society: History and Possibilities,* edited by Sudipta Kaviraj and Sunil Khilnani, 39–57. Cambridge: Cambridge University Press, 2001.

Eaton, Richard M. *The Rise of Islam and the Bengal Frontier, 1204–1760.* Berkeley: University of California Press, 1993.

Eldridge, C. C. *England's Mission: The Imperial Idea in the Age of Gladstone and Disraeli.* Chapel Hill: University of North Carolina Press, 1974.

Fabian, Johannes. *Time and the Other: How Anthropology Makes Its Object.* New York: Columbia University Press, 1983.

Feaver, George. *From Status to Contract: A Biography of Sir Henry Maine, 1822–1888.* London: Longmans, Green, 1969.

Freeden, Michael. *The New Liberalism: An Ideology of Social Reform.* Oxford: Clarendon, 1978.

Goldie, Mark, ed. *The Reception of Locke's Politics.* London: Pickering and Chatto, 1999.

Gopal, S. *British Policy in India, 1858–1905.* Cambridge: Cambridge University Press, 1965.

Goswami, Omkar. "Agriculture in Slump: The Peasant Economy of East and North Bengal in the 1930s." *Indian Economic and Social History Review* 21, no. 3 (1984): 335–64.

Gray, Peter. "The Peculiarities of Irish Land Tenure, 1800–1914: From Agent of Improvement to Agent of Pacification." In *The Political Economy of British Historical Experience, 1688–1914,* edited by Donald Winch and Patrick K. O'Brien, 139–62. Oxford: Oxford University Press, 2002.

Greenough, Paul R. *Prosperity and Misery in Bengal: The Famine of 1943–1944.* Oxford: Oxford University Press, 1982.

Grover, B. R. "Evolution of the Zamindari and Taluqdari System in Bengal." *Tritiya barshik itihas sammelan: abhibhashan, prabandhabali, o karja bibarani.* Dhaka: Bangladesh Itihas Parishad, 1975, 86–113.

Guha, Amalendu. *Planter-Raj to Swaraj: Freedom Struggle and Electoral Politics in Assam, 1826–1947.* New Delhi: Indian Council of Historical Research, 1977.

Guha, Ranajit.. "Neel-Darpan: The Image of a Peasant Revolt in a Liberal Mirror." *Journal of Peasant Studies* 2, no. 1 (1974): 1–46.

———. *Elementary Aspects of Peasant Insurgency in Colonial India.* Delhi: Oxford University Press, 1983.

———. "The Prose of Counter-Insurgency." In *Subaltern Studies II: Writings on South Asian History and Society*, edited by Ranajit Guha, 1–42. Delhi: Oxford University Press, 1983.

———. *A Rule of Property for Bengal: An Essay on the Idea of Permanent Settlement*. Durham, NC: Duke University Press, 1996.

Gunn, Simon, and James Vernon, eds. *The Peculiarities of Liberal Modernity in Imperial Britain*. Berkeley: GAIA and University of California Press, 2011.

Habib, Irfan. "Potentialities of Capitalistic Development in the Economy of Mughal India." *Journal of Economic History* 29, no. 1 (1969): 32–78.

———. *The Agrarian System of Mughal India, 1556–1707*. 2nd ed. New Delhi: Oxford University Press, 1999.

Hall, Catherine. *Civilising Subjects: Metropole and Colony in the English Imagination, 1830–1867*. Chicago: University of Chicago Press, 2002.

Hambly, G. R. G. "Richard Temple and the Punjab Tenancy Act of 1868." *English Historical Review* 79, no. 310 (1964): 47–66.

Hampsher-Monk, Iain. "Edmund Burke and Empire." In *Lineages of Empire: The Historical Roots of British Imperial Thought*, edited by Duncan Kelly, 117–36. Oxford: Oxford University Press for the British Academy, 2009.

Harvey, David. *The New Imperialism*. Oxford: Oxford University Press, 2003.

Hashmi, Taj ul-Islam. *Pakistan as a Peasant Utopia: The Communalization of Class Politics in East Bengal, 1920–1947*. Boulder, CO: Westview, 1992.

Hilton, Boyd. *A Mad, Bad and Dangerous People? England, 1783–1846*. Oxford: Clarendon, 2006.

Hirschmann, Edwin. *"White Mutiny": The Ilbert Bill Crisis in India and Genesis of the Indian National Congress*. Columbia, MO: South Asia Books, 1980.

Hobsbawm, E. J. *Industry and Empire: From 1750 to the Present Day*. Harmondsworth, UK: Penguin, 1969.

———. *The Age of Empire, 1875–1914*. New York: Pantheon, 1987.

Hobsbawm, Eric, and Terence Ranger, eds. *The Invention of Tradition*. Cambridge: Cambridge University Press, 1992.

Hollander, Samuel. *The Economics of John Stuart Mill*. Toronto: University of Toronto Press, 1985.

Holt, Thomas C. *The Problem of Freedom: Race, Labor, and Politics in Jamaica and Britain, 1832–1938*. Baltimore: Johns Hopkins University Press, 1992.

Hont, Istvan, and Michael Ignatieff, eds. *Wealth and Virtue: The Shaping of Political Economy in the Scottish Enlightenment*. Cambridge: Cambridge University Press, 1983.

Horne, Thomas A. *Property Rights and Poverty: Political Argument in Britain, 1605–1834*. Chapel Hill and London: University of North Carolina Press, 1990.

Hyam, Ronald. *Britain's Imperial Century, 1815–1914: A Study of Empire and Expansion*. Houndmills, UK: Palgrave Macmillan, 2002.

Iqbal, Iftekhar. *The Bengal Delta: Ecology, State and Social Change, 1840–1943*. Houndmills, UK, and New York: Palgrave Macmillan, 2010.

Islam, Sirajul. *Rent and Raiyat: Society and Economy of Eastern Bengal, 1859–1928*. Dhaka: Asiatic Society of Bangladesh, 1989.

Islam, Zafarul. *Socio-Economic Dimension of Fiqh Literature in Medieval India*. Lahore: Research Cell, Dyal Singh Trust Library, 1990.

Jackson, Ben. "Property-Owning Democracy: A Short History." In *Property-Owning Democracy: Rawls and Beyond,* edited by Martin O'Neill and Thad Williamson, 33–52. Oxford: Blackwell, 2012.

Jalal, Ayesha. *The Sole Spokesman: Jinnah, the Muslim League and the Demand for Pakistan.* Cambridge: Cambridge University Press, 1994.

Johansen, Baber. *The Islamic Law on Land Tax and Rent: The Peasant's Loss of Property Rights as Interpreted in the Hanafite Legal Literature of the Mamluk and Ottoman Period.* London: Croom Helm, 1988.

Kamal, A. H. Ahmed. "Peasant Rebellions and the Muslim League Government in Bengal, 1947–54." In *From the Colonial to the Postcolonial: India and Pakistan in Transition,* edited by Dipesh Chakrabarty, Rochona Majumdar and Andrew Sartori, 201–20. Delhi: Oxford University Press, 2007.

———. *State Against the Nation: Decline of the Muslim League in Pre-Independence Bangladesh, 1947–54.* Dhaka: University Press, 2009.

Kinzer, Bruce. *England's Disgrace? J. S. Mill and the Irish Question.* Toronto: University of Toronto Press, 2001.

Kling, Blair B. *The Blue Mutiny: The Indigo Disturbances in Bengal, 1859–1862.* Philadelphia: University of Pennsylvania Press, 1966.

Koditschek, Theodore. *Liberalism, Imperialism, and the Historical Imagination: Nineteenth-Century Visions of Greater Britain.* Cambridge: Cambridge University Press, 2011.

Laslett, Peter. "Introduction." In *Two Treatises of Government,* by John Locke. Cambridge: Cambridge University Press, 1988.

Lieberman, David. "From Bentham to Benthamism." *Historical Journal* 28, no. 1 (1985): 199–224.

———. "Property, Commerce, and the Common Law: Attitudes to Legal Change in the Eighteenth Century." In *Early Modern Conceptions of Property,* edited by John Brewer and Susan Staves, 144–58. London: Routledge, 1996.

Losurdo, Domenico. *Liberalism: A Counter-History.* London: Verso, 2011.

Ludden, David. *An Agrarian History of South Asia.* Cambridge: Cambridge University Press, 1999.

MacAskill, Joy. "The Chartist Land Plan." In *Chartist Studies,* edited by Asa Briggs, 304–41. London: MacMillan, 1965.

Macpherson, C. B. *The Political Theory of Possessive Individualism: Hobbes to Locke.* Oxford: Oxford University Press, 1970.

Majeed, Javed. *Ungoverned Imaginings: James Mill's History of British India and Orientalism.* Oxford: Clarendon, 1992.

Maksud, Saiyad Abul. *Maulana Abdul Hamid Khan Bhashani.* Dhaka: Bangla Academy, 1994.

Mamdani, Mahmood. *Citizen and Subject: Contemporary Africa and the Legacy of Late Colonialism.* Princeton, NJ: Princeton University Press, 1996.

Mantena, Karuna. *Alibis of Empire: Henry Maine and the Ends of Liberal Imperialism.* Princeton, NJ: Princeton University Press, 2010.

Marx, Karl. *Grundrisse: Foundations of the Critique of Political Economy (Rough Draft).* Harmondsworth, UK: Penguin, 1973.

———. *Capital: A Critique of Political Economy, Volume One.* New York: Vintage, 1977.

———. *Theories of Surplus Value*. Amherst, NY: Prometheus Books, 2000.

McCarthy, Thomas. *Race, Empire, and the Idea of Human Development*. Cambridge: Cambridge University Press, 2009.

McLaren, Martha. *British India and British Scotland, 1780–1830: Career Building, Empire Building, and a Scottish School of Thought on Indian Governance*. Akron, OH: University of Akron Press, 2001.

McPherson, Kenneth. *Muslim Microcosm: Calcutta, 1918–1935*. Wiesbaden: Steiner, 1974.

Mehta, Uday Singh. *Liberalism and Empire: A Study in Nineteenth-Century British Liberal Thought*. Chicago: University of Chicago Press, 1999.

Metcalf, Thomas R. *The Aftermath of Revolt: India, 1857–1870*. Princeton, NJ: Princeton University Press, 1964.

———. *Ideologies of the Raj*. Cambridge: Cambridge University Press, 1995.

Momen, Humaira. *Muslim Politics in Bengal: A Study of the Krishak Praja Party and the Elections of 1937*. Dacca: Sunny House, 1972.

Mukherjee, Tilottama. "Markets in Eighteenth Century Bengal Economy." *Indian Economic and Social History Review* 48, no. 2 (2011): 143–76.

Mundy, Martha, and Richard Saumarez Smith. *Governing Property, Making the Modern State: Law, Administration and Production in Ottoman Syria*. London: I. B. Tauris, 2007.

Murshid, Tazeen M. *The Sacred and the Secular: Bengal Muslim Discourses, 1871–1977*. Calcutta: Oxford University Press, 1995.

Muthu, Sankar. *Enlightenment against Empire*. Princeton, NJ, and Oxford: Princeton University Press, 2003.

Nasr, Seyyed Vali Reza. *The Vanguard of the Islamic Revolution: The Jama'at-i Islami of Pakistan*. Berkeley: University of California Press, 1994.

O'Brien, Karen. "Colonial Emigration, Public Policy, and Tory Romanticism, 1783–1830." In *Lineages of Empire: The Historical Roots of British Imperial Thought*, edited by Duncan Kelly, 161–80. Oxford: Oxford University Press for the British Academy, 2009.

den Otter, S. N. "The Political Economy of Empire: Freedom of Contract and 'Commercial Civilization' in Colonial India." In *Worlds of Political Economy: Knowledge and Power in the Nineteenth and Twentieth Centuries*, edited by Martin Daunton and Frank Trentmann, 69–94. Houndmills, UK, and New York: Palgrave MacMillan, 2004.

Palit, Chittabrata. *Tensions in Bengal Rural Society: Landlords, Planters and Colonial Rule, 1830–1860*. Calcutta: Progressive, 1975.

Pateman, Carole. *The Sexual Contract*. Oxford: Blackwell, 1988.

Perlin, Frank. "Protoindustrialization and Precolonial South Asia." *Past and Present* 98 (February 1983): 30–95.

Pincus, Steve. "Neither Machiavellian Moment nor Possessive Individualism: Commercial Society and the Defenders of the English Commonwealth." *American Historical Review* 103, no. 3 (1998): 705–36.

———. *1688: The First Modern Revolution*. New Haven, CT: Yale University Press, 2009.

Pitts, Jennifer. *A Turn to Empire: The Rise of Imperial Liberalism in Britain and France*. Princeton, NJ, and Oxford: Princeton University Press, 2005.

———. "Political Theory of Empire and Imperialism." *Annual Review of Political Science* 13, no. 2 (2010): 211–35.

Pocock, J. G. A. *The Ancient Constitution and the Feudal Law.* Cambridge: Cambridge University Press, 1987.

———. *The Machiavellian Moment: Florentine Political Thought and the Atlantic Republican Tradition.* Princeton, NJ: Princeton University Press, 2003.

Postone, Moishe. *Time, Labor and Social Domination: A Reinterpretation of Marx's Critical Theory.* Cambridge: Cambridge University Press, 1996.

Rao, Anupama. *The Caste Question: Dalits and the Politics of Modern India.* Berkeley: University of California Press, 2009.

Harun-or-Rashid. *The Foreshadowing of Bangladesh: Bengal Muslim League and Muslim Politics, 1906–1947.* Dhaka: University Press, 2003.

Ray, Rajat Kanta. *Social Conflict and Political Unrest.* Delhi: Oxford University Press, 1984.

Ray, Ratnalekha, "The Bengal Zamindars: Local Magnates and the State before the Permanent Settlement." *Indian Economic and Social History Review* 12, no. 3 (1975): 263–92.

Ray, Ratnalekha. *Change in Bengal Agrarian Society, 1760–1850.* Delhi: Manohar, 1979.

Robb, P. G. *Ancient Rights and Future Comfort: Bihar, the Bengal Tenancy Act of 1885, and British Rule in India.* Richmond, UK: Curzon, 1997.

Rosdolsky, Roman. *The Making of Marx's 'Capital'.* London: Pluto, 1977.

Rothermund, Dietmar. *Government, Landlord and Peasant in India: Agrarian Relations under British Rule, 1865–1935.* Wiesbaden: Franz Steiner, 1978.

Rothschild, Emma. *Economic Sentiments: Adam Smith, Condorcet, and the Enlightenment.* Cambridge, MA: Harvard University Press, 2001.

Roy, Tirthankar. "Indigo and Law in Colonial India." *Economic History Review* 64, Suppl 1 (2011): 60–75.

———. "Where Is Bengal? Situating an Indian Region in the Early Modern World Economy." *Past and Present* 213 (November 2011): 115–46.

Sarkar, Sumit. *The Swadeshi Movement in Bengal, 1903–1908.* New Delhi: People's Publishing, 1973.

———. "Two Muslim Tracts for Peasants: Bengal 1909–1910." In *Beyond Nationalist Frames: Postmodernism, Hindu Fundamentalism, History,* 96–111. Bloomington: Indiana University Press, 2002.

Sartori, Andrew. "The British Empire and Its Liberal Mission." *Journal of Modern History* 78, no. 3 (2006): 623–42.

———. "Abul Mansur Ahmad and the Cultural Politics of Bengali Pakistanism." In *From the Colonial to the Postcolonial: India and Pakistan in Transition,* edited by D. Chakrabarty, R. Majumdar, and A. Sartori, 119–36. New Delhi: Oxford University Press, 2007.

———. *Bengal in Global Concept History: Culturalism in the Age of Capital.* Chicago: University of Chicago Press, 2008.

———. "Global Intellectual History and the History of Political Economy." In *Global Intellectual History,* edited by Samuel Moyn and Andrew Sartori, 110–33. New York: Columbia University Press, 2013.

Seal, Anil. *The Emergence of Indian Nationalism: Competition and Collaboration in the Later Nineteenth Century.* Cambridge: Cambridge University Press, 1971.

Semmel, Bernard. *The Rise of Free Trade Imperialism: Classical Political Economy, the Empire of Free Trade and Imperialism, 1750–1850.* Cambridge: Cambridge University Press, 1970.

Sen, Shila. *Muslim Politics in Bengal, 1937–1947.* New Delhi: Impex, 1976.

Sen, Sudipta. *Empire of Free Trade: The East India Company and the Making of the Colonial Marketplace.* Philadelphia: University of Pennsylvania Press, 1998.

Sen Gupta, Kalyan Kumar. "Agrarian Disturbances in Eastern and Central Bengal in the Late Nineteenth Century." *Indian Economic and Social History Review* 8, no. 2 (1971): 192–212.

———. *Pabna Disturbances and the Politics of Rent, 1873–1885.* New Delhi: People's Publishing, 1974.

Simhony, Avital, and D. Weinstein, eds. *The New Liberalism: Reconciling Liberty and Community.* Cambridge: Cambridge University Press, 2001.

Solow, Barbara Lewis. *The Land Question and the Irish Economy, 1870–1903.* Cambridge, MA: Harvard University Press, 1971.

Steele, E. D. "Ireland and the Empire: Imperial Precedents for Gladstone's First Irish Land Act." *Historical Journal* 11 (1968): 64–83.

———. "J. S. Mill and the Irish Question: The Principles of Political Economy, 1848–65." *Historical Journal* 13 (1970): 216–36.

———. "J. S. Mill and the Irish Question: Reform and the Integrity of Empire." *Historical Journal* 13 (1970): 419–50.

———. *Irish Land and Irish Politics: Tenant-Right and Nationality, 1865–1870.* Cambridge: Cambridge University Press, 1974.

Stein, Burton. *Thomas Munro: The Origins of the Colonial State and His Vision of Empire.* Delhi: Oxford University Press, 1989.

Stokes, Eric. *The English Utilitarians and India.* Delhi: Oxford University Press, 1989.

Sturman, Rachel. *The Government of Social Life in Colonial India: Liberalism, Religious Law, and Women's Rights.* Cambridge: Cambridge University Press, 2012.

Subrahmanyam, Sanjay. "Historicizing the Global, or Labouring for Invention?" *History Workshop Journal* 64, no. 1 (2007): 329–34.

Tholfsen, Trygve R. *Working-Class Radicalism in Mid-Victorian England.* New York: Columbia University Press, 1977.

Thompson, E. P. *Customs in Common.* New York: New Press, 1991.

Thompson, F. M. L. "Changing Perceptions of Land Tenures in Britain, 1750–1914." In *The Political Economy of British Historical Experience, 1688–1914*, edited by Donald Winch and Patrick K. O'Brien, 119–38. Oxford: Oxford University Press, 2002.

Travers, Robert. *Ideology and Empire in Eighteenth-Century India: The British in Bengal.* Cambridge: Cambridge University Press, 2007.

Tully, James. *A Discourse on Property: John Locke and His Adversaries.* Cambridge: Cambridge University Press, 1980.

———. "The Framework of Natural Rights in Locke's Analysis of Property." In his *An Approach to Political Philosophy: Locke in Contexts*, 96–117. Cambridge: Cambridge University Press, 1993.

Uddin, Layli. "Pir, Politician and Peasant Leader: The Making of Maulana Bhashani in Colonial Assam, c. 1930–1947." Unpublished M.Phil. thesis, Oriental Institute, Oxford University, 2011.

Urban, Hugh B. *Songs of Ecstasy: Tantric and Devotional Songs from Colonial Bengal.* New York: Oxford University Press, 2001.

Vaughn, James. "The Politics of Empire: Metropolitan Socio-Political Development and the Imperial Transformation of the British East India Company, 1675–1775." PhD dissertation, University of Chicago, 2008.

Vaughn, Karen I. "John Locke and the Labor Theory of Value." *Journal of Libertarian Studies* 2, no. 4 (1978): 311–26.

Vaughn, W. E. *Landlords and Tenants in Mid-Victorian Ireland.* Oxford: Clarendon, 1994.

Washbrook, David. "Law, State and Agrarian Society in Colonial India." *Modern Asian Studies* 15, no. 3 (1981): 649–721.

Williams, Raymond. *Keywords: A Vocabulary of Culture and Society.* New York: Oxford University Press, 1983.

Wilson, Jon E. *The Domination of Strangers: Modern Governance in Eastern India, 1780–1835.* New York: Palgrave Macmillan, 2008.

Wilson, Kathleen. *The Sense of the People: Politics, Culture and Imperialism in England, 1715–1785.* Cambridge: Cambridge University Press, 1998.

Winch, Donald. *Riches and Poverty: An Intellectual History of Political Economy in Britain, 1750–1834.* Cambridge: Cambridge University Press, 1996.

Wood, Neal. *John Locke and Agrarian Capitalism.* Berkeley: University of California Press, 1984.

Woolhouse, Roger. *Locke: A Biography.* Cambridge: Cambridge University Press, 2007.

Zastoupil, Lynn. *John Stuart Mill and India.* Stanford, CA: Stanford University Press, 1994.

INDEX

Act X (1859), 45, 51, 71–72, 98; Bengal Tenancy Act and, 85; custom and, 47; "fair and equitable" rent stipulation, 48, 54; indigo cultivation and, 107; as Magna Charta of Bengal peasantry, 59; pergunnah rates and, 82–83; right of occupancy and, 49, 55, 123

Adam (biblical/quranic), as original cultivator, 9–10, 112, 146, 148

Administration of the East India Company, The (Kaye), 40

adverse possession, 120

Africa, 1, 36, 130

Agrarian Justice (Paine), 72

agrarian leagues, 134

agriculture, 14, 36, 50, 90–92; commercialization of, 109, 112–16, 129, 156; "foreign capital" and, 168; as foundation of government revenues, 151; improvement of, 85, 99, 100; industrially organized, 1; international commodity exchange and, 108; as source of wealth, 148; tenant right and, 77–78

Ahamad, Asimuddin, 166, 167

Ahamad, Kasiruddin, 166, 167

Ahmad, Abul Mansur, 177, 178–79, 180, 183, 195, 242n152

Ahmad, Kamruddin, 142

Ahmed, Rafiuddin, 158

Ahmed, Shamsuddin, 180

Ain-i-Akbari, 155

Ali, Syed Nausher, 163, 169

All Bengal Cultivators Association, 150, 151

Allen, W. J., 54, 55

All India Muslim League. *See* Muslim League

allodial title, 65

Ambirajan, S., 56

Anjuma-i-Islamia, 154, 177

Anjuman Ettefaque-i-Islam, 179

anjumans, 142, 179, 180

Argyll, Lord, 41

aristocracy, 25, 26, 214n65; Burke's defense of, 72; limitation on sovereign's power and, 69; surplus in hands of, 91

Ashcraft, Richard, 19, 211n14

ashraf (Muslim gentry), 137, 142, 195

Asquith, H. H., 95

Assam province, 42, 145, 150, 155, 185–192

Assam Provincial Muslim League, 189

Atiqullah, Syed Muhammad, 168

Aurangzeb, 224n67

Austin, John, 35

Awadh, 37, 63

Babeuf, Gracchus, 72

Baboo Dhunpat Singh v. Baboo Gooman Singh, 51

Bagehot, Walter, 35

Bakarganj district, 133

Bakarganj Proja Party, 181

Baksh, Kader, 163–64

Banerjea, Surendranath, 159

Banerjee, Mamata, 2